'Indispensable reading for anyone who has any significant interest in Australian politics.'

- Bob Hawke

'Kelly writes a gripping political narrative that also has the powerful over-tones of Shakespearian tragedy.'

- *The Australian Financial Review*

'Kelly at his best is a wordsmith and analyst without peer among those who make their living observing and reporting national politics.'

- Alan Ramsey

'A superb account of dramatic political events.'

- Laurie Oakes

THE
HAWKE
ASCENDANCY

A definitive account
of its origins and climax 1972–1983

Paul Kelly

ALLEN&UNWIN

For my wife, Margaret

First published in 1984
This paperback editon published in 2008

Copyright © Paul Kelly 1984 and 2008

Allen & Unwin
83 Alexander Street
Crows Nest NSW 2065 Australia
Phone: (61 2) 8425 0100
Fax: (61 2) 9906 2218
E-mail: info@allenandunwin.com
Web: www.allenandunwin.com

National Library of Australia
Cataloguing-in-Publication entry:

Kelly, Paul, 1947–

The Hawke ascendancy : a definitive account of its origins and climax 1975–1983 author, Paul Kelly

Crow's Nest, N.S.W. : Allen & Unwin, 2008.

ISBN 978 1 74175 497 1 (pbk.).

Includes index.
Bibliography.

Hawke, Bob, 1929–. Australian Labor Party.
Australia—Politics and government—1976–1990.

320.994

Set in 10/12 pt Times by Midland Typesetters, Australia
Printed by McPherson's Printing Group, Australia

10 9 8 7 6 5 4 3 2 1

Contents

PART III   THE CLIMAX

PART IV   EPILOGUE

Preface to this new edition

A few months short of the 25th anniversary of his 1983 election win Bob Hawke was on the campaign trail again. Aged 77, his tanned face more deeply lined, the silver mane as thick as ever, his glamorous wife Blanche d'Alpuget by his side, Hawke claimed a presence in Labor's victory over John Howard. He campaigned across the marginal seats, sometimes in royal blue pants, white shoes and a light blue sports coat that few men his age would dare to wear. Thoroughly enjoying himself, Hawke's vituperative attacks on Howard were not replicated by a more restrained Labor leader, Kevin Rudd, in his landmark campaign.

Rudd's victory followed in Hawke's footsteps. He became the third Labor leader since World War II to take Labor from opposition to government at a national election after Gough Whitlam in 1972 and Hawke in 1983. Rudd's swing was greater than Whitlam's and comparable with Hawke's. Measured by the two-party preferred vote, Labor's two greatest election results in the past half century are the Hawke and Rudd victories.

Hawke's participation in the 2007 campaign testified to his physical and political vigour. On the trail Hawke was proud of his fitness and aware that his status within the Labor pantheon was now beyond question. Indeed, with the passage of time his legend as Labor's longest serving prime minister has assumed a grander presence on Australia's landscape. Hawke radiated a satisfaction with his legacy rare for a retired leader. The brooding Hawke of 1992, encamped in a Sydney hotel, lamenting his loss of the prime minister-ship to Paul Keating and alienated from many of his colleagues, was long forgotten. Hawke was now reconciled with history, the Labor Party and the country.

The Hawke Ascendancy is the story of Labor's recovery from its 1975 debacle to its smashing victory eight years later. It is a political thriller. Its hero is Hawke, who saw himself as the irresistible political force. It features a rich and compelling cast including Whitlam, Bill Hayden, Paul Keating, Malcolm Fraser, John Howard and Andrew Peacock. In his unmatched personal popularity, television image, folk hero profile and unrepentant narcissism Hawke's quest for power was unique yet also reflective of a new political age. In the early 1980s he offered Labor both opportunity and temptation—it could surrender to Hawke in a gamble with its soul.

Hawke was elected to parliament at the 1980 election and the focus of this story is the 1980–83 term when that lethal and intimidating Liberal prime minister, Malcolm Fraser, struggled against Hayden as Labor leader and Hawke as Hayden's rival to save his government. Hawke's appeal was that he represented the future—he thrived in the 24-hour media cycle that was redefining politics and he symbolised the transition from party to people as the source of the leader's authority.

But the Hawke ascendancy reflected the idea, as the book argued, that he would become a prime minister of 'longevity and substance'. Hawke arrived with convictions about how Labor should govern and sure that most previous ALP leaders had been their own worst enemy. He came to govern for the long term, to entrench Labor in the institutions of power, to expose the conservatives as weak rulers and to alter the nation's direction through a sustained and calculated policy shift. A punter, sports fanatic and Rhodes scholar, Hawke satisfied Bagehot's description of a statesman, 'a man of common opinions and uncommon ability'.

When John Button wrote his famous letter to Hayden seeking his resignation—published in the prologue—he confessed that 'even some of Bob's closest supporters have doubts about his capacities to lead the party successfully'. But they were wrong. Hawke did more than deliver office. He won four successive elections and was never rejected by the people, being deposed instead by the Labor caucus in December 1991.

His enduring legacy, however, is as a reforming prime minister whose government was instrumental in dismantling the Australian Settlement of the early Federation era and constructing new policies based upon an open competitive economy, a diversified society, a stronger enterprise-based culture and a more mature international outlook. A generation after Hawke's arrival in office Australia is widely judged as a far more successful economy and nation, having moved significantly higher in international ratings with the benefits translated into higher living standards. Hawke and Keating seeded these changes that were enhanced further in the Howard era.

There were some notable failures on Hawke's watch—the 1990s recession, leading to the highest jobless figures since the Great Depression, and the stalling on Aboriginal advancement. His failure of personal judgement lay in mismanaging his transition to Keating.

However, when former Hayden supporter and Hawke minister Neal Blewett penned his chapter for the centenary of Federation publication *Australian Prime Ministers*, he concluded that Hawke 'must be rated the greatest prime minister since Menzies'. It is a well-based assessment. Hawke was instrumental in shifting Australia's political culture towards a more liberal, open and individualist outlook suited to the age of globalisation. He pitched to the people and the nation's interest and shunned the narrow and insular tribalism that has so often retarded Australia's progress.

In the Labor pantheon 25 years after his initial victory, Hawke is located alongside John Curtin, for whom he had such a high regard. Though they governed in different times, Hawke and Curtin tower as the two greatest Labor prime ministers, both being in the debt of their finance ministers, Keating and Ben Chifley. *The Hawke Ascendancy* is the story of how it began.

Paul Kelly, 2008

Preface to first edition

This book tells the story of Bob Hawke's ascension to power and the first phase of the Hawke Government. It begins with Labor's 1975 debacle and comes to its climax in the events of February–March 1983, which saw Labor return to office under Hawke. It is the story of the power struggle between three men: Malcolm Fraser, Bob Hawke and Bill Hayden, and the battle between the Liberal and Labor Parties for office.

It is a selective account and does not pretend to be comprehensive. It is written not to favour any individual or party over another. The perspectives are historical cynicism—that all governments make mistakes—and political optimism—that there should be a better way.

I would like to thank the very many people who assisted me with interviews, nearly all of whom would prefer to remain nameless. I also apologise to the many to whom I should have spoken but could not due to time constraints. I particularly thank my close friends and colleagues who helped me with their ideas, files and books. I have kept a set of confidential footnotes covering many of the personal conversations related in the book.

My publisher, Richard Walsh, was particularly helpful with his suggested changes to the manuscript and tolerant of my failure to meet deadlines. I would like to thank Betty Miller who typed most of the manuscript and also Margaret Hyslop who assisted. My greatest thanks go to Margaret Kelly who nursed the book with precision and its author with care.

Paul Kelly, 1984

Prologue

On the morning of 28 January 1983 the leader of the Opposition in the Senate, John Button, launched his final bid to change the leadership of the Labor Party. Button judged that Australia's premier politician and Prime Minister Malcolm Fraser was about to strike against Labor with an early election—an election he believed the ALP leader, Bill Hayden, could not win. The power-brokers of Australia's oldest political party had convinced themselves that Bob Hawke was their only hope: the saviour who could turn despair into triumph.

In the previous three weeks Button had made two visits to Brisbane to persuade Hayden, his best friend in politics, to resign the leadership in favour of Hawke. Both trips had been unsuccessful. Now Button made recourse to his own ultimate weapon of persuasion, the pen. His letter to Hayden was an appeal to Hayden's idealism and a dispatch of death for his ambition. Button was not just negotiating the fate of men. Subsequent events would prove that his letter was shaping the course of history:

> Dear Bill,
>
> I had hoped to talk with you in Brisbane regarding the matter of your leadership of the party. My impression was that you were anxious to discuss this matter too, but that you subsequently changed your mind, and certainly I was reluctant to raise it with you in the presence of Dennis Murphy. Hence this letter.
>
> My visit to Brisbane on 6 January was only undertaken after a lot of thought, and some discussion with several colleagues. During our talk on that

day I expressed, albeit reluctantly, the view that you should stand down as leader of the party, and I was concerned to put that view to you as a friend. It is still my opinion.

I felt I could talk to you about that issue, because since you became leader of the party I have been consistently loyal to you in every major difficulty you have faced. I am still loyal to you as a person and I hope I am still regarded as a friend. In part, I hope that is apparent from the fact that in spite of considerable discussion on this issue within the party, none of it has appeared in the press. My ultimate loyalty, however, must be to the ALP.

If we had had the opportunity of talking yesterday, I would have put the following points to you.

1   I believe that you cannot win the next election. In July last year I had doubts about this. Since the last leadership contest, it seems to me that your level of performance as party leader has declined considerably.

2   In discussions between us, you have relied on the polls as indicative of a reasonable level of performance by yourself and the party. It has been my view that with the recent economic performance by the Government, we should have been 10–15 per cent ahead of the Government consistently. We have not, and the last Morgan Poll shows us at four per cent ahead.

3   The worst feature of the last poll, however, is the approval rating amongst Liberal voters of Fraser's performance (69 per cent), compared with your approval rating amongst ALP supporters of 46 per cent.

4   The last figure reflects my view of the state of morale amongst party members and supporters, which I raised with you on 6 January. It is very bad, and you cannot win an election without the enthusiastic support of our own constituents.

5   Whilst 'the party' in July–August was divided on the issue of a change of leadership, it is not nearly so divided now. At least four of the state leaders, five of the six state Secretaries, the National Secretariat, and a majority of the parliamentary party favour a change.

6   The alternative leader (created as such by the last leadership ballot) is, of course, Bob Hawke. You said to me that you could not stand down for a 'bastard' like Bob Hawke. In my experience in the Labor Party the fact that someone is a bastard (of one kind or another) has never been a disqualification for leadership of the party. It is a disability from which we all suffer in various degrees.

7   I am personally not one of those who believes that we can necessarily coast into office on the coat-tails of a media performer and winner of popularity polls. On the other hand I believe Hawke's leadership would

give us a better chance of success, and if the ALP is to be defeated in the next election I would personally prefer it to be under his leadership than yours. That might provoke some really hard thinking about where we are going.

8   I must say that even some of Bob's closest supporters have doubts about his capacities to lead the party successfully, in that they do not share his own estimate of his ability. The Labor Party is, however, desperate to win the coming election.

If I might return to our discussions in Brisbane, I repeat what I said then: namely, that I did not approach you as an emissary from any group within the party, but rather to indicate my own perceptions and concerns. These are based on a lot of listening to many people who are your friends rather than your opponents.

You have, unhappily, a difficulty in working with colleagues, but it in no way diminishes their respect for your political career. I believe that respect and affection would be greatly enhanced if you stepped down from the leadership. The 'Macbeth stuff' which you gave me in Brisbane is really all bullshit. My own present wish is to see the election of a Labor Government in which you play a prominent and influential role.

Could we talk about this?

> With kindest regards,
> Yours sincerely,
> John

Four days before Button wrote this letter, on 24 January, Malcolm Fraser called the Federal Director of the Liberal Party, Tony Eggleton, to Kirribilli House in Sydney and told him to prepare for an early election in March. Fraser was anxious to exploit the new political climate revealed by the Flinders by-election the previous December, and surmount the world recession to win his fourth general election. It was critical to Fraser's prospects that his opponent be Hayden leading a demoralised Labor Party.

Hayden announced his resignation from the ALP leadership on 3 February, six days after Button wrote this letter. On that day he told colleagues that the letter had been the final influence in his decision. He called it 'brutal but fair'. The resignation announcement was made by Hayden to the ALP shadow Cabinet in Brisbane only 25 minutes after Fraser left Parliament House, Canberra, with his letter for the Governor-General requesting an election. Just 31 days later Bob Hawke became Prime Minister and the Fraser years became history.

Labor had waited seven years between the traumatic watersheds of November–December 1975, when it lost power, and February–March 1983, when it regained power. For Australia's new Prime Minister the Hawke ascendancy had begun.

PART 1

THE MEN

1
The seeds of conflict

Mr Hawke might find it best . . . to save politics for when he becomes a politician.

Bill Hayden, February 1976

On 14 December 1975, the day after his sweeping rejection by the people, Gough Whitlam offered the ALP leadership to two men—Bill Hayden and Bob Hawke in that order. Whitlam lacked the power to determine his successor but assumed the right. His instincts were sound and his judgement both of the men and the ALP were proved ultimately to be correct. Hayden and Hawke became his successors respectively. To them fell the arduous task of rehabilitating the image, policies and morale of Australia's oldest political party, negotiating the dark travail of the Fraser years and returning Labor to office. They carried the burden unequally, but that was to be expected. Hayden and Hawke marched together into the future, but they were soldiers moulded in different alloys and coloured in contrasting hues. United in Labor allegiance, they were divided by personality, history and ambition. The story of Labor's return from the wilderness is the story of their power struggle.

There were two contenders for the succession, not one, because Hayden and Hawke had never matched each other on the same terrain. Hayden was the outstanding contender from the parliamentary Labor Party and hence the logical successor; but Hawke's unprecedented career and character had established him as the extra parliamentary contender. These men climbed towards the apex of power from opposite sides of the mountain. When their power rivalry reached its climax in February 1983, it had eight years of contrasting endeavour and pent-up tension to release.

After Whitlam had been defeated, he had first rung Hayden with the message of succession on this December Sunday. Hayden later told

3

colleagues that Whitlam's offer had never been direct; it was merely a hint. But this is irrelevant. The leadership lay open for Hayden and Whitlam acted in recognition of this. But Hayden was emotionally exhausted and mentally demoralised. He had just received the biggest jolt of his career and was still fighting to hold his seat of Oxley which had been converted into an assumed safe Labor seat years before. Already sensing the wave of recriminations about to engulf the party, Hayden had no stomach for the challenge. He needed a rest. So he fell back into the bosom of his family and purged the guilty feeling that had mounted over many years as an absent father on political duty. He wanted to forget politics and renew his family ties. Hayden was not ready to be Labor leader because he did not want to be Labor leader.

Later the same day Whitlam asked Hawke to join him at The Lodge. He said that, because Hayden had refused, Hawke should enter Parliament as quickly as possible and take the leadership. Whitlam said he would stand down for Hawke midway through the coming Parliament, so he could lead Labor into the next election. Hawke recalled, 'I was so surprised that he'd turned so quickly to me. Not because I disagreed with his judgement, but because I wasn't even in Parliament. I thought Gough was quite right in wanting Hayden to take over . . .'[1]

That evening Whitlam issued a press statement which alluded to his understanding with Hawke:

> The President of the party, Mr Bob Hawke, and I met today to discuss the rebuilding of the Labor movement. In the immediate future we place ourselves at the disposal of the will of the party, to ensure that whatever arrangements are made about particular people, the high purposes of the ALP and those who believe in its cause shall continue to be served for the good of Australia and her people. Each of us is ready to serve in any capacity which the Labor Party chooses.

For Hawke, the Whitlam offer was proof that his manifest destiny was within reach. But his response showed that he lacked either the maturity or stability required for the leadership—apart from the difficulty of procuring a parliamentary seat. Late on the afternoon of his talk with Whitlam Hawke appeared highly excited and the next night he went on television saying Whitlam wanted him as successor and predicting he would defeat Fraser at the next election. While Hawke's deficiencies were of a different nature to those of Hayden, they were just as real; neither man was ready to assume the mantle. Hawke's comments generated a wave of recrimination. The Whitlam–Hawke understanding was anathema to the Labor Caucus; the 'parliamentary club' closed ranks. It attacked Whitlam with a vengeance, but Whitlam was one of its own. Hawke was an outsider and this made him unacceptable.

The 'parliamentary club' was the bastion of hostility towards Hawke, because he aspired to lead the parliamentary Labor Party but had still not joined it. This 'club' was the most powerful force in the ALP. Its power was underpinned by the rules of Caucus sovereignty and given reality in its election of the ALP shadow ministry and all of the federal parliamentary leaders. The reason so many shrewd judges believed for so long that Bob Hawke would never lead the party was their conviction that Caucus would never bow to Hawke and Hawke would never pay homage to the Caucus. It was only in July 1982 that Caucus hostility towards Hawke faltered and finally, in February 1983, that it folded.

The archetypal symbol of the 'parliamentary club' hostility towards Hawke was the Sydney solicitor and future deputy Prime Minister, Lionel Frost Bowen. Bowen sat in his electoral office on Monday 15 December and read the newspaper reports about Whitlam's move towards Hawke. Bowen blamed Whitlam for the defeat; he saw any transfer of leadership to Hawke as absurd. He decided then that he would challenge Whitlam for the ALP leadership, not just to oppose Whitlam, but to oppose his succession plan as well. Moreover, if Hawke came into Parliament to become leader, then Bowen would oppose Hawke directly.

Bowen spoke to a Whitlam supporter and indicated his intentions. About 20 minutes later Whitlam rang. 'Comrade, are you thinking of standing for leader?' he asked. Bowen replied, 'As a matter of fact, Gough, yes I am. And what about yourself?' Whitlam said, 'Oh, I'm still thinking about it.'[2] Bowen knew he had no chance; his candidature was symbolic. Whitlam retained the leadership in January with 36 votes from Bowen with 14 and Frank Crean with 11. But Bowen had laid a claim to the succession.

The most potent mixture for political upheaval is a power rivalry fed on a personality conflict. The personality differences between Hayden and Hawke originated in their family backgrounds 40 years earlier. Both men, born only three years apart (Hawke in December 1929 and Hayden in January 1933), became symbols of new generation ALP politicians. But they were very different men. Hawke was raised in optimism and confidence, Hayden in pessimism and frustration. As a child Hawke was drowned in love and security, pampered and spoilt, encouraged to believe that God watched his steps and inspired by a sense of his own destiny. In contrast Hayden was reared amid emotional and material deprivation, with a father ruined in the Depression who had recourse to the bottle and a mother to whom he became companion, son and father figure for the younger children.[3]

Hawke's father, Clem, adored his son, whose earliest memories were of 'love—an overwhelming love. I can't describe how passionately my father loved me.' In this way the emotional pattern was forged that would dominate Hawke's life—the need to love and be loved as a man and politician. Hawke's official biographer, Blanche d'Alpuget, calls this force 'the overwhelming magic'; it helped establish the deep emotional content not only in Hawke's personal relationships but in the public relationship between him and the community, which was quite unlike that of any other public figure. Hawke became an extrovert, not just in terms of personality projection, but by revealing his own emotions. During his life he has wept, raged and sworn with a recklessness that knew no precedent in public life and, in turn, become the object of an emotional response ranging from admiration and even love from strangers who identify with him to murderous hatred from enemies.

Hayden's father, William George, was a religious absconder who jumped ship in Australia, plied his piano-tuning trade in Queensland, moving in and out of work in the 1930s, and left to his wife the task of keeping the family together. One of Hayden's early memories is that of being awoken by the crash of his father's drunken body on their home veranda. For years as a boy Hayden had no room of his own; he slept on a bunk in the living room. He went to school barefooted because the family could not afford to buy him shoes. In this childhood environment he became emotionally and personally introverted. He never enjoyed the normal paternal ties that bound most homes, and years later strove to be the sort of father to his own children that he himself had never experienced. His mother, Violet, grew vegetables and kept chickens in the backyard to supplement both the family's food and income. She taught Hayden what her experience of life had taught her: never to be trusting of others. 'Never let your left hand know what your right hand is doing' was the message Violet imparted to her son. So Hayden struggled through genuine deprivation of the body and spirit. Privacy and suspicion became his protective shield to manage and combat the world.

The two young men moulded by these families could scarcely have been more different. Hawke's family security bred a physical exuberance, a breathtaking, unquenchable self-confidence; Hayden's insecurity fostered a worried frown and built an inferiority complex across his path in life. Hawke's emotional development meant that he was prepared to rely upon and trust others and the 'outflowing magic' would usually ensure that others, in turn, would rely upon and trust him. Hayden's emotional set told him that he should trust nobody unless he had no choice; in that case he should trust with caution.

This instinct was coupled by another which Hayden absorbed in his seven years as a Queensland policeman: never let anybody intimidate you! Hawke related easily to others. He was a natural communicator; he wanted to communicate himself. Hayden was reluctant to communicate himself or his emotions and years later, in the 1970s and 1980s, would have great difficulty with the politics of personality projection.

Education provided one of the sharpest contrasts between the two men. Education was the indispensable instrument through which Hawke set about realising his destiny. His mother was a schoolteacher and his father a preacher. The magic of books and words filled the Hawke household. 'Education is the key to the world' was the motto his mother, Ellie, engraved on the minds of her children. By contrast, there were few books in the Hayden household. Education was surrounded by a mystique typical of many working-class families who knew it was the means to social mobility but had little idea of where to begin the journey. Hayden failed to develop as a competent reader in his youth, a legacy noticeable four decades later.

Hawke was a scholarship boy. He won entry into the academically elite Perth Modern School, matriculated, completed a law degree at the University of Western Australia, won a Rhodes Scholarship to Oxford where he wrote a thesis on Australian wage fixation, returned home and went to the Australian National University in Canberra to begin his doctorate. Hayden left Brisbane State High at 16 with a sound pass in the Junior Public Examinations and joined the state public service as a clerk earning a wage to supplement the family income. A few years later, after his father died, Hayden joined the police force, which offered both more interest in life and an adult wage. He also became a vigorous sportsman participating in football, rowing and even woodchopping, for which he competed in the odd country show.

In 1956 Hawke, then 27, was studying for his doctorate in Canberra and had never held a full-time job. Despite the good life of drink, sport and academic challenge, he was being pulled elsewhere—towards politics (Hawke's uncle Albert had become Premier of Western Australia), public service and industrial affairs. He attended his first basic wage case in early 1957 and was soon ensconced in the ACTU as research officer.

At the same time, amid the sugarcane of central Queensland, Hayden was keeping the peace in Mackay where he taught himself German in his spare time. Then he was sent to a small station at Redbank near Ipswich where he lived in the police barracks. It was here that he joined the local Labor Party and first felt the onset of the obsession to fill his educational vacuum. Walking past the old Courier-Mail building in Brisbane, he noticed a window display about secondary correspondence school. Soon Hayden began studying for his matriculation by correspondence. In 1959 and 1960, when Hawke was appearing before the Full Bench of the Arbitration Commission as the brightest jewel to illuminate our wage cases, Hayden was getting up at 5.00 a.m. to study and, when on the beat, was going into the men's mealroom at railway stations to spend a few minutes studying a trigonometry text in his bid to secure university entry.

In 1956 Hawke married Hazel Masterson, daughter of a modestly well-to-do accountant; in 1960 Hayden married Dallas Broadfoot, daughter of a coalminer. Hawke and Hazel initially lived on the ANU campus; Hayden and Dallas rented a house in an Ipswich suburb where they had a wood stove, no hot water and no curtains.

In those days Hawke dreamt dreams about himself and managed to convince many of his friends that they would be eventually realised: he would become Prime Minister. Hayden was too uncertain of himself to accept even the most modest reality, let alone indulge in dreams. On the morning of his election to Parliament, the day of the 1961 General Election Hayden sat on his bed trapped in self-doubt about the wisdom of challenging the then sitting Member for Oxley, Menzies' Health Minister, Dr D. A. Cameron. 'This sort of thing isn't for you', he told himself. 'Working-class policemen don't defeat Liberal Cabinet ministers. You've made a mistake in all of this. You've got yourself into debt thinking you can toss a Cabinet minister.'[4] Hayden won comfortably. He won Oxley at the next nine general elections.

Hayden's rebellion was against the intellectual deprivation of his youth. It was a sustained, tenacious and deliberate struggle to reshape himself as a person. Over six years while serving in Parliament Hayden completed his economics degree as an external student and by the early 1970s his political outlook was transformed from what it had been a decade earlier. He was an economic rationalist and social libertarian. He had turned from a high-tariff into a low-tariff politician. His preoccupation was with economic efficiency, growth and redistributive politics. He not only advocated but campaigned for the abolition of censorship of films and books and the abandonment of homosexuality laws—significant liberal stances in the late 1960s for a Queensland member of the ALP Caucus. Hayden's transformation was comprehensive. He read ferociously from Shakespeare to Kafka, dropping quotations into his parliamentary speeches. The scope of his renaissance, although not its intensity, was suggested in a 1972 interview when he said:

> I am very conscious of the fact that I don't have middle-class values. As you know, I've got a degree in economics and I suppose people take a university standard of education as being associated with middle-class standards. But I'm

quite conscious of the fact that there are serious defects in my education that would have come through a middle-class home, like my lack of acquaintance with literature, art and music and my limited ability to discuss these things. I've tried to plug up these defects in more recent times . . . [5]

This was the pattern of Hayden's life. The awareness of his own deficiencies had created a deep-seated drive towards self-improvement through study. Hayden took an almost physical delight in this process. He said, 'There used to be times when I was swotting awfully hard and I used to come away feeling wrung out, but with that really wonderful feeling that you could get in the chest.'[6] Hayden's motivation was overwhelmingly internal, not external. His drive was to self-improvement not self-aggrandisement, unlike that of many other politicians. His working-class radicalism, which had drawn him to the left wing of the party both before and after he entered Parliament, was tempered in the 1960s by these intellectual changes and his sense of realism. The discipline and sacrifice he displayed separated Hayden from much of the Caucus. He spurned the bar and the long, idle hours his colleagues spent exchanging drinks and developing their skill as raconteurs. He became a shadow minister only after the 1969 election, six years after his first attempt. Gradually he built his expertise in areas such as economics, social security and even foreign affairs. Whitlam appointed him social security spokesman upon his election to the front bench—a post in which he would make his reputation and prove his mettle.

In personal terms Hayden was preoccupied with his next step, the next challenge. He had no grand vision for his own ambition. He was still fighting to overcome the handicaps of his youth. Hayden built himself as systematically as a bricklayer builds a house, but never worried whether the dimensions would be sufficiently impressive to inspire others when he became a major focus of attention. He saw himself as an outsider and retained a chip on his shoulder, the product of resentment over the denials in his youth. In 1972 he said, 'I'm really angry about the sort of society I grew up in. I blame the system for it . . . so you've got to try and change values.'[7] Yet education created in Hayden an impatience with his colleagues and a cockiness about his ability: 'If you're going to sit in a Cabinet with people you must never suddenly confront them with a new idea, because it will inevitably be defeated. They'll be frightened by it; you've got to work around to it slowly . . . to get too far in front of the masses is equally as dangerous a sin.'[8]

In the years before Whitlam's 1972 victory Hayden never saw himself as a future leader. In an immortal remark when asked about the leadership he said, 'I've got no aspirations in that direction. Not even slightly . . . first of all,

I'm sensible enough to realise that my Caucus colleagues would never make such a mistake as to endorse me for leader of the party. But to be Leader of the Opposition you'd have to almost totally destroy your family life. I'm not prepared to do that.'[9]

Hayden became an unusual mixture of the old and new. The working-class background was betrayed in his hesitant delivery and stumbling over words; yet Hayden gradually became one of the most widely read and policy-wise figures in the party, with academic friends and pretensions as a social theorist. When the tenacity of the old Hayden was combined with the skills of the new, he emerged as a formidable figure. He proved this in the 1972–75 period of the Whitlam Government. As Social Security Minister he introduced Medibank in the teeth of ferocious opposition. Then, as Treasurer, he had the economic nous and political strength to strip away Labor's ideological clothes and bring down a realistic and clever budget—a feat none of his colleagues could have matched. Whitlam belatedly realised his mistake in not making Hayden Treasurer much earlier. Labor's rearguard action to stay in office against Malcolm Fraser's assault was largely based on the popularity and responsibility of Hayden's 1975–76 budget. As the end approached, he was one of the few ministers whose stature had been enhanced during the three years of office, both in the party and in the community. The direction he gave the Government in its last four months led many to believe he had the best credentials as Whitlam's successor.

In 1969, three years before Hayden dismissed his own leadership potential, Hawke showed he had no reluctance about power by becoming ACTU President. It was his penultimate ambition. Hawke had always sought power, had always been fascinated by it. Now he had the chance to exercise that power. He shot into national prominence three years before Whitlam became Prime Minister and would remain there five years after Whitlam's demise. During Hawke's decade as ACTU President Australia was transformed and the naive optimism of the 1960s was lost in the deepening recession of the 1980s. Hawke also underwent a personal transformation. The angry left-winger turned into an arch defender of the political status quo. The man who frightened so many people as a ruthless manipulator of union power turned into an agent of national reconciliation. Hawke, in fact, brought not working-class tradition but middle-class radicalism to the union movement. He championed the political strike—in 1971 against retail price maintenance which threatened the ACTU–Bourke's store, against the Springbok Rugby Tour and the French nuclear tests.

Hawke's role in each case reflected his ultimate aspirations: to force social and political change as a politician using the muscle of the trade union movement. The dramatic impact of his initial achievements, notably the crushing of retail price maintenance, stunned both the Labor Party and the wider community. Many people became frightened of Hawke, others admired him as a leader who could bring genuine change. It was no wonder that Labor parliamentarians soon came to resent him. Hawke was a politician operating outside Parliament to achieve reform and succeeding when Labor parliamentarians were virtually powerless. It was only logical for Hawke to accept the most senior job that a non-parliamentarian could take: President of the ALP. His accession to this position in July 1973 created fresh dilemmas for both Hawke and the Labor Party. Hawke's response was typically ebullient: 'If you can't ride two horses, then you shouldn't be in the bloody circus.'

As ALP President, Hawke had a platform from which he could legitimately advise the Whitlam Government. His mistake was to do so, often and in public, when he felt Whitlam or his ministers had erred. Like many others he thought this very frequently. Hawke told Whitlam taxes should go up in 1973, attacked the Galston airport decision taken by Federal Cabinet the same year, fought the Whitlam Government on the 1973 prices–incomes referendum, broke with the Government over its even-handed Middle East policy, attacked the 25 per cent tariff cut, cautioned Whitlam over his sacking of Dr Jim Cairns, publicly warned the Prime Minister to heed Caucus sovereignty and blasted Whitlam's decision to allow Lance Barnard to resign, thus precipitating the disastrous Bass by-election. It was in those years that the hostile 'parliamentary club' view of Hawke formed among the Whitlam ministers and backbenchers. The issue to them was not whether Hawke's advice was right or wrong; usually it was right. The issue was that his advice was given so flamboyantly that it appeared to serve his own media interests at the direct expense of the Labor Government. Family disputes between the organisational and parliamentary heads of a political party are usually kept private, but Hawke kept them public. Many ministers resented the way he censured their mistakes and aspired to lead them, yet appeared curiously reluctant to enter the parliamentary cauldron. Whitlam's deliberate oversights only accentuated the problem. He never regarded consultation as a high priority and often gave it no priority. Consequently Hawke was rarely informed beforehand of major decisions, a right to which he believed he was entitled.

Hawke performed an invaluable service for the Labor Government in defusing dangerous industrial confrontations. Then at each election campaign—in 1972, 1974 and 1975—he would hurl himself into the fray to the point of exhaustion campaigning for the ALP. He soon became, at least after the 1974 election, the best campaigner in the Labor Party—a further paradox given his non-parliamentary status. In this way he would redeem himself for earlier indiscretions. It was a love-hate relationship between Hawke and the ALP Caucus but, as the decade progressed, the hatred became dominant.

In late 1975 an incident occurred between Hawke and Hayden which deeply affected their personal relationship and shook Hayden's view of Hawke. Hayden arranged for his economic adviser, Dr Peter McCawley, to brief Hawke about the 1975 budget on the afternoon of budget day. His purpose was to ensure that Hawke was fully aware of the Government's effort to secure maximum wage restraint through tax cuts. This briefing became relevant when the Opposition made the allegation that ACTU–Solo had had prior knowledge of the $2 per barrel budget levy on crude oil and hence had stolen a commercial advantage over its competition. In response to Opposition questions Hayden told Parliament that only three members of the Cabinet were aware of the budget revenue decisions; he told the House that the budget had been 'totally secure'.[10] Hayden made these comments forgetting about the Hawke briefing. But Hawke did not forget. A few days later Hawke arrived in Canberra and told ALP National Secretary David Combe, 'We've got a problem; Bill has unwittingly told a lie to Parliament.'[11] Hawke's position was that if asked he would reveal the briefing. In the political climate of October 1975 such an admission would have been lethal.

Hayden and Hawke discussed the issue late one night at Parliament House. Hawke was pressing for a reopening of the Royal Commission on Petroleum, which had made adverse findings about ACTU–Solo. He was anxious to clear the company's reputation. During their discussion Hayden felt distinctly uncomfortable at the prospect that Hawke might suddenly find the attractions of honesty irresistible on the budget briefing.[12] Such a revelation would have been deeply embarrassing for Hayden. His instinct was to reveal the briefing and accept the consequences.

After consultation with Whitlam and reflection during a weekend at Ipswich Hayden arranged to be interviewed on the ABC by Richard Carleton, to whom he revealed the Hawke briefing. His motive was to pre-empt a furore later and ensure that he did not become hostage to Hawke on the issue. Hayden came under attack for two days in Parliament and had a no-confidence motion moved against him by the Opposition. Then the matter died, overwhelmed by the mounting 1975 crisis. But an edge had been added to relations between Hayden and Hawke; it was an incident which Hayden would not forget.

The events of November–December 1975 swept away the existing order and established a new one. Whitlam publicly declared he would not be a candidate for Labor leadership if Hayden put his name forward. Yet Hayden retreated in determined fashion to cultivate his garden. He decided to pursue a fresh intellectual challenge and enrolled for a law degree. He refused even to stand for the ALP Shadow Cabinet and went into the Parliament as an Opposition backbencher, a retreat so comprehensive that his colleagues correctly identified it as self-indulgence.

Within days of the ballot that could have made him ALP leader, Hayden said:

> I am just not interested. I have said so for many years and I continue to say it. Some people are just not interested in wanting to run things from the top seat. Some people like to be technicians close to the top, playing a worthwhile role— at least I hope I played a worthwhile role—in contributing. I like to have a task, and give myself to that task fairly single-mindedly. I am not sure that I would be a satisfactory leader in the sense of working with a team of people. I have a record of being in conflict with the Caucus fairly frequently.
>
> I can look back at a number of instances where I warned them early, much earlier than just about anyone else in the Caucus, that certain courses that were being adopted were not the wisest and that they would present problems later on.
>
> Taking a Cassandra role is not always popular. I would also say that sometimes I have been quite wrong, too. I am not suggesting infallibility at all. But I do like that position of being able to assert my own independent judgement.[13]

This was the authentic Hayden, perfectly consistent with the 1972 Hayden. The quotations were almost exactly the same. Of course the circumstances of 1975 and the enormous personal letdown were important. But Hayden had not coveted the job; he had never seen himself as leader. This merely proved he lacked the furnace of ambition that drove so many other men to the leadership. It was not his intellectual ability that was found wanting; the fault, if one judges it a fault, lay in his personality. His reaction showed he was a normal man because only an extraordinary man would have wanted to become Labor leader at that time or, indeed, any other time.

Because Hayden was in no condition to become leader then, the decision was the right one for him. Yet it is only because he subsequently sought to become leader and Prime Minister that this decision, in retrospect, appears as a personal and political failure. It meant that Whitlam, not Hayden, led the Labor Party into the 1977 election. With Hayden as the leader instead of Whitlam, Labor's major electoral liability would have disappeared and Hayden could have won seats in 1977 to give himself a better platform from which to attack Fraser in the 1980 election.

In early 1976 the Iraqi affair burst upon the Labor Party and in the process reduced Hawke's standing to its nadir inside the ALP. This happened despite the highly constructive role he played at the vital National Executive meeting which reviewed the fiasco. The Iraqi affair had its origins in the decision by Whitlam, National Secretary David Combe and left-winger Bill Hartley to raise US$500,000 from the Ba'ath Socialist Party of Iraq to finance Labor's election campaign. But the funds never came. Hawke's initial view was that Whitlam should not and could not survive as leader. His mistake was to make these comments to journalists after a press conference at his Melbourne home on 28 February, the Saturday before the National Executive meeting. Hawke assumed his non-attributable comments would not be used. But they were and the headlines in *The Australian* read 'It's The End For Whitlam', while an accompanying story said there had been an increase in support for Hawke to become leader. The headlines in Sydney's morning tabloid *The Daily Telegraph* were 'Hawke To Axe Whitlam'. The overkill of these two papers from the Murdoch stable prompted a surge of sympathy for Whitlam and deep resistance to his removal at the behest of the Murdoch group which had campaigned so virulently against the Whitlam Government before it fell.

The apparent backing of the Murdoch press for Hawke against Whitlam did Hawke severe damage inside the ALP: he was seen to be sponsored by the party's enemies. Moreover, by his non-attributable comments Hawke appeared to assume a role for himself in the removal of Whitlam. The 'parliamentary club', already antagonistic towards Hawke, now began to loathe him. He would have to live with the resentment, even hatred, of senior figures in the parliamentary party who would campaign ceaselessly to deny Hawke's leadership ambition.

Just before the Iraqi affair broke, Hayden himself launched one of the strongest 'parliamentary club' attacks on Hawke. This time Hawke had given public advice to Caucus members not to boycott the opening ceremony of Parliament to protest against Sir John Kerr for his dismissal of the Whitlam Government. Much of the Caucus was infuriated by this gratuitous remark from a non-parliamentarian who, without being a member of the dismissed Government, purported to tell its former members and present parliamentarians how to react. Hayden bluntly told Hawke to keep out of politics:

> Mr Hawke was not always terribly helpful to the Labor Government with some of his impulsive, intemperate comments and his occasional emotional outbursts. The fact that many of those comments were made in distant corners of the world like London or Delphi didn't diminish the blow against the Labor Government. Mr Hawke has to make a hard decision. The decision is whether

he wants to be a politician making a reasonable appeal to our establishment endorsement [i.e., preselection process] or whether he wants to be a resolute trade union leader defending and promoting the interests of the workers. It is impossible to do both satisfactorily. Given the present industrial situation, Mr Hawke might find it best to give an undiverted commitment to the aspirations of the workers of Australia and to save politics for when he becomes a politician.[14]

Hayden believed that Hawke's conduct was disloyal to the ALP. Hayden and many other Caucus members had concluded that Hawke's penchant for public comment was imposing a burden that the party should not expect to carry. He saw it as Hawke promoting himself and damaging the party. It seems that Hayden, who had now retreated from his own hard decision to drop out, missed the irony in his suggestion that Hawke do the same. These remarks by Hayden reveal the contrast he implicitly drew between himself and Hawke. He identified Hawke as a man very different to himself, with different values, who used tactics that Hayden deplored. Meanwhile Whitlam, after surviving the Iraqi affair, said in March that Hawke 'is not, I believe, as intellectually well equipped for leadership as I know Bill Hayden to be'.[15] Whitlam never changed his mind again on the succession. The door of the 'parliamentary club' was shut firmly against Hawke.

For Hayden the Iraqi crisis was a second, although more difficult, chance to take the ALP leadership. Whitlam survived only because there was no suitable alternative, while Hayden, who would have been such a candidate, declined to run. However, the letdown from the 1975 defeat had worn off. When former Education Minister Kim Beazley (Sr) resigned from the shadow ministry in protest at the Iraqi affair, Hayden replaced him and became defence spokesman. He was back in politics. A few months later Hayden said of his December to March retreat:

It seemed to me I was being too self-indulgent and I think largely, unconsciously, was putting some of my own interests before greater responsibilities that I had . . . I suppose the biggest jolt I received was one night I was talking to my wife and referred to some criticism of myself, again that I was self-indulgent . . . and my wife who is fairly discreet, if not passive in her views on my involvement in politics, heartily agreed with the observation which had been made. I suppose it was a shock really.[16]

By now the impact of the Whitlam years on Hayden was more settled and easier to read. They had left Hayden with a deep appreciation of the difficulty

15

in introducing reformist policies inside Australia's political structure. Hayden was not just sceptical about his own talents—although aware of his superiority over most of his colleagues—he was sceptical about the scope for a Labor leader in the post-Whitlam era. Indeed, Hayden was dubious about the power of politicians to effect change. It seemed to him that power lay more with a diffused group within business, unions and the public service, all deeply conservative institutions. With the world economic crisis now superimposed on this structure of political inertia, Hayden was inclined to think a reformist government would be paralysed. The realist and pessimist in Hayden told him to stay clear of the leadership.

Meanwhile, Bob Hawke was assailed by a crisis that was both political and personal. The transition to Parliament was becoming a major hurdle in his own mind and a litany of lost opportunities. Hawke had been ALP candidate for Corio at the 1963 election but had lost. When the 1967 Corio by-election had been called, Whitlam visited Hawke at the ACTU and urged him to stand. Hawke had told Whitlam that his aim was to succeed Albert Monk as ACTU President. If he did, he would remain as ACTU President for six years. He was attracted to this post because it offered the permanence of power, unlike Parliament. So Gordon Scholes won Labor preselection in 1967, won the Corio by-election and held the seat at every succeeding election. Seven years later, on the eve of the 1974 snap election, senior Labor ministers wanted to boost the Government's chances by persuading Hawke to contest a Melbourne seat. Combe put the proposition to Hawke, who said he would consider it. But Clyde Cameron leaked the story that Hawke had been asked to run against Snedden in Bruce and effectively ended Hawke's chances. He would not challenge Snedden because the risk of loss was too great and he could not nominate for another seat without appearing to be running scared of Snedden.

The more Hawke lectured his Government, the more Whitlam tried to move Hawke into Parliament. In October 1974 Whitlam wanted to retire Treasurer Frank Crean to the Commonwealth Bank board, forcing a by-election for Melbourne Ports. Whitlam wanted Hawke to run and saw the by-election as a rallying point for his troubled Government. Hawke refused, telling Whitlam that a by-election would be crazy. Whitlam later recalled: 'His reaction was that we couldn't win a by-election in Melbourne Ports. If you look at the Melbourne papers of the time you will see that Bob Hawke aborted the proposal.'[17] But it was not Hawke's own work. Frank Crean changed his mind, stayed in politics, tried to keep his safe seat for another successor such as his son, Simon, was humiliatingly dumped as Treasurer by Whitlam and ultimately succeeded by former Victorian Opposition Leader Clyde Holding.

Finally in December 1975, Hawke seemed to be anxious to accept

Whitlam's offer and surge into the leadership. But within months the ALP Caucus presented such a formidable obstacle to Hawke's ambition that there was grave doubt that he would ever make such a transition. Hawke was deeply affected by the Iraqi affair, upset at the stain it left on the party, bitter at the internal hostility towards himself and almost demonic in his determination to destroy the left and Bill Hartley. But the crisis of his personal life was also looming. Blanche d'Alpuget described him at this time:

> While the forces upon him to enter Parliament—and those threatening him against trying—built up, the more serious dilemma for Hawke was a private one: alcohol . . . He knew that he could not achieve his dream unless he moderated his drinking. Already television interviewers were covering up for Hawke, by scrapping film of him recorded when he was drunk. When he was to be broadcast live, or to take part in important prerecorded debates, Hawke by 1976 would sometimes mutter, 'No, I mustn't drink. I mustn't drink.'[18]

2
Hayden as saviour

Hawke's not in Parliament and Whitlam's not taking us anywhere. You should run for the leadership.

Paul Keating to Bill Hayden, February 1977

By early 1977 Bill Hayden had abandoned his Hamlet-like equivocation, and accepted that fate had ordained him to challenge Gough Whitlam. Hayden had not aspired to this assignment and had long resisted pressure to resort to the knife. But he became a victim of his historical circumstances. It was his own decision, but it was made at the behest of others who insisted that Hayden had a responsibility to both himself and the ALP to step to centre stage and to assume the political burden of the Labor Party and responsibility for its electoral fortunes. Hayden was 'turned' on the leadership by his own friends. He was conscripted to become Labor's saviour.[1]

Hayden's career would unfold into a tragedy so cruel that only a Shakespeare could capture its magnitude. Hayden was a man who, under pressure from his peers, made a strike for power against Whitlam. Unlike Hawke, who always possessed this capacity, Hayden needed to bend himself consciously to the task and surrender his heart to ambition. Once committed to the path, he proceeded with grim determination and then mounting enthusiasm.

As leader, he was trapped in a search for electoral victory, learning as he went like a man in a maze, exploring one passage after another until he nearly broke right through. In the process he sacrificed much of his personal self to become the political man: idealism faded into cynicism, scepticism dissolved into aggression. Finally Hayden was ready and, hungry for power, closed on the elusive goal of the prime ministership. But at this point the forces of pragmatism which Hayden represented rose up to slay him in deference to the ultimate pragmatist, Bob Hawke, whose certainty as an election winner he could never match. In his final act of discretion Hayden volunteered to vacate the leadership to Hawke just as he volunteered to seize it from Whitlam. On both occasions Hayden used the interests of the Labor Party to legitimise his actions. Few politicians could so justifiably use such an argument.

Hayden's tragedy is exquisite because in both 1977 and 1983 his invocation of ALP interests was also designed to conceal his personal fears. In 1977 Hayden was persuaded to put aside the self-doubt that was integral to his character. He agreed to challenge Whitlam not just for himself but for the party, and in so doing he represented not just himself but the coming generation of Labor politicians. Yet all through his long leadership the self-doubt was never conquered. It lingered, disappearing and then reappearing; it was betrayed a thousand times in public and private, notably in Hayden's overcompensation to conceal it. In January–February 1983, when Hayden submitted to the internal party pressures on him and resigned, it was because his self-doubt re-emerged and prevailed. A leader confident in himself would never have resigned in the knowledge that an election was coming. Hayden never feared Fraser. But he feared his own capacity to beat Fraser at that time. The pessimism that permeated the ALP also claimed Hayden as a victim. It did so because he had never possessed the inner belief in self that so marked men like Fraser, Whitlam and Hawke. Deep inside, the doubts of 1976 were alive, still transmitting the messages that made him more a normal man and less a megalomaniac.

The final irony is that most of the Labor politicians who persuaded Hayden to undertake his 1977 leadership strike were the same men whose flight to Hawke in 1983 cost him the leadership—John Button, Paul Keating and Mick Young being three such notables. It was the misfortune of Whitlam and Hayden and these power-brokers that there was a power vacuum in the Labor Party post-1975. Labor had four deputy leaders in the two years from 1974—Lance Barnard, Jim Cairns, Frank Crean and Tom Uren—yet none was a leadership contender. There was no obvious successor to Whitlam. So Whitlam stayed and Hayden stepped into this vacuum and eventually became his challenger.

The Labor leadership is a cruel and contradictory post. A leader is expected to lead but also expected to be an equal. Most recent Labor leaders have gone the way of death, despair or dismissal. Curtin died in office; Chifley died as leader after losing office; Evatt went mad; Calwell, who came within a few votes of office, sank into despair; Whitlam was briefly triumphant and then dismissed, and Hayden, the reluctant leader, prevaricated on the edge of victory only to be betrayed by the curious combination of himself and his friends.

After 1975 Whitlam was unchanged but diminished. He was an extinct volcano, gigantic but expended, a memorial to past glories and brilliant performances. He was driven by a new overwhelming force: the thirst for vindication. Preoccupied with the past, he became an obstacle to Labor's march to the future. Whitlam's tragedy was that the political world he knew had been transformed. The system of parliamentary government in which he thrived had led to his sacking; the assumption of economic growth on which The Programme was based had been cancelled; the Whitlam panache remained but the Whitlam popularity was lost between dazzling horizons abroad and empty factories at home. Finally, the message of Whitlamism— bigger and more interventionist Government to promote equality and enlightenment—lay broken at the foundations of Fraser's edifice.

Whitlam had dominated four Liberal leaders—Holt, Gorton, McMahon and Snedden—and had pioneered a new vision for Australia. He was a great man, but not possessed of the multi-faceted greatness of a Churchill or De Gaulle. Whitlam had but one political career in him and that had effectively ended. He could not recast himself to face Fraser. So he persevered through 1976 and into 1977, Kerr's victim, seeking vengeance on both Sir John Kerr and Sir Garfield Barwick, but true to himself and the ideas he championed.

However the 1975 election debacle had not only reduced Labor's numerical strength in Parliament but had revoked Whitlam's mandate with the voters. His continued presence on the political stage in 1976–77 discredited the ideas he represented and guaranteed a demoralised ALP. The mood was captured by Peter Bowers:

> In opposition the Labor Party has become geriatrically introspective: it is tired and lacks confidence in itself. At question time Labor MPs wander into the House like Brown's cows, to browse a while amid the vacant acres of green leather on the opposition side. Mr Whitlam gives the impression of going through the motion of leading with the glazed instincts of a fighter out on his feet . . .
>
> Ministers blunt any criticism of the Government's economic performance—and there is much to criticise—by reminding anyone who may have forgotten of the sorry mismanagement that marked the Whitlam Government. The Government backbench openly mocks Mr Whitlam. No party, as Mr Snedden learnt, will sit for long behind a leader who is not taken seriously by his opponents.[2]

Whitlam was heroically unrepentant but electorally insensitive. Asked whether he interpreted the 1975 result as a rejection of his Government's programmes, Whitlam replied:

Of the programmes themselves, no. The people were only just beginning to see the benefit of those programmes. I interpret the result last December as a one-off verdict flowing from two factors. One, the election took place halfway through our term, as the previous election did. Secondly, Australia's isolation from comparable countries enabled the conservatives to assert that Australia's economic difficulties were exceptional and due to local factors alone . . . The changes I made in the middle of 1975 produced the best Government that Australia has had for very many years.[3]

Hayden's challenge was assisted by an important technical factor. After 1975 the Caucus rules were changed to allow for a midterm election for the leadership positions and the Shadow Cabinet. This meant the leadership would be vacated in May 1977 and nominations called, allowing Hayden to challenge Whitlam in a head-to-head contest. It enabled Hayden to surmount the major difficulty in any challenge, to secure beforehand a vote to declare the leadership vacant. Moreover, since the leadership was being thrown open, Hayden had a right to stand. After all, if Whitlam still adhered to his December 1975 position, then he would not recontest the ballot and allow Hayden to replace him.

The ALP Caucus of the 1975–77 Parliament was a cauldron of animosities given free licence by consignment to Opposition. The party was in transition. The former Whitlam Government ministers, having lost power, were ending their careers amid vituperative post-mortems. The younger generation was despondent but not so scarred, and was looking towards the future. It is nearly impossible to recapture the rancour that filled the Caucus at this time. Whitlam was alienated from his other three leaders, his deputy, Tom Uren, and Senate deputy Jim Keeffe (both of the left), and his Senate leader Ken Wriedt who, during the Iraqi affair, had attempted to force Whitlam's resignation. Lionel Bowen, whom Whitlam had groomed in Government, had broken with him irrevocably. Bowen intended to oppose Whitlam in the May 1977 ballot, just as he had opposed him in January 1976. Respected party figures such as Kim Beazley from the right and John Wheeldon, once from the left, refused to serve in Whitlam's shadow ministry. His most implacable enemy was Clyde Cameron, who plagued him at one Caucus meeting after another. Blessed with a sense of humour, a tenacity to pursue his enemies down the decades, skilful in debate, swift in counting heads, accurate in his reach for the political jugular, Cameron was a ruthless man. He would never forgive Whitlam for his humiliating removal in 1975 from the Labour and Immigration portfolio to Science and Consumer Affairs. Significant figures in the Caucus's left wing were scheming against Whitlam. In late 1976 the left

21

flirted briefly with the idea of promoting Mick Young as an alternative leader.

In this climate it is not surprising that before Christmas 1976 Whitlam sat by the pool at his new Sydney eastern suburbs address to analyse his future. At various stages Margaret Whitlam had told him to quit politics. Whitlam himself had wavered. On this day, his senior Private Secretary Richard Butler, later to become Ambassador for Disarmament in the Hawke Government, flew to Sydney to review the strategy. Four propositions were examined and conclusions reached. The first was that on any assessment of the numbers Whitlam could survive the May 1977 ballot. This was an imperative since it was agreed that Whitlam could not end his career in a humiliating rejection by the Caucus. Secondly it was agreed that Whitlam should be able to make significant inroads into Fraser's position at the next election. It was felt that a big increase in Labor's parliamentary strength, even short of victory, would enable Whitlam to retire having brought the party back to the brink of office. The third point was the succession and Whitlam reaffirmed that Hayden must be the next leader. But he felt that 1977 was not opportune for Hayden and that Hayden's leadership would be enhanced if he entered on a high note with the ALP in a strong position, as opposed to the huge margin Fraser currently enjoyed. Finally they discussed Whitlam's place in history. Whitlam said that he wanted vindication but he was aware that by seeking it he ran a risk. They concluded that the ultimate humiliation would be a defeat for Whitlam in the mid-1977 ballot. This must not happen. This long and emotional meeting closed with Whitlam deciding to stay on to fight again.[4]

Whitlam now went on to the offensive. He knew the party needed the tonic of revitalisation and he had the answer. He recognised that Hayden's confidence and aggression had returned as 1976 progressed. The most damaging blow the ALP had delivered Fraser that year was Hayden's statement that 'blind Freddie' could see a devaluation of the dollar was necessary.[5] During the 1976 budget session Hayden was chirpy and relaxed, belting out economic questions on his portable typewriter for colleagues to ask in Parliament. Whitlam decided he would use the May 1977 ballot to recruit Hayden as deputy leader in place of Tom Uren. In this fashion Whitlam would not only remove Uren, with whom he usually avoided conversation, but give the party a new-look Whitlam–Hayden ticket, tying Hayden's economic credibility to his own chariot wheels. But first some details had to be resolved.

In January 1976 Uren had won the deputy leadership 33–30 from Paul Keating. If Hayden were to replace Uren, then Keating would need to be neutralised. The man for this task was Senator James ('Diamond Jim') McClelland, a man of silver tongue, impeccable style and lightning wit who, if he had entered the House of Representatives rather than the Senate 15 years earlier, would have rivalled Whitlam for the leadership. McClelland shared many of Whitlam's traits and consequently was prepared to forgive his failings. In early 1977 he invited Keating to his Point Piper house for a chat. McClelland said Hayden should be elevated to the position of deputy and argued that a Whitlam–Hayden team was Labor's best. Keating agreed to talk to Hayden and indicated his willingness to stay clear of the deputy's contest. McClelland proposed that Keating support Hayden against Uren, thus giving Hayden a sufficiently broad coalition to win. Soon afterwards Whitlam told Richard Butler: 'It's all fixed, comrade. We'll have a Whitlam–Hayden team forming the next Government.' Hayden later came to Whitlam's office to seal the deal. He agreed to run for deputy and told Whitlam that he would not contest the leadership ballot.

Just before the Parliamentary session began in February 1977 Hayden and Keating went to dinner at the Taverna restaurant in Canberra. Keating had just turned 33 and had already been eight years in Parliament. Kim Beazley (Sr) once stood in King's Hall and, pointing Keating out to a journalist, predicted: 'You see that man; watch him because he's a political killer.' Keating brought to Caucus and machine politics the disciplined infallibility of his Catholicism. Dressed with the smart severity of a Jesuit, he slid along the parliamentary lobbies carrying ambition as an altar boy cradles his missal, reflexes sharpened to strike heretics. Although steeped in Labor tradition personally handed to him by Jack Lang and Rex Connor, Keating was unburdened by the dead hand of the past; he pursued his passion for French antiques at Paddington and cultivated leaders of the financial community at the big end of town. Keating prayed to God and waited on history; he was still to discover a more complex world. In the meantime his youthful energies were devoted to securing another ALP Government while he developed friendships with the press and enemies in the Liberal Party.

At their Canberra dinner Hayden told Keating, 'I intend to run for the deputy leadership.' Keating gently reminded Hayden that he thought the purpose of the meeting was to establish whether he would stand aside for Hayden. After further discussion Keating said, 'Hawke's not in Parliament and Whitlam's not taking us anywhere. You should run for the leadership. If you want to do both me and the Labor Party a favour, then challenge Whitlam. Why worry about the deputy's job? That will get you nowhere and achieve nothing.' Keating told Hayden he had always supported Whitlam, but knew that Whitlam was finished. If he remained leader, Labor would lose the next election. Hayden was interested in the prospect of Keating's support against Whitlam. He agreed to sound out others. Herein lay the origins of a difficult relationship which was eventually to founder on the twin reefs of Hayden's chronic suspicion of Keating and Keating's disappointment in Hayden.

Hayden found he had advocates everywhere. Senator John Button urged him to stand and wrote him a letter to this effect, so opening the fateful relationship in Hayden's career. Button would develop a personal and emotional intimacy with him that would prove so valuable for so long, but ultimately fatal. Button was a small man of quick wit, crafty calculation and intellectual provocation. In Victoria he was a champion of a small faction, originally called the Participants, opposed to the tyranny of the bigger factions on the left and right.

Hayden's bid for the leadership would herald the emergence of a new force in the ALP Caucus: the centre. It was not a faction as such but a group tied together by personal associations and shared policy commitments. As the friendship between Hayden and Button grew and put down roots, it became a symbol of the Caucus centre. It attracted younger and more intelligent politicians tired of the militarism of the ALP machine and the sterile slogans of yesteryear. The centre saw itself as both enlightened and realistic. It was economically responsible and socially progressive and depicted itself as the wave of the future in a party which desperately needed new policies and a new spirit. The centre was first identifiable as a group in this autumn of 1977 when Hayden bid for the leadership. Its most prominent recruits included Senator Peter Walsh, whose furious efforts to recapture the style of the late Eddie Ward long disguised the steel-trap brain he applied to economics and taxation, and Senator Don Grimes, a Tasmanian medico who was already slotted to become Social Security Minister.

Mick Young, who had become famous as part of Whitlam's 1972 'It's time' campaign, was a fervent Hayden advocate and began a friendship with him that would bloom brightly before it sank into an endless winter. Young would have been a caricature if he had not been authentic. A former shearer with a ruddy Irish complexion, he was also a champion prawn-peeler, beer-drinker, turf patron, China buff, media personality and inimitable raconteur whose grip on politics was pure instinct. He knew Whitlam was finished and Hayden was the best alternative. In 1977 Hayden and Young dined together at the Kingston restaurant in Canberra owned by Young's best friend, former Whitlam Press Secretary Eric Walsh. By the end of that year Hayden was saying he wanted Young as his deputy.

The pressures on Hayden to run were immense. Whitlam would be challenged by Lionel Bowen anyway. Long-serving figures such as Kim Beazley and Clyde Cameron both encouraged Hayden; Beazley believed Hayden would make a capable leader while Cameron saw him as a means of deposing

Whitlam. Wide sections of the left would support Hayden against Whitlam, but not Hayden against Uren. Hayden's prospects of building a broad base of support from right to left looked good. Late 1976 had seen subtle but important changes in the political climate. Opinion polls began turning against the Fraser Government and the economy languished in recession. The Government appeared susceptible to a powerful Opposition thrust. Whitlam was the stumbling block.

Hayden did not speak to Lionel Bowen, but there was delicate communication between them about the ballot. Bowen was a perplexing mixture of tradition and unpredictability whose roots lay in the NSW Catholic right wing and who sounded like a Chips Rafferty after law school. A father of eight who had spent years in Randwick politics, Bowen was an old-fashioned, straight-talking, laconic Australian. He had a great feel for humour and always stayed his own man. But he did not want to stand aside for Hayden and suggested instead that both men run and exchange preferences against Whitlam. Hayden refused. He wanted a clear run at Whitlam. Bowen, recognising Hayden's position as stronger than his own, reluctantly pulled out.

Clyde Cameron launched an early assault on Whitlam too vicious to be productive. In a letter on 21 February to all Caucus members Cameron managed to attack Whitlam while not mentioning his name:

> Australians will not tolerate a one-man dictatorship; nor should they. Prime Ministers John Curtin and Ben Chifley proved that competent leaders can afford to be democratic. Neither of these great Labor Prime Ministers found it necessary to ape the pettiness, petulance and arrogance of Liberal Prime Ministers . . . Both found it possible to govern better by taking Caucus and Cabinet into their confidence—they never used the weapon of pre-emption against their own colleagues . . .

As February turned into March Hayden's position firmed. Then on 8 March he had a meeting with Hawke, after which he moved decisively and informed Whitlam of his challenge. Hayden met Hawke at David Combe's home to discuss the problems of the ALP in Queensland. But the most significant discussion was not about Queensland but about the leadership. Hawke at this meeting appeared preoccupied by his own ambitions and quizzed Hayden intensely on the prospect of Hawke becoming leader after he entered Parliament. He asked Hayden whether he would challenge Whitlam in the mid-year ballot. Hayden prevaricated, but said he had a high enough opinion of himself to run for leader some time. Combe was convinced that Hayden had been put on notice once again by Hawke, in the most unmistakable fashion, that the ACTU President was obsessive about his transfer to Parliament and the leadership. He was worried that Hayden would think he had been 'set up' and lured to meet Hawke under false pretences. Hawke was clearly betraying his frustration: he saw a leadership ballot only three months away with a possible transfer from Whitlam to Hayden, an event he was impotent to influence.

Now Hayden acted to lock out Hawke.[6] That night political spirits effervesced throughout the lobbies, courtyards and dining rooms of Parliament House. It was a royal occasion. Her Majesty, the Queen of Australia, was in attendance and there was strong clapping during the King's Hall reception from Liberals anxious to upstage the republican sentiments of Labor members. As usual Fraser was dreary and Whitlam stole the show. Alluding to Fraser's gift of a thoroughbred to the Queen, Whitlam parried: 'I have never heard a horse praised so fulsomely since Caligula made one a consul.'

After the Queen had left, it became an old-fashioned but expensive Australian party. Hayden was upstairs in the members' dining room, which had been thrown open for the night; Dallas was by his side, mixing with the swirl of Caucus and the press gallery. With a cocky manner and happy spirit Hayden punched adrenalin with his friends thereby reinforcing his sinews of confidence. Messages were flashed about the room: Hayden was running; Dallas was encouraging him. That night the new order appeared imminent.

Hawke was dining downstairs in the courtyard at a table of black comedy: Sir Warwick Fairfax and Lady Fairfax, Fraser's Press Secretary David Barnett, Whitlam's Private Secretary Richard Butler, Hawke and several journalists. Hawke had not been restrained by the magnificence of the occasion. He drank up and spoke out. His targets were Sir Warwick and the Fairfax press and his style was bantering and colourful. The main burden of his remarks was the need for the Fairfax papers to adopt a more constructive attitude to Labor in general and Hawke in particular, although the conversation was sufficiently wide-ranging to embrace Catholicism and royalty. Occasionally Hawke appeared diverted when, for instance, he put his arms around Lady Fairfax who was wearing an attractive, off-the-shoulder summer gown. Hawke's evening finished with a Labor staffer pouring a glass of beer over his head.

In the clear light of the next morning Hayden went to Uren's office and told the deputy he would oppose Whitlam. Uren promised his support to Hayden, but warned that it would be a difficult challenge. The left did not persuade or trap Hayden into the challenge—a claim subsequently made by Whitlam. Indeed the Caucus figures who encouraged him were from the centre and the right, but Hayden correctly assumed that once he declared himself he would have significant left-wing support.

Uren, a former Changi POW, a Labor battler and romantic, had replaced his anti-Vietnam crusade of the 1960s with an anti-uranium campaign in the 1970s. Uren's misfortune, upon which he had seized, was to become titular leader of the ALP left after the demise of Jim Cairns, its figurehead, and the departure of Lionel Murphy, its brains. Uren aspired to become an ideological leader of the left as well as a Caucus organiser. His relationship with Hayden was curiously lopsided in a way which Uren failed to perceive and which Hayden ruthlessly exploited. Influenced by his paternal pride in Hayden, Uren was the challenger's champion in forums of the left. He was proud of his own role in Hayden's development as a man and as a politician, and felt he had a stake in a future Hayden leadership. But Hayden privately described the left as 'intellectually suffocating', criticised Uren's overbearing tactics and scarcely reciprocated Uren's affections. Uren gave him two pieces of advice: stay off television during the contest and tell Whitlam of his decision.

The next night, 10 March, Hayden left Keating's room for his personal confrontation with the longest-serving Labor leader. Keating had warned Hayden that Whitlam was a 'jungle fighter' who would use any weapons to hold his position. But Hayden believed he had to inform Whitlam, given their previous talks about the deputy leadership. Hayden's personal code made such notice imperative.

Whitlam's experience in personal confrontation had a history so rich and so violent that Hayden was easy prey. Hayden had no chance even to ask Whitlam to stand down as leader. Whitlam pre-empted his request by confirming that he would be re-contesting the leadership in the May ballot. Hayden told Whitlam that he would also be a contender. Whitlam asked: 'Why, Bill?' Hayden replied that it was because others had asked him to run; even if he declined, Bowen would still be a candidate. Whitlam said: 'Bill, I intend to keep my hand on the tiller.'

Hayden left after five minutes and returned to Keating's office. He was unnerved and Keating offered him a Scotch. Later Keating said, 'Whitlam always backed Hayden for his successor but he knew that, while Bill might be the best man, he was no match for Gough himself in a face-to-face encounter.'

Whitlam's attitude was that Hayden had declined the leadership when it was available. Now he would have to fight for it. The next day Whitlam and Hayden held another talk. This time, significantly, they discussed Hawke. The essence of Hayden's challenge was to push Whitlam aside and seize the leadership before Hawke came into Parliament. Whitlam agreed with Hayden's objective but not his timing.

Animosity towards Hawke unified Whitlam and Hayden and left- and right-wing factions. The most vehement anti-Hawke section of the Caucus at this time was the right wing Bowen–Wriedt axis. Bowen was prepared to stand aside for Hayden's challenge in order to cement a succession that kept out Hawke. Wriedt's hostility for Whitlam was only surpassed by his even more profound hostility for Hawke. The left remained anti-Hawke but was chiefly preoccupied with debating the merits of Whitlam and Hayden. Clearly Hawke was already shaping the tempo of ALP power politics.

It soon became apparent that Hayden's position was not as strong as assumed by his backers and the press. Whitlam was fighting to avoid a humiliation and he fought superbly. He had three sources of advantage. The first was his incomparable leadership profile and on 10 March he delivered a parliamentary attack on Fraser literally beyond the capacity of anybody else in the ALP. Secondly Whitlam was the symbol of Labor sentiment and devotion throughout the rank and file of the party. The Caucus knew another Whitlam; but in the branches and trade unions the faithful had shared Whitlam's 1975 martyrdom and worshipped him with passion. The ALP had never deposed its leader mid-term and Whitlam was able to mobilise the sentimental loyalty of the movement to himself. Finally Whitlam campaigned as the more substantial and appealing leader, bluntly asserting that since Labor would win the next election the party must decide who it wanted as Prime Minister.

There was an initial foray by Hayden's backers to precipitate the contest and force it the following week. But under the strategic influence of Clyde Cameron, they decided during two meetings in Wriedt's office on 15 and 16 March to wait until May. The reasons were uncertainty about Hayden's core strength in the Caucus and the view that a delay would assist Hayden. Cameron disputed the prediction by the Whitlam camp that Hayden would wilt under pressure. He said:

> I always make it my practice to study the man I am promoting. I have watched Hayden for some time. I've watched his eyes; I've watched his hands; I've watched the way he moves; I'm convinced he won't crack.[7]

The most contentious debate centred around the real worth of the challenger. Over the next two months Hayden was branded everything from a weak, unsure man to an economic genius. In public and in private the Whitlam forces probed for Hayden's susceptibility. Whitlam declared it was 'amazing' that certain people had changed their attitudes on the leadership now that Labor's prospects had improved. Laurie Oakes put the big question in a column headed 'How tough is Bill Hayden?':

> Bill Hayden has a slightly off-beat sense of humour, and there is one joke he likes to play over and over. He will invite someone to his office but when they

open the door they find an apparently empty room. Mr Hayden will be hiding either in a cupboard or on hands and knees under his desk. Hiding as a joke is one thing. What worries some of Mr Hayden's colleagues is what they fear may be a tendency to hide on occasions when things are serious . . .

Political leaders are supposed to be hungry for power and supremely confident of their own ability. Mr Hayden is not—or has not been in the past . . . Many in the party see the present leadership crisis as the ultimate test of Mr Hayden's character.[8]

Hayden passed the toughness test and eventually the debate moved to other qualities. Hayden's supporters believed he offered a return to a more orthodox Labor leadership than Whitlam. Hayden would consult with Caucus while being less authoritarian and brilliant; the days of crashing through or crashing would be over. Hayden would be a safe choice, strong on economic management when it was the chief issue. His former Cabinet colleagues testified that, although an agoniser, Hayden was not a weak man. The acid test was whether he could develop from being a competent minister into a leader.

Two inescapable facts, however, should have been accorded priority in the debate over Hayden's merits. The first was that Whitlam could not recover politically and this was obvious. The second was that Hayden was the best alternative leader in the Caucus and this was also obvious. This analysis means that Hayden should have won. The Labor Caucus usually displays a sound judgement in leadership battles. Its May 1977 decision was one of its worst.

In power terms Whitlam solidified his base, the NSW right. He met the NSW Party President John Ducker at the Parramatta Travelodge one weekend: 'Comrade, I think I'm entitled to one last go.' Ducker replied, 'Gough, we've never let you down. We're not going to now.' Ducker delivered a few votes for Whitlam, decisive in such a close contest.[9] Keating was in a difficult position, isolated from his NSW machine and under pressure to join it. He felt later that his own relations with Ducker never fully recovered from his support for Hayden. The operating axiom of the NSW right was, 'All for one and one for all', but Keating put his own judgement of Caucus politics and personal ambition ahead of his faction. He wanted to see a new ALP Government installed as fast as possible. But his split with the NSW right had an impact which Keating still remembered in 1982.

The logical left-wing ticket was Hayden–Uren, but at first the left was divided. The mix of factors which split the left's solidarity included rank and file support for Whitlam and concern that Hayden was an economic conservative who lacked leadership strength. Finally the bulk of the parliamentary left united behind Hayden. Some veterans, however, preferred their old enemy to the young upstart. It was widely believed that men such as Rex Connor, Frank Crean and Gordon Bryant voted for Whitlam despite their titanic battles against him in past years, notably the period of Labor Government.

The truth about the challenge is that Hayden wanted to win on ability alone. He ran as an individual not as a factional candidate. Although his colleagues urged him, the final responsibility belonged to Hayden, who conducted the challenge as he conducted his political life: as a loner. There was no 'fix', no factional guarantee of votes. There was a mood for change and Hayden was trying to tap it. In this first bid for power, even with his supporters gathered around, Hayden remained a solitary man on a solitary mission, sustained by his friends from the centre group yet still distant from them.

This challenge is an important example of Hayden's approach to power politics and a study of the code in which he believed. Hayden told Whitlam at the start. Then he stayed silent during the two months before the ballot. Finally he was prepared in his heart to accept the decision either way. It was because Hayden believed that Hawke, as challenger, flouted this code against him and, in the process, damaged the party, that he became so resentful towards Hawke in 1982 and 1983. The Hawke challenge to Hayden was the product of a different personality; it resembled a public cavalcade, an open assault on Labor ranks which Hayden, as challenger, could never have attempted. In 1977 Hayden hunted Whitlam according to his own introverted style. In 1982 Hayden looked back to see Hawke following in his own tracks; but Hawke hunted his man in a different fashion. He used tactics which, in Hayden's view, lacked integrity and ultimately with which Hayden could not cope.

On 30 May 1977 the ALP Caucus voted 32–30 to retain Whitlam and consign itself to the wasteland for a full parliamentary term. Peter Walsh walked out of the party room declaring: 'What we need now is a hit man.' It was a victory for the old against the new, for complacency against realism. Whitlam won on votes from the right, sections of the left, the sentimentalists and his son, Tony. His victory press conference was a nasty affair. He was appalled by the opening question from Brian Toohey, who asked when he would finally retire as Labor leader. Whitlam replied that he would do so two years after he had won the next election! The immediate impact of the result was to weaken further Whitlam's leadership and demoralise the party. Labor's dilemma was summarised by the author:

> The extent of the current division within the party is shown by the fact that of the top ten Labor figures below Whitlam, only one, Senator Doug McClelland,

supported Whitlam. The rest, deputy leader Tom Uren, the Senate leader Ken Wriedt, and the top seven figures in the vote for the front bench, Ralph Willis, Bill Hayden, Chris Hurford, Lionel Bowen, Mick Young, Paul Keating and Senator Don Grimes, were widely seen as Hayden voters and many of them were active Hayden lobbyists. Each one of these nine has been vehemently critical of Whitlam's style and tactics as leader and was associated at one time or another with the move to dump him.

To a big extent the future cohesion of the party will depend upon cooperation between these frontbenchers and the leader they wanted deposed. Yet within hours of the ballot, Mr Whitlam was making the precise type of remark that turned so many members against him. After scraping home in the ballot, he told a press conference that 'many' of his colleagues were out of touch with the electorate, later qualifying this to 'some' colleagues.[10]

Hayden lost, but emerged with his grip on the leadership enhanced. Significantly Hayden accepted the decision and did not try to regroup his forces for a second assault. This was despite pressure within the Caucus for Hayden to do exactly this. It reached a peak in late September after a violent clash between Whitlam and the Caucus over his alleged breach of ALP policy on East Timor. In early October Hayden, after consultation with Whitlam and other leaders, publicly dissociated himself from any attempt to overthrow Whitlam and tried to kill speculation on the issue.[11]

Bob Hawke was also a winner in the May ballot although in a negative sense. It meant the leadership transition to Hayden would be delayed until after the next election, thereby keeping a flicker of life in Hawke's prospects. Certainly it only sharpened the rivalry between Hayden and Hawke. This was revealed six months later when Hawke attacked Hayden for his acquiescence in Whitlam's decision to make abolition of payroll tax the centrepiece of Labor's 1977 election campaign. In an extremely risky trade-off Whitlam proposed that the Government would 'recover' the lost funds by abolition of the personal income tax cuts which Fraser had promised in his August 1977 budget. Hawke rang Hayden in protest when he first learnt of this proposal, but Hayden said that Whitlam had rung him and presented it as a *fait accompli*. Two days before Whitlam's Sydney Opera House policy speech on 17 November Hawke flew to Sydney in a bid to reverse the decision. He failed; Whitlam's response was: 'Thank you, but we need something dramatic.' Late on election night, 10 December, at the national tally room in Canberra when the sweeping dimension of Labor's tragic defeat was revealed, Hawke savaged Hayden in talks with journalists and Labor people.[12] How could he have allowed Whitlam to proceed with such a disastrous tax policy?

Some time later Hawke admitted that since he had failed to persuade Whitlam, it was perhaps understandable that Hayden had also failed.

During the 1977 election campaign Labor was bedevilled by internal divisions and Whitlam publicly clashed with his shadow ministers. One reason Malcolm Fraser had called this election a year early was to ensure that he faced Whitlam and not Hayden. Liberal Party research had revealed that Whitlam was a liability and the Liberal campaign tried to make his leadership an issue.[13] Fraser's majority was reduced from 55 to 48 seats, which meant that Fraser had followed the biggest election win in Australian history in 1975 with the second biggest in 1977. But 1977 was a greater political victory because it was a normal election and not held in the extraordinary circumstances of 1975 when the public's rejection of the Whitlam Government was comprehensive. The swing to Labor in 1977 was only 1.1 per cent. The message was that, despite an uneven and sometimes unimpressive Fraser Government performance, the electorate was no more prepared to vote ALP than it had been in 1975.

There were three reasons for the ALP debacle. The first was Whitlam's leadership, which was unacceptable to the community and caused disruption inside the ALP itself, culminating in lack of judgement in the vital campaign period. The second was the Fraser Government which presented itself as a strong administration and had only been in office for two years. In this sense, the 'fair go' effect was present in the electorate, which was prepared to suspend its doubts about the Government until a later date. The parallel to this was the electorate's retention of the Whitlam Government at the May 1974 election because of the feeling that it deserved a 'fair go'. The third factor in Labor's defeat was more deep-seated because it involved ideology and public perception. Separate from specifics such as taxes, unemployment and interest rates, the electorate perceived the Fraser Government as the party of economic management competence and the Whitlam Opposition as the party of economic incompetence.

The tragedy of Hayden's career is that he was not leader for this election. Hayden believed that Labor could win because economic recovery had not come. One feature of Australian politics is that Opposition leaders usually perform very well in their first election contest. The lucky Opposition leaders are those, like Fraser and Hawke, who spend little time in Opposition and are able to maintain their initial leadership momentum to carry them into Government. The argument is not that Hayden would have beaten Fraser in 1977. But Hayden would have denied Fraser a repeat of the 1975 result, reduced Fraser's majority to a reasonable size and reached a position from which to launch his 1980 bid for Prime Minister.

The truth is that Hayden succeeded Whitlam too late to escape from Hawke. Hayden's succession, delayed until after the December 1977 election, postponed Labor's revival and allowed Fraser to consolidate. It gave Hayden only one election as leader before Hawke entered Parliament. It meant that Hayden, although leader from December 1977 to February 1983, had only one election campaign. He had to wait a full three years as leader before facing his first campaign and was under pressure from Hawke all the time. If Hayden had won the leadership in May 1977 he would have been assured of two election campaigns against Fraser in his first four and a half years as leader. Finally it should be noted that, with the exception of Ben Chifley, every ALP leader since Scullin has produced his best voting swing at his first election.[14]

On 22 December 1977 Hayden defeated Bowen 36–28 and became ALP leader. The vote was close with Hayden winning on left and centre votes and Bowen having the right wing. Bowen had come under pressure to run from veterans such as Frank Stewart and Clyde Cameron. After a careful assessment he had agreed because he had a chance of winning. In the event Bowen defeated Uren 33–29 to become Hayden's deputy. In the Senate Wriedt was unopposed as leader and Button became deputy.

Hayden told the Caucus on his election that he had been inspired by Whitlam's 'untiring application and industry in achieving targets Labor had set' and described Whitlam as one of Labor's greatest leaders. Hayden said the challenge ahead would be demanding 'but no more daunting than Curtin faced in the 1930s'. Bowen told the Caucus that Hayden supporters were good judges of integrity and ability. In welcoming Hayden's election Bowen declared that the party made its leaders, not leaders the party.

But this Labor tradition would die with Hayden's own demise.

3
Born to rule

A man really needs three things or some of them anyhow: a hide like a rhinoceros, an overpowering ambition and a mighty conceit of himself.

Stanley Melbourne Bruce on the qualities needed
for an Australian Prime Minister

In 1977 Malcolm Fraser reached the zenith of his power in a career which would establish him as Australia's second-longest serving Prime Minister to Sir Robert Menzies. He would soon lay claim to being the best Prime Minister produced by the Liberal Party, even including its founding father. His record as a power politician is rivalled in Australian history only by Billy Hughes and Menzies. Fraser's assets were an iron resolution, immense physical stamina, dominance of his party, extensive political management skills and his economic policy—despite the celebrated deviations from it. The 1977 election had reaffirmed Fraser's control of both the House of Representatives and Senate, originally won in 1975; this meant he bestrode the nation, dominant in Parliament, the Cabinet and the Liberal Party in a manner so comprehensive that it is not likely to recur for many years.

Fraser was a Prime Minister of complexity, turbulence and patience, a 195 cm physical giant, thickset, cumbersome, but lethal. Elected Prime Minister at 45 and re-elected at 47, he was then a young man but a political veteran. Indeed when he lost office at age 52 after seven years in power, he was one year younger than Menzies when he won the 1949 election and began his 16 year record term, retiring at 71.

Politics was Fraser's life and he was the complete professional. Influenced by Menzies' leadership, a friend of Lord Casey, a penetrating student of the leadership of Gorton, McMahon, Snedden and Whitlam, Malcolm Fraser, once he assumed office, exuded executive competence, political cunning and brute strength. He devoured paper at work, at The Lodge,

34

at Nareen, in cars and planes, at home and abroad, at any hour of the day or night. He processed information, recycled it, recalled it; the telephone was his companion in calm, conundrums and catastrophes. Fraser was a dour talker but compulsive consulter: on the phone to ministers, at home, at work, on Friday night, Saturday night, Sunday morning, from anywhere in Australia or the world. Cabinet sat until ministers got tired, got sick and refused to come. Then Fraser would call another Cabinet meeting. Firstly Ivor Greenwood died; then Eric Robinson died. Peter Durack had a heart attack; Phillip Lynch became terribly ill; everybody worried about their health and their wives told most of them to quit politics to escape Fraser.

Fraser dominated his ministers yet hated overruling them. He wanted the respect of his senior colleagues while he tutored the junior ones like schoolboys. Fraser would keep the Cabinet sitting until ministers broke, conceding his case. Facing defeat, he would defer the issue for another day and procure another submission with another argument. Sometimes Fraser played devil's advocate, at other times he would steamroll the Cabinet. Fraser governed by exhaustion, not by edict. He rarely acted alone, not because he was afraid, but because he understood the force of collective power. He could switch from one issue to another and then to something else—from uranium safeguards to Zimbabwe to the national wage case. Fraser was headstrong and stubborn, yet prone to sudden switches of mind. He demanded answers with such ferocity that he frightened people from giving them. He had no conversation except politics, cars, the farm and then politics, politics, politics. The public service creaked, groaned and staggered under his demands, then it adjusted. He demanded options, more options and still more options. The head of the Prime Minister's Department, Sir Alan Carmody, dropped dead; his successor Sir Geoffrey Yeend paced himself and took sick leave. Fraser could not live without crisis. A manager of Nareen, Russell Paltridge, described Fraser as a man 'who thrives on crises and emergencies . . . when it's quiet in Canberra he will come here and pick out little things to complain about. When the whole world is against him, he is happiest.'[1]

Fraser could only put other people under such pressure because he was addicted to putting pressure on himself. His motivation, like that of Hayden, was strictly internal. He drove himself relentlessly at a pace and pressure which would have cracked most men much earlier. Fraser found it almost impossible to forget work, to relax and enjoy himself. Such escape was possible only in passion, and Fraser's passions were cars and fishing. Finally he was persuaded to take up golf, the sport of statesmen. But at one practice after throwing a hundred balls on the ground, Fraser swung, strained his back, then foolishly kept swinging. The result was three months' sick leave for a serious operation. Fraser punished himself along with everybody else; finally the huge frame broke and Fraser spent a total of six months of his last three years indisposed with pneumonia or pleurisy or his bad back.

Fraser excelled at learning his brief, honing the argument, beating his ministers in Cabinet, savaging his opponents in Parliament. He liked testing people: his backbenchers, his ministers, his bureaucrats. Fix this; tell me how to do that. Often he knew the answer to the question he asked. He would test public service advice against business and then test business against the public service. Fraser had deep instincts and powerful prejudices. His was an intuitive mind, but not flexible. He was not an original thinker and, in many ways, was profoundly anti-intellectual. He liked being surrounded by his professors, but this time, unlike at Oxford, they were subordinate to him. He scoffed at journalists reading, let alone writing books on contemporary politics, declaring with the arrogance of the participant that nobody could ever get it right. In books he liked detective thrillers; in music Frankie Laine. The suppressed larrikin in him would emerge behind the wheel of a car trying to escape from his security guards behind.

Fraser was never overawed by power. He accepted it as his natural course and he had a capacity to assume great responsibilities. But he expected his own staff and the bureaucrats to service the demands of that power with haste and efficiency. There was little reward working for Malcolm Fraser. On his 50th birthday, at a party given by his staff, David Barnett made a speech in which he hailed Fraser as a great Prime Minister but added that he was not the easiest person for whom to work. This was an understatement. In reply Fraser thanked Barnett then, alluding to this remark, said in a deadpan voice: 'It's all voluntary, you know.' The reward in working for Fraser was working for Fraser. The Prime Minister that Bill Hayden faced had the countenance of an Easter Island statue and the drive of the Lancia that he fancied, but never its grace or its style.

Fraser's record is littered with paradox. No Government adhered to such a rigorous economic policy for so long, yet policy somersaults were a striking feature of Fraser's administration. The reason that there is no agreement on the Fraser record is because each side can extract evidence for its arguments. The Liberal Party right wing has attacked Fraser as a leader who failed to follow his free-market philosophy and succumbed because of this ideological lapse. The Labor Party left wing still regards Fraser as the villainous enemy of public enterprise, income redistribution, detente and our constitutional integrity. His prime ministership was marked by consistency yet contradiction, ideology yet pragmatism, radicalism yet conservatism. The reason for this is that his Government, throughout its long life, was always dominated by the personality of the Prime Minister and it mirrored the complexities of the man himself.

Three character traits shaped Fraser's approach to office. They were his natural sense of superiority, his deep loneliness and his notion of public service. Fraser was one of the richest men who ever sat in federal Parliament and his inherited patrician superiority was reinforced by upbringing. Fraser carried with him a sense of class nurtured in the rural aristocracy and social heirarchy of Victoria's Western District. His early education was received in irregular tuition from the schoolmistress who once taught Stanley Melbourne Bruce; then he went to boarding schools and Melbourne Grammar. Social awkwardness long concealed the certitudes of the rural aristocracy which Fraser carried into his political life. Money and establishment gave him a strong core of values and identity. He was above the swirling questioning of social values in the 1960s and it is not surprising that he appeared a reactionary at the time. His strengths were his confidence in himself and his conviction that there were established values, practices and procedures to be upheld. Fraser possessed the surety founded in genuine conservatism that there was an intrinsically proper set of relations between institutions and people and a proper *modus operandi* for elites whether in Government, business or public service. He embodied the notion of being born to rule. Unlike Menzies, Fraser was born to the purple. This patrician superiority pervaded Fraser's career and was the source of his strength.

An intensely lonely childhood bred an aloofness in Fraser and an incapacity to relate to his fellow man. His childhood was spent in farmhood isolation where he was reared with a sense of duty, hard work and, perhaps, a touch of cruelty. Fraser only described his childhood twice when he was Prime Minister. The first time was in the 1977 campaign:

> What was Mr Fraser's most frightening experience as a child? . . . Well, he said there was this time when his father took him on a picnic during a flood in the Riverina. He was left on an island in the middle of the flood and his father rowed off. Young Malcolm knew that snakes made for higher ground in a flood and he was terrified snakes would get to him before his father got back.

Then the Prime Minister recalled his funniest boyhood experience:

> The sulky got bogged and his father told him to unharness the horse. When the shafts were released from the harness, the sulky overbalanced backwards, catapulting his mother into the mud. His father was ready with his camera to photograph the incident.[2]

Finally, in the last week of the 1983 election campaign, Fraser, under intense pressure and sensing defeat, lapsed into reminiscence:

> I can remember three years in a row knocking lambs on the head as they dropped, trying to save the ewes. Now that was as a very young child. I think I was eight in the last of those particular droughts . . . The nearest neighbour was 50 miles away and, well, there was somebody across the river, but you had to go a long way around to get there . . . In one of these years when we had floods instead of drought, we went six months without a wheel getting on the place.
>
> We had quite a bit of forest country on this Riverina property through which the Edward River meandered and one of the things that I suppose as a kid I prided myself on, I was always warned about not getting lost, because people had been lost, people had disappeared in the forest and were found years later . . . My father would test me and try to take me around this way, around that way and say 'What direction is home, is it over there?' I'd say, 'No, it is over there.'[3]

Fraser was moulded by a blend of paternal toughness which bred aggression, isolation which formed a solitary man, and obligation which forged a sense of purpose. Later in politics while he had the power necessary to run the ship of state, his personality was too aloof ever to capture the public's imagination in the television age. He lacked the warmth of Gorton, the appeal of Hawke, the wit of Whitlam. There was no streak in his personality which would compromise the dull solemnity he conveyed. Fraser would never be loved by the public, nor would they ever identify with him. The most Fraser could expect, and the stone on which his Government would rest, was public respect for his strength. Fraser understood this but did not like it. He recognised his limitations but still regretted that he did not receive affection. Fraser always had difficulty in relations of equality. He was more at ease in an hierarchical relationship such as when he deferred to Menzies or Casey or, later in life, when most people deferred to him as Liberal leader. Some ministers settled for subordination as the basis of their relationship; others, like Eric Robinson and finally Andrew Peacock, who found this intolerable, broke with Fraser and resigned. Only a few such as Peter Nixon could, while respecting the office of Prime Minister, deal with Fraser as an equal.

Fraser's sense of public service, inseparable from his personal ambition, was also inspired by his background. It is not generally remembered that Fraser came from a political tradition. His grandfather, Simon Fraser, was a member of the original Australian Parliament and a Victorian senator who served for 11 years. Fraser possesses his papers from the Federation debates. Simon Fraser was a tough, shrewd and flamboyant conservative and the first two of these qualities were passed to his grandson. Malcolm went to Melbourne Grammar and then Oxford, where he absorbed the great spiritual virtues of the British tradition: belief in God, faith in country, dedication to public service and commitment to self-improvement. It is not surprising in the light of this background and education that Fraser entered politics. He had only two choices: the farm or Parliament. For a man with ambition and sense of purpose the decision was obvious. The extraordinary feature of Fraser's ten years on the backbenches and then of his ministerial years is that his repeated rejection by his colleagues in leadership ballots and on other issues never caused him to question his beliefs, change his style or doubt his inheritance.

Within Fraser himself there was a deep personality clash, a contradiction so great that it ran through his entire career and that of his Government—the struggle between order and violence. Fraser led the party of conservatism and tradition yet he bathed it in blood and cloaked it in radicalism in his climb to power. The three great eruptions in Fraser's career, which now dot the landscape of history like gigantic volcanoes, were his resignation and successful strike against Gorton in 1971, his successful coup against Snedden in 1974–75 and, most dramatic and enduring, his forcing of the 1975 political and constitutional crisis which led Sir John Kerr to sack the Whitlam Government and thereby procure the election which gave Fraser the biggest majority in history. The man responsible for these actions was no ordinary politician.

The real warning came in 1971 and *The Sydney Morning Herald* correspondent Ian Fitchett wrote that Fraser's resignation from the Gorton ministry 'must bring a complete reassessment of his motives, aims and ambitions'. It was the first significant sign that Fraser was overwhelmed by his own leadership vision. By striking against Gorton Fraser purported to tell the Liberal Party who was fit to lead it and by what code its leader should operate in the office of Prime Minister. It was precisely because Fraser had his own established set of values and relations, which he believed Gorton had transgressed, that he sought such dramatic recourse. The Gorton crisis was fair warning to everybody that Fraser was no retiring conservative who would let politicians, the Liberal Party or the political system evolve as they might. Fraser was in politics to insist upon the proper values, the right way for the Liberal Party. His ego was so enormous that he was prepared to take decisive, even violent action to further this cause, a cause indistinguishable from his own vaulting ambition. But the Gorton crisis taught Fraser that political violence is only acceptable when gloved in morality and principle. He absorbed the lesson. Thus garbed, he struck against Snedden in the interests of the Liberal Party, and against Whitlam, to use his own rhetoric, to save Australia.

Much of the analysis of Fraser's career is based upon these three events which revealed Fraser's utter belief in himself and his clever command of power. Each was a progressive step towards making the Liberal Party his own. They showed Fraser not as a reckless gambler but as a politician prepared, after careful thought, to take a very calculated risk. With each success an aura of invincibility began to surround him and finally by 1983, to cloud his judgement.

Fraser was always plagued by the discord he created in 1975. He was unlucky in that a more competent Governor-General than Sir John Kerr would have obtained a more satisfactory, less divisive resolution to the political stalemate. In his decision to use the Senate to force the election Fraser was hungry, determined and self-righteous—but the failures of the Whitlam Government also put much pressure on Fraser from the non-Labor forces to terminate swiftly the Government's life. The result was that Fraser sacrificed the quality of his mandate and any breadth of community goodwill. He was elected in the teeth of implacable and continuing hostility from the Labor Party and its not uninfluential supporters throughout the electorate. The endurance of these perceptions was obvious eight years later when Bob Hawke defeated Fraser by depicting him as an agent of division and by campaigning on the slogan 'Bringing Australia Together'. To the extent that this campaign symbolised Hawke's commitment to consensus against Fraser's capacity to divide, it represented Labor's revenge for 1975 through its use of the flaw those events had left in Fraser's image. In 1983 Hawke was elected with goodwill from wide sections of the community—including the non-Labor side—in dramatic contrast to the rancour generated by Fraser's 1975 triumph.

The 1975 crisis left a legacy of paranoia and bitterness on both sides of the great divide. It lost Fraser much of the opinion-making elite in the media, notably the press, the intellectuals, the writers and, of course, the trade unions. Fraser did not betray any concern and in turn deeply distrusted and resented the opinion-makers. He shied away, dismissing most of them as pro-Labor or incompetent, and played to the few he knew would treat him favourably. Fraser looked to the Murdoch group, distanced himself from the press gallery and concentrated on the electronic media to communicate directly with the people. The 1975 crisis virtually established the pattern of the early years in power. Fraser practised the politics of divide and rule and played to his silent, middle-class majority at the expense of the minority. He depicted himself as a leader of the radical right wing and was therefore seen as confrontationalist. His strong rhetoric and to a lesser extent his policies accentuated the gulf between employers and trade unions, public servants and private employees, the employed and the unemployed, many of whom were branded dole bludgers, and finally between rich and poor, since the redistribution effects of Fraser's early policies, notably changes to the tax system, benefited the wealthy at the expense of the underprivileged. He proceeded to dismantle the Whitlam programmes and displayed a mean vindictiveness in refusing the request of Foreign Minister Andrew Peacock to sponsor Whitlam for the International Court of Justice, a prestigious post for both individual and country.

The 1975 crisis naturally generated a huge debate about Australia's political and constitutional system—a healthy debate but also a diversionary one, necessitated only by the event itself. Fraser never spoke about the Whitlam dismissal and he gave no sign that it affected his capacity. But its influence was insidious and it undermined the opportunity for radical change suggested in the size of Fraser's mandate. In the 1975–77 period Fraser sought to legitimise the power which many believed he had illegitimately obtained. Fraser had to defend Sir John Kerr's action and honour since Kerr had appointed him Prime Minister, yet he knew that Kerr's presence was a continuing liability for his Government. His offer of the UNESCO ambassadorship to Kerr was considered improper by many and provoked such an outcry that Kerr withdrew, leaving both himself and Fraser exposed, along with their motives, in a failed and squalid deal. In every campaign he fought—1977, 1980 and 1983—Fraser was forced to defend his 1975 blocking of supply and he always promised he would do it again if he felt it was necessary. Only when Fraser left the political stage could his successors, Andrew Peacock and John Howard, abandon this line.

The two great dominating themes of the Fraser Government—economic management and ministerial propriety—have their origins in the 1975 crisis. Fraser's charge against Whitlam had always been twofold: that Labor was destroying the economy and that it was without integrity. On becoming Prime Minister he accepted the obligation to revive the economy and restore integrity. This was the burden which office bestowed upon him, a responsibility far greater because of the claims Fraser made when forcing the great constitutional crisis. Nowhere was Fraser's penchant for putting himself under pressure more obvious than in 1975 and the consequences it created for the new incumbent.

It was the ministerial resignations and upheavals which studded the Fraser years with drama and personality conflict. Fraser's house was plagued from the start. In early 1976 Posts and Telecommunications Minister Vic Garland resigned and appeared in court on a $500 bribery charge that was subsequently dismissed; the 1977 crisis over Treasurer Philip Lynch's business affairs was the turning point from which Lynch's career became a downhill slide; the next year Finance Minister Eric Robinson was damaged when he stood down and Senate leader Reg Withers was destroyed when he was sacked in a complicated issue of personal propriety involving the electoral system; later Primary Industry Minister Ian Sinclair resigned pending his trial before the NSW Supreme Court; his successor Peter Nixon was the subject of damaging allegations concerning his pecuniary interests and political conduct; finally in 1982 two of the brighter Liberals, Health Minister Michael MacKellar and Business and Consumer Affairs Minister John Moore, were forced to resign over the colour TV cover-up. Fraser claimed a higher moral authority throughout this period. His detractors pointed to the resignations and argued his Government was a scandal, the most scandalous since Federation. The Prime Minister pointed to the resignations as proof that he was upholding exacting standards.

The Lynch affair was the gravest crisis Fraser faced in his early years as Prime Minister. It inaugurated ministerial propriety as a cardinal weakness of the Government and, briefly, threatened Fraser's very survival in the 1977 election. Fraser forced Lynch to resign under threat of sacking yet he realised post-election that Lynch was essential to his own power structure. If Lynch had not returned as deputy then it was more likely that a Fraser rival, Andrew Peacock, rather than an ally, Tony Street, would have secured the job and the seeds of destabilisation during the second term would have been sown.

The self-interested but acute analysis by Lynch himself at a post-election meeting on 13 December 1977 with Fraser, Street and Nixon made this point. The record of the meeting says:

> He [Lynch] was aware that Snedden and Peacock were considering standing for the deputy leadership and that both Street and Howard had an interest in doing so . . . Lynch said that he believed Fraser would not be well served by either Snedden or Peacock who would, in a sense, be adversaries to him as deputy leader. Both Street and Howard, because they were close to him, would not be seen by the party as being an adequate counterbalance.
>
> Lynch said his decision to step aside was right and had been vindicated by the election result. Resolution of the Lynch issue was important both for the Prime Minister and the party at large. Because of the very large majority there was the environment for the seeds of discontent to grow. The handling of this issue was important for the stability of the Government over the next three years.

Lynch said the Prime Minister had handled the whole matter in an indecent, uncivilised and ruthless fashion . . . The Prime Minister had prejudged the issue before even receiving any of the statements that had been prepared . . .

Lynch said he could not help having the feeling of being let down. This was all the more difficult because he had been one of the few who had always played it straight and had given him full support and loyalty . . . When Ian Sinclair had been subject to serious charges, the Prime Minister had seen fit to accept his word. He had not had Sinclair investigated . . .

From his establishment heights Fraser was suspicious of the techniques a man such as Lynch had used to claw his way to wealth. Fraser always distrusted 'new money' and the men who peddled it. The crisis ended any prospects of further political advancement for Lynch and cost him the Treasury—but Lynch returned as deputy to become an invaluable sheet-anchor for the Government and Fraser. Finally the affair convinced Fraser of the need to ensure the propriety of his Government and that the means to guarantee this was independent assessment, a far-reaching conclusion.

The first step involved asking Justice Sir Nigel Bowen for a report on public duty and private interests. The Bowen Report set out a code of conduct for ministers, parliamentarians and public servants. The Fraser Cabinet endorsed the report as policy but then applied it selectively. Ministers were required to furnish Fraser with a private statement of their pecuniary interests and accept the onus on them to avoid conflict of interest situations.

Fraser's zealousness to enforce standards required courage because it damaged his Government internally and externally. The greatest example is the 1978 Queensland electoral redistribution affair in which Fraser appointed a royal commission and, when it found against Withers, sacked him. This decision was opposed by both the deputy Prime Minister, Doug Anthony, and the deputy Liberal leader Phillip Lynch, proof that Fraser was insisting on standards higher than his senior colleagues felt necessary.

The origins of the hostility that built up towards Fraser among his senior ministers lay partly in the Prime Minister's streak of self-righteousness. In 1975 Fraser had justified his strike against Whitlam by appeal to moral principle. Yet Fraser's career was littered with the shells of men whom he had destroyed: Gorton, Whitlam, Connor, Snedden. Nobody in politics had displayed such ruthlessness. Fraser's senior colleagues—and Reg Withers and Doug Anthony were among the toughest—had nothing but respect for his tactics. Yet Anthony and Withers were honest about what they did: they lived by that great axiom of politics: 'If you see a head, kick it.' Now they saw Fraser falling victim to some of his own propaganda about principle.

Withers simply dismissed Fraser as a hypocrite when Fraser sacked him from the ministry. Withers told journalists: 'When the man who's carried the biggest knife in this country for the last ten years starts giving you a lecture about propriety, integrity and the need to resign, then he's either making a sick joke or playing you for a mug.'[4] Anthony criticised Fraser to his face, arguing that loyalty was more important than morality: 'Menzies and McEwen would never have gone on like this. They would have stood up for their ministers and got their ministers to stand up for them.'[5]

This underlines probably the most remarkable aspect of Fraser's character: his total absorption and belief in the morality of his own position. Once embarked on a course of action, Fraser was unwilling to concede the slightest morality or validity to the opposing side. He became the embodiment of justice and virtue; his opponents became tainted with iniquity. Just as Fraser assumed a superiority in his dealings with others, so he assumed a higher morality for his own actions.

Fraser paid a high price for his vindictiveness against his Liberal enemies in the early years. Senior Liberals such as Victorian Don Chipp and Tasmanian Senator Peter Rae should have been members of Fraser's Government. He excluded them because he disliked them. Rae became a constant thorn in Fraser's side through his skill and use of the Senate committee system. Chipp left the Liberal Party and used his personality and media skills to form the Australian Democrats—an event Fraser would have considered inconceivable.

Both in the nation and in the Senate the Australian Democrats caused Fraser immense difficulty. It was all his own fault; the breakaway was his creation. In December 1976 Chipp had written Fraser a letter expressing concern about his autocratic methods of government. Fraser called Chipp to a Melbourne meeting in January 1977 which, to Chipp's surprise, was also attended by Fraser's friend and ministerial colleague Tony Street. Chipp was upset to find that Fraser had shown his letter to several Cabinet ministers. Chipp said later:

> Fraser then replied that he had brought Tony into the discussion to assure me that he, Fraser, did not dominate the Cabinet. He then said, 'Tony, you tell Don that.' Tony, with Malcolm towering above him, dutifully complied.
> I burst out laughing, but neither Fraser nor Street could understand why. I remember thinking, 'What's the bloody use!'[6]

Economic management is the big test by which Fraser will be judged. His 1975 election programme offered full employment, economic revival and an end to inflation. Fraser promised full personal income tax indexation, tax indexation for companies, protection from competitive imports for industry, full wage indexation, cuts in Government spending and an investment-led recovery. This programme was naive, idealistic and a misreading of the economic problem.

The story of Fraser's first two years was the battle between Malcolm Fraser and John Stone, between Fraserism and the Treasury philosophy. The dynamic of Fraserism was small Government and lower taxes; but the Stone prescription was to 'fight inflation first' through comprehensive fiscal, monetary and wage restraint. The first lesson Stone taught Fraser was the evil of wage inflation. In January 1976 Fraser, on Stone's advice, broke his full wage indexation promise and moved to a partial indexation position at the start of the long and sorry struggle for wage restraint.

On assuming office Fraser had little understanding of the intractable nature of Australia's economic problems. His misplaced optimism led him to begin implementation of the neoconservative economic reforms his rhetoric championed. In fact Fraser insisted upon his reforms in a similar fashion and haste to that of Whitlam. Like Whitlam he possessed an implicit faith in his own leadership and therefore in his capacity to bring change. Like Whitlam, Fraser believed that genuine leadership could triumph over adverse circumstances and bend history to its own will.

The result was that there were three phases in the economic management of the Fraser years. During the first phase, in 1976, the Prime Minister retained the whip hand over Stone and the Treasury. This was the period of Fraser innovation. The second phase, starting in 1977 and going through till 1981–82, saw Fraser accept more of the Treasury prescription in the ongoing tussle between that department and himself over policy details and direction. The third and final phase, leading into the 1982–83 budget, saw Fraser turn away from the Treasury and a near-collapse in Government–Treasury relations. In this period Fraser searched unsuccessfully for a new direction.

The Government's May 1976 mini-budget represented the high tide of Fraser innovation, partly due to the influence of the Prime Minister's chief adviser-philosopher, Professor David Kemp. The spending cuts were modest but the revenue reforms were radical. Fraser insisted that full personal income tax indexation (the discounting of tax increases due to inflation) be implemented immediately. This was the equivalent of a significant tax cut automatically built-in each year. Stone warned that the revenue loss would mean a significant blow-out in the budget deficit with dangers for inflation. Treasurer Lynch accepted this warning and sent his senior aide to Nareen with Stone's memorandum under Lynch's name; it was the first act of defiance against Fraser. But Fraser dismissed the Lynch–Stone advice and plunged ahead. He told the joint parties meeting at the mini-budget briefing: 'We promised to introduce tax indexation over three years. Would any of you have believed that we could do it in six months?'[7] The reform was agonisingly abolished over the next several years. The same fate befell the trading stock valuation for companies—a system of company tax indexation—introduced quickly and later cancelled.

The climactic break with the Treasury came in November 1976 when Fraser devalued 17.5 per cent in the teeth of Treasury resistance. But the move succeeded. Devaluation did not produce the inflation whirlwind the Treasury had feared, while the boost to Australian competitiveness produced a healthier export performance. The competitive advantages of the devaluation helped offset the competitive penalty imposed on industry through wage rises given by the Arbitration Commission.

The next year, in the 1977–78 budget, the Government reformed the tax scales, converting them from seven steps to three, and gave a significant tax cut on top of tax indexation. The new rate scale was to operate from 1 February 1978. In the December 1977 election campaign these tax cuts became the 'fistful of dollars' which appeared in the famous Liberal Party television election advertisements—one of the most blatant appeals to greed for many years. Stone had opposed the tax cuts as an indulgence the Government could not afford. Fraser was soon to agree—but only after his 1977 re-election on the 'fistful of dollars'.

Fraser was too restless, too active, too searching and too ambitious for his own self-interest. The result was that overkill bred retreat, on every front and on almost every issue. The 1975 policy speech was absurdly optimistic and so were the tax concessions of 1976 and 1977 whose subsequent cancellation cost Fraser much credibility. There were many other examples. After promising in the 1977 campaign that interest rates would fall two per cent, he saw his predictions dashed and as a result virtually abandoned interest rate forecasting. But in 1980 he talked up the resources boom and once again went too far, only to see much of the boom fade away. For a Prime Minister traditionally seen as preaching sacrifice Fraser's mistake was to hail too many false horizons and build up expectations rather than play them down.

Fraser was a Prime Minister with a tremendous sense of how to handle the instruments of power. This became one of his cardinal assets. He was elected not as a popular personality, but precisely because he was an 'insider' and a power politician. The instruments through which he governed were the Cabinet, the public service and the Liberal Party. He knew exactly what type of relationship was needed in each case. He used each instrument as an organ of Government and a means of consolidating his own authority.

Fraser's ultimate instrument of power was always the Cabinet. He chaired Cabinet according to the strict rule of Cabinet solidarity which produced effective Government and ministerial discipline. Cabinet solidarity meant that the Government spoke with one voice; ministers were not permitted private views in public. On Fraser's orders, most had no press secretaries. Cabinet secrecy was assumed to be binding and this precluded the ventilation of the different views ministers put before any Cabinet decision was reached. Without the imprimatur of Cabinet, ministers had only limited authority and discretion. So reluctant were ministers to act alone that Cabinet became weighed down with business, the Government became tied to the Cabinet table and finally new procedures had to be adopted in a bid to facilitate ministerial freedom and Government efficiency. The crisis was very real. One minister said: 'The sheer volume is quite enormous. It's nothing to cart two linear feet of Cabinet documents to Cabinet.' Another minister admitted that he read only ten per cent of Cabinet submissions thoroughly—'and if anyone claims to read more, he is lying'.[8]

Cabinet ran the nation; it was not run by the media, big business or the unions. But Fraser dominated the Cabinet. So Fraser's policies were given the stamp of collective responsibility; everyone was locked in, everyone was responsible. In the early days Fraser would lobby his senior ministers on the big issues before Cabinet met: Anthony, Lynch, Withers and sometimes Sinclair were the key ministers who operated as an informal 'kitchen Cabinet'. Once they had agreed, the rest was a formality. Fraser's patience and persistence knew no limits except those defined by his determination and ruthlessness. In its seven years the Fraser Cabinet took very close to 18,990 decisions, which is of the order of 2,710 on average each year. This, in turn, is about ten decisions by Cabinet each working day for seven years. Some of these decisions were nominal or incidental; others involved intricate and voluminous detail.

Whitlam was a great parliamentarian and kept Parliament sitting as the forum of his dominance; Fraser relied upon executive power so he kept Cabinet sitting as the instrument of his power. Fraser believed that Government had to lead and that people had to be led. His notions of authority and hierarchy left him with no sense of participatory democracy. Fraser once quoted with approval the observation on the 1960s protest cult: 'In the disturbances caused by the scarcity of food, the mob goes in search of bread, and the means it employs is generally to wreck the bakeries.' [9]

Fraser believed the public service existed to serve the Government.

Rather than being impressed by good advice Fraser expected it. One of his great skills was management of institutions. In late 1976, after the devaluation crisis, Fraser split the Treasury into the two departments of Treasury and Finance—an action which the Whitlam Government had never steeled itself to take. This diversified the sources of economic advice and it was a lesson in power politics to the Treasury's then Deputy Secretary John Stone that bureaucrats existed to serve Government and not dictate policy. Fraser changed the law and the guidelines in an effort to ensure that bodies such as the Industries Assistance Commission and the Australian Schools Commission gave the type of advice that Government wanted.

Fraser reaped the full fruits of the beefing-up of the Prime Minister's Department originally undertaken by Whitlam. Its two chief functions were to provide across-the-board policy advice to Fraser, thereby ensuring that he was briefed on every minister's area, and to administer the Cabinet, which meant drafting the agenda, commenting on the submissions, writing and circulating the decisions and follow-up action to ensure decisions were implemented. The department became an engine room of power. Then Fraser created the Office of National Assessment under the umbrella of his own department to provide him with advice and intelligence analysis on international events. During an overseas crisis such as the Chinese invasion of Vietnam, the Iran–Iraq war or the Soviet invasion of Afghanistan, the Prime Minister would receive an intelligence brief from ONA early each morning. He wanted everything on tap.

The third instrument of Fraser's power was the Liberal Party and he recognised it as his daily weapon and ultimate power base. He made contact almost every day with the Federal Director of the Liberal Party, Tony Eggleton. He was meticulous in attending Liberal Party Federal Executive meetings. Whenever he faced a serious party crisis Fraser went straight to the Liberal Party Executive and obtained a resolution supporting him. The challenge from Andrew Peacock and the revolt within the party over the bottom-of-the-harbour tax legislation are the prime examples. No Liberal leader had ever put such store by party consultation. Gough Whitlam called the 1975 Bass by-election without even consulting his own party, an action that would have been inconceivable for Malcolm Fraser.

Fraser's other institutional strength was his commitment to, and operation of, the conservative political coalition. He dismissed the long debate which had plagued the Liberals about relations with the National Country Party: the coalition was an essential requirement for conservative power. Under Fraser there were not two parties in Government; there was one Government which contained two parties. In Cabinet there was no discrimination according to party allegiance and ministers voted as individuals. When there was trouble within the Government, then Fraser called in his best negotiators to fix it. Peter Nixon was his best negotiator, so he took a role in both the Lynch and Peacock crises. Some Liberals said this was tantamount to Country Party interference in Liberal business. But to Fraser it was always Government business. Malcolm Fraser and Doug Anthony had a truly professional relationship. Fraser's country background and Liberal politics meant that he combined in himself the attributes of both Country Party and Liberal Party leadership. Consequently the problem of coalition division—a potential minefield—was virtually eliminated from the Fraser years.

Fraser was deeply influenced by Whitlam's mistakes. He absorbed lessons from the collective and individualistic flaws which he perceived had undermined Whitlam. Consequently Fraser sought to differentiate himself from his predecessor. Whitlam had bought himself a Mercedes, saying the Prime Minister should have the best; Fraser made do with a Holden instead, and at first flew commercial rather than VIP charter when overseas, at great discomfort to himself. Only later did he buy VIP planes for this purpose. Fraser was loath to sack or reshuffle his ministers, partly a reaction to Whitlam's ministerial reshuffles and the controversy they created. Fraser's basically introverted political nature was reinforced by Whitlam's perform-ance as the extrovert. Fraser, unlike Whitlam, never assessed his ministers in public like a schoolmaster, never criticised them, always minimised the media's scope for playing with personalities. Whitlam indulged his personal-ity; Fraser was a natural repressive.

Fraser knew that the most important task of leadership was to formulate philosophy and set policy direction. The chief architect of Fraserism as a philosophy was Professor David Kemp, the intellectual and wordsmith who became his Private Secretary in Opposition and served two stints as Director of the Prime Minister's office. As early as 1973, in his 'A Leader And A Philosophy', probably the most influential Liberal essay over the past 12 years, Kemp charted the future direction:

> The most obvious explanation for the Liberal Party's troubles with the
> electorate has been the inadequacy of its leadership since the retirement of Sir
> Robert Menzies, or at least since the death of Harold Holt . . . The leadership
> issue cannot be resolved into a simple popularity contest between the two men
> at the head of the major parties. This was the error of many Liberals—including
> the author of this piece—at the time of Mr Gorton's selection as leader of the
> party . . . Seeing leadership in terms of 'image' misses its most important
> ingredient. The leader's first task is—as the very word implies—to lead the
> party he heads.

The key requirement of the successful leader is the sense of inner
security which means that he is neither afraid to consult, nor afraid to act
alone . . . The ultimate support of a leader's authority is his role as
expounder of a philosophy or ideology which commands common consent
and adherence in the party . . . A revival of concern for the philosophy of
liberalism and its implications for policy is essential to give the party that
sense of common purpose and motivation it needs to be an effective
opposition.[10]

Kemp defined the Liberal goal as the realisation of human dignity for all.
The fundamental instrument to achieve dignity was freedom, individual
freedom. This philosophy became both a guide to policy and an appeal to beat
Labor. It meant 'the more the individual and the family man retain the right to
spend their own income the more mature and responsible the individual will
be'. So the Liberals were the party of low taxation and of family responsibility. The onus lay with the state to justify taxation. Because Liberals had more
faith in people than in Government they opposed centralisation of Government
power and supported decentralisation, in which people had a greater say. This
philosophy meant support for private enterprise, opposition to Government
regulation, incentive for private schools, a smaller public sector and all the
rhetoric of the Fraser years. The political beauty of the philosophy was that it
was comprehensive. By supporting the individual, the Liberals refused to
declare themselves between competing interest groups. It made for a pervasive
political appeal.

For nearly eight years, in Opposition and then in Government, Fraser
championed this philosophy. It became the text for the Liberal revival and
eventually the credo for the right-wing radicals who had sprung up post-1980
in bitter criticism of Fraser for not applying his philosophy. But as early as the
1977 election it was clear that Fraser, an Australian farmer and professional
politician, actually believed in Government intervention and Government
control. In the 1975–77 period Fraser supported high protection for industry,
experimented with a prices–incomes freeze to control inflation, backed regulation of the financial system and manipulation of interest rates to guarantee
below-market-rate home finance.

The reality is that Fraser used his philosophy more as a tool of leadership
authority than as a guide to policy. He always used ideas as a means to power.
But his personal commitment to those ideas fluctuated depending upon
whether or not he believed they were valid for the circumstances. Judged by
his actions Fraser was a pragmatic realist and not an ideologue. His major
reform, tax indexation, was abandoned because he was not prepared to consis-

tently cut the level of Government spending to make tax indexation consistent with anti-inflationary deficits.

When Fraser went to the people in 1977 his record was undistinguished. True, he had restored confidence after the Whitlam years. Inflation had fallen from 13.0 per cent in 1975–76 to 9.5 per cent in 1977–78. But unemployment had risen swiftly. The average jobless level had increased from 269,000 in 1975–76 to 378,600 in 1977–78. Economic growth was weak.

During his first two years Fraser had talked loudly but his actions had fallen short of the radicalism he espoused. The pragmatic realist who was now apparent beneath the rhetoric of the strident ideologue was immensely powerful after his 1977 triumph. But Fraser interpreted the result as vindication of his performance so far. Now he moved to institutionalise himself as Australia's natural Prime Minister.

4
Hayden as leader

As far as I'm concerned Hayden is dead.

Bob Hawke, July 1979

Bill Hayden brought to the leadership of the ALP diligence, determination and direction at a time when the party's electoral relevance had been cast into doubt. Hayden never possessed the inspirational flair or granite strength that immediately distinguishes a leader from his followers. But in the 1977–80 period Hayden took Labor to the brink of electoral success and killed the notion that Fraser had reduced Labor to a spent force.

The challenge for Hayden's leadership was always a personal challenge. It was whether he could continue to grow under pressure and finally bloom as a substantial leader and Prime Minister. This struggle was waged inside the man himself between his past and his future.

Hayden's five years as leader were conducted amid three looming shadows—Whitlam's record, Hawke's rivalry and Fraser's dominance. Each one became a benchmark against which he was compared and eventually found wanting. Hayden struggled to escape from these shadows into daylight where he could be assessed in his own right. But the Government, the Labor Party and the media conspired against him. His leadership struggled between the sluggish Opposition benches, to which he rarely gave the touch of life, and the isolation of his Ipswich home, which became a retreat from pressure. At his best Hayden displayed the experience, toughness and intelligence to take the ALP to power. No student of his leadership can dispute this. But his best was reserved for too few occasions—the 1980 campaign, federal conferences, the July 1982 Hawke challenge. These were dashes of fire in a career of grey. However Hayden's achievements were far-reaching and must be measured against the magnitude of the difficulties he faced.

The Labor Party that Hayden inherited in December 1977 was weary and confused. Cleverly exploiting Whitlam's mistakes, Fraser had moulded the intellectual climate of the nation. The years 1976–80 were highlighted by the so-called tax revolt, hostility to big government and public servants, union bashing and the dole bludger slur as Australia drifted towards understandable but ugly right-wing shibboleths. The community blamed unemployment on the trade unions and the deceased Whitlam Government far more than on Malcolm Fraser. But unemployment was not the political issue; subtle and deep changes were underway in community expectations.

Bad times had led the electorate in two different directions, both of which Fraser had detected far earlier than the ALP. The first was a willingness to vote for the party of perceived economic management competence. The second can be brutally described as the resurgence of greed. The recession made the hip-pocket nerve more sensitive than ever; the desire to maintain living standards was converted into a powerful lust for tax cuts. The idealism and optimism of the Whitlam years had given way to a selfish pessimism. This was in large part because of Whitlam's own economic failures. The nation was still adjusting to the collapse of the era of steady economic growth.

The intellectual crisis facing the Labor Party was serious and its specifics lay in the two priority areas of economic policy: spending and wages. Fraser had created a pervasive illusion of support for smaller government and less spending in order to reduce inflation. To respond to this Labor had a fundamental choice: it could accept or reject the smaller public sector as expounded by Fraser. Because Hayden was an honest economist, he would not allow Labor to promise more public spending without financing it through higher taxation. But higher taxation was politically unacceptable. So the dilemma for Labor was how could it win votes and yet adhere to its support for a big public sector?

There was a converse to this question. If Labor did not support a bigger public sector and a more compassionate society through a better welfare system, why should people vote ALP anyway? The danger for the Labor Party was that in making economic management the key issue, it would play to the strength of the party of capital. Fraser would set the terms of the debate.

Labor's second dilemma stemmed from the wide community acceptance that excessive wage rises were responsible for inflation and therefore recession. Labor needed a wage policy which confronted this reality since it could not be escaped if Labor did form another Government. But the party's ties with the trade union movement meant its wages policy had to be broadly consistent with the aspirations of the trade unions. Many ALP figures believed this reconciliation was impossible. The more wages loomed as the most critical economic issue, the more it appeared that Labor's industrial wing was a political dead weight. Moreover community hostility towards unions over strikes damaged the ALP by association. Some senior party figures such as Ken Wriedt and John Wheeldon inclined to the view that the ALP should sever its trade union connection.

This crisis led some astute observers to venture that Labor's fortunes would never recover. Max Walsh, in his 1979 book *Poor Little Rich Country*, wrote:

> At the end of the seventies it was possible to pose seriously the question as to whether Labor would remain a sufficiently powerful political force within Australia ever to govern again in its own right . . .
> Labor had reverted to its pre-1963 condition of waiting for the Government to fall, of believing that it was just a matter of sitting. Labor, of course, accompanied this waiting exercise with ritual calls to the public conscience about the plight of the unemployed, the underprivileged and the disadvantaged. Lacking an alternative economic strategy, Labor's conscience-pricking humanism underlined the negativism of its approach and the fragile base on which its future was predicated.[1]

The conflict Hayden faced on attaining the leadership was between economic conservatism and Labor traditionalism. Hayden himself was a blend of both. His achievement was to pilot the ALP through its loss of innocence in the Whitlam programme and provide it with a new-found commitment to economic responsibility. He managed the necessary blend of principle and pragmatism which kept Labor unified but moved it significantly towards a realistic and less exciting policy framework. Hayden was both the inheritor and repudiator of Whitlamism. He accepted the Whitlam strategy of moving the ALP into the centre to win office by adding middle-class votes to its working-class base. But Hayden abandoned Whitlam's programme of big government.

The character of Hayden's early leadership was marked by three tendencies: orthodoxy in Caucus, conservative 'responsibility' in economics and a drive to reinvigorate the relationship between the political and industrial wings of the movement.

In his relationship with the party Hayden was imbued with the old-fashioned spirit of the Labor movement and reverted to tradition. He was more prepared than either Whitlam or Hawke to work through party structures and, notably in the earlier 1977–80 period, to keep open the leader's door. He had patience for internal dialogue and would resort to the leadership steam-roller less often than his predecessor or successor. In short Hayden was seen as a more orthodox leader, who would try to carry the party with him from within its own ranks.

Hayden's early leadership years were spent lecturing Labor on the necessity of economic responsibility. This was also an appeal which reinforced the only plus in his image with the electorate. Hayden's most trenchant declaration was made to the 1979 ALP National Conference:

> We will not find our future in the past. Much and all as we may regret it, now is not the time for the visionary reform programmes of earlier years. This is the period of the hard slog and the scope for reform will have to be won by hard work, by discipline, and by a commonsense approach to policy. There is frankly no easier way and we can't fool ourselves, or the people, by thinking that there is . . .
>
> First, and above all else, we must demonstrate beyond doubt that we are competent economic managers. That competence and the public's recognition of it is the absolute essential underpinning of everything we want to do. Without it, without an unqualified commitment to pursue responsible, economic management then we might just as well pack our bags and give the game away. It is, I believe, as crucial as that.
>
> While I admit there are times when even my best friends seem irritated by my personal commitment to responsible economic management, it seems to me the alternative can only be irresponsible economic management.

Hayden spelt out what he meant by responsibility in his reply to the 1978–79 budget, his first as Opposition leader. He proposed a 'modest expansion', an $840 million increase in the Fraser deficit of $2,800 million. Much of the expansion would come via extra spending on capital works and housing to create jobs. The basic position of the Hayden years was thus established. It would remain the same through each succeeding budget. Hayden stood for a cautious expansion, just a bit more than Fraser.

The defect in this policy was that Hayden defined his own position by reference to Fraser's economics. If Fraser stood for, say, deficit D, Hayden's policy would always be D + 1. Such derivativeness meant that Hayden still needed a different conceptual appeal to the electorate. Economic responsibility just short of Fraserism might be a necessity, but it could never win office.

Hayden's initial answer to this problem lay in micro-economics. He once said of himself: 'I am a conservative in macro-economics; I am a radical, whenever I can be, in micro-economics.'[2] Hayden's aim was to run the economy responsibly but win votes through the politics of redistribution. Again his intention was spelt out in his 1978–79 budget reply and in March 1979 when he took the fight to Fraser. Hayden proposed to change the taxation mix and make redistribution an election issue—a crucial decision which influenced his 1980 election defeat. Hayden's carrots were a cut in indirect taxes, a freeze in oil prices and a possible easing of the income tax burden. The lost revenue would be regained by a capital gains tax on assets above $200,000, a resource rent tax, income tax rises for the top two per cent of income earners and a crackdown on tax avoidance through family trusts. The new tax package would raise about $1,000 million. Hayden declared: 'The dispute between Mr Fraser and me is one of major principle . . . The argument boils down to the interests of the people against the rights of privilege.'[3]

This was a risky but legitimate approach. Hayden was promising tax increases but was creating room for tax cuts as well. This redistribution was the reformist element in his policy. But, fatally, he lacked the nerve to pursue it. Hayden was left stranded in the 1980 campaign having enunciated the policy but not having sold it—a mistake Whitlam would never have made. Hayden became a target for an unscrupulous attack and Fraser seized his chance in the campaign.

The third hallmark of Hayden's leadership was his search for closer ties between the parliamentary and industrial wings. In doing so, he also came to grips with Labor's wages policy dilemma. Herein lay the origins of the ALP–ACTU prices–incomes accord which is so central to the political and economic strategy of the Hawke Government. The accord was championed by Hayden from mid-1979 onwards and it assumed a greater importance each year. The irony for Hayden is that the policy was a perfect instrument for Hawke's appeal to consensus. Post-1980 it would become an area of difficult negotiation between the ALP and the ACTU, Hawke's industrial friends. Hayden perceived the accord as central to Labor's strategic position. He never realised that circumstances would conspire so that the accord would move to finalisation in late 1982 and early 1983 simultaneously with the climax of the leadership crisis. It would become decisive in Hawke's triumph over Hayden.

The idea for the accord came from Labor's Shadow Treasurer, Ralph Willis, who had studied European and British experiences during a 1978 overseas visit. The intellectual origins of the accord were to give an ALP Government a mechanism to prevent a wages explosion during periods of economic growth. Experience had shown that this was probably Australia's major short-term economic problem. As the economy began to pick up, rapid wage rises fanned inflation and thus choked off the recovery. Willis, Hayden and Hawke all believed that if the next Labor Government failed due to a wage explosion, thereby repeating the fate of the Whitlam Government, the long-term damage to the party would be catastrophic. The solution was to reach an accord with the unions under which they agreed to moderate wage demands and thereby ensure a sustained economic recovery that would gradually lower unemployment. The objective was to avoid the British 'disease', where the unions had thwarted recovery. The concept of a social wage was devised as the trade-off which would allow unions during recovery to accept less than they could obtain in the marketplace. The social wage was based on the recognition that real living standards were a function not just of income but of the additional mix of benefits stemming from tax policy, health insurance and welfare payments. This view assumed cooperation between an ALP Government and the union movement in shaping the economic and welfare policies which made up the social wage.

The defect in this strategy was the decentralised nature of the Australian union movement and the confrontational rather than consensus tradition in Australian politics. It was one thing for the ALP to reach an accord with the ACTU. But the ACTU lacked the power or sanctions to guarantee the compliance of its own members for a deal struck with Government and authorised by the Arbitration Commission. It was a weak central body which reflected the aspirations of its constituents. Implicit in the strategy was an effort to enhance the authority of the ACTU. However, the problem was not restricted to union structure but affected attitudes. Cooperation between the Whitlam Government and the union movement had been a dismal failure. This was because of the Labor Government's reluctance to share its power with the unions and the union movement's refusal to recognise the conflicting pressures on a Labor Government. Fraser's instincts were right in detecting and exploiting the gulf between the often disaffected union rank and file and the trade union leadership. Trade union leaders had too often sacrificed the cause of national economic progress on the alter of short-term sectional interest. They had done this through demanding, often with strike action, wage rises which exceeded profitability, resisting technological change and insisting on outdated employment practices which retarded productivity and growth. In this sense many wage gains were phoney, the product of a selfish and reactionary union movement, and their result meant more unemployment and less economic growth. Many union leaders did their members the disservice of denying the link between excessive real wage rises on one hand and higher inflation and unemployment on the other.

Hayden believed an ALP Government armed with the accord could establish the industrial conditions to achieve sustained economic growth. This became the new orthodoxy in the party. Labor's ties with the unions were to be revitalised and used as an electoral asset and not discarded. This strategic decision was undoubtedly correct. The notion that the ALP would benefit by cutting off its union wing was a fanciful mirage usually peddled by editorials in right-wing papers. By such action it would lose its sheet anchor, much of its financial base and, most dangerous of all, run the risk of a new party springing up on the left representing the union cause. It was true that the trade unions were unpopular institutions, but the very notion of the accord implied an effort to reform the attitudes which made them unpopular.

In 1979 Hayden began one of the seminal transformations of his leadership: from economic rationalist to political pragmatist. This transition was decisive and if he had made the journey more quickly he might have won the 1980 election. Hayden underwent his own road to Damascus. But it was not light that came into his soul, it was iron. Two years earlier Hayden had given himself to personal ambition when he challenged Whitlam. Now he believed that the imperative for a man seeking power was to compromise himself in order to achieve it. Hayden's path was soon littered with discarded relics of his political conscience.

He abandoned his espousal of lower tariffs to promote economic efficiency in order to deny Fraser this avenue of attack on him. Then Hayden qualified his support for world parity oil-pricing, which meant pricing a resource at its true value, in order to give Labor the chance to win votes by offering lower petrol prices than Fraser. Finally he decided to steal Fraser's 1977 clothes and twist his income redistribution pledge to offer a modest tax cut to a majority of income earners. Cynicism joined caution as the byword of the Hayden Labor Party. But Hayden's final hardening towards Fraser and his ministers occurred over the issue of ministerial propriety.

The puritan instincts of Hayden's working-class background had been supplemented by his careers as an honest cop and straight politician. A formidable duo. In 1975 he had drawn the lesson that Fraser would threaten national institutions to preserve his own power. Hayden then watched the litany of ministerial scandals: Garland, Lynch, Withers and finally Sinclair, who was charming, ruthless and brazen. Labor believed he was as guilty as hell. Hayden spearheaded the attack against Sinclair and on the afternoon that the Finnane Report into Sinclair's business affairs was released in the NSW Parliament, the federal Parliament was engulfed in wild scenes. When the Government moved to gag the debate, Hayden, Young and Keating hurled their fury back in its face screaming, 'Resign, resign' at Sinclair. Keating spat out, 'It's a dirty, rotten corrupt Government.' Hayden called, 'The Fraser family fortune came from a railway swindle; you can understand why they're covering up.'[4] Hayden believed the Fraser Government was filled with too many crooks. This was conviction, not mere rhetoric. When a man starts to see his opponents as the embodiment of iniquity, then he is far advanced in the self-justification of any tactic needed for their removal. Fraser was rapidly making Hayden over in his own image of toughness and pragmatism.

But Hayden's greatest failure was his inability to communicate either himself or his policies to the electorate. In no other area was his insistence on following his own instincts and rejecting advice more obvious or damaging. Hayden's attitude was old-fashioned and uncompromisingly working-class: what you see is what you get. His inability to communicate was a highly personal matter and Hayden would rarely take advice on personal, as distinct from political, matters. But communication is the essence of contemporary politics. Hayden was guileless and lacking in the personal vanity which the television age has bred into its political practitioners. Hawke was careful about his appearance, Hayden was disinterested. The man being projected as the alternative Prime Minister would just stroll into his Ipswich barber; Dallas would buy his shirts at the local shops; Hayden would appear on television with his uniquely Queensland sense of colour contrast: open-necked blue, white and pale blue sports outfits. His staff would cringe. The Labor campaign managers would crawl up the wall. Hayden was defying their judgement and insisting that he knew better.

Hayden set himself against the greatest revolution of *The Age* by denying the notion of a television image separate from personal identity. Hayden believed that by being himself he would communicate himself to the nation. This was a grand delusion upon which Hayden persisted for too long. Even a casual glance at Neville Wran would have reminded Hayden of the huge contrast between the television image and the real man. But Hayden insisted that ideas and policies would bring their own reward. He filled his television comments with economic jargon and his parliamentary speeches with too many statistics. When he took advice, it was grudgingly: he did smile on television and slow his delivery. But his suspicion that making himself into an effective media politician was either dishonest or effeminate remained. Hayden said:

> The important thing is to be yourself and not get into the hands of people who want to mould you as a sort of cellophane packet and present you as soap powder or that sort of commodity. That's artificial: I couldn't bear with that.[5]

Hayden found it demeaning and intolerable to curry favour with powerful media figures. He despised Rupert Murdoch's publications, displayed suspicion towards those of Kerry Packer and tried to cultivate the senior Fairfax editors. He found talk-back radio identities boorish and the most powerful of them, John Laws, both pretentious and a menace to ALP interests. Hayden had to summon all his discipline to be polite to Laws and on one spectacular occasion abandoned discipline for opinion, telling Laws he was 'totally prejudiced against the Labor Party at the federal level'.[6]

There was a sad dimension to Hayden's incapacity to handle the media. He was always sensitive to the criticism that he lacked strength and was self-conscious when he began wearing glasses. But his final humiliation was kept in his desk drawer: a hearing aid, which he needed but could never bring himself to wear, except once at a Newcastle function when his staff suddenly noticed it. They did not see it again. Meanwhile, in Parliament, Hayden struggled with poor timing and terrible intonation. He fluffed interjections, often because he could not hear them. Chatting to Fraser over the front table he reached forward, hand cupped over his ear, trying to catch the words.

Hayden always longed to possess the oratory skills of old-time Labor figures who could hold a meeting spellbound with their words and jokes. He insisted that his staff fill his speeches with as many jokes as possible; when they failed, Hayden would use his own. His humour was deficient and his timing worse. One of his speech writers quipped: 'What do you want to win, an election or an Emmy?' In the 1980 campaign Hayden addressed a breakfast for Labor's women candidates at Sydney's Wentworth Hotel. He delivered an effective fighting speech but referred to 'deep throat' as his witty allusion for the morning. The feminists were horrified.

Hayden's Press Secretary, Alan Ramsey, told him later to cut out the 'bloody awful jokes'. Hayden pressed his finger in Ramsey's chest saying, 'Listen, you've got no sense of humour. If you can't write some decent jokes for me, then get someone who can.' Suddenly Susan Ryan appeared, kissed Hayden and said, 'Bill, that was wonderful, but please stop telling those awful jokes.' Hayden paused and then laughed. The tension seemed broken. But no, Hayden then turned to Ramsey and said: 'You put her up to that.'

Hayden's experience as a Queensland cop left him with a deep sense of defiance when intimidated. A stunning example was his decision to visit the Middle East in 1980 and see, among others, PLO leader Yasser Arafat. The powerful Jewish lobby had launched a vigorous campaign against this trip. But Hayden only decided to go after pressure from the President of the Executive Council of Australian Jewry, Isi Leibler. Leibler, one of Hawke's closest friends, rang Hayden and the two men had a fiery exchange in which Leibler asked him to cancel any plans to see Arafat. Hayden, rightly, or wrongly, felt that this was an act of intimidation and decided then that he must proceed.[7]

For a political leader internal rule is as important as external appeal. Hayden's management of the ALP in the 1977–80 period was personally courageous and politically dangerous. His upbringing fated him to be a loner in politics. His geographical isolation in Ipswich tended to accentuate this personality trait. Hayden was divorced from the great states and factions that dominated the Labor movement and whose weight determined its leadership and policies. He was his own man and never the representative of any faction. Because neither left nor right owned him, there was always a tension between the leader and the factions. Hayden governed not in the interests of the right or left, but according to his own interpretation of Labor interests.

Hayden was elected leader in December 1977 on centre and left-wing votes against Bowen, who relied on right-wing votes. This established the pattern of Hayden's leadership. There was never a threat to him from the left; the threat was always from the right. Initially it was Bowen; some speculated that it might become Wran; it was always assumed to be Hawke. As a result Hayden was suspicious of the right, particularly the powerful and ruthless NSW machine which would be the engine room for any challenge in the right-hand lane—from Wran or Hawke. The left was in decline, not numerically but in terms of ideological relevance and leadership candidates. As the left strategists had cast their eyes across the political spectrum looking for a successor to Whitlam, Hayden was the first candidate they had encountered and he was firmly of the centre, not of the left. So Hayden had become the recipient of the left-wing vote.

In essence Hayden had a hard economic centre surrounded by a soft social-welfare surface. This enabled the left to depict or rationalise Hayden as a left-leaning politician. But when the political temperature rose, the surface melted to reveal the hard centre. Hayden's economic credo for the ALP in recession made him a natural right-wing politician. It was obvious at an early stage of Hayden's leadership that there was a contradiction between his policy stance and his power base. This guaranteed tensions, which remained contained before 1980 and only exploded in 1981–82. The danger for Hayden was that if he gave the left no policy returns and essentially forced it to select between right-wing politicians, for example, himself and Hawke, then the left would choose whomever was most likely to win.

The 1979 Adelaide Conference highlighted Hayden's dilemma between his policy and his base. At his first conference as leader Hayden, despite the vulnerability of his position, put his own indelible stamp on Labor's future. On the two critical policy platforms, economics and energy, he led the way and thrashed left-wing amendments seeking more public ownership and greater economic expansion. Hayden carried the conference with him, relying on centre and right-wing votes. The engine room for his policy support was the NSW right represented by Wran, Keating, Ducker and Richardson. Hayden was in a curious position. The men whose votes he needed for policy were those with whom his personal relations were marked by uncertainty and suspicion. The leftists, whose policies he had repudiated, were the men whose support he needed in order to stay ALP leader.

In his early days as leader Hayden was taken to lunch at Le Café in Sydney by Ducker and Richardson. But the relationship never flourished. Ducker told friends, usually in an amused or exasperated tone, about his 'typical' conversation with Hayden when they met at airports:

> Hayden would say to me, 'Uren and Gietzelt tell me not to trust you because you are too treacherous. You seem all right to me but I just wonder what you're doing behind my back.' I just tell Hayden that we support the leader of the Labor Party. But he seems to have a bit of trouble accepting this. He'd better bloody well make up his mind.[8]

Keating had similar experiences. Hayden was antagonistic towards Keating after May 1977 because he believed that Keating, after encouraging him to run against Whitlam, had finally voted for Whitlam. Keating denied this. Six months later Keating told Hayden he would be voting for Bowen against him in the December 1977 contest. At this stage Hayden began to think that if Keating told him the truth once, then he may have told him the truth twice.

But Hayden never trusted the NSW machine and it, in turn, never trusted him. He lacked the personality to forge ties with the right wing. Although a Catholic by birth, Hayden fell outside the Irish Catholic Labor tradition and thereby forfeited the gift for hard drinking, personal rapport and native cunning which gave automatic membership of that clan. He was fascinated by its exponents and his personality opposites, such as Mick Young and Eric Walsh, and at various stages sought out their company.

Hayden's rock was the Caucus centre. During the 1977–80 period John Button became Hayden's key confidant and ally. There was a mutual respect, emotional warmth and intellectual spark in their relationship. The centre group lacked a power base at grassroots level in most states but became at Caucus level the political cement in Hayden's leadership. Hayden always paid his respects to the left wing but made fewer concessions to them as his leadership advanced.

The other asset Hayden enjoyed, rare in the Labor Party, was a leadership team with whom he could work. He, Bowen, Wriedt and Button comprised an unusual quartet, not devoid of tension but certainly without venom towards each other. Relations between Hayden and Bowen were strictly business-like and never personal, but their vast personality differences were not accentuated by political disloyalty.

Hayden's most traumatic and important party move was his spearheading of federal intervention into his own state branch of Queensland in 1980. Until then it had been run by an incompetent and narrow right-wing junta, which presided over Labor's declining electoral fortunes. Hayden decided that Labor would never win office federally until Queensland was cleaned up. The exercise involved giving the branch a new administration and ensuring proper power-sharing between its right-wing, left-wing and centre groups. At the national level the left and centre had pressed for intervention, and intervention meant that Queensland's representatives on the ALP National Executive and Conference would cease to be dominated exclusively by the right wing and would represent other factions. Consequently, national right-wing forces opposed a thorough purging of the Queensland 'old guard'.

In February–March 1979 Hayden had agreed on intervention—despite threats from the Queensland ALP to secede. But at the penultimate moment he was persuaded to back off by Bowen, Keating and Young. They argued the move would give the left too much power and weaken moderate ALP strength. Hayden, still hesitant and inexperienced in machine politics, concurred.

One year later he returned to the fight, convinced his instincts had been correct. Hayden brought more tenacity and care to this task than to any other internal issue he faced. He knew there would be a showdown with the NSW right, so he personally lobbied all National Executive members and counted the numbers himself. When the right warned him he faced defeat, Hayden told them he had the numbers. Button, who was his indispensable ally in this, drew upon his personal experience of Victorian intervention a decade earlier and drafted all the necessary National Executive motions. David Combe worked tirelessly to ensure intervention succeeded. Hayden refused to be intimidated by further Queensland warnings that intervention would create two Labor Parties in the state. Keating came to the National Executive meeting with a compromise he had organised with the Queensland branch, but Hayden was done with compromise.

The NSW right was furious. Intervention proceeded and the 'old guard' defied it. The issue went to court, which found in favour of the federal party in a landmark decision. Three years later Bob Hawke led the ALP to a sweeping five-seat gain in Queensland at the 1983 election and so reaped the benefit of the seeds Hayden had fought to sow.

A leader is both a tool of the faction he represents and a manipulator of that faction. Hayden showed that, far from being a prisoner of factions, he could manipulate them for his own ends. In power terms Hayden ran the party by relying on the centre group and stitching alliances together with either the left or right depending upon the issue. For his leadership position he relied on left–centre votes; to maintain his economic policy he relied on right–centre votes; Queensland intervention was achieved on left-centre support, while at the special 1981 National Conference Hayden relied on right–centre votes to defeat the left's drive to harden up the party's socialist objective. This technique infuriated the faction leaders, but the approach was sound. Over time it gave both the left and the right their own wins within the party. It helped maintain the ALP as a broad coalition of forces. On nearly all these key issues Hayden's decisions as leader were utterly sound for the party's long-term interests. The technique had one flaw and Hayden was susceptible to it. It had the potential to cast doubt on the leader's personal trustworthiness.

At the 1979 Adelaide Conference this vulnerability was evident when a spectacular Hayden–Hawke brawl began over whether the ALP should include in its prices–incomes deal with the unions provision for a referendum to give the national Government power over prices and wages. Hawke and Willis, who presented the economic policy, recommended a referendum. Hawke's strategy was to secure its endorsement from the ALP as a prelude to putting it to the ACTU Congress. But Hayden had nagging doubts about a referendum and on the eve of the conference, left-wing leaders Tom Uren and Victorian President of the Amalgamated Metalworkers' and Shipwrights' Union Jim Roulston warned Hayden they would defeat the prices–incomes recommendations to the conference. On the morning of the debate Hayden had breakfast with about 20 right-wing delegates drawn heavily from New South Wales and Queensland, including Wran and Ducker. Hayden begged them to support the Hawke committee's proposals in the economic debate. They gave their word. Hayden went into battle with his right–centre coalition behind him. By late in the morning Hawke, tanned and fit, was in the President's chair, furiously making speech notes and preparing himself for a major attack on the left.

The attack never came because Hayden reached a compromise with the left over lunch which preserved the rest of the policy but dropped Hawke's referendum. Hawke, outraged at Hayden's switch, refused to deliver his speech. He was tempted to publicly attack the compromise but he retreated, later confiding that 'John Ducker saved me'. Hawke admitted: 'There was no way I could speak without opposing Hayden on the conference floor.' His strategy of carrying the conference and taking the resolution on the referendum to the ACTU Congress was in ruins.

Hawke's fury was not isolated. Ducker, Wran and Willis all expressed their displeasure during the debate. But Hayden was ecstatic. He called a press conference to unveil the future accord between the Labor Party and the union movement, and brushed aside the row emerging over his own tactics. Hayden told the media: 'I made up my own mind on this and I carried the conference and that's what matters.'[9]

Hayden had won and he revelled in that win. But discontent swirled about him. Young warned that Hayden would rue the day he had doublecrossed the right wing. Ducker saw the issue simply: it was an 'unnecessary betrayal'. Hayden had cast doubt on his capacity for personal trustworthiness. The suspicion between Hayden and the NSW right became mutually deeper.

The event triggered one of the most publicised explosions of Hawke's career. That evening he repaired to the Gateway Inn and the red-walled Rotunda Club Bar where, by dint of sheer perseverence, he transformed a minor setback for himself into a major one. The ALP President had apparently forgotten the homily offered earlier to the conference by former ALP Senator Jim Toohey—'the unity of Labor is the hope of the world'. Hawke told half a dozen journalists, 'As far as I'm concerned, Hayden is dead.' Warming to his theme, an emotional but not very tired Hawke labelled Hayden 'a lying cunt with a limited future' and offered the opinion that, 'As far as Bill Hayden and I are concerned, it's finished.'[10] After Adelaide no-one either inside or outside the ALP could doubt that Hawke's entry into Parliament could mean anything but a sustained and damaging public brawl between Hayden and Hawke while Hayden stayed leader. But Hawke even speculated that he might remain in the trade union movement with his friends like John Ducker. He left Adelaide depressed and with a heavy cloud over his future.

Hayden left Adelaide with his leadership enhanced, anxious to plan the 1980 campaign, but more personally antagonistic towards Hawke than ever. He had been outraged at Hawke's autumn 1979 statement that he would decide over the next several months whether or not to seek ALP preselection for the 1980 election. Hayden believed this move was designed to attract publicity to Hawke at the expense of Hayden's own efforts to beat Fraser. Nonetheless once Hawke did become an endorsed candidate Hayden displayed great pragmatism in burying his animosity so as to attempt to realise his political ambition.

In mid-1980 Hayden and Hawke held their most important talk on the leadership before Hawke's entry into Parliament. They faced each other, declared a truce, and laid the ground for the remarkable ALP troika. The meeting was at John Curtin House in Canberra during a break in a National Executive meeting. Hawke told Hayden he wanted to make his position clear. 'I will work my guts out in this campaign to get you elected as Prime Minister,' he said. 'I will go to the last ounce of my energy to do this. It would be dishonest of me if I didn't say the embers of Adelaide remain in my mind, but I want you to know I can put this away and work for the party and your success.'

Hayden told Hawke that since he had preselection, he should come into Parliament as soon as possible. Hayden wanted a by-election for Wills; Hawke agreed. There was a strange community of interest between them. But it foundered because the member for Wills, Gordon Bryant, resisted all pressure to leave early.

The incident showed Hayden's determination to harness Hawke's popularity for his own ends. At the same meeting the two men also discussed the future leadership if Hayden lost the election. Hayden said that in this event he would probably stand down. He had discussed this very question with Dallas recently. Hayden said the worst result would be for Labor to lose narrowly because in this situation he would feel entitled to have another shot at the next election. Hayden told Hawke that if he did lose and stand aside, he would probably remain in Parliament. He had no other profession. They discussed what job Hayden might occupy if he did stand aside. Hayden stated that he would prefer Foreign Affairs and Defence to an economic portfolio.

Hayden's ambition overcame his pride in his embrace of the troika— Hayden, Hawke and Wran—as the symbol of moderate Labor leadership against Malcolm Fraser in the 1980 elections. Hayden had made almost no impact on the electorate after nearly three years as Opposition leader. His campaign strategists told him that when it came to swinging voters:

> they don't know who you are and care even less. They're vaguely interested in what the leader of the ALP stands for, but so far don't have a clue . . . they will be only vaguely interested in voting for Bill Hayden if, and only if, they can get some kind of line on him, preferably one involving some sense of hope for Australia's future.[11]

The troika arose from the fortuitous opportunity presented when Neville Wran replaced Neal Batt as ALP National President. Batt had had to retire for personal reasons and Hayden had then decided he wanted Bowen as the new president. Combe agreed and rang Bowen with the proposition. Bowen was initially reluctant, but accepted on the basis that he was the choice of Hayden and the party. At this time Neville Wran had had severe problems with his voice and was recuperating in the far north. Wran would have been the preferred choice, but it was assumed by NSW Secretary Graham Richardson and others that he was not available. So Combe began ringing delegates to the ALP National Executive, lobbying them for Bowen. He planned to make an announcement the next morning.

Suddenly Richardson rang Combe: 'Mate, you wouldn't believe this. I've just had a phone call from N. K. Wran whispering: "I want to be the fucking National President and you fix it up".' Combe and Richardson quickly agreed to switch horses. Hayden was on a boat at the time and desperate efforts were made to reach him by radio telephone to avoid a fiasco in the changeover. When he was finally contacted, Hayden agreed. That night Richardson announced on television that Wran would be a candidate, but nobody had told Bowen, who was furious and told Hayden so. Bowen felt the anger of a man who had been unceremoniously dumped when on the verge of accepting the honour.

Labor's 1980 election strategy began to evolve in mid-1979, about the time Hayden had a long dinner in Sydney with National Secretary David Combe and ANOP Managing Director Rod Cameron. Combe and Cameron wanted to discover Hayden's preliminary ideas about an election strategy. Hayden had in fact independently reached the same conclusion that Cameron had formed as a result of his survey work and decided the ALP would campaign to restore family living standards. The idea was old-fashioned. It was a politician promising to give people money. But Hayden's economic nous and Cameron's market research suggested that such an appeal would be powerful precisely because people were worse off than before. Labor would use a moderate economic stimulus to repair the fall in family living standards. It was an uninspiring appeal which went back to bread-and-butter basics. The grand vision and broad sweep of Whitlamism was pushed aside. This was a strategy conceived in caution, which accepted Fraser's own terms of debate but which fingered the exact weakness of his Government in the electorate.

Labor's 1980 campaign was a carefully planned and thoroughly researched effort. Cameron's ANOP research found that 'swinging voters for the first time in memory believed their living standards were falling and would continue to fall'. Their mood was summarised by David Combe:

> Swingers believed that Fraser was out of touch with their problems . . . For swinging voters the issue was personal living standards and how to maintain them in the face of inflation, taxes, rising petrol prices, increased housing costs, interest rates and a growing burden of health care and health insurance.[12]

In late 1979 Hayden got this advice from his campaign strategists:

> Remember that the next election will be decided solely on the votes of the 15 per cent of 'swingers' who show any willingness to change. Remember that virtually all of them must have voted for Fraser in 1977 . . . They are not

discerning upper middle-class professionals who carefully reason through their vote. They are basically ignorant and indifferent about politics. They vote on instinct for superficial, ill-informed and generally selfish reasons . . . They believe politicians are irrelevant charlatans, and that the country survives despite them.[13]

The 1980 campaign contrasted sharply with Whitlam's 1977 strategy. Whitlam made an appeal to the nation which misread its mood. Hayden made an appeal to swinging voters confident that his pitch was right. The campaign technique of the future, which focused on the swinging voter, had been established.

In his policy speech Hayden offered a very modest $300 million income tax cut, a cut in sales tax and a 12-month freeze in petrol prices. Labor pledged to make health care free for children and expectant mothers; but it was too economically risky to return to full Medibank. Home buyers were offered assistance, a job-creation scheme was launched and a family income supplement promised to the needy. Hayden resisted pressure to go further and offer a cut in petrol prices. Cameron urged this on him because ANOP research revealed the doubling in petrol prices as a critical issue. But Hayden was anxious to hold the line on economic responsibility. Hayden's economic conscience betrayed him when he told the press that Labor would 'consider' reverting to world parity pricing when inflation was lowered.

Significantly Hayden had retreated on his capital gains tax. The income redistribution theme had been played down. Hayden promised instead, on Willis's advice, an inquiry into wealth after winning office. This was the chink in a carefully designed opportunistic strategy. The Fraser Government spent the final week in a saturation media effort impaling Labor on its alleged 'wealth tax'. During most of the campaign Hayden was defiantly conservative. He said John Stone would stay at the Treasury, departmental changes would be kept to a minimum and there would be no one-man Government but collective decision-making.

This campaign revealed the convergence that had taken place in Australian politics. The Government and the Opposition had moved together on policy in a fashion that defied the rhetoric on both sides. Convergence was a major feature of politics in the late 1970s and early 1980s yet it was not until the early phase of Hawke's administration that it was widely recognised. However by 1980 the Hayden Labor Party was well down the road from Whitlamism towards a more conservative and managerial bent with the economy its chief preoccupation. But it remained far from a new home base and in the interim was relying more upon Fraser's mistakes than Hayden's strengths.

Hayden believed the campaign polls which pointed towards his winning the election. On voting day, 18 October 1980, he drove around Ipswich, distracted, hoping to be Prime Minister within hours. The defeat came as a bitter blow. Labor gained 49.6 per cent of the two-party preferred vote as compared to the coalition's 50.4 per cent. But Fraser's majority was 23.

Labor had waged a better campaign than the Government. It had exposed Fraser's vulnerability and his complacency. Hayden could conceivably have won with a more ruthless policy which clarified at an earlier stage Labor's revenue-raising measures. But Hayden had lost his main chance. He had performed beyond all expectations in the campaign, but his failure came later when he could not sustain that performance.

5
Boom and bust

*This development promises to be as important to Australia and
individual Australians as anything in the last 35 years.*

Malcolm Fraser on the resources boom in his
1980 policy speech

One of Malcolm Fraser's most emotional political beliefs, documented in his
1956 maiden speech to Parliament, was his vision for a grand Australia. Fraser
was an aristocratic but repressed version of Rex Connor, the Labor Minister
whose destruction he used as a trigger to assume office. Beneath his rhetoric
and action to promote private enterprise and liberate market forces Malcolm
Fraser harboured a secret dream—to pioneer Australia's great resource devel-
opments. When his chance came Fraser seized it, not just as a welcome
departure from the long negative grind of beating inflation but as the realisation of the development-nationalist within him.

Students of Fraser's 22 February 1956 speech would have found a young
man of lofty idealism and ambitious horizons. He tied both Australian defence
and development into the rope that would make Australia strong. Fraser
applauded the Snowy Mountains Scheme and called on the 'Australian
Government' to embark upon a 'national project' and dam both the Ord and
Fitzroy rivers in the north in a great irrigation scheme. He also urged the in-
itiation of a 'national communications plan' for Australia by recalling that
'when the Romans made a conquest they followed up their victories with the
construction of some of the best highways the world has known'. The young
Malcolm declared:

> I am sure that I shall live to see the day when we shall have 25 million people in
> Australia and then we shall be able to look the world in the face far more boldly
> and play a more effective part in the maintenance of world peace and freedom.

Fraser had no ideological bias against public sector involvement. Indeed these projects were so grand that only Government could manage them. He advised: 'Public bodies have an important part to play in our national development because many things are too big in scope or too important for private people or even groups of people to undertake alone.' He concluded with an appeal to idealism. Where would the investment capital come from for these projects? Australians had to choose; they should sacrifice higher spending now and save more to create investment funds in the cause of a bigger, better, braver Australia 25 million strong.

Twice in his prime ministership Fraser reached back to resurrect his developmentalist roots—first in 1980 and again in early 1983. Both times he was authentic but both efforts were dashed. They revealed Fraser as a multi-faceted politician who, depending upon the circumstances, would produce another side of his identity for the occasion.

In 1980 Fraser embarked on potentially one of the biggest expansions of the public sector since Federation in order to provide an infrastructure for the gathering resources boom. At the mid-1980 Premiers' Conference, the Loan Council approved, on Fraser's initiative, total infrastructure borrowings over the rest of the decade of $4,700 million. This was to be raised both at home and abroad principally for state electricity commissions to boost power gener-ation across the nation, to provide new ports, coal loaders, gas pipelines, electrification of rail lines and backing for the huge North-West shelf project. The aim was to provide adequate support for the resource investment surge.

The Fraser Government did not merely approve the state Government requests. The Prime Minister solicited such requests and was determined that the federal Government would oversee the pace and priorities of this develop-ment. In one of the great ironies of politics Fraser, who destroyed the Whitlam Government over its $4,000 million loan-raising, presided just five years later over Loan Council approval of his own $4,700 million loan for many of the identical purposes that Whitlam and Connor had intended.

Fraser's stance was opposed by both Treasurer John Howard and Secretary John Stone because it contradicted the fight against inflation. They argued that the infrastructure borrowings were a further strain on capital markets at the very time corporate demand was buoyant, with the result that interest rates were likely to be pressed upwards. But Fraser was in an inspi-rational mood and rejected this advice. He was realising his dream and the bulk of the infrastructure programme was taking place in the public sector. The programme itself was administered under a new category of Loan Council borrowing which enabled both the Prime Minister and premiers to highlight the funded projects for their own political benefit.

The origins of the resources boom lay in the second OPEC oil shock in 1979, which increased the real price of oil so spectacularly and quickly. This had two significant impacts on industrial, oil-importing nations. Firstly it provoked a new search for energy substitutes for oil. Secondly it led to a major economic downturn in the OECD nations. Australia was the beneficiary of the first trend because it was energy-rich. Consequently there was an upsurge of interest in Australian energy exports, notably steaming-coal for electricity generation. The resources boom was an investment boom directed towards the opening-up of new coalmines, coal loaders and ports, the North-West shelf, power stations and aluminium plants. It was primarily funded with foreign capital and had a long time-lag between the investment itself and the export revenue years later. It was characterised by a flurry of activity in which more projects were planned than would be realised.

However it was not until 1982 that the second impact of the 1979 oil shock, the downturn in the industrial nations, was proven to be more important than the first effect, the competitive energy advantage bestowed upon Australia, with the result that new investment dried up. But in the 1979–80 period Fraser responded enthusiastically to initial pressure from Western Australian Premier Sir Charles Court and persuasive advice from economists in his own department, notably Ed Visbord on the infrastructure scheme.

The driving force behind the boom remained the private sector, and its ardour was matched only by the Government's own propaganda. The Department of Industry and Commerce under Sir Phillip Lynch released reports estimating the size of prospective resources investment; this was the origin of the famous 1980 figure of $29,000 million, which was always likely to be a phoney estimate. Such calculations were tricky by nature and evidence from inside the public service reveals the belief that the estimate was exaggerated. The June 1980 report of the IDC on economic strategy which was dominated by Treasury and the Prime Minister's Department warned:

> The figures assume away possible mutual exclusivity among projects; they also assume that firm decisions to proceed will be taken on all those projects currently under final feasibility study and that all projects will be completed according to present plans. The subdued medium-term outlook for the world economy could lead to the delaying of some projects, as may environmental and other concerns.[1]

Manufacturing industry, through its umbrella group the Australian Industries Development Association (AIDA), complained that Government surveys and statistics were leading to 'an overoptimistic and simplistic picture of the general level of investment in the 1980s'. AIDA said only an immigration programme or guest worker plan could solve the labour demand. It feared the bidding-up of wages in the resources sector might extend through other areas of the economy. Beneath its concerns was a 'gut' fear that manufacturing industry would suffer in the adjustment process. The AIDA Director was Geoff Allen, former Press Secretary to Snedden and well-known to most Liberal ministers. After AIDA's criticism Lynch called Allen and gave him a rap over the knuckles, which forced a form of retraction.

The Prime Minister's 1980 policy speech reflected an unquenchable confidence in the boom. It revealed a politician anxious to recreate the exaggerated optimism of the goldrush days when the bonanza for some fired the enthusiasm of all. So confident was Fraser that he offered the boom and not income tax cuts in the 1980 campaign. He declared in his policy speech:

> Five years ago we committed Australia to a new sense of direction and national purpose. We have fulfilled that commitment . . .
>
> In my policy speech of 1977 I said Australia could look forward to $6,000 million in development. Some amazement was expressed in this—even disbelief . . . And now prospective development is $29,000 million. This development promises to be as important to Australia and individual Australians as anything in the last 35 years. Already new aluminium smelters and mines are being established in Australia along with the associated new towns, railways, roads and port facilities. The benefits of this will be felt nationwide . . .[2]

Fraser said the boom would create 60,000 jobs directly and many more indirectly. But there is no escaping that the apostle of hardship rekindled the cargo-cult mentality. Fraser felt that after five years of fairly tight economic management a boom was long overdue. When it came he rushed to embrace it.

In the 1980 campaign Fraser was a victim of complacency and a superior Labor election strategy. He called the election in supreme confidence and ran on his performance as an economic manager, the gathering resources boom and the rising concern about defence following the Soviet invasion of Afghanistan. In 1979–80 inflation had crept back to 10.2 per cent, but jobs were being created and unemployment that year was going down, being 6.1 per cent, compared with 6.2 per cent and 6.3 per cent for the two previous years. During the 1978–80 Parliament Fraser had displayed considerable managerial fortitude in reducing the deficit and restoring Australia's international competitiveness. Government spending was held to 8.4 per cent in 1978–79, the smallest increase for ten years, and 9.1 per cent in 1979–80, while the estimated rise for 1980–81 was 13.7 per cent. Overall the Common-wealth budget deficit as a proportion of Gross Domestic Product had fallen from 4.9 per cent in 1975–76 to an estimated 0.9 per cent in 1980–81.

These figures, which gave Fraser a great sense of achievement, concealed the reality. The cut in the budget deficit had been achieved more through higher taxation than spending restraint. The cardinal feature of these years had been the Fraser Government's far-reaching decision to price local oil at the world parity price. This decision to price a vital resource at its true value was both economically rational and one of the significant political advances of the Fraser administration. The spin-off for the Government was a new growth tax—at least for a few years—with much of the higher petrol prices being paid by ordinary Australians now going to the Government. For instance in the three years from 1977–78 to 1980–81 the revenue from crude oil and LPG rose from $476 million to $3,108 million—a sixfold increase. This windfall was used not to ease the tax burden, as Fraser had once pledged, but to reduce the deficit in line with Treasury's prescription. Fraser was a high tax and low deficit Prime Minister, not an attractive package.[3]

The 1980 election, in which Labor made significant gains, burst the myth of Fraser's electoral invincibility. It was not until the day before the election that Fraser got his first poll showing a Liberal win. Much of the Government camp had been running scared and the campaign polls, which consistently predicted an ALP victory, were counter-productive for the Opposition. The outlying states of Queensland, Western Australia and Tasmania saved Fraser. The Government kept Labor to only eight out of 35 seats in these states, thereby providing a conservative bulwark which Labor could not overcome. The most ominous warning for Fraser, however, was Victoria where Labor won a ring of seven seats and finally overcame the terrible legacy of the 1950s DLP split in that state.

While Hayden had not established a leadership ascendancy over Fraser, the 1980 election imposed far-reaching limitations upon the Prime Minister's power. The Government's House of Representatives position was significantly weaker—despite a 23-seat majority, partly inflated by the gerrymander. The national uniform swing needed to unseat Fraser was only 1.4 per cent. This put the Government on a knife edge for the next Parliament. Fraser had now lost his Senate majority, effective from 1 July 1981, to a combination of the ALP and Australian Democrats. For the first time he faced an unpredictable, poten-tially hostile Senate. The golden years now lay behind him.

Fraser was shocked by his close brush with defeat and the failure of the resources boom to inspire the electorate's imagination. The explanation in the Liberal Party was that the voters had not benefited personally from the boom and that many of them doubted whether they would benefit. The upshot was Fraser's January 1981 Australia Day television message to the nation. The Prime Minister drew a direct comparison between the goldrushes and the resources rush of the 1980s. Reaching for the hip-pocket nerve, Fraser pledged:

> I express tonight the firmest possible determination to see that the prosperity flowing from these great ventures will lift the living standard of every Australian family, not just of those immediately involved.

The test for Fraser now became his management of the boom, which by its nature brought uneven growth. The bigger the boom, the more economic dislocation it would create. Some people would be worse off while others rode the financial roller-coaster to success. The resources boom began to transform the agenda of Australian politics. Inevitably it sharpened competition for a slice of the new wealth. It set wage-earners against employers to take some of the higher profits in wages. The import-competing manufacturing sector felt threatened by the burgeoning export sector. Resource-rich states entered a new rivalry with the older industrial states whose manufacturing base was in decay.

In this unfolding vision of prosperity there were clear challenges to economic policy, all with deep roots in Australian history and identified ahead of time. The first was to facilitate the contraction of less efficient industry as growth took off; the second was the need to reduce the borrowing demands of Government in order to promote the financing of the boom at the lowest possible interest rates; the third was the need to avoid a wages explosion. Failure on one front, let alone three, would only hasten the bust via the needle of inflation.

John Stone identified the first necessity as early as 19 November 1979 in a major speech. He argued that the logical course for the Government was to 'facilitate the entry of imports by a gradual dismantling of our present import protective regime . . .'. If such an adjustment were not made, economic forces 'will quite inevitably compel us towards other paths'. The other paths would be either revaluations of the dollar, which would mean a competitive disadvantage to local industry, or acquiescence in the inflationary consequences of a relaxed monetary policy as export revenue increased. Stone's prescription was favoured by a majority of public service advice. The 1980 IDC report on economic strategy argued:

> The expansion of new industries with higher profits and productivity is a major source of growth, but inevitably involves the relative contraction of other less

productive industries. Resource development is merely one example of this ongoing process . . . Structural adjustment and economic growth are linked, curbing one will curb the other . . .

The majority of the IDC considers that it would be desirable to initiate substantial early moves towards structural adjustment through, for example, the removal of quotas and lower tariffs over a relatively short period.[4]

Fraser knew that reductions in industry protection were good economics but bad politics. In 1981 the Government established a committee to examine an across-the-board tariff cut; it also sent a reference on a general reduction in protection to the Industries Assistance Commission. The Government had an opportunity to act, but it declined. It was saved from its agony of indecision by the collapse of the boom itself, and by the economic downturn. One loss from this period is that the boom was not sufficiently sustained to force the Government into such industry readjustment decisions.

However the Government responded to the second challenge and during 1981, climaxing in its budget, it accepted the Howard–Stone advice that a severe deflationary policy should be adopted. The Government's aim was to reduce its own demand for funds and, by squeezing the public sector to create room for private-sector expansion, not just in resources but in business investment generally. Treasury warned that the condition of the economy made this stance necessary:

The current surge in investment in resource projects is but the latest in a series which have occurred intermittently throughout Australia's history. The important differences from the last 'mining boom' of the late 1960s, however, are that inflation was then running at between three and four per cent annually, compared with about ten per cent now and that the public sector is now commanding about 38 per cent of total resources compared with about 32 per cent at that time.[5]

There was a unity of purpose between economic and political strategy in the 1981–82 budget. This was the post-election budget, so political logic dictated a tough approach to pave the way for tax cuts in a later budget closer to the 1983 election. Malcolm Fraser adjusted to the changed circumstances and read a new text to the states at the mid-1981 Premiers' Conference. The previous year he had championed the infrastructure programme; now he cut it back, worried that the economy might overheat and anxious to reduce both interest rate and inflationary pressures released by the boom.

The economic and political strategy of the August 1981 budget was to ease interest rate pressures and allow growth to continue. For this reason the budget was almost balanced, which meant that after seven years the Fraser Government was on the brink of wiping-out the budget deficit. It was the most deflationary budget of the Fraser years.[6] The irony is that it was brought down at the precise time the economy started to turn down. The Treasury did not detect or predict the economic deterioration about to begin. The Government accepted the challenge of economic growth in this budget and stuck by its principles. The problem was that it devised a policy for an economic environment which was being transformed and its deflationary policy would only accentuate the looming downturn in 1981–82 and thereafter.

It was in wages policy, the third challenge posed by the boom, that the Government failed significantly and the consequences accompanied its defeat in March 1983. During the 1983 campaign Fraser attributed the broken condition of the Australian economy to three factors: the world depression, the drought, and the 1981–82 wages explosion. He argued correctly that his Government could not be blamed for the former two factors. Australia is a boat on the sea of the world economy. Droughts belong to the providence of God, not Malcolm Fraser. But the Government could not avoid responsibility for the wages explosion which was the rock upon which its reputation for economic management was dashed long before the 1983 campaign began.

In one sense Malcolm Fraser was elected Prime Minister on the basis of the 1974 wages explosion, which had destroyed the confidence of the financial community in the Whitlam Government. Fraser campaigned on wage responsibility in 1975. The necessity for wage moderation was the first major lesson Stone taught Fraser. It is hard to think of a single policy imperative more prominent in Fraser's rhetoric. Yet wages policy presented the most intractable institutional problem for the Fraser Government. The response needed was a wages strategy; tactics would never suffice in the long-term. The Fraser Government never confronted the need for a new wages strategy and fiddled with tactics until events in the marketplace overwhelmed it.

The Government accepted and worked within the system of centralised wage fixation and indexation which it had inherited from the Whitlam years. The change was that the Government, with support from employers, secured a form of partial rather than full indexation, which meant that wages were adjusted for only about 80 per cent of price rises. Fraser and his ministers would publicly attack the Arbitration Commission when it handed down judgements they disliked; they even grumbled in private over favourable decisions. But the truth is that they never devised any alternative to Arbitration. While economic activity was low, the Government could muddle along in this fashion and this is exactly what it did.

The resources boom meant a new wage push. The more the Government talked about a $29,000 million boom, the more the unions were provoked into a new wage round. But the same Government which insisted upon wage restraint to sustain the boom had no means to achieve its aim. Benefits of economic growth will always be distributed as wages. The Government's task was to allow wages to rise but not so far as to choke off the 'goldrush' itself. The challenge was to find a mechanism, underpinned by social attitudes, that made it viable. Wages rose 14 per cent in the year to December 1980—a rise of 4.7 per cent in real terms—too much of a grab too fast. The Government was already put on notice. The system of centralised wage fixation was being stretched to breaking point.

In April 1981 the Aribitration Commission, deeply sceptical itself about the system, accepted a submission from the federal Government for a tight set of wage indexation guidelines. Within months, if not weeks, these guidelines were under attack from the unions, who could smell profits in the market-place. Much of the attack came from within the public sector—Fraser's own employees. Telecom unions managed to extract agreement from their management for a significant rise which was inconsistent with the guidelines. In mid-July 1982 the Cabinet submitted to pressure from its own employees and private employers and decided the indexation guidelines should be widened to provide for a 'safety valve' to permit higher pay increases. The Government strategy was to concede a little within the indexation system rather than concede a lot in the marketplace. Unions in the transport, postal, Telecom and waterfront areas all took industrial action in pursuit of new claims.

The flash point was the claim by the Transport Workers' Union for an extra $20 a week. The TWU Executive began its industrial campaign on 23 June 1981. On 17 July it resolved to stay on strike until progress was made. On 21 July the Victorian Government declared a state of emergency because TWU bans had left the state without milk or groceries and meat was running out. Australia faced an industrial crisis. Fraser was due to leave for London and the wedding of Prince Charles and Lady Diana. On 22 July the federal Government decided to suspend and stand down thousands of Telecom workers and deregister the TWU. Two days later ACTU President Cliff Dolan phoned Fraser at The Lodge and asked for a meeting: 'The situation is desperate and is going to get worse . . . Can we talk about it?'[7] The upshot was a meeting that day in Canberra involving senior ministers, the ACTU and Commission President Sir John Moore. Significantly the employers were excluded.

Fraser and Dolan did a deal at this meeting in the cause of industrial peace. The federal Government would drop its threats; the unions would agree to return to work; both the Government and the ACTU would agree that the indexation guidelines needed to be interpreted more widely to allow the pay rises to be ratified inside the system. Sir John Moore was a pained observer. Sitting through this summit while Fraser and Dolan designed a means of getting the wage rises yet having the Arbitration Commission legitimise them, Sir John at some stage decided he would not be manipulated for these purposes.

The joint press statement by Fraser and Dolan after this conference said that both the Government and the ACTU agreed that a 'contributing factor in the current industrial situation' was the rigidity in the commission's wage-fixing principle which prevented the processing of higher wage claims. On the same day, 24 July, the Director-General of the Confederation of Australian Industry, George Polites, wrote a biting letter to the Prime Minister attacking this conclusion:

> The fact is that there is nothing in the principles which prevents any union or employer from taking any matter to the commission for determination . . .
>
> We would urge that greater care be taken to ensure that statements made by Government representatives reflect the facts.

Meanwhile Tamie Fraser flew off in the VIP plane with the Governor-General, Sir Zelman Cowen, and Lady Cowen for the royal wedding. Fraser stayed at home to negotiate the industrial truce. Despite Fraser's deal with the ACTU, Cliff Dolan had trouble finding and then convincing TWU Secretary Ivan Hodgson to end the strike. Fraser warned Dolan that his postponed trip to the royal wedding might have to be cancelled outright. Dolan replied: 'Well, I'm a republican so the wedding doesn't matter to me. But I appreciate that as Prime Minister you should be there.' On Monday 27 July in the Arbitration Commission deputy President Isaac concluded the TWU claim was unjustified and dismissed it. But outside the hearing the employers, the Australian Road Transport Federation (ARTF), struck a deal with the TWU on a wage rise which was more than the union demanded. The settlement was swift. Just before midnight Malcolm Fraser left Melbourne for London on a British Airways jet and arrived only hours before the wedding. He had phoned Dolan to thank him: 'Cliff, if ever you see any problems arising that we can straighten out, don't hesitate to ring me.'[8] The crisis was over. Fraser and Dolan had a new mutual respect and Malcolm got to the wedding. But while he was away Sir John Moore dynamited the seven-year-old indexation system which both Fraser and Dolan had undermined.

On 31 July Sir John announced the Full Bench National Wage Case decision which criticised both the Government and the ACTU. The bench said:

The events since April have shown clearly that the commitment of the participants to the system is not strong enough to sustain the requirements for its continued operation. The immediate manifestation of this is the high level of industrial action in various industries including the key areas of Telecom, road transport, the Melbourne waterfront and sectors of the Australian public service. In many cases action was taken on the pretext that the claims could not be processed because of the principles. Some of these disputes have resulted in substantial increases being agreed without regard to the test of negligible cost or the implications of flow-on.

To accommodate these strong pressures the ACTU and the Commonwealth proposed widening the safety valve provided by the principles dealing with anomalies and inequities. The belief that the answer lies in greater flexibility of the kind proposed is illusory. Such flexibility would resolve sectional claims at the expense of national adjustments and destroy the priority expected of a centralised system. It cannot be otherwise.

For these reasons we have decided that the time has come for us to abandon the indexation system.

The end of indexation was neither planned by the Government nor part of its strategy. The irony is that Malcolm Fraser, after criticising the system for so long, was still trying to preserve it when Sir John Moore recognised the farce had to be ended. Wage policy as an arm of economic strategy had virtually ceased to exist for the Fraser Government. The Prime Minister had helped negotiate the industrial truce, but he had treated the TWU dispute as an industrial issue when he must have known that its real import was economic. The employers attacked the Government, and Fraser's former speech writer Alan Jones, Director of the NSW Employers' Federation, said they had been 'sold out'.

The collapse of centralised wage fixation through the Arbitration Commission ushered in a period of collective bargaining. Yet the new wage round which helped to smash the indexation system continued with even more momentum in the decentralised wage fixation framework. The pace-setting agreement came in December 1981 between the Metal Trades Employers' Association and Australia's militant Amalgamated Metal Workers' and Shipwrights' Union (AMWSU). It provided for a 38-hour week and two pay rises totalling a basic $41 a week extra for 500,000 workers. The agreement included a provision for no extra claims during its 12-month duration. The initial instinct of the federal Government was to oppose the agreement when it came before the commission for ratification. On 7 December Industrial Relations Minister Ian Viner foreshadowed this action. But the next day the President of the Metal Trades Industry Association, John Dixon, told Fraser by telegram that his executive was alarmed at the prospect of government intervention resulting in the commission's refusal to ratify. Later that day federal Cabinet decided that it would try to isolate any flow-on rather than oppose the agreement. Metal trades employers had warned of an 'industrial holocaust' if it was not approved. So the agreement was ratified. Six months later the same John Dixon attacked demands by the Liberal Party free-market lobby to lower protection for the metal industries on the grounds that this would cause unemployment.

Alan Jones warned after ratification:

> It is industrially naive for top ministers to say there will be no flow-on from the Metal Trades agreement. And it is economically naive to say this deal will not lead to higher inflation, increased interest rates, unemployment and bankruptcies.[9]

When it ratified the agreement on 18 December, the Full Bench said it would be unrealistic to assume there would be no flow-on of the wage agreement. The bench pointed out that there had been little opposition to ratification. The decision was applauded by National Director of the MTIA, Bert Evans, and National Assistant Secretary of the AMWSU Laurie Carmichael, who described the decision as the biggest advance for two decades. The MTIA said the agreement would contain wages rather than trigger an explosion. The Treasury had another view. In a dire prediction it said that the agreement was 'unsustainable for the economy'. In the event thousands of jobs were lost.

The result was that the rise in average weekly earnings for 1981–82 was about 14 per cent with the big increases coming towards the end of the year. This explosion was significantly less than the 26 per cent in 1974–75, but inflation was also less. In 1974–75 average real male weekly earnings had risen 6.4 per cent compared with an estimated 4 per cent in 1981–82. Clearly the Fraser Government's wage explosion was not as powerful as that under the Whitlam Government, but 1981–82 saw the biggest real wage increases since the Whitlam period. The impact on employment was significant because profits were not as strong and real interest rates were greater than in 1974–75. Moreover the very experience of the Whitlam years meant that inflationary expectations were more quickly assumed in financial markets.

In its analysis of the reason for the wage explosion the Treasury (in other words Stone, who was responsible for the draft of the budget document, and Howard, who authorised it) unmistakably criticised Fraser, Lynch and Anthony who, had led the resources bandwagon. It said one underlying factor in wage rises in the 1980–82 period was:

> an apparent development of exaggerated expectations about the increases in national income that would be generated by the resource investment 'boom' and, perhaps even more importantly, the speed with which this additional income would accrue. As a result, wage claims were formulated in anticipation of benefits which had not, in fact, yet begun to flow.[10]

The failure of the Fraser Government was its lack of any wage strategy to combat the pressures unleashed by the boom. The Government was virtually impotent. It responded to the new wage round on a week-by-week crisis-by-crisis basis. The record shows the Government had no answer to the wage pressures which eventually blew apart the indexation system. It tried initially to bolster that collapsing system; then when confronted with collective bargaining, it could merely hope for the best. In fact, the consequences of the wage explosion plagued Fraser throughout the 1983 campaign. He was never able to spell out the Government's wage policy because it was never able to formulate one. The demoralisation of 1981–82 ran deep.

The abandonment of indexation had presented a chance for the Treasury. The period after July 1981 became a test of the collective bargaining system which Treasury advocated. Howard and Treasury preferred collective bargaining because they said it allowed wages to reflect market realities. High wages in boom areas would not flow across the economy, which meant that wages would not increase as fast as they would under a centralised system. These propositions were certainly debatable. But the 1981–82 experience proved that Australia lacks the institutional structure to make collective bargaining work. Treasury admitted this in the 1982–83 budget papers. It said that 'with the benefit of hindsight' the collective bargaining process of 1981–82 was 'still far too centralised'.[11]

Treasury's conclusion was that for collective bargaining to work, the traditional craft-union structure in Australia would need to be disbanded; this would amount to social engineering. It would mean negotiations on a company-by-company basis—one of the most radical social changes in Australian history. Treasury and Howard were forced to this conclusion by the failure of the collective bargaining experiment in 1981. The more sophisticated advocates of a decentralised system within the Liberal Party recognised that the transition would be both long and difficult.

Assessed both in retrospect and at the time the 1980 election was the watershed which broke the Fraser regime into its two periods—the opening five years of dominance and the final two-and-a-half years of decline. It was only the daunting personality of Fraser himself which clouded the crumbling of his own political edifice. In the post-1980 period Fraser no longer enjoyed the untrammelled power of his early years. Simultaneous with the decline in his power came an increase in the magnitude of the economic challenge.

The vision splendid of a resources boom generating rapid economic growth was lost between the severe international recession of the early 1980s and a domestic wage explosion. Malcolm Fraser's economic challenge became not that of managing wealth as he had assumed in his 1981 Australia Day message but distributing the burdens of a brutal recession. The economic cycle had been in harmony with Fraser's political cycle in his 1980 election victory. But the world recession hit Australia later than other nations and would therefore present a formidable obstacle to Fraser's subsequent re-election. The ultimate irony for Fraser was that the resources boom which he championed finally took him as its victim. It exposed the Government's wages policy failure. But Fraser's complete intellectual bankruptcy would be his attack on the ALP–ACTU accord during 1982–83, Labor's response to the very industrial-wages issue that had defied Fraser.

The limitations upon Fraser's political power as a result of the 1980 election were threefold. Firstly his government had lost its comprehensive dominance of the Parliament. Secondly there was a growing division of power and assertion of opinion within the Liberal Party itself. Forces and figures frozen for half a decade under the Fraser glacier were thawing out. On the one hand, the anti-Fraser ginger group on the backbench became increasingly bold. On the other, the 1980–83 period would see the emergence of the free-market lobby or 'drys' under the informal leadership of Western Australian backbencher John Hyde, which spearheaded criticism of Fraser from the right and exercised intellectual and numerical power within the party. The climax of this fragmentation was the challenge to Fraser by Andrew Peacock, a challenge which Peacock tried to mount with a foot in both the alienated wings of the party. The third factor was the entry of Bob Hawke into Parliament, an event which always had the potential to threaten the Government from without. Success was no longer a question of economic management for Fraser. The prior test was how to confront both the Hawke emergence and the Peacock challenge.

6
The irresistible force

This is probably the biggest decision I have had to make in my life.

Bob Hawke, September 1979,
on his decision to seek Labor preselection

From the day Bob Hawke walked up the stairs of Parliament House as the Member for Wills, politics was transformed. Hawke's arrival was unique. In the previous 50 years no new member had entered federal Parliament as a national figure with such a long-sustained popularity and with such a strong claim on the prime ministership. His very stature was a measure of the subjugation of Parliament to television as the forum of national debate. Hawke came not as an unknown but as a champion, not to languish on the backbench but to take the prime minister's chair, not to reshape his political character but to reconcile the Parliament to his destiny. Above all Hawke came to lay siege to the parliamentary Labor Party, its traditions, its prejudices and its crumbling ideology. Hawke offered Labor power; the price was the surrender of its identity to the seducer. Hawke went into Parliament to allow the party to submit to him.

The story of the 1980–83 Parliament is the contest for the prime ministership and Government between three men and two parties. This Parliament, unlike others, was not dominated by the orthodox and exclusive struggle between the Prime Minister and leader of the Opposition. This was a three-way struggle: Fraser, Hayden, Hawke. The contest began slowly and its real nature was not obvious even at mid-point. When Hawke did break out in 1982 the structure of the three-cornered competition became obvious. Fraser sought to maintain himself and to maintain Hayden as his opponent; Hayden sought to defeat Fraser yet simultaneously beat-off Hawke; Hawke sought to overthrow Hayden before overwhelming Fraser. Each man had two opponents and his success against one inevitably affected his success against the other. The nearest parallel was the 1975 three-way struggle between Whitlam, Fraser and Snedden. But the 1980s contest was far more extended and was conducted between combatants very different, yet more evenly matched, with the outcome uncertain up to the penultimate moment as to which of the three would triumph. For half of the Parliament it was a four-way struggle with Andrew Peacock providing the symmetry, but in autumn 1982, Fraser resolved his own leadership problem.

It was the irresistible force of Hawke that made this a three-way contest. There had been other 'established' candidates who entered Parliament with illustrious reputations. Sir Robert Menzies in 1934, Sir Garfield Barwick in 1958 and Dr Herbert Vere Evatt in 1940 are obvious parallels. While each of these had leadership claims due to outstanding careers, they were products of a different world. Although superior intellects to Hawke, none could match on entry to Parliament, the populist figure Hawke had become. So his leadership claim was of a different dimension to such men. Hawke's challenge was like no other. From the day he entered Parliament, within hours of taking his place as a Caucus member, Hawke was the alternative leader. He did not see himself as Hayden's heir apparent or eventual successor in the next Parliament, next year or even next week. Hawke wanted the leadership now. Immediately. His arrival occasioned the event. His was an ambition impervious to objective political factors such as his lack of numerical support. Possessing a messianic view of himself, he saw no need for an apprenticeship; with his experience and record Bob Hawke, aged 52, presented himself to the party.

Hawke's arrival put Hayden under immense pressure. It was because the Opposition leader initially coped so well that its magnitude was underestimated by many. The reality is that, with Hawke in Caucus, the margin for mistakes by Hayden was virtually eliminated, an essential point that was not initially understood. All leaders sooner or later make mistakes. One test of leadership is the capacity to recover from such mistakes, minimise the damage and refloat the ship. This was precisely where Hawke's presence became a material threat to Hayden. Hayden now faced Malcolm Fraser in front of him and Bob Hawke behind him.

After 1980 Hayden was the politician under greatest pressure because he was fighting on two fronts simultaneously. Fraser's fight was against the Labor Party. Hawke's struggles came in sequence: first Hayden, then Fraser. This meant Hayden's performance would be the most important in determining the fluctuations in this tripartite rivalry. Hayden was enhanced by the 1980 election results, but the Hawke factor defied measurement. It was a challenge that owed more to psychology than arithmetic. Numbers were not as important as usual, because Hawke's influence spread like an infectious gas: pervasive, insidious, invisible. Everyone knew the Hawke factor was present, but nobody could ever quantify its impact.

Hawke's attitude towards Parliament had been deeply ambivalent for many years. Parliament would test whether the obsessions of his career would turn into reality or be dismissed as fanciful. Because the stakes were so great, so was the temptation to avoid the test. For a long time Hawke created both political and psychological hurdles for his entry into Parliament. Perhaps the most graphic demonstration of this was his performance at the Perth Press Club in 1977 when, answering questions with a glass of wine in his hand, Hawke said:

> I think I have, on any objective judgement, one of the most responsible and, I suppose if you want to use the word, powerful and influential positions in the country. I enjoy the position and I do it well, and I have no ambition in terms of seeing Parliament as the apex of a man's achievement. If I am going to change from a position where I am, which I enjoy and do well, it would not be sensible for me to put my bum on a backbench. So if I move, it will only be in terms of a judgement of my colleagues about another form of leadership.[1]

When asked whether he thought he was being 'slightly presumptuous' in making the ALP leadership the condition for his entry into Parliament, Hawke replied:

> I could have fluffed around and said my obvious part is to go and serve my apprenticeship and wait, and so on, but I prefer to be straightforward and tell you. If your judgement or the judgement of others is that this is a brash statement, by an opinionated middle-aged man, so be it. I'm telling you what I think.[2]

The more Hawke aspired, the more resentment grew inside the ALP 'parliamentary club' and within the powerful left wing which hated Hawke. It was a vicious circle and Hawke appeared caught in it. The transition to Parliament became a litany of dashed hopes and forsaken opportunities. The problems remained: Hawke's reluctance to surrender genuine power at the ACTU; opposition by his enemies on the left; his own secret fears.

Post-1976 several backbenchers were approached about moving aside for Hawke, but they declined. Clyde Holding spoke to Gordon Bryant about moving to the Victorian Legislative Council and allowing Hawke to replace him in Wills. Bryant refused. Another approach was made to Horrie Garrick, the Member for Batman, but he also declined. Hawke briefly flirted with moving to Adelaide if he could obtain preselection for the safe seat of Bonython and canvassed the idea with Mick Young. But Bonython went to Dr Neal Blewett in 1977.

The Victorian branch, inspired by the socialist left, called nominations for ALP preselection for the 1978 election by 30 September 1976; it provoked an agony in Hawke. If he ran, Hawke believed he would become a 'lame duck' ACTU President for the intervening two years. Hawke took a week's holiday, went fishing and then announced that he would stay at the ACTU. In late 1977 a redistribution meant fresh nominations. Hawke's faction controlled the Lalor seat; supporters begged him to stand but he refused. The 1977 election came and went; Hayden replaced Whitlam.

Hawke's champion was Victorian centre-unity machine man Bill Landeryou, who wanted him to lead the party. Hawke had little 'feel' for the Labor machine or desire to count heads. He was dependent upon Landeryou's organisation of the centre-unity faction, of which Hawke was the figurehead. But Victorian centre-unity lacked the factional strength, ruthlessness or professionalism of its NSW counterpart. The NSW right-wing machine was the most formidable and successful Labor force in Australia. Its leaders were John Ducker, Graham Richardson and Paul Keating. If Hawke had come from NSW, his seat would have been delivered to him. The contrast between Hawke's dilemmas and the way in which Neville Wran's transition from the NSW Legislative Council to the Lower House was organised in the early 1970s is illustrative of the NSW professionalism.

Hawke's political future was now tied to his war with the Labor left. This battle was accentuated by the crises in his personal life which, in 1979, took Hawke to his lowest ebb. His mother was dying, his wife was estranged, the long-deferred decision about a parliamentary career could be delayed no longer. Hawke's campaign against the left revealed him as a deeply emotional politician but never a tactician. He was prone to sudden changes of mood: understanding dissolved into intolerance and Hawke's messianic view of himself was often exposed.

A trinity of influences provided the poison in the division between Hawke and the left. There was his passionate identification with Israel, which was increasingly linked with South Africa as the left's main antagonist. The second factor was Hawke's pragmatic support for uranium mining coupled with strong safeguards at the very time when the left's anti-uranium drive had become a crusade. Finally Hawke's refusal to use union power on 11 November 1975 in the cathartic aftermath of Whitlam's dismissal had assumed its own mythology within the left. Hawke had been worried that the sacking could have provoked violence and street riots and had seen his national responsibility as one of ensuring calm and order, while Whitlam had appealed to Labor supporters to 'maintain your rage'. Hawke's response to the 1975 crisis provides a penetrating insight into his character.

In late 1978 Hawke and Landeryou activated a new scheme to expel their arch demon, the Victorian far left-winger Bill Hartley, from the ALP. Hawke had wanted to expel Hartley during the 1976 Iraqi crisis; in 1977 Hawke and John Ducker had discussed another expulsion move. This time the trap was laid for the February 1979 ALP National Executive meeting. Hawke and Landeryou had the support of the NSW right and consent from Victorian ALP leader Frank Wilkes. Landeryou told the left-wing but pragmatic Victorian ALP Secretary, Bob Hogg, of the plot. Hogg was appalled. He replied: 'We may as well cut our budget to two dollars and forget the state election.' Hogg told Landeryou the expulsion move would force the left to close ranks and provoke a factional struggle of renewed ferocity. Hogg rang National Secretary David Combe saying it had to be aborted, and his advice prevailed. The 'cooler heads' argued that Hartley was of diminishing relevance to the Labor Party and an expulsion move would make him a martyr. But news of Hawke's intentions had spread throughout the Victorian party and the hatred for him from the socialist left intensified.

At the ALP Victorian Conference on 19 March 1979 Hawke branded Hartley and his supporters as 'a canker' and ridiculed them as 'a telephone box minority'. In a later defence of his attack given to Blanche d'Alpuget Hawke revealed the depth of bitterness dividing the Victorian party:

> Centre-unity people came up to me after and said 'That was a very good speech, but you shouldn't have done it'. I said, 'Why not? They're bastards—but you don't tell them.' It was just too much, part of this weakness syndrome: you're allowed to see the canker, but you're not to say or do anything about it. For a decade we'd been putting up with the [socialist left] and I was sick and tired of the number of times I'd been told that they were changing, they were becoming more reasonable; but every time they opened their mouths they became less reasonable.[3]

In the next six months Hawke was humiliated by Hayden at the Adelaide National Conference, was fooled by the Russians over the release of Soviet Jews, then absorbed the shock of his mother's death, suffered a rebuff on uranium at the ACTU Congress and finally decided to seek preselection for Wills. The socialist left had its own candidate, Victorian organiser Gerry

Hand, who nominated before Hawke. Hawke deeply resented having to fight a normal preselection contest and felt that his record entitled him to special treatment, but the Labor Party recognises no such law. He relied on Landeryou's operation to guarantee the numbers. Although Hawke was a former ALP National President, he rarely went to branch meetings; he needed political managers to organise on his behalf. Hawke's media image was that of an essentially 'ordinary bloke', yet inside the ALP he was aloof from the rank and file.

Ever distrustful of Hayden, Hawke told the ALP leader of his decision only on the morning of his announcement, 23 September 1979. His trade union friends were reluctant about his departure and apprehensive for his future. Charlie Fitzgibbon said, 'If he thinks he must, I suppose he must.'[4] John Ducker had warned Hawke, 'Caucus is a closed club; I worry that you could become a frustrated and embittered man if you lose out in Caucus.'[5] But these men knew that Hawke was a consummate politician-actor and he was seeking a new stage. At his press conference Hawke put Hayden on notice regarding the leadership:

> I haven't got any timetable. I think the point needs to be made clearly that the leader of the Labor Party is Mr Hayden elected as he is and must be by the federal Caucus. While he's the leader so elected he has my support. If that position becomes vacant, I would be a candidate.

This declaration of political intentions by Hawke was far-reaching and he underlined its enormous personal nature:

> This is probably the biggest decision I have had to make in my life and it does involve closing a chapter and opening a new one. I would have thought I was well enough known now in the community to be [seen] as a person who has emotions. I'm just not cool and calculating about those things.

The stakes involved both for Hawke and the Labor Party in the Wills preselection were huge. Bob Hogg had spoken to Hawke before the decision and advised him to reassess his outlook. He said that Hawke's conference speech attacking the left had been counterproductive to his own interests and damaging to the party. Hogg feared that the mutual hatred between Hawke and the left had a force of its own and could split the Victorian ALP if it was unleashed. Hogg spoke to the left leadership at the start of the Wills preselection contest to make three points. If the left defeated Hawke it would be a pointless victory. The party could not accept Hawke's defeat and recourse would probably be taken by the right wing at National Executive level. Finally the community would never understand Hawke's defeat and would retaliate against the ALP.

Hogg's assessment was that Hawke was in an unstable period of his life and that his defeat might facilitate a split in the Victorian ALP. This was one point of concern he raised with senior ALP figures. Hayden was told about these fears and Hogg's assessment of the danger of a schism if the socialist-left candidate Gerry Hand won Wills. Few can doubt that Hawke, who resented the left running a candidate, would have been outraged if he had lost. His rage would have been not just the product of thwarted ambition but almost certainly a crusade against the left to preserve the ALP. What would have been the consequences of Hawke's preselection defeat? The bottom line is that Hawke would not have campaigned for the Labor Party at the 1980 election. Hawke told colleagues: 'If I am rejected by the Labor Party as a candidate, how can I campaign for the party at that election and maintain my own credibility and integrity?' Hawke's non-appearance would have been a huge propaganda weapon in Fraser's hands. It would have doomed any Labor chance of victory in 1980 even before the campaign had begun.

Hogg correctly recognised that the move to keep Hawke out of Parliament, if it succeeded, would have been a catastrophe for the Labor Party. The consequences above the bottom line are a matter of almost endless spec-ulation in doom. But in these 1979 events lie the seeds of the left's analogy between Hawke and the great Labor traitors, Billy Hughes and Joe Lyons, both former Prime Ministers at the centre of two of the three great Labor splits. Hawke was disgusted by such comments. He believed he was located more in the mainstream of the ALP tradition than the socialist left which attacked him virulently. But the Hawke–Hughes–Lyons analogy was drawn by senior figures such as the late Jim Roulston, then President of the Victorian Trades Hall Council and Vice-President of the ALP.

In the event Hawke defeated Hand 38–29, thereby confirming the view of his backers that the centre-unity group always had the numbers in Wills. If the preselection voting was relatively close, however, a survey taken at that time shows how enormous was his popularity in the country at large. In May 1979 an ANOP survey asked 1,800 voters to select from given candidates who would make the best Prime Minister. The results were: Hawke 31 per cent, Wran 17 per cent, Peacock 16 per cent, Fraser 12 per cent and Hayden 11 per cent. ALP voters nominated: Hawke 42 per cent, Wran 21 per cent, Hayden 20 per cent and Fraser zero. Coalition voters nominated: Fraser 32 per cent, Hawke 19 per cent, Wran nine per cent and Hayden two per cent. This gave Hawke a decisive edge over both Hayden and Fraser. One in five coalition voters selected Hawke as Australia's best leader, while no Labor voters nominated Fraser. Hawke's potential to persuade coalition voters to switch made him a certain election winner.

When Hawke came to Parliament his power base was the Victorian centre-unity faction. His closest colleagues in this faction were Clyde Holding and Gareth Evans, both friends of long standing; others included Joan Child, Barry Cunningham, David Charles and Senator Robert Ray. The obvious opposite end of Hawke's political axis was the NSW right, which had recently been renamed centre-unity. Its Caucus leader was Paul Keating and its organiser was Graham Richardson. Hawke moved instinctively towards Keating. Just before he nominated for Wills, Hawke rang Keating and proposed a Hawke–Keating leadership ticket—but no definite time was specified. Keating reserved his position but told Hawke that, despite his standing in the nation, his future would depend upon his performance after he entered Parliament. Keating had been impatient with Hawke for delaying so long. He said there was deep opposition to Hawke from the left and centre of the ALP. While the NSW right had much in common with Hawke, its support would be conditional. Keating said that if Hawke did not perform 'then there's one body you'll have to step over—and that's mine'.

The Hawke–Keating relationship was established initially during two long conversations in Sydney in 1980 before the election following an approach to Keating by Barry Unsworth. They met first at the Hyatt Hotel above Kings Cross and later at the Boulevard Hotel. Hawke's message was that he wanted an alliance with Keating so the two men and the factions they represented would effectively run the party together. The arrangement was a good balance: the older man from Victoria, the younger man from NSW, both from the centre-unity faction. They were divorced as direct power rivals by an age difference of 14 years: Hawke was 50, Keating was 36. They shared a pragmatic approach to politics. Keating said he would help Hawke, but he did not want to pull down Hayden. Yet he embraced the alliance as a natural development. There was, however, a proviso. Keating told Hawke: 'The first Labor leader I tear down will be the one I replace.' The import of Keating's message was that Hawke should aim for the leadership as fast as possible, probably in his first Parliament. Otherwise he might face Keating as an opponent post-1983. Keating's ambitions were inevitably tied to the Hayden–Hawke rivalry. His assessment in 1980 was that there were two avenues before him. Keating could either 'throw in' with Hawke, possibly becoming his deputy and thereby the obvious successor, or he could support Hayden and try to succeed Hayden, preferably in office, at the first chance.

The decisions Keating made would be vital to the future of both Hawke and Hayden. But this was not Keating's decision alone; his power stemmed from his faction, which meant that his own decision would need factional approval and notably Richardson's backing.

The significance of Hawke's approach to the NSW right is that he was building his power base. Hawke went to the people with whom he felt common interests. There were only two men who, in an ideal world, Hawke would have chosen as his deputy. They were Mick Young and Paul Keating. But Keating was preferable because his NSW position gave him far more power than Young. Hawke was not just trying to stitch together the numbers to make him leader, he was taking a long-term view and identifying the power bases upon which he would rely as ALP leader. His judgement was sound. When the NSW right was linked with Hawke's Victorian centre-unity group, an axis would be established with near majority support in the party. It would serve as a platform from which Hawke could attack or isolate the left.

During 1980 the left had adopted one defensive position after another to stop Hawke. After Hawke obtained preselection, Uren developed a short-term and long-term strategy to halt his arrival. In the short term the left would support the existing Hayden–Bowen leadership. If Labor performed badly at the 1980 poll and Hayden was either unable or unwilling to remain as leader, then the left would support Bowen as successor. Bowen had won significant left-wing support in the previous three years due to his highly protectionist stance. In the longer term Uren was prepared to move behind Keating on the calculation that he might be the only man who was strong enough to hold out Hawke post-1983 if Labor remained in Opposition. There could have been no greater demonstration of the left's hostility towards Hawke than Uren's contemplated embrace of Keating, who had been one of its most deadly enemies for years.

The tensions within the Caucus over Hawke were exposed in December 1979, after Hawke obtained Wills preselection, when Ian Viner taunted Hayden in Parliament, 'Every day that the leader of the Opposition sits in this House, Bob Hawke will be breathing so closely down his neck and he will be so worried that there is no possibility at all that he will be able to have a profile within the House or among the voters.' At this point Uren stood up, walked to the centre table and asked Viner whether he'd 'put his money on it that Bob Hawke will be the leader of the Labor Party'.[6] The Government benches howled with delight. Their bait was taken. But Uren did not mind. He wanted to put on notice that the left wing would halt Hawke's leadership drive.

The previous month, in November 1979, Hawke had launched another vitriolic assault on the left at the Victorian state conference. He reaffirmed his determination to expel left-winger figures Bill Hartley and Tom Ryan, chief organiser of the left-wing Food Preservers' Union. Hawke's attack split the 400 delegates into two snarling factions and he refined his description of them from that of 'a canker', to 'an eating, spreading sore, an ulcer, a gangrene'. But Hayden, also at the conference, took a different line warning that, 'It is perhaps timely to suggest that all of us should not forget just who our real opponents are.'[7] Hawke's comments reflected his determination, now that his entry to Parliament had been confirmed, to cleanse the ALP of its impurities. The elimination of the extreme left was necessary to make Labor the party which reflected the aspirations of the Australian people. Hawke's second purpose was to reduce the influence of the socialist left in the party in order to increase his numbers in the Caucus.

Throughout this crisis in the Victorian ALP Bob Hogg tried to contain the damage. He spoke to Hawke after his preselection win and urged him to moderate his stance. Hogg was actually relieved at the November conference and believed the war between Hawke and the left could have been far worse. In his own speech to conference Hogg warned against the cycle of retribution:

> When we get to that point of talking about expelling people we have, in my view, reached a politically bankrupt position.
>
> It is a bankrupt position because we are an umbrella organisation and none of us can clearly define the limits of who should be in and who should not. It's a very, very grey area and once you get to that we would have problems.[8]

In mid-1980 Hawke visited the United States, where his comments betrayed the inevitability of his power clash with Hayden. In talks with the US administration Hawke put forward what became dubbed as his 'Washington scenario'. He told US officials that Labor under Hayden would easily lose the 1980 election and that he would take over after the debacle. At the next election Labor would be elected on a Hawke–Keating ticket. In Washington Hawke stayed with Australian journalist John Edwards, who assisted in arranging his appointments. His 'Washington scenario' was presented, not just to the US Government, but to American journalists—one such meeting was conducted in the presence of two Australian journalists—and to functions he attended in New York, such as a dinner organised by Australian lawyer and former Stephen, Jacques & Stephen representative in Manhattan Howard Schreiber. Hawke was deeply embarrassed when his comments were reported in *The Sydney Morning Herald* and *The National Times* by Mike Steketee and Brian Toohey. Back in Australia he denied the stories. Edwards subsequently approached Toohey and related that in a phone call Hawke had asked whether the journalists would be willing to retract their stories. The upshot was that Toohey wrote a more detailed version of the original story.

The four parliamentary leaders of the ALP in 1980 were Hayden, Bowen, Wriedt and Button. These men were not just anti-Hawke, they were passionately anti-Hawke. They represented the continuation of the 'parliamentary club' hostility to Hawke which had deepened in the past seven years. When the combined weight of the left was added to this group, along with the emerging Caucus centre led by Hayden and Button, and the unwillingness of Keating actually to move against Hayden, the anti-Hawke forces in the Caucus were formidable indeed. While opinion in the community was that Hawke would lead the party, the conventional wisdom in Caucus was the opposite.

Hawke's strategy then was to storm the Caucus. He would appeal directly to the public over the heads of the Caucus in classic presidential style, thereby maximising public pressure on the party to change leaders. Hawke would play to his strength. It was the strategy of the irresistible force being applied to the Caucus which, with its anti-Hawke bias and natural inertia, was the immovable object. Hawke's strategy sprang from his supreme ego and was founded in an arrogant assumption: that only Hawke, certainly not Hayden, could beat Fraser. This was bound to generate a backlash in an organisation such as the Labor Party, so committed to egalitarianism, but it had one critically redeeming virtue: it might be true.

Hawke was running for Prime Minister as a means of becoming Opposition leader. He was aiming to beat Fraser and to present irrefutable evidence from opinion polls to the party with the argument that he must therefore replace Hayden. Hawke offered to deliver Labor to Government and argued that the party must recognise its paramount self-interest. Thus armed, the most popular man in Australia entered the Caucus determined to convince the party to accept the public's own decision. The irresistible force had arrived.

7
The Peacock crisis

*I believe you have engaged in acts of gross disloyalty to me and
my office.*

Andrew Peacock to Malcolm Fraser,
April 1981

The personal friction and power conflict between Malcolm Fraser and Andrew
Peacock was a fault in the earth that bonded the Liberal Party, running from
the late 1960s until Fraser's 1983 retirement. No rivalry in recent decades
matches its longevity, no other Liberal Party struggle its intensity. Almost from
its inception this conflict was over the Liberal inheritance. Such different men
brought to their leadership claims contrasting policy, style and personality.
The battle was not just between themselves but within the party and about
its destiny.

The two great factors in Fraser's success as Prime Minister in the
1975–80 period had been his electoral success and his leadership authority.
The latter was partly due to the absence of any leadership rival in the way
McMahon had been an alternative to Gorton and Fraser himself had been the
alternative to Snedden. Consequently, despite growing ministerial crises,
Fraser survived his second term during the 1977–80 Parliament without any
challenge to his own position. That challenge eventually came from Peacock
only in late 1980 and the break between the two men became public in 1981
with Peacock's resignation. So the 1980 election represented a turning point
for the Fraser Government. It ended five years of leadership stability, reopened
Fraser–Peacock rivalry at a more intense level, and produced an image of
disunity which would harm the Government's electoral prospects.

From its first sighting Peacock's star was prematurely hailed as a new
sun: a Liberal Party member at 16, Liberal candidate at 22, President of the
Young Liberals at 23, President of the Victorian Division at 26, successor in

Kooyong to Sir Robert Menzies at 27 and a federal minister at 30. It was a career of unparalleled promise. Such a brief résumé cannot convey the enthusiasm which Peacock displayed and the admiration he engendered. Andrew was tanned, elegant and dashing; his wife Susan was pretty, glamorous and publicity-conscious.

Where Fraser was aloof, Peacock was a participator; Fraser championed the ideological status quo of the 1960s which Peacock dismissed as obsolete as he moved towards the progressive wing of his party; while Fraser was genuine establishment and impervious to the new values of the 1960s, Peacock was fascinated by the latest trends in society and culture. Finally in their home state of Victoria, Fraser supported the conservative wing of the Liberal Party, which upheld the coalition strategy. Peacock was closely aligned with those Liberals who wanted to distance or even break ties with the Country Party.

During his early years in Parliament Peacock paid his way on a 'fact finding mission' to South-East Asia and joined the diggers on patrol north of Nui Dat. Then he went to Europe and caught a bus to Paris at the height of the 1968 student riots. Peacock had incorporated what he wanted from the style of the youth generation. This was seen in his predilections for rock music and jazz, a taste for informal but elegant clothes, literary dabbling from André Malraux to Arthur Schlesinger on the Kennedys, and a fascination for the cultural centres of North America. In politics it was reflected in Peacock's campaign to lower the voting age to 18, an emphasis on civil liberties, support for liberalised censorship and opposition to capital punishment. Overseas Peacock backed the Liberal foreign policy of the day but softened it around the edges.

He became Gorton's boy minister, aged 30, running the Army during an increasingly unpopular war, dealing with generals, men twice his age. Yet Peacock succeeded where his Army predecessor, Phillip Lynch, had stumbled. In his portfolio Peacock also displayed that keen sense of anticipation of change that has become his hallmark, of knowing when to shift position. A supporter of Vietnam in his early days in Parliament, he warned in 1970, when US withdrawal was obvious, 'We must seek to dissolve the myths that have masked the emerging reality to lead the nation beyond the obsessive issues of the past . . .'[1]

Peacock and his department had to cope with an awesome duo in Defence—Fraser and Sir Arthur Tange—both committed to centralisation of political and bureaucratic control. Fraser ruthlessly interfered in the narrow domains of his service ministers. Peacock believed that Fraser as Defence Minister was trying to undermine the Army and strike at him. Fraser believed that Peacock in defending the Army was resisting civilian authority over the military. This tension was instrumental in creating the distrust that culminated when Fraser resigned from his Defence portfolio and brought down Gorton. While Peacock had previously attracted media attention, Fraser was clearly the power politician. But Peacock, previously a Gorton man, was sufficiently adroit to make the transition to the McMahon ministry, unlike his friends and fellow Gorton-backers Jim Killen and Tom Hughes. Killen languished on the backbench; Hughes returned to the Bar. Andrew was a survivor.

As Minister for External Territories under McMahon Peacock turned a graveyard of reaction into a beacon of achievement. He committed himself to independence for Papua-New Guinea and established a close personal relationship with its Chief Minister Michael Somare, testimony to Peacock's ability to forge ties with overseas politicians. This portfolio was perfect for the wider image of himself which Peacock was then cultivating. He was inevitably depicted as the wave of the future in a party beset by old men, reaction and internal division. The national sentiment of the day was leftward, accentuated by disillusionment with Vietnam and the gathering tide of Whitlamism, whose essence was confidence in Government intervention. Peacock declared: 'Those of my vintage don't shrink with fear at the mention of economic planning or a greater government control here or there. We've grown up with an acceptance that the Government must play greater roles in certain areas.'[2]

His progress was assessed not as a normal young politician but as one whose destiny was The Lodge. The inevitable parallel with the Kennedys was suggested by the Peacocks themselves. Susan drove an E-type Jaguar; the Peacocks flew to Italy for the weekend on an Alitalia inaugural flight, and Susan water-skied off the Great Barrier Beef on the shoulders of Pierre Trudeau. The level of expectation rose simultaneously with the pressure to succeed. The Peacocks had a glamour unmatched in the dreary halls of Australian politics. Andrew enjoyed good relations with the media and was frank and communicative. But he was sensitive to criticism, a vulnerability he concealed beneath a haughty pose switched on and off with ease. Peacock benefited from the Kennedy comparison, but he became a victim of it.

The chink in the Peacock pose was revealed in his 1970 offer of resignation over Susan's advertisements endorsing Sheridan sheets in *The Australian Women's Weekly*. Peacock reacted with a sensitivity out of proportion to the event, a response that would recur in Peacock's career. It exposed tensions in the relationship between Andrew and Susan; it also revealed an emotionalism that betrayed sound judgement. Susan was forced into a humiliating apology and became a wife who had jeopardised her husband's position. Yet she had had her own aspirations and had wanted to go into politics herself.

Peacock had deterred her. When questioned once about Susan's leanings, he explained with a grin, 'somewhere right of Goldwater'.

After the 1972 election defeat Peacock lost by one vote to Lynch in the deputy's ballot. Lynch was a loyal deputy to Snedden and Peacock was Snedden's close friend. Fraser waited in the wings, the alternative leader. Fraser–Peacock rivalry now intensified because, as shadow ministers, their status was more equal than before. They competed furiously for the Foreign Affairs shadow ministry, which Snedden eventually gave Peacock so that the younger man moved ahead of Fraser for the first time in their careers. John Edwards wrote of their contest that it:

> continued unabated with a ferocity that astonished their colleagues. Peacock believed that Fraser was responsible for a letter critical of Peacock's foreign policy appearing in a newspaper, a letter which he discovered came from a fictitious address. He was upset by stories about his marriage circulating within the Liberal Party.
>
> Fraser too was nettled by persistent rumours that he had separated from his wife and was under treatment from a Melbourne psychiatrist. Both stories, the truth of which Fraser absolutely denies, were fair indications of the level at which the party conflict was being fought. Each hired public relations consultants to defend themselves against each other as much as to promote themselves in the electorate.[3]

The 1974 election triumph of Whitlam over Snedden was a watershed for the Liberal Party. Within months the Whitlam Government's economic crisis made its subsequent re-election virtually impossible. Whitlam had Snedden's measure, yet his Government was failing. It needed only a strong Liberal leader to marshal his forces and sweep away the ALP Government. Fraser depicted himself as such a man and he offered a new brand of leadership authority. Fraser, on the right, now saw the Liberal tide coming back towards him and his philosophy of free enterprise sharpened the differences between Labor and Liberal. He benefited from the new breed of Liberals, some hard-headed, others merely ambitious. Men such as Tony Staley, Ian Viner, Vic Garland, John Howard, Eric Robinson, John Bourchier, Ian Macphee and Reg Withers wanted to win with a leader they respected, who could provide longevity in office. When the Liberal Party embraced Fraser as its new leader, it rejected not only Snedden but Peacock.

The Fraser coup against Snedden was influenced by the tempo of Fraser–Peacock rivalry and it was Peacock who precipitated the showdown. Realising that Snedden was doomed, Peacock called for a party meeting in a bid to force the issue before the Fraser camp was ready and, if Snedden could not be saved, then challenge Fraser himself. Peacock's judgement was badly astray. He alienated Snedden and delivered the leadership to Fraser.

Many Liberals at this time took the view that Peacock lacked the nous and toughness for power politics. As Fraser made the Liberal Party over in his own image, Susan drifted away to Robert Sangster and a 24-room manor on the Isle of Man. Peacock had tried to live out the Kennedy image; now he retreated with damaged pride into Foreign Affairs and a new phase of life.

In his new portfolio Peacock mastered the issues and enjoyed an unparalleled range of political and social contacts. Cy Vance, Teddy Kennedy, Fritz Mondale. Often when Fraser travelled overseas he was dependent upon Peacock to make the contact. In Peking in 1976 it was Peacock who rang Henry Kissinger and then handed over the phone to Fraser. It was Peacock who organised Fraser's first talk with Jimmy Carter before the Georgian became President. Peacock was friends with Andrew Young, Barbara Walters and, most famous of all, Shirley MacLaine, who added lustre to the illustrious Peacock reputation. ('If Australia ever decides it doesn't want him, the world will take him with open arms.') Peacock developed a new perspective on life: a single man overseas, a father at home. He became more American-orientated, attuned to the Californian awakening with its jogging, yoga and karma. He would holiday in New York, travel with his surf ski and reflect on the lyrics of John Lennon: 'As I sit down and listen to some of those lyrics now, I read more into them . . . Lennon's lyrics are even more meaningful to me now.'[4]

Fraser and Peacock made a successful but contrasting foreign double for Australia, cooperating on a wide range of policy issues. Fraser was all grit and determination, Peacock was quick and subtle. Fraser warned the tsar; Peacock softened the message. In foreign affairs Fraser was an ideologue who understood that the man who closes-off his options is the man who enjoys real power. Peacock liked to keep his options open by being more circumspect. Fraser championed the peacekeeping commitment to Zimbabwe while Peacock was cautious; Fraser launched his attack on the EEC over agricultural protectionism, when Peacock saw little to gain; Fraser appointed Sir John Kerr UNESCO ambassador against Peacock's silent opposition; Fraser proclaimed the end of détente after Afghanistan, but Peacock shunned such historical conclusions; when Fraser campaigned to have Australia boycott the Moscow Olympics Peacock was nowhere to be seen. A yardstick by which to judge a minister overseas is whether he casts a bigger shadow than does his country. Perhaps Peacock did, but Fraser's shadow was bigger.

Ultimately Peacock's relations with Fraser were dominated by his political strategy which, in turn, was shaped by his ambition to succeed Fraser.

Peacock's strategy was to bide his time and judge when to stake his claim. By 1980 he had grown restless and frustrated and, sensing that the Government's electoral position was fragile, he was ready to begin his move. Yet as a man Peacock was still caught up in the emotional swirl of his personal past and political destiny. Perhaps the real nature of his decision was to relax his self-discipline and let his emotions respond to the provocation of Fraser's intransigence.

The public split came in July 1980 over recognition of the murderous Pol Pot regime. Vietnam had invaded Kampuchea in 1979 and installed the Heng Samrin Government in Phnom Penh. Since then international pressure from the USA, China and South-East Asian nations had been to continue recognition of the former Pol Pot Government in order to deny legitimacy to the Vietnamese invasion. The mass brutality of Pol Pot made this policy potentially difficult if public opinion was aroused against it. Peacock was determined to change the policy, but Fraser wanted to retain it for the time being. The issue arose when George Negus from '60 Minutes' spent three days with Peacock and his companion (later wife), Margaret St George, for a television profile. It was a provocative exchange:

PEACOCK: I may move to a situation where I don't recognise anybody . . .

NEGUS: Let me ask you a question I don't think you could answer or would want to answer. Do you think you could convince the Prime Minister that we should adopt that sort of neutral position?

PEACOCK: I can answer that. I believe I would.

NEGUS: It remains to be seen. That's very interesting . . .

PEACOCK: All right, you wait and see. This programme will be aired before I seek to persuade him.

NEGUS: It would be interesting though, wouldn't it . . .

PEACOCK: But the conduct of foreign policy is left with me . . .

NEGUS: He's so anti-Vietnamese and so anti-Russian, if you can convince him to adopt a neutral position on this, you've really achieved something in a lot of peoples' eyes.

PEACOCK: Well, you've said it, haven't you?

Peacock's comments were cabled to Fraser overseas. The Prime Minister had just held talks in Tokyo with China's Premier Chairman Hua Guofeng, and Thailand's Prime Minister General Prem, in which the latter asked Fraser to reaffirm existing policy. Fraser scheduled the item for the next Cabinet meeting and upon returning home told colleagues that no minister in his Government was to trumpet: 'I will do'. On 15 July, two days after the

'60 Minutes' programme went to air, Fraser rebuffed Peacock in Cabinet. The policy was confirmed and Peacock was isolated. Peacock had convictions on the same issue, but it is idle to believe he was not searching for a cause on which he could confront Fraser.

After Cabinet Peacock went to Fraser and offered an oral resignation, but Fraser refused to accept it. Obviously Fraser believed it was negotiable. He sensed that Peacock's pride as well as his policy was involved. Fraser asked Peacock to discuss the matter with other ministers and called in Anthony and Nixon. Eventually a compromise was produced. Fraser agreed to amend the Cabinet decision to include the words: 'The Cabinet agreed that, as in the past, the matter would be kept under continuing review. The Cabinet also agreed that, if in the judgement of the Minister for Foreign Affairs circumstances alter, the Minister will re-raise the submission with the Cabinet.'[5] Peacock said he would consider overnight his resignation and the next morning he withdrew it, accepting the compromise. Peacock was determined to take the issue back to Cabinet.

In early September Peacock received a report from his department on two hapless Australian yachtsmen who had been imprisoned by the Pol Pot regime. The report concluded that in all probability they had been gruesomely tortured before being executed; it described the forms of torture. Over 2–3 September, *en route* to New Delhi for the Commonwealth Heads of Government Regional Meeting (CHOGRM), Peacock told Fraser the circumstances had changed. Peacock, knowing that Fraser set the Cabinet agenda, asked him to list the Pol Pot recognition at the 'earliest possible opportunity'; Fraser declined. One reason which Fraser did not give Peacock was that he planned to call an election. He was seriously contemplating mid-October which meant an announcement almost immediately on his return to Australia. Another reason was that Fraser, unlike Peacock, never saw the issue in terms of principle. The Prime Minister believed it was more a matter of timing, that sooner or later the policy would change, but in the interim Australia should support its allies.

During the New Delhi meeting the issue was discussed between Fraser, Peacock and Singapore Prime Minister Lee Kuan Yew. Afterwards Fraser gave Lee a ride back to Singapore on his VIP plane. At New Delhi Lee had embarrassed Fraser when he had said it was support for the Pol Pot regime in the United Nations that counted and that 'nobody was fussed or excited about diplomatic recognition'. While Lee preferred both, he was merely identifying the top priority. But his remarks offered a political hook for Peacock. If Lee, a spearhead of the international effort, did not mind Australia embracing derecognition, then why should Fraser? Fraser moved to plug this hole and initiated talks between the three men on Pol Pot as the plane neared Singapore.

The Prime Minister said that Lee's New Delhi remarks were ambiguous, warned Lee there was public concern in Australia and suggested he make a clarifying statement. Of course Fraser would use this statement against Peacock in their struggle.

Fraser and Peacock discussed the issue further in Singapore. Peacock left these talks with two understandings: firstly that Fraser would not publicly comment on the Pol Pot issue and secondly that Fraser would allow Cabinet to consider it.[6] The Foreign Minister flew to Australia, arriving on the morning of 10 September, and began preparing the Cabinet paper. Fraser later denied that he had given any such commitment to Peacock. The Prime Minister held further talks with Lee in Singapore and flew to Canberra, arriving on the evening of 10 September, whereupon he held a press conference as his office distributed Lee's release.

An unusual aspect of Lee's statement was that it quoted from a recent exchange of letters between Peacock and Singapore's Foreign Minister, Rajaratnam. They showed that Singapore had urged Australia to continue recognition of Democratic Kampuchea (the Pol Pot regime) and that Rajaratnam had warned derecognition 'will become a weapon in the hands of the Soviets and the Vietnamese'.[7]

Peacock was incensed about Lee's statement and its distribution by Fraser. Fraser said later that he did not know Lee would quote from the private letters and, if he had known, he would have tried to deter Lee. But the exercise had too much Fraser overkill.

Peacock rang Fraser that evening and accused him of disloyalty. Fraser rejected the charge, saying the statement was Lee's and not his own. Consequently he had not been obliged to inform Peacock beforehand. Peacock asked Fraser to have the Cabinet meet the next day to discuss the issue, but the Prime Minister told Peacock to see him instead. Fraser was by then preoccupied with another matter. He was finalising his election and planning to call on the Governor-General the next day. The Pol Pot issue would have to wait.

Peacock wound himself into a tension so tight that its release would soon endanger the Government. He tried to see Fraser the next morning, but failed. He spoke to Fraser just after Parliament sat at 10.30 a.m. and was told to arrange an appointment later. But the two men had not spoken again when Cabinet sat at 2.25 p.m. to debate the election. All ministers, including Peacock, endorsed the election. Significantly Peacock said nothing of the Pol Pot issue and his failure to raise it at Cabinet was critical; this was the proper forum for his complaint.

However Peacock waited until Cabinet broke and then went to Fraser's office for the showdown. He told Fraser he had been placed in an intolerable position. Fraser knew the credentials vote in the United Nations could arise as early as 15 September, so it was imperative that the issue be considered before then. But Fraser had not allowed Cabinet consideration; he had breached his undertakings. The Prime Minister called in Anthony, Sinclair and Nixon to discuss the matter with Peacock. The Foreign Minister gave them three options which he later described:

> First, I could resign. Second, the Cabinet could change its policy. Third, in the event that the Government did not change the policy, I could remain silent until after the election and then decline a portfolio in a new Government. When discussing the options I made it clear that, if the policy was not changed, the third option was acceptable to me.[8]

Peter Nixon handled the negotiations with Peacock, which lasted many hours. He said later:

> The truth of the matter is that option one was a gun at the head of the Government; option two was also a gun at the head of the Government; and option three was not accepted as a real option by anybody present in the room, because the Government was about to go to the country at a general election and if the story that Mr Peacock would not accept a portfolio in a new Government had broken, it would have brought down the Government.[9]

The Peacock crisis was the most serious threat to Fraser since the Lynch affair three years earlier. Again it came on the verge of an election, thereby magnifying the danger. The Prime Minister was 'on the brink', almost beyond the stage of retreat in his election advance, yet his traditional rival was threatening resignation. The situation was similar to that faced by Fraser in 1983. The election decision was taken, the ministers consulted. Then came the crisis. In 1980 it was Peacock's resignation threat; in 1983 it was the chance that Hawke would become his opponent. Both times Fraser pressed ahead and on both occasions Nixon urged him on. Fraser left for Government House after 5.00 p.m. and secured Sir Zelman Cowen's approval to the dissolution— the simplest of the four dissolutions Fraser sought from 1975 to 1983. As Fraser was leaving his office Peacock reiterated that he would accept option three. Peacock has a clear memory of Fraser saying 'Thank you, Andrew', but Nixon later denied this, saying agreement was not reached until 11 p.m. that night.[10]

Nixon devised a compromise acceptable to both Fraser and Peacock. Australia would support Pol Pot in the UN vote, but then announce its intention to derecognise. This would be put to the next meeting of Cabinet. In the interim both Fraser and Hayden launched into the election campaign.

Peacock left for New York and the General Assembly session. Fraser put the proposal to Cabinet in Melbourne on 23 September and Nixon briefed the meeting. Incredulity dissolved into fury. Ministers were dismayed about the events and hostile to Peacock. Carrick, Killen and Howard expressed deep concern. The initial mood was one of outrage; opposition was vented to the Cabinet succumbing to Peacock's threat. No single action of Peacock so isolated him in the Fraser Cabinet. The reason was that, despite its vigour, its brawls and its underhand tactics, the Fraser Cabinet did not operate according to the rules of resignation threats. All ministers were united against Peacock. He was threatening each of them individually and the Cabinet collectively.

Fraser sat back and let Nixon persuade his colleagues to accept Peacock's proposal. Finally Cabinet agreed and Peacock was informed. The issue was resolved but the origin of the crisis remained—Peacock's essential refusal to accept any longer the way Fraser handled his Government and his ministers. It was inevitable that it would recur in another guise.

Peacock returned to Australia for the campaign. His threatened resignation was not known then to the electorate and he did receive significant popular kudos for prevailing on the Pol Pot issue. If Fraser lost the election, he would contest the leadership. Peacock was preparing himself for this possibility which, until the last few days of the campaign, seemed a probability.

Fraser's victory saved the Liberals from a poisonous power struggle. If Fraser had lost, then the full weight of the outgoing Liberal Cabinet would have been thrown against Peacock's leadership drive. But Peacock still scored his own victory. After the election he ran against Lynch for the deputy's job and lost by only 47–35.

In challenging Lynch Peacock openly staked his claim, not just to the deputy's job, but to succeed Fraser. Peacock polled half-a-dozen more votes than his opponents expected, which reflected a substantial anti-Fraser vote. The result served notice that Lynch's capacity to hold the deputy's post, and thereby protect Fraser, was diminishing. Yet Lynch remained the only figure sufficiently strong to keep out Peacock. Lynch flirted with the idea of standing aside as deputy as a prelude to leaving politics. He wanted to become Australian High Commissioner to London. But Fraser appealed to him: 'I can't work with Peacock. I want you to stay on as deputy.' The wheel had turned full circle. Three years earlier Fraser had almost disposed of Lynch, now he needed him. So Lynch stayed and became Sir Phillip soon afterwards.

While Peacock was moving to fill the vacuum created as Lynch's position weakened, Peacock still had his own rival. In the 1977–80 period John Howard had proved his mettle as Treasurer and hence had a claim on high office. Peacock was propelled into the challenge for the deputy leadership by the additional need to stay ahead of Howard. Howard decided not to challenge Lynch because his strategy was to act as part of the Fraser–Lynch–Howard troika to beat off Peacock. This contest was really between the maintenance of Fraser's power structure and the threat to that structure from Peacock.

In Fraser's new ministry Peacock made his long-awaited switch to a domestic portfolio and became Minister for Industrial Relations. But this move only increased tensions inside the Government and between Fraser and Peacock. It ended the quarantining of their rivalry in foreign affairs and brought it into domestic matters. Fraser held some fears that Peacock and Hawke, both anxious to overthrow their respective leaders, would accommodate each other to further their mutual interest. Industrial relations was an area where Fraser's interest always ran high and where the different styles of the two men would be accentuated. Peacock stood for consensus, Fraser for confrontation.

Peacock's decision to hire Barry Simon as his Private Secretary significantly increased the chances of an early clash with Fraser. Defeated at the 1980 elections, Simon had been a Liberal backbencher who had previously provoked terrible trouble for Fraser by arguing that the Liberals should run against Peter Nixon in Gippsland. Over the previous two years Simon had shifted his allegiance from Lynch to Peacock.

From the start of his employment by Peacock Simon ran a highly political operation. Journalists were briefed and information was fed out about Peacock's view on Cabinet items; activity such as this was anathema to the Fraser Government. Simon circulated among his former backbench colleagues, cultivating Peacock's interests. His hostility to Fraser mirrored that of Peacock. The Prime Minister disliked Simon and was apprehensive about his activities. Very few defeated politicians ever took jobs as ministerial advisers. All Fraser's defence mechanisms were alerted by the unmistakable pattern in Peacock's activities: threatened resignations, the challenge to Lynch and the hiring of Simon.

Peacock remained only six months in the ministry. It was a period of simmering discontent, not just between Fraser and Peacock, but between the Cabinet and Peacock. After the election Fraser had left Peacock off the major Cabinet committees dealing with economic policy. Peacock complained and Fraser promised to act, but did not do so. Ministers felt Peacock was defying Cabinet solidarity through press briefings given by his office; Lynch and Viner were particularly upset. Peacock fell out with Fraser, Lynch and the Country Party trio over an early 1981 ACTU black ban on Qantas flights. The Prime

Minister initiated an emergency Cabinet meeting which authorised a huge RAAF airlift of about 1,000 stranded Australians home from New Zealand. Peacock opposed the provocative public comments by senior ministers. Fraser and Lynch believed Peacock was negotiating with the parties without prior Cabinet agreement.

The tensions reached breaking point over the Government's efforts to delay introduction of the 35-hour week. This issue is a classic study of Fraser's interventionist style. The Arbitration Commission had paved the way for the 35-hour week for chemical workers. Chemical giant ICI Australia was negotiating a package of wages and conditions, which included shorter hours. Peacock and Simon were in close touch with ICI and Peacock's approach was to encourage firms to resist if they could, but not to threaten them if they submitted to the unions.

Peacock on 26 March made a ministerial statement along these lines which Fraser approved before delivery. That evening Fraser, after a *Melbourne Herald* report on the union push, became seized with the urgency of halting the 35-hour week stampede. Addressing the Melbourne Chamber of Commerce he threatened reprisals by use of tariffs against companies negotiating any log of claims containing a 35-hour week claim. This was aimed squarely at ICI. The next day Fraser summoned ICI executives to his Melbourne office for two meetings and laid down the law. Peacock was furious; so was ICI. The company and Peacock had an understanding, but Fraser had usurped Peacock's strategy and substituted his own. Fraser was careful to ask Peacock to attend his meeting with ICI, but Peacock was busy. So Fraser and Lynch carved out the new approach.

It was a significant switch which broke public promises given to the chemical industry 18 months earlier and on which its own investment plans had been based. ICI threatened a 'shutdown' of $900 million worth of investment projects and the bluff and counter-bluff continued for days.

On 10 April Simon addressed businessmen in Canberra, and when the ICI case was raised, he said industry 'ought to be appalled' at the Government's performance. In an obvious reference to Fraser Simon said the Government had 'bullied', using a 'very large stick' and that there had been 'a lack of an honest approach by certain people'.

The Prime Minister rang Peacock saying Simon was a troublemaker and should be sacked. But Peacock argued that dismissal was an overreaction. On Sunday 12 April Fraser increased his pressure, speaking to a number of Cabinet ministers to gather support. He spent 30 minutes talking to Peacock, who still refused to remove Simon. Thereupon Fraser asked whether Peacock would discuss it with the Cabinet on Tuesday. Peacock initially refused but then he agreed on the basis that Cabinet had a right to canvass the matter. It was obvious the circle was closing, not just on Simon, but on Peacock himself. Fraser's intention, if Peacock refused to dismiss Simon, was to obtain a Cabinet instruction to this effect. At this point Peacock would have to accept the Cabinet decision or himself resign.

The irony was that Peacock and Simon were essentially correct. Fraser's 35-hour week intervention was autocratic and probably counterproductive. Several ministers held reservations about threatening ICI. But all ministers had to tolerate interference from Fraser to a greater or lesser extent.

Simon's comments were an indulgence that gave Fraser the chance to lop off his political head. The Prime Minister chose to insist on the application of Cabinet solidarity which, in other circumstances such as breaches by Country Party ministers, he overlooked. That afternoon Peacock made a statement dissociating himself from Simon's comments. But the deadlock remained and Peacock was left to face a Cabinet showdown the next day.

The crisis took a new turn on Tuesday morning when Peacock open *The Australian* and saw a page-one report from its political correspondent Malcolm Colless that revealed Peacock's resignation threat over the Pol Pot issue the previous September. Colless called it one of Canberra's best-kept political secrets and said that Peacock had threatened resignation after Fraser had been to see the Governor-General. Peacock saw the story as a damaging leak against him and his paranoia about Fraser flared. Peacock's first suspicions were that Fraser had inspired the story.

Peacock stayed in his office on Tuesday and declined to attend Cabinet. Two of his Cabinet friends, Jim Killen and Dame Margaret Guilfoyle, came to urge him to remove Simon and deny Fraser the chance to get at Peacock himself. They said that Fraser had persuaded the Cabinet that Simon had to be dismissed. But Peacock was more worried about *The Australian* article. He called Nixon into the office and claimed that there were inaccuracies in its account. Peacock said he wanted Fraser to clarify the facts now that the issue had become public.

Nixon wrote out in longhand the vital words which Peacock wanted in Fraser's statement: 'There are some significant inaccuracies in that report.' Nixon, accompanied by Killen and Guilfoyle, conveyed these words to the Prime Minister. Fraser agreed. The three ministers returned to Peacock's office. Guilfoyle told him: 'You have got the words that you wanted.'[11] However Peacock was already considering resignation since he knew that was the logic of his defence of Simon. He had perused Fraser's famous 1971 resignation speech against Gorton. Before lunch Peacock conferred with Simon and reported that Cabinet was united against him. At this point Simon said

Peacock had to face reality and accept his resignation. Simon's fall was a triumph for Fraser and a blunt assertion of his authority over Peacock.

That lunchtime Peter Nixon had obtained from Fraser's office a copy of the Prime Minister's press release on *The Australian* story. The full text which Nixon took to Peacock read:

> I have seen the statement on the front of today's Australian concerning events that occurred last year. There are some significant inaccuracies in that report.

Peacock was dismayed by its brevity: he had expected more clarification. Nixon said that any inadequacies were 'a matter for the Prime Minister or David Barnett to explain'.[12] Peacock believed Nixon had indicated that Fraser or Barnett would give the press more information by way of background.

As the day progressed Peacock seemed satisfied that the leak had not originated with Fraser; he believed it had probably come from Lynch's office. Peacock asked Fraser to organise a meeting between the two of them and Lynch. He wanted the Prime Minister to pursue the source of the article and seemed confident that Lynch would be embarrassed. But later Peacock told Fraser he was tired and wanted this meeting deferred. Obviously Peacock was both tired and emotional.

At about 8.00 p.m. Fraser's Press Secretaries David Barnett and Jim Bonner bumped into Peacock and Simon. In a note for Fraser Barnett recalled the exchange:

> BONNER: See you tomorrow!
>
> PEACOCK: You may well see us both in different circumstances. You with your back to the wall. I mean that. You've been dribbling too much tonight.[13]

That evening at his motel Peacock flicked on the television to see Richard Carleton on 'Nationwide' say of *The Australian* story:

> There is little doubt that this story was planted by Mr Peacock's enemies . . . The story is not a scoop in the old-fashioned journalistic sense; rather it is an exclusive handout. Mr Fraser's hand can be detected behind the story, but even more clearly can be seen the hands of Sir Phillip Lynch's team of political operators and schemers.

Within minutes David Barnett on Fraser's orders had rung the ABC requesting an apology for Carleton's assertion. Barnett said Fraser's office did not originate the story nor convey it through another outlet. At the end of the 'Nationwide' programme its compere Clive Hale said Fraser's office had just denied that it or anyone else named by Carleton (that is, Lynch's office) was responsible for the story. This was not in fact what Barnett had said. His statement was specific to Fraser's office as the originating source.[14]

Peacock went into a fury over the programme. He concluded that Fraser had doublecrossed him. The Prime Minister was publicly denying that either his office or Lynch's office was responsible for the story, thereby pre-empting the discussions which Peacock had sought with both men to pursue this issue. Peacock rang Carleton, Barnett and the ABC in Sydney. He told Carleton he had believed that 'Fraser was going to give Lynch a kick in the head'. Carleton urged Peacock to 'be careful'. Barnett explained to Peacock that the ABC had misinterpreted Fraser's denial. The ABC in Sydney, still confused, told Peacock their denial was accurate. Peacock called Fraser and there was an angry row between them. Fraser rang Nixon and reported, 'The young man seems agitated . . .' A few minutes later Peacock, at his motel, wrote a draft resignation letter.

The long-simmering Fraser–Peacock clash, fed on the Pol Pot issue, industrial relations differences and the Simon affair had exploded. Peacock, teetering on the edge, finally jumped after the manoeuvrings on *The Australian* story. The next morning he went for a jog and then dictated a resignation letter, emotional in tone and accusatory in content; a declaration of war against Fraser:

> I believe you have engaged in acts of gross disloyalty to me and my office. I believe you have consistently allowed false and damaging reports to be published about me and my capacity as a senior minister. I find this constant disloyalty intolerable and not to be endured. As you are aware, it is quite impossible to carry out effectively the duties of a sensitive and extremely important portfolio while a Prime Minister, both overtly and covertly, undermines the authority of a senior minister. This you have done.
>
> It should not be thought that acts of recent days alone have forced me to this position. I believe you have cast aside the stability and sense of direction of the Government. Indeed you have a dangerous reluctance to consult Cabinet and an obstinate determination to get your own way . . . this decision is irrevocable . . .[15]

For months he had been working towards an assertion of himself against Fraser and had decided, at least subconsciously if not consciously, to break from the Prime Minister if their divisions reached crisis point. Peacock intuitively understood the political primitivism which was the ultimate law that governed the Liberal Party. He knew that assassination was the typical, often the most respected, method of leadership transfer. Peacock knew Fraser's own bloody trail to glory. A man proved his leadership mettle by assassinating his predecessor. The technique was never put in these terms, but it was understood. Peacock knew the combination of Fraser's electoral decline and internal party hostility would make him increasingly vulnerable.

The words of Peacock's resignation and the language of his press conference were deliberately borrowed from Fraser's strike against Gorton. But herein lay a tactical mistake on Peacock's part. By invoking Fraser's words against Gorton, he asked to be judged by Fraser's results. Gorton had fallen almost immediately, but Fraser was too powerful to succumb to Peacock's resignation. Consequently Peacock was creating expectations he could not immediately satisfy. When he subsequently denied his intention to challenge for the leadership, he convinced nobody. The obvious conclusion is that the timing of Peacock's resignation was influenced by his emotions and not by a cool appreciation of the politics.

Peacock's tactical mistake was that the issue of his resignation did not provide a platform from which he could attack Fraser. The Parliament was not sitting so there was no backbench to which Peacock could air his grievances. But the problem was more fundamental: Peacock did not resign on a clear-cut issue of principle which could be used to mobilise support against Fraser. Indeed there was terrible confusion for weeks among ministers, journalists and backbenchers as to exactly why Peacock had resigned. His letter to Fraser made accusations that undertakings given by the Prime Minister the previous day had been broken, but Peacock avoided saying what undertakings he meant. Indeed that afternoon Peacock even told Nixon that he did not see Nixon as party to any broken undertakings.[16]

While he remained confident, Fraser viewed Peacock's resignation with the utmost seriousness. He moved immediately to extract full Cabinet backing for himself against Peacock's accusations. After a major Cabinet row Anthony and Lynch released a joint statement denying that Peacock resigned because of a 'personal conflict' between himself and the Prime Minister. They asserted that 'the conflict is between Andrew Peacock and the Cabinet'. Fraser held a full-scale press conference on the afternoon of the resignation to 'reject utterly' the Peacock charges. The next day, 16 April, he launched into a series of background briefings for senior media correspondents—probably the most intensive briefings of his entire period in office. Then he went on talk-back radio and television.

Fraser's approach was to dismiss Peacock as a threat and patronise his resignation. Fraser said, 'It is not the first time that Andrew has been close to resignation. On other occasions we have dissuaded him from resignation and the issue has just gone past.' The Prime Minister said he used National Party ministers to negotiate because Peacock had regarded senior Liberals as 'competitors and rivals'. In terms of working in a Cabinet team Fraser said of Peacock, 'There are some people who are maybe unmouldable.' It was difficult not to detect petulance in Peacock's action and Fraser played cruelly on Peacock's emotionalism: 'Mr Peacock's feelings and his frustrations in his ministry have obviously become too strong . . . it was never my intention to contribute to the strain which Mr Peacock so clearly felt.'[17]

However, Peacock's standing in the community, the Liberal organisation and the parliamentary party—if not the Cabinet—guaranteed that he would be taken seriously. His resignation solidified the anti-Fraser forces in the Liberal Party and gave them an alternative leader, behind whom they could rally for the first time. In the fortnight between Peacock's 15 April resignation and his 28 April speech to Parliament the Liberal Party split began to widen. The mischievous Senator Reg Withers, fiddling on the backbench for so long, now put his violin away and took out his dagger to support Peacock against Fraser.

The voice of reconciliation was that of Federal Director of the Liberal Party Tony Eggleton, and in a note advising on tactics for Fraser's parliamentary reply to Peacock he said:

> I would tend to think that the Prime Minister has nothing to lose, and potentially something to gain, by leaving open the possibility of Mr Peacock's re-entry—although in the words he uses to make the point, it may do no harm to give Mr Peacock something of a kick in the tail . . . If Mr Peacock is going to be destroyed, the destruction will not stem from the present statement. And a note of magnanimity can do a great deal of good, and no harm, in the parliamentary statement.

Fraser's patience and Peacock's worry were revealed in a 20-minute phone discussion between them on 27 April, the day before Peacock's resignation speech. Mr Richard Searby, QC, a director of Rupert Murdoch's companies, was the intermediary, contacted initially by Peacock. During their phone call Fraser told Peacock the course he had chosen was 'painful and lonely'. He suggested that Peacock come up and have a few drinks. Fraser asked: 'Why is it in your view impossible to say that you hold to the charges, etc., but in the interests of the Liberal Party you don't want a public brawl over it?' Finally Peacock said he had to follow the course he had set. Fraser philosophised that the die was 'never cast until the pebble is actually in the pool . . . Somebody can stop even in the act of throwing.'

The next day Peacock denounced Fraser and gave the ammunition to his charge that the Prime Minister had 'a manic determination to get his own way'. Peacock said: 'I resigned because of irreconcilable differences between the Prime Minister and myself about his method of government . . . By reposing too much power in the Prime Minister, the system of collective responsibility within Cabinet is destroyed.' Peacock again declared that there was 'no conspiracy to overthrow the elected leader of the party'. Fraser gave a rigorous defence of himself and his Government and said, 'I approach the future without rancour.'

But the Liberal Party was now divided against itself and consequently would be debilitated until the division was resolved. The consequences of such a division for the Government would be measured in a direct loss of electorate support. Malcolm Fraser knew that, unless he could settle the issue between himself and Peacock, his survival as Prime Minister was in jeopardy. Peacock knew the political logic of his position meant a leadership challenge against Fraser.

PART 2

THE BATTLE

8
Hayden surges

The polls indicate that the party would do better under my leadership.

Bob Hawke to Bill Hayden,
February 1982

Bill Hayden's leadership reached its zenith in early 1982 when he began to prevail in the three-way struggle for power between himself, Fraser and Hawke. As Hayden contemplated the outlook mid-term he was *en route* to The Lodge. The polls showed it; then Hayden read the world economic trends and saw a downturn about to overtake Fraser. In the 18 months since the October 1980 election the Fraser Government had slid into decline and division. Inside the insulated world of Parliament Hawke appeared to have lost that special status which had made his reputation. Hayden was on top and he was ebullient.

The thrust towards power had continued to change Hayden. He was thriving in his drive for Government and radiated ambition for office. Hayden knew that a swing of only 1.4 per cent lay between him and his elusive goal. This dictated his approach of political aggression and electoral caution. At the start of his fifth year as Labor leader Hayden had long been purged of his last remnants of political innocence. The economic rationalist had virtually surrendered to the political pragmatist. Hayden was returning to his Labor roots and resurrecting the old-fashioned populist style to which he had secretly aspired for much of his political life. He said on television that he found economics boring and irrelevant. When Hayden's former economic adviser, Australian National University economist Dr Peter McCawley, warned that he had 'gone soft' on economics, Hayden snorted: 'I'm not after the Coombs Building Economic Prize.' Inside Caucus Hayden, once the consensus leader, was displaying autocratic assertion.

The striking feature of Hawke's initial year in Parliament had been the discrepancy between aspiration and reality. In neither the Caucus nor the Parliament had Hawke performed as an alternative leader. He became an orthodox frontbencher whose primary focus was his industrial and employment shadow portfolio and whose attack was centred on his ministerial counterpart, Ian Viner. During 1981 there was grave doubt even among Hawke's own supporters as to whether he possessed the capacity and judgement to mould himself as the ALP parliamentary leader. Hawke's low point came at the special ALP National Conference in July 1981 to modernise the party's socialist objective and to expand both its National Conference and National Executive structures. Hayden relied on right-wing votes and conspicuous support from Graham Richardson to defeat the left-wing move to deepen Labor's commitment to socialism and nationalisation of industry. Then Hayden spearheaded moves to double the size of the National Conference and insert tough affirmative action provisions in the ALP rules. Hawke was low-key during the debate and his only intervention came on the socialist objective when he accused the left of 'intellectual wanking'.

However Hawke's most abject performance occurred at the main conference dinner in the banquet room of Melbourne's Southern Cross Hotel, which was attended by several hundred people. A number of Labor notables had been asked to tell their best jokes with an award for the wittiest performer. It was a formidable cast: Gough Whitlam, Bill Hayden, Bob Hawke, Lionel Bowen, Mick Young, Clyde Holding and others. Hawke's main joke was told with an accent, an Indian accent. Almost each sentence seemed to start with 'Oh dear'. The build-up involved Indian Prime Minister Indira Gandhi agreeing to run a 'monster national lottery with three mystery prizes' in order to divert national attention from her political mistakes. Third prize was a free trip around the world on Air India; second prize was a fruit cake. The 'little man' who won second prize complained that the third prize was better. Mimicking the lottery compere, Hawke then moved smoothly to the denouement: 'But this is a very, very special fruit cake. It was baked by our glorious Prime Minister Mrs Gandhi.' The little man, according to Hawke, replied 'F— Mrs Gandhi', to which the compere said, 'Oh, no, no, no, you will be wanting first prize.'[1] The audience was unimpressed; Labor women, who had come to the conference to achieve stronger affirmative action, were hostile. The Indian High Commission later made a formal protest to Hayden as ALP leader. Hawke said that anybody familiar with his record would realise it was 'absurd' to brand him a racist. Yet the joke revealed Hawke's lack of judgement as an aspiring Prime Minister.

The next day Hawke went to Graham Richardson on the conference floor and asked for a dispensation from voting with the right wing against some of the more extreme affirmative action proposals being put by women delegates. He explained: 'The women see me as sexist; I don't want to compound it.' Richardson shook his head. He was a great admirer of Hawke, but he knew that future leaders were not supposed to act like that. Hawke left the Melbourne conference with his party standing undistinguished and his parliamentary contribution unspectacular. Hayden emerged enforced.

Hawke's personal transition to Canberra was smoother than his political transition. He stayed in a Kingston town house overlooking Telopea Park which he purchased in mid-1980. Hawke enjoyed Canberra and had many fond memories of it from his student days at the ANU. There was a curious harmony between the solitude and tranquility of the national capital and the new Hawke, who was more at peace with himself than he had been for many years. Within the Caucus Hawke rarely carried his ambition on his sleeve, it was more an integral part of his nature. His strength was his inner belief in himself. He could recover quickly from mistakes and this capacity encouraged others to forget them as well. His talent as a media performer remained without peer in federal politics. Hawke had the skills of a television professional in his own right. The proof of this was the invitation which he accepted in 1981 to host Australia's most popular daytime television programme, 'The Mike Walsh Show', when Walsh was indisposed. However a fairly accurate assessment of Hawke's first year in Parliament was provided the next day by Laurie Oakes:

> Since Mr Hawke entered Parliament he has not done himself justice. He does not perform nearly as well in Parliament—or in Caucus by all accounts—as he did yesterday as a television compere. His media skills are unquestioned. But a politician requires other skills as well . . .
>
> Mr Fraser so far has not found Mr Hawke much more difficult to deal with than a number of other Opposition frontbenchers . . . There is more to politics, especially in the big league at the national level, than making like a television star.[2]

Fraser himself declared: 'Mr Hawke will find Mr Hayden harder to push out than he thinks.' Asked why he thought this the Prime Minister replied, '[because of] my judgement of Bill Hayden'.[3] But Fraser was taking no chances. When the opening came, he moved to discredit Hawke as brutally as possible. The issue was the Fraser Government's decision for Australian participation in the multinational peacekeeping force in the Sinai Desert to supervise the Israeli withdrawal under the Camp David accords. Hayden and Lionel Bowen had declared Labor's opposition without reference to Caucus.

At a subsequent meeting of the Caucus Foreign Affairs and Defence Committee Hawke criticised the comprehensive nature of the ALP opposition to the force. But Hawke knew he could not reverse the basic position. The upshot was a Caucus decision opposing any multinational force not under the auspices of the United Nations. Labor's opposition had majority support from the public as shown by opinion polls. On 22 October 1981, when justifying the ALP stance, Hawke said, 'I am not prepared to support a position in this matter clearly against the view expressed in the polls.' This struck a nerve centre in Fraser's brain. The Prime Minister's rhetoric had always loathed politicians pursuing popularity at the expense of principle.

A week later, on 29 October, Fraser gunned Hawke in Parliament saying he had 'embarked on the greatest betrayal of the only thing in which he ever had a really sincere belief in his whole life—the people and the state of Israel'. During the debate Hawke defended Labor's position, but indirectly criticised Hayden who had called Israel's Prime Minister Begin the greatest threat to peace. Hawke, to his credit, dismissed the dishonest analogy being peddled in the ALP circles between the Vietnam and the Sinai commitments. But towards the end of his speech, Hawke broke down. He left the chamber in tears as Government backbencher Jack Birney rose and attacked him for a 'sell-out of Israel'.

During the year Hawke had given several well-researched speeches on the need to boost economic growth, develop a skilled work force, tackle the unemployment crisis and confront the wages policy dilemma. Drawing on his vast knowledge of Australian wage fixation, Hawke produced his own wages initiative. In an August 1981 address to the Industrial Relations Society of NSW Hawke called for the reintroduction of the basic wage which had been abandoned in 1967. This concept provided a minimum wage for workers plus margins for skill. Hawke emerged as a trenchant critic of the existing system of across-the-board partial indexation of wages. He said:

> We have indeed travelled a strange path. We have moved from an early position where, in difficult economic circumstances, we fully indexed a basic wage to protect those most in need of protection to a position where, because of difficult economic circumstances, we do not fully index wages and in so doing impose the greatest burden on those least able to bear it . . .

During Christmas 1981 and into New Year Hawke considered his position and began 1982 with the conviction that this must be the year of the challenge. Hawke's ego was impervious to objective evidence that his challenge had more reality in his own head than it enjoyed in the party room. The moral of

1981 was that Hayden would not surrender and seemed unlikely to falter. The prospect for 1982 was a restless Prime Minister, predictable only in his pragmatism, searching for a re-election strategy for his failing Government. Hawke had to assert himself, otherwise he would become a victim of history and not its architect, stranded between the combative Hayden and despotic Fraser, gladiators flaying each other, yet curiously growing alike.

As it unfolded 1982 would become the most remarkable year in federal politics since 1975. The opening event, so vital for both Hayden and Hawke, was the Lowe by-election, precipitated by the retirement of former Liberal Prime Minister Sir William McMahon. The by-election came at the right time and in the right seat for the ALP. The Opposition needed a swing of only 1.2 per cent to win the Sydney western suburbs seat and demonstrate that the Prime Minister was on the political rack. The onus now lay on Hayden; but if the swing to Labor was insubstantial then Hawke would benefit. However, the by-election forced an alliance between Hayden and the NSW machine, both of whom had an interest in a convincing victory.

McMahon reported that Fraser was 'horrified' when told of his resignation intentions. It was not surprising. Lowe was the first by-election he had had to face in a marginal seat since he had taken office. It covered an area where the long-term demographic trend was towards Labor. It was also a seat where grassroots Labor strength combined with NSW machine professionalism to produce an excellent Opposition candidate. Bill Hayden told the NSW Party President, Paul Keating, that he would like to see the Chairman of the Law Reform Commission, Michael Kirby, as the ALP candidate. But this was a fanciful delusion. Keating said the best candidate was the state Labor Member for Drummoyne, Michael Maher, a politician of exceptional popularity. So the NSW machine, with Hayden's blessing, organised the candidate. Hawke also campaigned in Lowe, trying to conceal his frustration as his NSW allies worked with Hayden for an ALP victory.

Lowe propelled Hayden to neutralise the policy weakness which Fraser had exploited during the previous election: Labor's capital gains tax. The issue was again relevant because the Caucus economic committee was in the throes of finalising a new Labor policy. In November 1981 this committee met in Melbourne and considered a detailed submission from Ralph Willis for a comprehensive capital gains tax. The ALP left was committed to the Willis concept and saw capital gains as a symbolic issue which would determine whether a Hayden Government was genuine about income redistribution. The left-wing chairman of the economics committee, Brian Howe, had asked Hayden to attend the November meeting and was bitterly disappointed when he stayed away. The meeting deferred the Willis proposal through fear of its electoral impact and accepted instead an amendment from Shadow Attorney-General Senator Gareth Evans to tighten existing law rather than imposing a new law. Keating was a powerful opponent of the Willis proposal; along with Neville Wran, he believed the issue had lost Labor NSW seats in the 1980 federal election.

Hayden had moved a long way from his 1978–79 position of championing income redistribution through a radical change in the tax mix. He felt it was difficult, perhaps impossible, to market a capital gains tax from Opposition. The revenue return could not justify the political risk. He decided to steer the issue along the lines suggested by Gareth Evans and Victorian backbencher Michael Duffy. In this way Labor's commitment to taxing capital gains could be placed squarely in the context of tax avoidance. The party would pledge to implement Section 26(a) of the Income Tax Assessment Act so that speculative profits were taxed—the original intention of the law.

In order to finalise this stance before the March by-election Hayden needed to intervene and short-circuit the deliberations of the Caucus economics committee. He went for the quick fix. On 26 January Hayden informed Willis and senior officials, Mick Young as ALP Vice-President and Bob McMullan as National Secretary, of his intentions and secured their approval. Hayden was determined to deny Fraser any avenue of political escape in the Lowe by-election. The left watched stunned while Hayden systematically demolished a touchstone of its ideology in league with the 'big guns' of the ALP right.

But the left had another reason for concern. The Labor candidate for Lowe at the 1980 election had been a left-wing woman, Jan Burnswoods. Naturally she expected to become the candidate for the by-election. Hayden did not intervene in the preselection process; but he endorsed the successful campaign of the NSW right to promote Maher against Burnswoods.

On 3 February Hayden prevailed in the party room on capital gains tax policy, but only after a damaging row with Willis and at the cost of alienating the left. Willis told Caucus that Hayden had been 'undemocratic and pre-emptive' in his actions. He said the Hayden formula was no solution to Labor's commitment to impose a tax on capital and that it would not close off tax avoidance. Both Hayden and Bowen attacked Willis on the grounds that he had endorsed the new policy at the previous week's meeting. Hayden said that 'like a good policeman' he had notes of the meeting where Willis had approved the approach. Hawke did not speak during the meeting on either of the two main issues—capital gains or health policy—and this fact was tucked away in stories which both *The Sydney Morning Herald* and *The Age* carried of the Caucus debate the next day.

Hawke betrayed acute sensitivity about Hayden two days later when he attacked 'deliberate and contrived leaking' from the Caucus as designed to undermine him. The fact that the leak was a report of Hawke's silence did not modify his concern. It was a petty incident but revealing of the growing leadership tensions.

At the next Caucus meeting Hawke named Hayden's Press Secretary Alan Ramsey as the source of the reports. These remarks were seen as an indirect but obvious criticism of Hayden for trying to undermine his position. These allegations triggered the first personal clash between the two men inside Caucus since Hawke's entry into Parliament 16 months earlier. Hawke defended Willis, claiming that Hayden had altered the terms of their understanding and, significantly, he argued for a capital gains tax on the grounds that it was necessary to underpin the ALP–ACTU prices-incomes accord.

Hayden emerged from the spat more cocky than ever and tried to highlight his own toughness against Hawke's sensitivity. He said, 'I'm too thick-skinned now to feel as pained as I once did when I was a victim of [leaking].' Hayden recalled the story of the famous ALP politician, Reg Pollard, who said that he had always believed he had a good idea of the identity of the half-a-dozen or so people behind Caucus leaks. But eventually they all left Parliament, leaving only himself—and he knew it couldn't be him.

The capital gains tax issue had cast Hayden in the role of a strong, even autocratic leader, an image he seemed to relish after being depicted as weak for so long. But it was also an omen of danger for it signalled deep tension between Hayden and the left. Hayden revelled in his dominance over Hawke and senior Caucus members remarked upon Hawke's inability to adapt to his new forum. Hawke was such a natural leader that he felt uncomfortable with shadow ministry status—one of the team under Hayden. Hawke was constrained. The low profile of his early period in Parliament was partly deliberate. But as the by-election intensified the political climate, both in the Caucus and in the electorate, Hawke took his first decisive and overt step to secure the leadership—he confronted Hayden.

Hawke saw Hayden in the leader's office late one night, probably 18 February, just after Hayden's win on capital gains tax. The challenger spoke in measured and confident tones, careful to look Hayden in the eyes. Hawke had only one weapon: public opinion polls. In the coming months he would deploy them against Hayden with the furious firepower of a battalion. This night Hawke did not actually ask Hayden to resign, but he put to him an argument which led directly to this conclusion. Hawke went through the opinion polls and argued that Labor was doing badly. Given the abject record of the Fraser Government, Labor should have been in a far better position.

Hawke said Labor was doing better in the states than federally and that the party was not realising the potential of its position. Hawke told Hayden he believed the ALP would do better under his own leadership and that this view was held by many people in the party.

Hayden replied quickly and strongly to this frontal assault. He said the Labor leadership was determined not by opinion polls but by the Caucus. Hayden was telling Hawke that the 'parliamentary club' was sovereign in ALP politics and, now that Hawke was a member of Caucus, he could no longer avoid this fact. Hayden said he had Caucus support; it would continue to support him. Moreover he had every confidence of leading Labor to win the next election. The polls indicated that Labor would win. Hayden told Hawke he had no doubt about his own ability to turn this lead into an election victory.

After this meeting Hayden was buoyant and excited. He always believed that in a face-to-face encounter Hawke was no match for him, that as a politician Hawke needed 'handlers' to help him. Hayden, being a loner, did his own work. He felt the thrill of satisfaction at checking and then rebuffing Hawke's personal probe. Hayden was convinced of his own ascendancy. Hawke left empty-handed, but he had made the gesture. Hayden had been put on notice. Psychologically Hawke had purged himself for the challenge. Both men awaited the 13 March Lowe by-election result—a poll that counted.

Labor won Lowe with a two-party preferred swing of just under nine per cent, thereby delivering Fraser the biggest electoral defeat so far in his career as Prime Minister. Hayden said a national swing only one-third as great in a general election would give a Labor Government a 23-seat majority. The win was greater than expected, but it fell short of the cataclysmic proportions of the 1975 Bass by-election which had signalled Fraser's utter ascendancy over Whitlam.

Hayden interpreted the result as a repudiation of both Fraser and Hawke. Certainly it indicated that Labor was 'on line' to win the next election. But the Liberals took solace from the big personal vote Michael Maher attracted for the ALP. They said the party swing was much less than Lowe suggested. Hawke was not fazed by the result; he never betrayed any sign of doubt that he was the only man equipped to lead Labor back to Government. Even when few others believed this, Hawke's confidence was unshaken.

In a paradoxical fashion Lowe contained the seeds of hope for Hawke precisely because it precipitated the first of Fraser's major political offensives during 1982. The day after the by-election Paul Keating sank the political knife into Fraser by declaring that Labor should look for an election at a time of its own choosing by using the Senate's power over supply. Keating was baiting Fraser. But Fraser lashed back and oblivious to the historical irony, declared that the ALP would be guilty of 'the greatest hypocrisy of all time' if it blocked supply. Many people must have felt a tinge of satisfaction at having Fraser's 1975 tactics turned on himself. But the Prime Minister was determined to make attack the best method of defence. He warned both the Liberal Party and the nation that they must prepare for an election in the light of comments by senior ALP figures. Fraser began building the election climate which would have such a profound impact during 1982. Having tasted defeat, he started to turn the pressure back on Hayden.

The reality behind Fraser's rhetoric was the Government's reassessment of Senate obstructionism. In November 1981 Fraser was relaxed about the Senate, declaring: 'Overwhelmingly our legislative programme has gone through.' The Prime Minister said there was 'no justification' for anyone to think 'the Senate is behaving impossibly and that therefore there will be an election very soon'.[4] The pivot on which the Government's attitude changed was the package of bills to effect the extension of sales tax announced in Howard's August 1981–82 budget. The Labor Party opposed the bills; for months the Australian Democrats agonised between expediency and principle. On 16 February 1982 the five Australian Democrat Senators decided to reverse their position of the previous year and defeat the bills which would impose sales tax at 2.5 per cent on basic necessities and other items. Senator Don Chipp said the Democrats' previous position was an 'error of judgement'. The revenue involved was an estimated $330 million in a full year. The decision caught the Government by surprise and it had two consequences.

The first was that Fraser's capacity to introduce personal income tax cuts was reduced. The Government's sales tax strategy was to broaden the indirect tax base, thereby creating room for personal income tax cuts. The thwarting of this strategy by the Australian Democrats was a damning commentary on the political incompetence of the Fraser Government. The Government had controlled the Senate until 1 July 1981, during which period it had a golden opportunity to introduce and pass such legislation. Cabinet had considered a submission from Treasurer Howard for a broadly based indirect tax in early 1981. Howard almost prevailed, but he was beaten by Fraser. The Prime Minister opposed the concept as did his office staff chief David Kemp and top economist Professor John Rose, who both wrote Fraser a powerful memo opposing the indirect tax on grounds of consistency and simplicity. The danger was that it would fuel inflation. Both Howard and John Stone were convinced that, like the move to world parity pricing for oil, the immediate inflationary consequences had to be accepted for the greater longer-term gain. Having decided against a broadly based indirect tax in early 1981 the Government, when it got to the budget, decided upon sweeping extensions in indirect taxation for revenue reasons. But it was too late and a hostile Senate threw most of them out.

The second consequence was that Fraser now began seriously to contemplate an early double dissolution election. The Senate's rejection of the sales tax bills would give him the trigger for a double dissolution under Section 57 of the Constitution. Later it became clear that the Australian Democrats made the Senate not so much obstructionist as unpredictable. But Fraser thrived on the unpredictable and he was determined to exploit the latest assertion of Senate power for his own ends. Caution dictated that Fraser be prepared in case the ALP and the Australian Democrats, in a fit of absence of mind and honour, blocked supply. But opportunity dictated that he stoke the election fires so that he could strike if Hayden stumbled. Government Senate leader Sir John Carrick told the Liberal Party federal Executive in late February that the blocking of supply was a real possibility. This was far too alarmist. But it helped create, along with the comments of Fraser and Keating, an unreal, almost feverish, election atmosphere. Fraser was not yet ready for any immediate election, but he began to consider seriously the need for an election short of his full parliamentary term. He would use this threat to marshal his own forces and intensify pressure on the Opposition. Meanwhile Fraser turned to confront the internal challenge to his authority.

9

Fraser defeats Peacock

*I just think Andrew Peacock has been an ego-tripper from way back . . .
He throws a few crumbs and calls gully, gully, gully.*

Tamie Fraser, March 1982

In April 1982, the month after the Lowe by-election, Malcolm Fraser effected one of the major power strikes of his career when he precipitated and then put down the Peacock challenge. Fraser displayed both patience and precision in his elimination of the pretender. He had waited while Peacock grew more audacious trying to gather support about him, then Fraser struck while Peacock was still cleaning his weapons and rehearsing his drill. The contrast in their careers was again revealed: Fraser's mastery of power; Peacock's obsession with style. In the process Fraser removed his politically ailing deputy, Phillip Lynch, and replaced him with John Howard, thereby preserving his own power structure within the Liberal Party. Fraser's defeat of Peacock was a housekeeping necessity before he could turn his full attack back on the Labor Party.

The cauldron of Liberal politics from late 1981 onwards became more fluid and unpredictable. Deep animosities swirled through the top of the party, released by the Peacock threat; the frayed nerves of worried backbenchers provoked criticism of policy and insolence towards the leadership. The Fraser Government displayed the internal divisions and external confusion which spelt decay and almost inevitable defeat. New scandals erupted; old economic problems, notably inflation and unemployment, were about to return. Ian Viner incurred the hostility of both business and unions in his Industrial Relations and Employment portfolio; Ian Sinclair faced a fresh crisis over the so-called 'Asia dairy' affair, being probed by a Senate committee headed by Peter Rae. Meanwhile Fraser conducted one of the grandest political diversions in Australian history: the mammoth Commonwealth Heads of Government Meeting in Melbourne.

In spring 1981 Peacock accepted his destiny and began preparations for his challenge. Fraser's base was at its most vulnerable since his election as Prime Minister six years earlier. The main figures in the Peacock cabal were Reg Withers, whom Fraser had made an implacable enemy, former South Australian Premier and Liberal movement leader Steele Hall, who had rejoined the Liberal Party but never abated his deep hostility towards Fraser, and Barry Simon, a victim of Fraser who now returned as a member of Peacock's backbench staff. The return of Simon, whose job was to assist Peacock with the political bricks and mortar, was the effective starting point for the challenge.

Peacock did not have the numbers to make him Liberal leader. His strategy was to highlight the Government's weakness and define an authentic Liberal philosophy in a bid to gather majority support. Peacock was trying to mould a climate of opinion, both inside and outside the Government. He appealed to the Liberal backbench hoping to ride to power on the tide of disillusion running out from the Fraser Cabinet. Peacock aimed at the biggest identifiable backbench group, the free-market lobby (or so-called 'drys' under the informal leadership of John Hyde). While Peacock declared there was no challenge to Fraser, he launched his campaign. Peacock, who had always been associated with the left wing of the Liberal Party, was attacking from the right. The strategy seemed dubious at the time; it was later revealed as misconceived.

Peacock called for almost immediate cuts in personal income tax, a more broadly based indirect tax, a fundamental reassessment of welfare and the payment of benefits on a needs basis, a cut in industry protection, support for collective bargaining instead of centralised wage fixation and deregulation of the financial system. Significantly these policies were all espoused by John Howard, not just in rhetoric but at the Cabinet table. During his own stint in Cabinet Peacock had shown only a meagre commitment to the goals he now championed. In power terms his mistake was to underestimate the emerging axis between the free-market lobby and Howard.

Peacock's central weakness was that his challenge was rooted more in disaffection with Fraser than support for himself. This meant that he lacked the ability to initiate Fraser's downfall; he had to exploit the mistakes of Fraser and his Government and highlight its declining electoral fortunes. His success would be a direct function of Fraser's failure. Although Fraser was a more vulnerable leader, he remained incessantly active, patient and ruthless. There was one certainty about Fraser in this situation of hunter and hunted: at some bend in the political path he would wait to ambush Peacock and end the hunt. All challengers must rely upon the media to promote their cause and undermine the status quo. Peacock, Withers and Simon were adroit at this task. Perhaps they spent too much time on the media and not sufficient on the Liberal Party. A mini publishing boom took off around Peacock with books, biographies and articles. Meanwhile Reg Withers unnerved the Liberals by publicly naming the Peacock hit list. Its most prominent members included John Carrick, Tony Street, Peter Durack, Ian Viner, Wal Fife, Kevin Newman and, of course, Tony Eggleton. Withers carried his hatchet for Peacock over his shoulder. He declared: 'The colt from Kooyong has embarked on a journey for the jugular.'[1] There was no turning back.

The major impetus Peacock got in late 1981 stemmed from the inept effort of his successor, Ian Viner, to discredit him on the floor of Parliament. Viner's attack followed a rigorous session he endured at an estimates committee when Peacock quizzed him about deregistration of the Builders' Labourers' Federation (BLF). To defend himself Viner got informal Cabinet approval to table documents in the House showing he had moved promptly to deregister the BLF in contrast to the delay under Peacock's administration. Viner made two mistakes. The first was that he tabled papers which named the Costain construction group as a cooperative employer in the deregistration campaign. The BLF immediately placed a national ban on Costains and a building industry spokesman said the Government had broken its promise to keep secret the identity of the contractors assisting its efforts. The second mistake was that confidential papers which were subsequently leaked appeared to contradict Viner's claim that the deregistration case was in a 'state of unpreparedness' when he became minister.[2] The incident captured the Cabinet paranoia about Peacock and riled much of the Liberal backbench. It produced a fertile field of hostility for Peacock to cultivate. While some Peacock supporters urged an immediate challenge to Fraser, Peacock knew his hand was still far too weak.

The first sign of publicity overkill in the Peacock challenge came during the Melbourne CHOGM in early October 1981. With about 40 Government heads in Australia Fraser was subjected to prominent newspaper reports that Peacock would challenge him within weeks. Other reports hinted that Fraser was ill and had been attending a cancer clinic. The Prime Minister was furious both with the press and with Peacock. The Commonwealth meeting which had been planned meticulously for more than a year was partly sabotaged by this combination. Fraser was an embarrassed host; he received condolences from fellow Commonwealth leaders with thanks but assured them the reports were fanciful. The fury burnt into Fraser's brain cells and the imprint remained.

During CHOGM both Howard on 5 October and Lynch the next day felt obliged to go public. Lynch defended Fraser; Howard denied that he would run as deputy on a Peacock ticket, the great delusion being promoted by the Peacock camp.

Peacock himself was doing little lobbying, and the 'legwork' was being left to Withers and Simon. Withers was trying to forge a Peacock–Howard ticket with the aim of winning the 'drys', already unhappy with Fraser, to the new leadership team. The logic in this tactic was that a Peacock–Howard ticket was the most viable and attractive for the long-term; but the tactic foundered on personality and power problems. Curiously Peacock did not appear enthusiastic about running with Howard and told colleagues there was 'no ticket', so Peacock and Withers had their wires crossed.

Howard was the obvious long-term rival to Peacock for the Liberal leadership. Both men had chosen different roads to the top. Peacock had broken from the Fraser Cabinet in a bid to establish himself as the alternative, appealing to both the party and the people, strutting the stage and displaying his plumage. Howard stayed within the system to prove his strength and capacity as Treasurer and deputy leader, aiming to beat Peacock through substance and stamina. The competing strategies reflected contrasting personalities. Peacock was flamboyant, elusive and mercurial; Howard was suburban, straight and stolid. Peacock was a gifted public performer with a great sense of nuance; Howard was more the private technocrat with a grip on practical politics.

The 1981–82 contest in the Liberal Party was between Fraser and Peacock, but in its resolution a new network of alignments was being forged. The Fraser power structure needed to be replenished because another fundamental change underway was the decline of Sir Phillip Lynch as a political force. This was not obvious at the time and as Lynch battled to survive, many outsiders and even some Liberals mistakenly concluded that he was trying to undermine or even overthrow Fraser. In fact, Lynch was fighting to keep his political head above water, but in the process confusion abounded. The combination of Peacock's challenge simultaneous with Lynch's decline presented Fraser with a serious problem. However the answer was obvious. Fraser had to promote Howard as quickly as possible into the Lynch vacuum to protect his political underbelly and assist him to defeat Peacock.

The origins of Lynch's political demise lay in his greatest Cabinet success: the Lynch plan for the Australian car industry. This was achieved in two stages, 1978 and 1981, and the concept was based on the General Motors world car strategy. The spirit of the policy was the Liberal Party's special deal with a powerful company or industry; the strategy was devised in Detroit. Its essence was to restructure the local industry through an export programme, concentrate on specialisation and help car makers at the expense of parts manufacturers. In December 1981 a total of 33 Government backbenchers spearheaded by the 'drys', John Hyde and Jim Carlton, launched a last-ditch assault on the Lynch plan, already progressing through Cabinet, demanding an end to the special deal, a cut in Government protection and a more efficient car industry. At stake was the fundamental issue of how the Liberal Party governed: whether it stuck by protection for inefficiency or demanded a more efficient industry base. Despite their differences over the years the 'drys' had always supported Lynch. This was the issue on which they broke. Hyde and Carlton were categorical after federal Cabinet in December 1981 accepted the Lynch plan: Lynch was finished as a political force. Few politicians have lost their power base so swiftly. Hyde and Carlton spoke only for themselves but they represented the thinking members of the 'drys'. The politician to whom their allegiance was now given was John Howard. This power shift had occurred before the parliamentary session began in February 1982.

In early March 1982 Lynch tried to resuscitate his career and he emerged from the depths thundering about 'millionaires on the pension' and pointing towards the need for a means test on pensions. Lynch said that by the year 2000 the number of Australians over 65 would have risen by 60 per cent and the welfare burden would be crippling. Much of the Liberal Party was agog with disbelief. The Lowe by-election was only days away and every Liberal knew that Lowe was heavily populated with pensioners; in the older suburbs like Strathfield they were better-off pensioners. Lynch's political judgement was known to be deft. Liberals asked each other how he could have made such a blunder. The 'smart' answer was that Lynch was trying to undermine Fraser on the eve of the Lowe by-election, because he wanted Fraser's job. But in politics the 'smart' explanation is often too Machiavellian by half. This was such a case.

On 3 March during a Cabinet interlude in sultry Brisbane reporters met with Lynch to sort out the mystery of his intervention. 'It's an issue that's meant a great deal to me personally over a long period,' Lynch said, balancing his hefty cigar on an ashtray. The media asked Lynch when the Government would act. Ah, that was a trickier matter, Lynch replied. The problem was really a 20-year one, but of course, Governments could not wait 20 years before tackling it. Someone had to start the ball rolling. The media probed Lynch: how long could the Government wait? Lynch volunteered five years. When asked if he felt Governments could afford to wait *that* long, Lynch was uncertain. But he was certain that the people in Lowe were not involved 'in this exercise at all'.[3] Bill Hayden, determined to cruel the Government's chance of rationalising welfare in the same way Fraser had intimidated him from his low protection stance, declared: 'It's another kick in the teeth for tens of thousands of aged and retired people.'

The obvious reason Lynch unburdened himself was to regain currency with the free-market lobby which was gaining more publicity for itself and its ideas month by month. Lynch had read the Liberal climate correctly but his response was so clumsy that it accentuated his decline. The incident also revealed the political difficulties of taking the tough decisions on welfare, protection and wages which the politicians usually sought to avoid. What Lynch did not say was that the previous year during the budget Cabinet had taken an initial decision to impose an income test for pensioners over 70. But it was reversed at Fraser's behest a few days later on political grounds.

As Andrew Peacock scanned the political horizon in early 1982 searching for the hills from which he could attack, one vantage point lay outstanding. It was the Victorian state election at which the oldest peak on the Liberal map would almost certainly fall. Victoria was the cradle of the Liberal Party and with the exception of McMahon had produced every Liberal leader. Much of the coalition success at federal level had been based on the chronic divisions inside the Victorian ALP. But politics is never static and Victoria was being transformed by the dual forces of Liberal decay and Labor resurgence. The full fruits of Whitlam's 1971 federal intervention in Victoria were about to be reaped. Peacock saw the inevitable demise of the 27-year-old Liberal state Government as a political and psychological lever which he could use to highlight the need for a new Liberal leadership at the national level.

The Peacock challenge bore a striking similarity to the Hawke challenge. Both pretenders remained somewhat distant from the parliamentary parties whose support they were trying to secure. But Peacock unlike Hawke lacked the surge of popularity in the electorate which ultimately carried Hawke to power. Peacock also confronted a more formidable opponent in Fraser than Hawke did in Hayden. Peacock's mistake was that he did not sufficiently control his own challenge and insist on rigorous tactics from his supporters. The 'leak' can be a potent political weapon, but without shrewd judgement it can be lethal for the originator. Peacock's closest supporters gave an unmistakable signal of the challenge to senior press gallery reporters. The story created its own momentum, but it came far too early for Peacock who was well short of the numbers.

On 24 March 1982 Michelle Grattan wrote in a front-page report in *The Age*: 'Mr Andrew Peacock is poised to challenge the Prime Minister, Mr Fraser, for leadership of the Liberal Party if the Liberals lose next week's Victorian election, his supporters say.' The Peacock supporters kept confirming the story and the press kept writing it. Fraser knew the showdown was imminent. He spent most of 24 March conferring with his senior ministers, Lynch, Carrick, Howard and Street. The ministers correctly judged that the leak would damage Peacock since it portrayed him as the architect of division—despite Peacock's denial that he was responsible for the story. At this stage Lynch argued that a statement should be issued to reaffirm confidence in Fraser. Lynch saw this as a chance to repudiate the speculation that he was trying to distance himself from the Prime Minister. Tony Eggleton felt a statement was unnecessary and would only maintain the momentum of the challenge story. But Lynch, whose deputy's job would be in grave jeopardy in any challenge, carried the day. In a statement issued at 9.15 p.m. after a full ministry meeting Sir Phillip said:

> The Prime Minister has the full support of all Liberal ministers and this statement is made with their full knowledge and concurrence. I have a very close and effective relationship with the Prime Minister. Suggestions to the contrary are false and mischievous.

The next day Eggleton's judgement was vindicated as the Lynch statement tended to depict Fraser as a beleaguered Prime Minister weaker than the numbers indicated. The Peacock supporters had tentative plans for a spill motion against Fraser on 21 April, the first scheduled party meeting after the 3 April Victorian poll. Fraser, as usual in a crisis from within, became accessible to the media. But Tamie Fraser trumped him when she declared: 'I just think Andrew Peacock has been an ego-tripper from way back . . . He throws a few crumbs and calls gully, gully, gully . . .' Malcolm was delighted; the press debated the meaning of gully, gully, gully.

Meanwhile the Liberal Party opened its divisions to the world. Peacock challenged Fraser to settle the issue by calling an immediate party meeting. In the curious doubletalk of politics Peacock then claimed that he was not challenging 'at the moment'. He attacked Lynch for creating a furore which could only distract the Liberal Party's energies. But the concern which Fraser and Peacock both vented for their Victorian brothers was more feigned than real. They had written off the Victorian Liberal Government and were engrossed in their own power struggle.

Two of Peacock's most trenchant critics inside the Government, Carrick and Howard, went public dismissing Peacock's claims to be taken seriously. Howard again punctured the myths still alive in the Peacock camp that he would join the challenger in a joint assault. Carrick branded the Peacock move as 'outrageous' and concocted in order to damage the Victorian party. The same day Malcolm Fraser went to a Treasury Gardens lunch for the

Australian Children's Television Foundation and tumbled off his chair onto the ground amid much laughter. Fraser denied it was an omen.

The true complexities of the struggle now emerged. The Peacock supporters did not have sufficient numbers to carry a leadership spill in their own right. Their numbers were accurately judged by Fraser's supporters at no more than 25 in contrast to their claim of 40 out of the 81-strong parliamentary party. Peacock could only get a spill by attracting another block of votes and the most obvious group was the free-market lobby. In his capacity as informal leader of the 'drys' John Hyde favoured a spill motion to dispense with Fraser, whom he regarded as a Prime Minister compromised too often. Hyde had already repudiated what he branded the 'Führer principle'—denying the existence of genuine problems—which he considered dominated Fraser's outlook. But if a spill motion were carried, Hyde wanted to make Howard, not Peacock, Liberal leader. He launched his own campaign to this end, provoking a response of generous embarrassment from Howard himself. Howard's position was that he would support Fraser as leader and that meant opposing a spill motion. But Howard now decided that if the spill motion were carried and Fraser deposed, then he would run for leader against Peacock. But because of Hyde's position Howard made a public appeal to his supporters so they could be in no doubt of his own attitude. The Treasurer said he was 'implacably opposed' to a spill and asked his supporters to vote accordingly.

Lynch went to Fraser on the weekend of 27–28 March and effectively passed in the deputy leadership. Lynch had been considering a business career for some time. He remained in 1980 at Fraser's request in order to deny Peacock the deputy's job. But Lynch knew that his position was in jeopardy in the latest Peacock challenge which was likely to open up both leaderships. He suggested to Fraser that he might step aside rather than be defeated; they both knew that Howard had sufficient standing to assume the deputy's job and, if necessary, fight Peacock for it. The logic behind Lynch's decision was the fear of Fraser's supporters that Peacock, having been defeated by Fraser for the top job, might challenge and defeat Lynch for the deputy's job. This would produce the unworkable, a Fraser–Peacock combination.

Lynch's decision would have far-reaching consequences for the course of politics beyond anything that could have been predicted at the time. Once Lynch went as deputy he would leave the Parliament soon after. This, in itself, would not shake politics but it would mean a by-election in Flinders, a difficult seat for the Fraser Government. So this prospect loomed on the horizon, but still far off.

Fraser and Peacock went to ground during the week before the Victorian election. Both men were closeted with their confidants discussing their tactics.

Tony Eggleton virtually moved onto Fraser's personal staff for the duration of the party crisis. The big question for Fraser was whether to call an early party meeting after the state election in a pre-emptive strike against Peacock. The issue for Peacock was how to gather his support without appearing to undermine the Liberal Party itself. Occasionally there was a break in the latent pressure. Press gallery members were startled one evening to get phone calls from NSW backbencher Jack Birney saying he wanted a 'high noon' between Peacock and Fraser and calling upon them to come out in the street with guns blazing.

On Friday 2 April Fraser spoke to both Lynch and Howard and finalised his strategy. Lynch would stand down thereby allowing Howard a clear run at the deputy's job. The transition from Lynch to Howard would please Hyde's free-market lobby and it would also advance Howard to the point of seriously challenging Peacock for the leadership succession. This scenario assumed a special party meeting.

Fraser had also decided that unless Peacock formally declared the challenge after the 3 April Victorian election then he would seize the initiative and declare it himself. Fraser's calculations were assisted by further publication of Peacock's plans. The Peacock camp told the media that Peacock would hold a full-scale press conference in Melbourne on Sunday 4 April, but that he was not expected to call a showdown. Peacock, in fact, was caught in a dilemma of his own making. He had precipitated the leadership crisis but could not bring it to a climax because he lacked sufficient support in the parliamentary party to win or even make the contest close.

John Cain became the new Victorian Premier with a sweeping mandate on 3 April and the next afternoon Peacock called upon the Liberal Party throughout the nation to make 'a new start'. Peacock declared:

> The Liberals lost ground because the electorate no longer believed the Liberals
> to be the party of economic growth, social progress and opportunity . . .
> Today the situation confronting an unpopular federal Liberal Government
> is that without a new start in policy and approach, including new policies for
> growth, we face federal defeat.

However, despite the best efforts of the press, Peacock declined to challenge Fraser.

As soon as the Prime Minister's aides told him of Peacock's reluctance, Fraser moved in for the kill. At his Treasury Place office that evening he announced a special Liberal Party meeting for 8 April, just five days later. He told colleagues the Liberal Party was 'bleeding to death' over the leadership issue and insisted that the party meeting must 'face the issue and end the speculation once and for all'. This decision was taken only after exhaustive personal consultation between Fraser and senior Liberals in both the parliamentary and organisational wings. Fraser left nothing to chance. He was aiming not just to defeat Peacock, but win by a convincing margin which, in itself, would silence the pretender. In his statement Fraser said:

> Speculation about leadership challenges in the Liberal Party has continued for virtually a whole year and it has obviously been promoted. It has come to a head twice, in the middle of CHOGM and then again ten days before the Victorian election. It has distracted Australia and disturbed the Liberal Party profoundly . . .

The next day, 5 April, Fraser flew to Tasmania for a sweep from Burnie to Hobart. During the morning he visited the Edgell potato factory with Ray Groom, the man he had once sacked as Housing Minister and an assumed Peacock supporter. Fraser concentrated as the management explained the intricacies of potato-chip production; but he also had a word with Groom. Later that day Groom enunciated from Burnie the Liberal vision of the future by calling for a Fraser–Howard leadership team. The Peacock camp was dismayed. Then Jim Killen, a longstanding Peacock friend, declared for Fraser. Peacock belatedly announced that he would in fact challenge Fraser at the Thursday meeting. Fraser in turn welcomed the statement: 'I think I am glad that Andrew has announced what he did about wanting to stand against me.' That night ministers gathered at Hobart's Wrest Point Casino for the next day's Cabinet meeting. Lynch arrived about 9.00 p.m. and went into talks with Fraser and Eggleton.

Tuesday 6 April broke on Tasmania as a bitter autumn day with howling winds. Lynch told Howard that morning that his decision was final. Just before Cabinet broke for lunch he announced his intention to resign as deputy leader. Several ministers were stunned. A long session ensued with minister after minister showering praise upon Lynch, who had been deputy since he was elected behind Snedden after the fall of the McMahon Government ten years earlier. But the Liberal announcements to the media were made in the gutter and on the kerbside of the Hobart Commonwealth Centre; ministers were waylaid by a stampede of journalists amid the Hobart gale. It was typical of the Fraser years that such a historic transition was handled with little dignity for its participants.

Howard announced his candidature but declared that he would not conduct a public campaign: 'My colleagues know me well enough.' He added that he did not need Fraser's permission to seek the post. Tasmanian identity and minister for the Capital Territory Michael Hodgman described Lynch as 'my mentor, counsellor and friend'; as a fellow Catholic he applauded Lynch's 'deep commitment to our faith' and announced that he would enter the ballot. The main message Fraser conveyed was that a 'sad day' had come with Lynch's exit as deputy. Health Minister Michael MacKellar signalled he would probably become a candidate. But the big surprise came during the Commonwealth Reception that evening at Wrest Point when Ian Viner, sensing the waning of his political star, told reporters he 'would consider running'. Lynch showed that the anti-Peacock sentiment lingered to the end by declaring it would be 'impossible' for Fraser to work with Peacock. Leah Lynch re-entered the public arena with a pithy summary of the power realities. She explained that Lynch had wanted to quit last time, but 'John Howard didn't have the numbers and they didn't want to wear Peacock. It was as simple as that.'[4] Lynch had the satisfaction of knowing that his resignation would contribute to another Peacock defeat.

The real fight was virtually over; the final figures were tallied at the party meeting two days later. Fraser declared the leadership vacant which allowed a head-to-head contest. He defeated Peacock 54-27, an exact two-to-one margin. The Prime Minister had achieved his aim since this majority buried the Peacock putsch. But Fraser did far more than simply defeat Peacock. He facilitated the transition from Lynch to Howard, thereby refurbishing his own structure. Howard defeated MacKellar 45-27 in the deputy's ballot. (Hodgman had polled 22 votes and Viner 5 in the first ballot.) Peacock's challenge had produced the ironic result of confirming Fraser's leadership and promoting Peacock's long-term rival to the deputy leadership.

However in the longer term the result guaranteed Peacock's future. It proved that one-third of the Liberal Party wanted him as leader. Those numbers would stick by Peacock when Fraser finally left and the contest became Peacock versus Howard. Peacock himself admitted that Fraser polled a big majority from within the existing ministry. That is to say, on the Liberal backbench the numbers for Fraser and Peacock were fairly evenly matched. The result was a relief for Peacock in that it brought to a climax the course upon which he had embarked with his April 1981 resignation. The experience was valuable in Peacock's maturity as a power politician and party operator. When he eventually returned to the Fraser Cabinet in late 1982 he seemed purged of his earlier paranoia about Fraser and better equipped to become the eventual successor. It should be noted that the Prime Minister could have avoided much of the trouble with Peacock if he had been prepared to identify Peacock as his expected successor. Peacock had always been the front-runner.

Howard had appeared to be closing the gap at various stages, but Peacock's appeal was too strong. However Fraser could never reconcile himself to this reality even though he acknowledged it.

The Prime Minister used the settlement of the Liberal leadership issue as a platform from which to fire his political artillery at the Labor Party. His own house had been chronically divided for most of the period since the 1980 election. Now this division had been resolved Fraser exploited his enhanced leadership stature and redoubled his attack on the Labor Party. Fraser launched his assault on Bill Hayden with a new vigour at exactly the same time that Bob Hawke began to move on Hayden from behind.

10
Hayden stumbles

Look, mate! If Rin-tin-tin was around now at the peak of his popularity, he'd be killing Hawke and myself and everyone else.

Bill Hayden, June 1982

Bill Hayden was a victim of the more scientific and psychological approach to politics symbolised in the 1980s by opinion polls, market research reports and a new breed of party professionals. The ALP machine was proud of its election campaign expertise. Its backroom strategists diagnosed the electorate the way a psychologist probes the psyche of an emotionally agitated patient. One of the keys to the revival of ALP fortunes around the nation in the 1982–83 period was the strength of the party organisation and its election professionalism. The professionals in turn exercised a pervasive influence upon the party and facilitated its embrace of pragmatism. Labor Premiers John Cain in Victoria and Brian Burke in Western Australia both won elections after internal party coups in which their documented electoral appeal was decisive. Years earlier Neville Wran had shown the way. Bill Hayden did not lose the Labor Party in one stroke, but one of the first and most important groups he lost were the election professionals—the men who would run Labor's campaign for office.

The most important survey work for the ALP was conducted by its commissioned agency, Australian National Opinion Polls (ANOP), whose Managing Director was Rod Cameron. In his decade-long association with the party Cameron had become a principal architect of its campaign strategies at both federal and state level. In March–April 1982 ANOP conducted a major, Australia-wide qualitative assessment involving 30 discussion groups with swinging voters. This survey work required a skilful discussion leader to extract from the small group of swingers their real perception of issues, leaders and parties. Most of this qualitative research was conducted under the supervision of Cameron's colleague Margaret Gibbs. After Cameron had written the report, he warned National Secretary McMullan that Hayden had shown up very badly, but he intended to give Hayden a full briefing. McMullan agreed.

On 18 May 1982, when Cameron, Gibbs and McMullan went to Hayden's Parliament House office for the session, they found the Opposition leader in a supremely confident mood. He pointed to the Morgan polls which had shown Labor about four per cent ahead for a long time, convinced it meant certain victory. Hayden had not performed so well in the poll of leadership ratings measured against Fraser. But Cameron had previously advised him that it was possible to win office even with a low personal rating on the leader's poll. Margaret Thatcher's first win was a classic example, as Hayden kept reminding himself. But this qualitative work was a disaster for Hayden. Its significance was the perceptions swinging voters held of Fraser and Hayden. Fraser was seen as arrogant and deceitful, generally disliked, a snob, a squire, out of touch, aloof and unpopular. But he had one major redeeming feature. Fraser was a strong leader: hard, tough, dominant, ruthless (evidently a plus) and willing to stamp on misbehaviour. Cameron then described Hayden's own image. He said something along these lines:

> Your image is very much as it was two years ago. You are seen as competent, smart, a good bloke, you have made progress in grabbing the theme of looking after the family, you are seen as honest and modest, but also as weak, wishy-washy, a whinger, and people often just cannot understand what you are saying. They see you as carping, supercritical and never having a good word for anyone. You are not seen as a strong leader.

Cameron read out a number of comments made by swinging voters, the archetypical line being, 'I hate Fraser, but I'll probably vote for him because I don't think Hayden has the strength to lead.'[1]

Cameron believed that Hayden's image was irretrievably bad. He thought this perception of leadership weakness could not be overcome as Hayden was now in his fifth year as leader. His image was too entrenched; he was no longer a new leader whose image was still capable of being adjusted significantly. Cameron told Hayden that in his assessment, the qualitative work meant that in an election Labor's current four per cent lead would be eroded so that only about two per cent was really solid. This meant a close result. Cameron continued, saying he believed Hayden could still win. Fraser's image was bad. Overall the question was whether the Government's poor record would nullify

Fraser's perceived leadership strength over Hayden. Cameron said strength was the most important leadership quality influencing swinging voters.

Hayden said nothing in response. Cameron's instincts told him that beneath the silence there was a strong reaction. Leaving Parliament House he said to McMullan, 'I think he took that very badly.' McMullan disagreed. In fact, Cameron's report was a lethal document for Hayden. One Hayden staffer said later that it 'put a conclusion which could only lead you to believe Hayden had to be replaced as leader'. The seeds of mutual distrust were sown between Cameron and Hayden. This was a significant falling out between the party leader and party pollster. Cameron later remarked about this briefing: 'Hayden was the only leader I knew who couldn't cope with this sort of news.' Cameron contrasted Hayden unfavourably with other former Labor leaders to whom he had given adverse reports, including Harry Holgate, Tommy Burns, Clyde Holding and Don Dunstan.

After Cameron's briefing Hayden's staff drew on the resources of the parliamentary library from which they got a second opinion critical of ANOP and challenging the validity of Cameron's results. Hayden even contemplated using this document inside the party to rebuff Cameron. He took the report to one strategy meeting that Cameron attended, showed him the paper and warned him to 'be careful' about the rigour of ANOP's work. Hayden believed he was being 'set up' by Cameron. He had every reason to be worried both for his election and leadership prospects, since the ANOP research would inevitably be used by the Hawke forces against Hayden. Cameron briefed key party figures on his qualitative research. They included National President Neville Wran and the two major State Secretaries, Graham Richardson and Bob Hogg. Hawke was also well acquainted with the ANOP results either directly from Cameron or through another source.

Cameron assessed politicians in terms of their effectiveness in the marketplace. He strove to educate both ALP politicians and party workers to understand the 'new politics' that had been shaped by mass communications, particularly television. Cameron tried to persuade Labor to take a more pragmatic approach towards winning elections, not just in the campaign period but in shaping the agenda during the parliamentary term. He had formed a natural alliance with the 1970s generation of powerful and astute ALP secretaries and machine men. The first had been David Combe, and Cameron and Combe collaborated on every federal campaign from 1974 onwards. Cameron also acted as pollster for every state Labor branch and had formed close ties with Graham Richardson, who embodied the NSW machine philosophy of power through pragmatism, and Bob Hogg, who got much credit for the Victorian election of the Cain Labor Government. Cameron slid easily into a working relationship with Combe's successor, Bob McMullan, who had previously been the Western Australian Secretary. Throughout 1982 there was a deepening belief among these party professionals who had to organise and run the ALP campaign that Hayden was unlikely to win.

Cameron's research did not have a seminal impact in its own right. Its function was to hasten the assessment the party professionals and many Caucus members were already making. Graham Richardson said later: 'The truth is that we were always going to challenge; the research made it legitimate.' In fact the research tended to gain the status of documentary proof of political instinct. The party professionals would never admit it shaped their outlook; but to those not automatically pro-Hawke it must have been a significant influence.

At a different level the Caucus itself always had trouble actually identifying the 11 seats needed to fall for Hayden to win Government. It was one thing to read the Morgan polls pointing to an ALP victory, it was another for the politicians to be convinced that particular seats had been won or lost. Many Caucus members harboured grave doubts, fearing that on voting day the swing to Labor might suddenly evaporate. Backbenchers knew there was little fire for Hayden among the party rank and file. It was a conventional wisdom within Caucus that Labor's lead was because of Government failure and not Opposition success. Caucus felt that if Labor won it would merely reflect that ancient axiom: 'Governments lose office'. The doubts about Hayden's capacity to win were not new; they were a permanent feature of his leadership.

For most of the previous Parliament during 1977–80, the Caucus had never expected Hayden to perform and poll as well as he did in the October 1980 election. In his post-election report, David Combe captured the mood:

> For many months there was a spectacular dichotomy between the party's own assessment of its prospects (shared by most media observers and evidently the Government), and that reflected in the opinion polls. Hence we found the leader spending much of his time persuading the party and the media to entertain more seriously the likelihood of an ALP victory. It was only in the campaign's final phase that the possibility was given any credence.

The same malaise was afflicting the party in the next Parliament and it betrayed one of Hayden's great leadership defects. He lacked the inspirational ability to enthuse the Labor Party at almost any level from grassroots to shadow ministry. The result was that the party, rather than radiating confidence of inevitable victory which a margin of only 1.4 per cent should justify, was uncertain and unsure. The 'will we or won't we?' syndrome was rife throughout the ALP. It seemed that even when he was on top, Hayden lacked the stature to convince his own colleagues.

It was in this climate in June 1982 that Hayden stumbled badly—the decisive break for which Hawke had waited for 20 months. Within a few weeks all the doubts about Hayden were reinforced and given fresh credence. The issue was nuclear warships, one so far on the periphery of politics as to be almost irrelevant. But Hayden reached out and seized defeat from the jaws of victory. He was revealed as a leader lacking authority, judgement and stature in a fashion so comprehensive that his greatest supporters were shocked.

The issue began when newly elected Premier John Cain moved to implement the Victorian ALP policy on uranium and declare Victoria a nuclear-free zone, a mere gesture since it had no uranium mining or nuclear industry but one that would placate the socialist left. Cain wrote to Fraser on 27 May saying that Victoria 'will not permit visits of nuclear-powered or nuclear-armed vessels'. He said:

> It would be appreciated if your Government could advise relevant foreign
> Governments . . . In each case of a proposed visit to Victoria by a naval vessel
> of a country controlling tactical nuclear weapons, it would also be appreciated
> if you could obtain from the relevant foreign Government an assurance that no
> nuclear weapons are carried.

This letter intruded into the federal Government's constitutional responsibility for defence and foreign affairs; it was ignorant of international conduct in its assumption that Governments gave 'non-nuclear weapon' assurances; it enunciated a policy with the potential to affect foreign policy and the ANZUS. It was patronising and foolish.

In his reply of 3 June Fraser explained that in 1976 after a major review the federal Government had announced the resumption of visits by nuclear-powered ships. (There had been a ban on such visits since 1971 pending the inquiry.) Fraser said that since 1976 there had been 44 visits with 'comprehensive radiation monitoring' undertaken in each case. But the key part of Fraser's letter concerned ships that carried nuclear weapons, such ships being either nuclear-powered or conventional. Fraser said nuclear-weapon states had a 'long-standing policy' of not disclosing whether or not nuclear arms were carried on a particular warship. The Prime Minister's reply continued:

> Australia must be a reliable partner to the United States because of our ANZUS
> obligations, and to the United Kingdom because of our traditional links. In the

discharge of our responsibilities Australia must be able, at the very least, to provide ports and port facilities for the replenishment and servicing of warships of those and other friendly nations.

Implementation of the policy set out in your letter would have the effect of excluding from Victorian ports all warships of the navies of the United States, the United Kingdom and France. In the last eight years there have been over 500 visits to Australian ports by warships of our nuclear-capable friends and allies. You will see, from these numbers, that prohibition of entry by these vessels would cause serious damage to our relationships with those countries . . .

Fraser said Gough Whitlam had accepted this position and quoted from Whitlam to demonstrate. He asked Cain to 'look again' since ANZUS was at issue. A few days later the issue became public and Fraser released the letters.[2]

Significantly Cain had alerted Hayden. There had been an exchange of letters between them on the issue. Hayden indicated he was not worried about visits by nuclear-powered ships but shared Cain's opposition to ships carrying nuclear weapons. So Hayden had his own considered position.

Fraser sought advice from the Commonwealth law officers on the steps needed to assert the federal Government's constitutional powers and prevent Cain implementing his policy. Federal Cabinet considered the issue when it met in Darwin on 8 June. Fraser was incensed at the implications of Cain's stance and set out to mobilise public opinion against Cain and the ALP. As usual when his position was strong, Fraser escalated his rhetoric. He warned:

We will do anything we can within our power to stop Mr Cain destroying Australia's defence and foreign policy, to stop Mr Cain destroying ANZUS and to stop Mr Cain in the name of the socialist left of Victoria leading this country towards a non-aligned defence and foreign policy . . . We have the constitutional authority. If it needs a change to the Commonwealth statute, then the Commonwealth statutes will, in fact, be changed.[3]

Hayden was in Hobart the next day, 9 June, for an ALP National Executive meeting to authorise federal intervention into the Tasmanian branch in a bid to improve the vote in Labor's weakest state. Late that afternoon he left the meeting and gave an interview to *The Sydney Morning Herald* and *The Age*, in which he declared himself. A Hayden Labor Government would not allow warships carrying nuclear weapons access to Australian ports. Hayden said, 'It would be totally undesirable for Australia or any parts of Australia to become nuclear weapon arsenals or storage or transit points.'[4] He made it clear that his intention was not to ban all warships. He wanted to persuade the

Americans to modify their 'non-disclosure' policy so that non-nuclear-armed warships, of which there would be very many, could still enter our ports.

Suddenly the nuclear ships issue became more important. The criticism Fraser deployed against Cain on foreign policy grounds now applied to Hayden. But it assumed greater force because Hayden was the alternative Prime Minister. The timing was perfect for Fraser. The ANZUS council meeting with representatives from the United States, Australia and New Zealand was due to be held in Canberra on 21–22 June. Discussion of the nuclear issue was now inevitable.

Contrary to popular views at the time Hayden had not made an inadvertent lapse. His miscalculation sprang from the deliberate foreign policy thrust which he and his deputy and Shadow Foreign Minister Lionel Bowen had developed. Hayden was a radical on the Australian–American relationship and had very little intellectual commitment to the alliance. By 1982 Hayden had been Opposition leader for five years without making a substantial visit to the United States, but he had been to Europe, Asia, the Middle East and South America. Hayden had a keen interest in foreign policy and had developed a framework in which he perceived the alliance.

His position was outlined in a major interview in mid-1981 and began with the need for drastic changes in the alliance. Hayden believed that ANZUS 'had to be kept within its context', defined by 'the limitations that American support would only be provided according to the constitutional processes of the USA and that means very simply on the decision of the American Congress'. He then argued that American support was not automatic and that on the occasion when Australia had wanted to invoke the alliance—the crisis in relations with Indonesia over West Irian in the early 1960s—the Menzies Government found that 'there was no succour or consolation from the Americans'. Therefore, on balance, the alliance had 'worked very much in favour of the USA' which enjoyed, among other advantages, a very large level of foreign investment in Australia. Hayden believed in a more independent Australian foreign policy, arguing that 'it would be quite wrong to presume that the alliance means that there is no room for disagreement and that there is no justification for striking out very much on an independent role'. Finally he said that while a Labor Government would accept the operation of US bases in Australia, this was conditional, and 'we would not be prepared to have ourselves locked in by default to a situation where a whole chain of events is unleashed which drags us into a nuclear conflict'.[5]

After the 1980 election Hayden and Bowen began to apply this approach. For example, Labor opposed Australian participation in the Sinai multinational peacekeeping force. Hayden and Bowen visited the major US bases in

Australia in March 1981. While they endorsed the basic operations at the two most sensitive facilities, Pine Gap and Nurrungar, they concluded the operations of the North West Cape base infringed Australia's sovereignty. The base was a relay station transmitting messages from US command centres elsewhere in the world to its nuclear submarines in the Indian Ocean; any firing orders sent to these submarines would go through North West Cape. Hayden warned that a Labor Government would seek to renegotiate the agreement to provide that 'Australia's consent is mandatory for all orders to initiate military action which flows from the station'. Secondly it would seek assurances for Australia that the station would not be used to transmit messages for a 'first-strike nuclear attack'. Hayden said that if the United States refused to accept such provisions, 'then we would ask them to wind down the operations of North West Cape as rapidly as possible'.[6] This policy held grave implications for ANZUS. It was only later that Hayden retreated and Bowen produced a political formula—the stationing of a special Australian officer in Washington liaising with the US command structure—that resolved the deadlock.

In May 1982 when US Vice-President George Bush visited Australia, Hayden pressed him during their talks on the CIA's role in local politics. Bush assured Hayden there had been no interference. Hayden accepted Bush's word but then asked the Vice-President whether he had personally investigated the allegations about the CIA, the Nugan Hand Bank and the destabilisation of the Whitlam Government. Bush said no. Hayden replied that the ALP could not be certain unless Bush had personally investigated the matter. The two men then discussed the best way the US administration could assure the Labor Party. Later Bush told a National Press Club lunch that the US could work with either side of Australian politics: 'I am convinced that we would be able to work well with whomever the people of Australia put in, and I don't see any specific item being a stumbling block to that.'[7]

The real prelude to the nuclear ships crisis was ALP opposition to the B–52 agreement between the Fraser Government and Reagan administration in early 1981. Fraser had a global view of politics and believed that Australia, as part of the Western alliance, should assist America's international position both politically and militarily. The Prime Minister's most important offer to the US was Cockburn Sound near Perth as a home port for the US Navy, but he also offered to assist in B–52 surveillance and training. The US declined the first offer but accepted the second. Fraser tabled the agreement on 11 March 1981. The B–52s were based at Guam and one of their basic purposes had always been the delivery of nuclear weapons onto the Soviet Union. The agreement provided for B–52 staging operations through Darwin and low-level navigation training *en route*, which involved Cape York

Peninsula. Both Fraser and Defence Minister Killen made it clear that the agreement was part of the overall US build-up in the Indian Ocean and Middle East following the Afghanistan and Iranian crises. Fraser put the agreement squarely in the context of the ANZUS Treaty, another example of practical defence cooperation.

The agreement did not mention nuclear weapons and this was consistent with US policy never to admit or deny whether its planes carried such weapons. But the Fraser Government had penetrated at least one step into this orthodoxy. Foreign Minister Tony Street received an assurance from Secretary of State Al Haig, documented and witnessed during their Washington talks, that the B–52s would be unarmed and would carry no bombs. When Fraser's statement to Parliament was being prepared, the contents of this Street–Haig understanding were incorporated word-for-word into the Prime Minister's text. Therefore Fraser was able to tell Parliament that the B–52 flights 'will be unarmed and will carry no bombs', although the agreement as such did not mention this issue. This was certainly a diplomatic concession to Australia. The assurance allowed Australian politicians to say at home that there would be no armed nuclear weapons carried without our consent, yet the agreement itself would not create trouble for the US with its other allies because it did not contain explicit concessions breaching the 'non-disclosure' rule on nuclear weapons.[8]

Hayden took note of the firm position and guarantees Fraser was able to give about nuclear weapons. But the Opposition leader was also influenced by Bowen, who argued that the US should give more definite assurances in the agreement itself. In Parliament Hayden recalled 'the deceit, the downright lying' by President Nixon and Secretary of State Kissinger over America's bombing of Kampuchea. Hayden and Bowen opposed the B–52 agreement and committed a Labor Government to renegotiate it with a view to having Fraser's assurance on no nuclear weapons written into the agreement itself.[9]

In June 1982 Hayden saw a parallel between the warships issue and the B–52 bombers. Before he went public in Hobart, his two main staffers, Mike Costello and Alan Ramsey, told him to couch his position towards nuclear-armed warships in exactly the same context Fraser had put the Government's position in relation to nuclear-armed bombers. They believed that if Hayden did this, he would remain on safe political ground both at home and abroad. Hayden tried to follow this formula but went too far. The irony of his position was that he had been sucked into it by Fraser's B–52 agreement. He felt that if Fraser was able to say whether or not the B–52s carried nuclear weapons, then he should be able to persuade the Americans to say whether or not their warships carried such weapons. It was one of his greatest follies and directly contributed to his political demise.

Hayden made two critical mistakes on this issue. Firstly he enunciated a position as a *fait accompli* which the US had to accept or reject. Secondly he misjudged the difference between operations of aircraft and ships. Fraser had pointed out that while Australia needed to agree with the tactical and strategic objective of any B–52 mission launched from Australian soil, this was quite different to providing rest and replenishment for ships which come to port in the course of normal patrolling duties.[10] However in a wider context Hayden had been taking too assertive a position on the Australian–American relationship across too broad a front, too confident that both public opinion and the Americans would follow him. Sooner or later the probability was that he would push too far and run into Uncle Sam. The Americans had observed Labor opposition to the Sinai force, North West Cape and the B–52 agreement, but on nuclear warships Hayden overreached himself. It was to prove a salutory lesson in the politics of the alliance and in defining the domestic political limitations imposed by ANZUS. Hayden was repudiated by both the Reagan administration and his own deputy Lionel Bowen.

In response to questions from Australian journalists in Washington the State Department issued the following comment:

> We believe this issue is a domestic one in which US intervention would be inappropriate. However, quite apart from the present dispute, it should be clear that access to allied ports and airfields for US ships and aircraft is critical to our efforts to maintain a strategic deterrence. It would be difficult, if not impossible, for the US to carry out its responsibilities to assist effectively in the defence of its allies if it is denied the use of their ports.

This US statement left no scope for interpretation. It put the ANZUS Treaty on the line. Hayden's office was furious, bitter at what it branded American intervention in domestic policies. The US was intervening to defend its interests. Access to ports, notably in the South Pacific, was becoming a political issue as the movement for a nuclear-free zone intensified. The US wanted to spell out the consequences for its allies.

The Fraser Government knew every move the Americans made. In mid-June Doug Anthony was in America and in regular phone contact with Fraser. On 14 June Tony Street told the Australian media that Vice-President Bush had expressed his concern about the warships issue to Anthony during their talks. Bush not only expressed concern, he allowed the Australian ministers to make his concern public. The Fraser Government and Reagan administration were orchestrating a campaign in harmony. Fraser had impaled Hayden on the ANZUS spike; now the Americans were turning him in the wind.

Shadow Foreign Minister Lionel Bowen was furious about Hayden's warship stance having been made without any reference to him. Bowen was responsible for the draft foreign policy going to the July ALP National Conference for approval. This document was available to Hayden, but he had not absorbed the message. The key paragraph said that Labor would 'oppose the storage of nuclear weapons on Australian territory and staging of operations involving nuclear weapons from Australian territory'. This formula allowed the transit visits of nuclear-armed ships. On 14 June journalists asked Bowen for his views and the deputy leader said the ALP accepted that the US could not identify which warships carried nuclear arms: 'We would not approve them basing nuclear-armed ships in Australia, but our policy has been to allow visits. They have always been allowed to come and, as far as the defence aspect is concerned, we should follow this practice.'[11] Hayden had been openly repudiated by his deputy.

After this statement the most important issue for Hayden became his own leadership. A humiliating retreat was as inevitable for Hayden as was the continuance of ANZUS under any Labor Government. Hayden had transgressed the line of electoral survival. He had also moved beyond the limits of party opinion; only the left would support his position. In a policy sense he had jeopardised the more independent foreign policy line which both he and Bowen had advocated. More significantly the fragility of his own leadership was being exposed. The whispering campaign against him had intensified dramatically as his warships torment continued. Some of his closest supporters were worried at Hayden's lack of judgement; their worry also deepened when Hayden sat pat, showing no signs of withdrawal. After five years as leader and a successful previous six months, one major mistake had provoked leadership speculation. Hawke could not fail to read the trend correctly. This was his main chance and he would seize it.

The warships issue came to a climax at the ANZUS council meeting in Canberra on 21–22 June. During the previous week Hayden had held out, waiting to talk to the Americans in a bid to reach some accord with them. It was another miscalculation. In the interim Fraser continued his campaign, arguing that Labor would smash ANZUS; the Labor Party grew more worried about the damage being inflicted on its electoral position and the poor leadership shown by Hayden. On the eve of the thirty-first ANZUS council Hayden gave his strongest endorsement of the alliance for some time saying, 'We are neither isolationist nor neutralist . . . We are committed to doing nothing that puts the alliance at risk.'

On Sunday evening, 20 June, Fraser hosted dinner at The Lodge for the ANZUS delegation leaders. Among those present included leader of the

US delegation and deputy Secretary of State Walter Stoessel, along with his Assistant Secretary, John Holdridge. The next morning both men were in Bill Hayden's office for talks with the Opposition leader. The meeting only lasted 30 minutes, but its impact was enduring. While Stoessel was subtle, Holdridge defended US interests in a ruthless and belligerent fashion, telling a surprised Hayden that the US would make no exceptions to its policy of 'non-disclosure' about nuclear weapons on planes or ships. If the Labor Party persisted in demanding such disclosure, then the United States would make it clear that under such ALP policy US naval ships would not visit Australia and B–52 bombers would not stage through Australia. It was made clear to Hayden that, on this basis, the ANZUS alliance would be in question. The Americans offered no concessions. They said they would make their deep concerns about Hayden's position a public matter.

Hayden said later he wished Australian diplomats would defend their national interests as vigorously as Stoessel and Holdridge had defended US interests against him. Holdridge's manner was aggressive, almost threatening. Hayden told the Americans that Labor policy would be finalised at the National Conference and explained the policy proposal. Stoessel told Hayden the US would not support any doctrine of a nuclear first-strike. He said visits to Australia of US naval ships were part of the maintenance of the US nuclear deterrent. He agreed with Hayden that the ANZUS Treaty was different from NATO and did not oblige the partners to react automatically.[12] The Americans left Hayden with nowhere to go but backwards.

The ANZUS meeting highlighted one of the basics of Australian politics over the past 30 years: that the alliance has been the property of the coalition. After the first day of the meeting Foreign Minister Street told the press that Stoessel was still concerned about the ALP's nuclear ships position—despite his meeting with Hayden. Practical cooperation between the Fraser Government and the US administration seemed to be flourishing. Meanwhile Hayden arranged a Sydney meeting with Bowen and other Caucus members to end Labor's debacle.

At the conclusion of the ANZUS meeting on 22 June Stoessel faced the press. He reiterated US policy and declined to comment on his meeting with Hayden. He pointed to the communiqué which said that the partners recognised American access to ports as a 'critical factor' in its efforts to 'carry out its responsibilities under the terms of the treaty.' Under questioning Stoessel refused to state his confidence in the capacity of the US to work with the ALP as an ANZUS partner. By this refusal he showed that the Americans remained unhappy about Labor's position. The ANZUS meeting finished as a triumph for Fraser and the US. The communiqué underlined the importance of port access and thereby legitimised the entire campaign the Prime Minister had waged in the previous three weeks.

Five hours after the release of the ANZUS communiqué in Canberra Hayden announced his backdown in Sydney. This followed a meeting with Bowen, Shadow Defence Minister Gordon Scholes, Gareth Evans, former Defence Minister Bill Morrison, and backbenchers Kim Beazley, Clyde Holding and Ralph Jacobi. In his press statement after the meeting Hayden adopted the Bowen position. It was the position which the press and the ALP always expected to be his only fallback.[13] Hayden succumbed to American pressure and the demand of the alliance. His retreat was more humiliating because it was made at the behest of the US. By waiting so long he further damaged relations between the US and the ALP. He failed to see the imperative of clarifying ALP policy before the ANZUS meeting, and not after. The three-week crisis had virtually transformed the political climate. It revealed the fragility of Hayden's authority. It suggested that Fraser, despite the immense political damage he had sustained in the previous 18 months, had a resilience and durability to hit back effectively; Fraser had secured US support in his campaign against Hayden.

The warships issue was a body blow for Hayden in his simultaneous struggle against both Fraser and Hawke. It was proof of all the opinion-poll results, namely, that Hayden lacked Fraser's strength. No other conclusion could be drawn from the incident. It was an injection of life into the confused ranks of the Fraser Government after more than 18 months of divisive upheaval, because it suggested that Fraser might still be re-elected. This very fear was accentuated throughout the Labor Party to Hawke's benefit. The challenger had always believed that Hayden lacked the true mettle of leadership. The warships issue reinforced this perception and reflected Hayden's continuing inability to sustain his performance.

By June 1982 it was obvious that the sweeping victory of the Victorian ALP under John Cain at the April state election was being turned against Hayden. Melbourne was the cradle of Hawke's support and the influence of the Melbourne opinion-making elite was starting to shape the political debate. Melbourne was the home of Hawke's centre-unity group, the ACTU, which was committed to his leadership, and the Melbourne *Age*, which ran a number of influential pro-Hawke pieces by its journalists and columnists. Finally Melbourne provided a prototype for the Hawke strategy. In an operation of surgical precision the Victorian ALP had removed its leader Frank Wilkes in favour of John Cain quite close to the state election and had then won a smashing victory. The moral drawn was that Canberra should act accordingly. The Victorian experience showed that any time before the election was soon enough; the closer the election the more imperative was the need.

In politics the dividing line between myth and reality is always fine and sometimes indiscernible. Politics is about mood and a great political leader by changing mood can change reality. As the vapour of defeatism swirled about Hayden, perceptions of men and events began to alter. The Victorian state election was initially seen as indicative of the national swing to Labor and hence a pointer to federal success. But the perception faded and then turned so that the state poll became a benchmark of Labor potential which Hayden could not himself repeat. The ALP fell victim to the opinion polls. The fortnightly Morgan poll published in *The Bulletin* began to cast a curious spell on the Caucus. Minuscule fluctuations had a ludicrously dramatic impact as Caucus shifted from despondency to delight. This was a great victory for Hawke, whose political career was fuelled by opinion-poll injections. Hawke studied the polls and distributed the opinions.

One poll on which either Hawke or his supporters were briefed was conducted by the market-research company Quantum, whose Managing Director was George Camakaris. Quantum had done extensive work for the Liberal Party for many years, mainly qualitative research. Camakaris was looking for a bigger slice of the political market and conducted a major qualitative survey on his own initiative, sending the results to Tony Eggleton. In May–June the Quantum survey was leaked to the media and received extensive coverage. It reinforced Cameron's ANOP research. Its significance, like that of the ANOP material, was that it undercut predictions of an ALP win based on quantitative, two-party preferred results which showed a swing of about four per cent to Labor. Both Cameron and Camakaris were saying that in an election campaign Hayden's weakness would cost him votes to Fraser. The Quantum report stated:

> Of the voters who claim the Liberal Party is effective in Government, the major unprompted or unaided reason being put forward is Fraser's strength and dominance . . .
>
> When compared with Fraser in the Liberal Party, Hayden's leadership appears an insignificant influence in the fortunes of the ALP . . .
>
> There is little doubt in our experience that Fraser has the very real potential to win through again. We cannot see this potential existing in Hayden . . .

The Camakaris survey showed Hawke excelling Fraser on almost every personality variable, including leadership strength. On the strength variable the main politicians rated out of ten: Hayden 5.3, Peacock 6.3, Fraser 7.9 and Hawke 8.4. The survey said:

> In times of insecurity people look for strength in their leaders. Fraser's got strength but he's also got the capacity to frighten them. Hawke's strength surpasses Fraser's, yet he's also got an image of a compassionate person who understands people.

The Quantum survey was publicised in both *The Sydney Morning Herald* and *The Age*.[14] In one sense it told the ALP nothing new, in another sense it told everything. In the context of the nuclear warships issue, such polls assumed a new force because they were being verified on the political stage.

The most potent and persuasive advocacy for Hawke came from his friend and social critic Phillip Adams, writing in *The Age* of 26 June, by which time the Hawke challenge was underway. Adams said:

> I've often seen Hawke walk into a room full of people and, within seconds, take command. Like it or not, he's a natural leader in a country crying out for leadership . . .
>
> The impact of media on Australian politics has been to create, for good or ill, a focus of attention on the leader—and Hayden is as stricken in that spotlight as one of the kangaroos in 'Wake in Fright' . . .
>
> In any case, if Hawke doesn't get the leadership, how will the ALP explain that to its party membership? More importantly, how will the party explain it to the voters at large? If Hawke doesn't lead the party, and lead it soon, a lot of Labor support will just fade, fade, fade away. It seems that the ornithological conflict between a hawk and a peacock may never take place, but in Hawke, Malcolm Fraser will confront someone in his own weight division.

This pressure took its toil on Hayden because he never knew how to combat it. He lapsed into excesses of justification and overcompensation which were never part of his real character. Hayden was always prepared to fight, but Hawke was too elusive an opponent and his ally was the communications industry itself, the medium through which politics was conducted. In late June 1982 Hayden declared:

> If you can't be tough in this game and take the strain then you should give it away . . . I can take the strain. If you look at my background, from a kid up, I've had to take the strain. I've had to fight my way through. Everything I've got, I've got because I was prepared to fight, I was prepared to hang in there and I've never given up on things that really count . . .[15]

In these comments Hayden betrayed his own desperation to convince himself, and the constraints of his own background. Knowing that he could never project a popular media image, he took refuge in self-assertion. He said:

> I can only be myself. I am not going to be a humbug. I am not going to be artificial. I'm certainly not going to be a half-baked vaudevillian to entertain people. I'll just rely on what I am and what I've got and the more important thing is the sorts of policies a party comes up with at election time . . . I was brought up in a community where it was generally regarded as the height of vulgarity to draw other people's attention to what you regarded as your virtues.[16]

Bob Hawke lacked these inhibitions and, with Melbourne cheering him on, he flew to Sydney to stitch together the alliance to make him leader.

11
Hawke strikes

Hawkey went over the top while the rest of us were still in the trenches putting on our boots.

Graham Richardson, July 1982

Hawke needed to win the NSW Labor leaders to transform his challenge from potential into reality. His invaluable NSW ally was the State Secretary, Graham Richardson, who had claims to being the best organiser and numbers man inside the Labor Party. Richardson and Hawke had a relationship of personal warmth and political rapport. They were constant companions in Sydney, having breakfast together in the presidential suite of the Boulevard Hotel, Hawke's Sydney base. Richardson had a commonsense view of Hawke and saw him as a great vote-winner, a natural leader and the obvious champion of the ALP right wing. Years earlier, during the 1972 and 1974 campaigns, Richardson had been Hawke's car driver and consequently knew more of Hawke's secrets and understood him better than most people. 'He helped me when I was a nobody,' Richardson said, underlining one of Hawke's great virtues: his capacity to treat men as equals. But Richardson was no longer a nobody. He was the chief organiser of the powerful NSW machine and believed that, at the right time, NSW had to move behind Hawke.

In May 1982 Hawke had visited both the National President, Neville Wran, and the ALP deputy, Lionel Bowen, in their Sydney offices. Hawke's advocacy at both meetings was that only he could assure the party of winning the next election. Hawke thought he had Wran's support, but the National President's view was that with rising unemployment Hayden should win anyway. Wran did not see a role for himself on the leadership issue and stayed neutral. Bowen was more important. The deputy was typically blunt with Hawke: 'You're right, I don't think we can win with Hayden.' Hawke asked

Bowen whether Labor could win with Hawke as leader. He replied, 'Perhaps. But I doubt if you can get the title.' Hawke proceeded to point out to Bowen that he was not sufficiently strong in Caucus to become leader himself. Bowen reluctantly admitted this fact and summed up: 'You've got to understand that I won't vote against Hayden. I can't be deputy to a man and do that to him. But I don't believe he'll win an election.'

Bowen was distant from the NSW machine and over the years had carved out his own special place in the ALP Caucus. He had no power base as such and in any contest had to rely upon the NSW right. But as deputy there were a number of Caucus members scattered across the states with whom Bowen had a personal relationship and hence an influence. Hawke's aim was to secure Bowen's support and, if not his backing, then his neutrality. Bowen remained resolutely anti-Hawke, but he mirrored the deepening scepticism towards Hayden's election capacity.

Hawke had been encouraged by his old friend and former NSW Labor Party President John Ducker, who was now at the state public service board. Ducker's advice to Hawke about securing NSW support was brutally simple: 'Get in and do it. If you prove you're determined, then I think they will support you.' Hawke told Ducker that he was working on a general timetable of a challenge about budget time in mid-August. He could not afford to wait longer. Fraser was stomping the nation in a fashion that suggested an election sooner rather than later.

Towards the end of the nuclear warships issue Hawke's power base, the Victorian centre-unity group, met one Sunday to plan the challenge. Those present included Hawke, Holding, Evans, Landeryou, ACTU Vice-President Simon Crean, and other Caucus supporters of Hawke. It was assumed that Hawke would have NSW right-wing backing and the conclusion was that the key figures were Lionel Bowen and John Button. Both were seen as having the potential to influence a small group of votes that would spell the difference. Bowen had recently repudiated Hayden on the warships issue and the Hawke backers believed he was more likely to switch since his position was more anti-Hawke than pro-Hayden. Uranium was mentioned, but Hawke said he would not abandon his opposition to the ALP anti-uranium policy in order to curry favour with the left. The timetable was confirmed for a challenge by August.

Hawke saw Richardson in his Sydney office at 11 a.m. on 25 June. He told Richardson he wanted the challenge as soon as possible. He said Victoria was ready and the ground swell was strong and continued that Richardson had been 'in bed with Hayden for too long'.[1] He believed there was some movement on the left, a few defectors he could win, such as George Georges and Andrew Theophaneous. But Hawke did not see any significant left-wing defection. He was irritated by Richardson's hesitation. The NSW Secretary felt the timing was wrong: the Parliament was not sitting and the 1982 ALP National Conference was about to begin. Richardson knew that while some NSW right-wing members wanted Hawke, enthusiasm among the majority was barely luke-warm. It would be no easy task to persuade NSW. Richardson enunciated the 'official' NSW stance on the challenge: 'We will need to evaluate your position and your support; you can't automatically count on our backing.' But Hawke knew he had the power to puncture this 'official' line by launching the challenge. He had waited long enough; now he would force the party to choose.

Hawke's timing was fortuitous because a convulsion was about to shake the Labor Party which, in itself, would have forced a challenge if Hawke had not already been planning one. The key figure in Labor politics would soon become NSW left-wing champion Tom Uren, and the issue, uranium. It was over uranium that Hawke had fought with his friends, suffered repudiation as ACTU President by the union movement, and saw his own children divide against him. Yet it was over uranium that the barricades of left-wing support for Hayden against Hawke split and nearly broke. Uren would lead the left defection to Hawke on the very issue over which the left had once tried to destroy Hawke. The next fortnight of ALP politics would verify the axiom that there were no permanent friendships in politics. Labor would live up to its reputation as the party of labyrinthine intrigue. So dramatic was the Uren 'breakout' and so spectacular did it become in merely a few days, that the accepted conventional wisdom was that the left had activated the Hawke challenge and Hawke's own backers did not discourage this opinion.

Uranium had been the area of traditional dispute between Hawke and Uren. The biggest victory of the left since Vietnam had come at the Perth National Conference in 1977 when it tied the ALP to a rigid anti-uranium platform. This was probably the biggest win of Uren's career. Uranium was also the one major issue in the post-Whitlam years on which the left's position had become the party's position against the will of the ALP leadership. Whitlam, Hayden, Hawke and Keating were bound to a party policy they opposed. In one of the few contemporary examples of the rank and file over-whelming the leadership, the ALP became the first major political party in a uranium-producing nation to declare against uranium and the nuclear industry.

The Perth conference had been a high tide of Hawke–Uren animosity. Uren had tried unsuccessfully to remove Hawke as National President. Hawke survived and said later of uranium: 'My heart says no but my head says yes . . .' But Uren had had the numbers on the conference floor. The conference agreed to a policy which opposed the mining, processing or export of Australia's uranium. But it went one step farther. Significantly it committed a future ALP Government to 'repudiate any commitment' entered into by a non-Labor Government. The aim was to scare away multinationals and investment in the Australian industry.

It was a policy devised for Opposition not for Government. Not surprisingly, it failed. The Fraser Government proceeded with uranium exports and so did the companies, thereby challenging Labor's threat to repudiate contracts. As ALP leader Hayden was stranded between popular ALP anti-uranium sentiment and a dangerous policy which pledged an ALP Government to repudiate huge overseas investments that sustained uranium mining and export. In 1982 the conventional wisdom was as strong as ever that ALP uranium policy could not be changed. But leadership is about defying old norms and creating new ones.

In February 1982 the South Australian branch had written to the ALP National Executive seeking clarification of the existing policy. As a result the National Executive had asked John Button and Gareth Evans to prepare a legal opinion on implementation of the policy. The big question was whether a Labor Government would be liable for huge compensation payments to the uranium companies for cancellation of their contracts. The left was worried. In the interim Shadow Resources Minister Keating finalised his proposed policy for the July National Conference with no change in the anti-uranium platform.

Evans's advice was that Labor would not be liable to compensation payments and this opinion seemed to leave Hayden and his deputy Lionel Bowen, who was a bitter opponent of the policy, with no recourse. The National Executive met in Sydney on 7 May to hear Evans's report. The turning point came with the speech from the Northern Territory delegate, Bob Collins, who stunned the meeting. Collins said he had recently visited Jabiru, one of the Northern Territory uranium towns, near the Ranger mine. He continued:

> It's full of working class people who have their homes, their schools, their shops and other facilities and it's all based on uranium mining. What I want to know is which one of you is prepared to go up there and tell these people that they have to pack up and leave, that it's all finished, that they have to close everything down and go onto the dole.

Collins cracked open the political shell in which the tough questions about the anti-uranium policy had been hidden.

Hayden and Bowen suddenly found that the executive was receptive to a uranium rethink. It decided 'that a further study of the financial, economic and social implications of implementing our policy be considered by a subcommittee comprising the national officers, Hayden, Bowen, Hogg, Richardson, and the Secretary and President of the ACTU'. The motion was moved by Hayden, seconded by Bowen. Three left-wing delegates opposed it. Hogg was reluctant to serve on the committee but agreed to do so, as the only figure from the left to maintain an anti-uranium platform.

Hayden had embarked upon one of his most significant and fateful tasks as ALP leader. He was determined to bring realism and acceptability to Labor's dogmatic anti-uranium position. His motivation was the same as on capital gains tax: he wanted to deny Fraser a weapon against him. But uranium was an issue that tapped the wellsprings of emotionalism within the Labor movement. Hayden's course was certain to provoke a profound and unpredictable brawl. Both Keating and Richardson were impressed by the courage with which Hayden set about this task. The May–June 1982 period was the high tide of Hayden's relations with the NSW right and, in particular, with Keating. Keating saw that Hayden in his bid for victory was prepared to fight for the moderate and pragmatic policies which had always been espoused by the NSW machine. Hayden was behaving like a right-wing leader—on capital gains tax, uranium and then federal intervention against the left-wing dominated Tasmanian Labor Party.

When Hayden addressed the NSW Labor Conference on the weekend of 26–27 June, Keating introduced him from the stage of the Sydney Town Hall with fulsome praise. Keating said: 'He has taken on the hard decisions that none of us like to take on, but which have to be taken if we are to win Government. He is a leader of courage and determination, a man of integrity and principle.' The omen was clear: Keating would be a reluctant convert to Hawke.

The danger for Hayden was that as his relations with the right warmed, so his links with the left cooled. For some time there had been a debate within the left about its cost–benefit return for supporting Hayden's leadership. The convenor of the Caucus left, Brian Howe, was a Hayden supporter but upset about Hayden's ditching of income redistribution. Uren and other left-wingers were now deeply resentful of Hayden's private denigration of them to others. This was one of Hayden's unattractive traits; far too often he would criticise people behind their backs. The rumour mills usually recycled the story to the offended party. Uren was sick of Hayden's cracks at the left, such as 'the purists have been to see me again'. Consultation with Hayden, which the left valued so highly, had become infrequent. Trust began to disintegrate. Uren had been the main, almost the sole channel of communication between Hayden and the left. But he was becoming jaundiced; the lopsided Hayden–Uren relationship was deteriorating. Uren felt that Hayden took both himself and the left for granted; in his heart he suspected that Hayden had made him look a fool. Uren began to reassess his relationship with the Opposition leader and his view of him as a man. He suspected that Hayden might try to weaken the anti-uranium policy, but he could scarcely believe it. Uren had always assured the left and often boasted that he would keep Hayden behind the existing policy.

This was Uren's mood when he eventually confirmed on 28 June that Hayden was determined to assault the anti-uranium policy at the July conference. One of the Labor State Secretaries had told the left that lobbying would begin very soon. Hayden rang Uren that day on another matter, and during their conversation Uren confronted him on uranium. 'You're a stupid bloody fool, Bill,' Uren said. 'We've been friends for a long time but this goes beyond friendship.' He accused Hayden of 'prostituting' the ALP policy. Hayden said he would like to discuss the issue with Uren, but Uren replied he had no wish to talk about it. This exchange took place the week before the National Conference began. The ALP was on the brink of upheaval.

The next morning, on 29 June, there were as usual about one million people listening to the ABC's 'AM' programme. It featured the lethal and legendary Clyde Cameron, who had been at the centre of so many power struggles and whose retirement from Parliament would not exclude him from this one. Cameron, with a clarity that was uniquely his own, declared:

> We've got to face facts. The public opinion polls show that Bob Hawke now commands more support than any other politician ever registered in these public surveys, and Labor would romp home with Hawke as leader. There's no doubt about that. Some will say, so can Hayden, but I've had a lot of differences with Bob Hawke, and I've been forced to change my mind about him. And I can say this, that if I was still in Caucus, I would have to vote for him . . . there may be an election, a snap election, this year, and I just don't want the party to be caught with its pants down with a leader that can't win enough public support to take us to victory.

The public dimension Cameron's comments gave to the Hayden–Hawke rivalry was such that it would be difficult for the party itself to ignore. This was precisely Cameron's intention and the pressure on Hayden was intensified.

June 29 would be a fateful day. That morning both *The Sydney Morning Herald* and *The Age* carried stories about Hayden's drive to soften the anti-uranium policy. *The Age* also published an interview with Hayden in which he went one step further. Hayden said the existing ALP platform would allow a future Labor Government to approve uranium exports if and when it was satisfied that the conditions the policy laid down—on waste disposal, nuclear safeguards and adequate public debate—had been met. Hayden believed the conditions could be met fairly soon: 'I'm not going to put a date on it, but I'm fairly optimistic that it's not that far out of the way.' This was a public warning by Hayden that he had no faith in the platform and would implement his own policy anyway.

Brian Howe rang Uren and told him about the *Age* interview. Uren promptly told Howe that Hayden had cancelled his leadership credentials and should be replaced. Uren was galvanised into action and he proceeded to break one of the cardinal rules of left-wing politics; he acted unilaterally.

Uren then phoned Hawke. The challenger was sitting in his Coburg electoral office, still enjoying the feedback from the Cameron interview. Hawke's secretary said, 'It's Mr Uren on the phone.' Hawke said, 'Who?' She repeated that it was 'Mr Uren'. Hawke took the call thinking to himself, 'Tom Uren doesn't call me up.' Hawke was right; Uren had a very definite purpose in his call. The leader of the left, the faction that detested Hawke and whom Hawke equally detested, was now promising Hawke the leadership.

Uren began by asking Hawke outright: 'If you were Labor Prime Minister, would you implement ALP federal policy on uranium?' Hawke said that he would. It was the natural answer; the obvious answer. Leaders are bound by policy. Hawke then raised the uranium debate at the following week's National Conference meeting. He said that if the Victorian delegation caucused and decided on a position, then he would vote for that agreed position. If he was allowed a free vote, he would cast that vote according to his own judgement. Uren replied that he was not really interested in the conference and took the discussion back to whether Hawke as a Labor Prime Minister would stick by party policy which, at that time, was solidly anti-uranium. Hawke answered, 'Unequivocally I would stand by the policy.' Hawke asked Uren to look at his performance in the 1980 campaign when he firmly adhered to party policy at all times. Uren said that Hayden had transgressed in his statement that morning which indicated he would defy the policy. He asked what good was served by policy if the leader said it could be overruled. Hawke agreed with Uren's argument, calling Hayden's statement to *The Age* 'stupid'. Uren said, 'Hayden is finished; he is a dead duck leader.' Uren made it clear that Labor must have a new leader and have one soon. But the party needed a leader who accepted policy and would implement it. Hawke told Uren that he would not bargain over uranium policy for the leadership, a statement Uren understood. But he was convinced that the left could withstand Hayden's attempt at the conference to change the policy. Uren told Hawke he would get back to him. Hawke was anxious; he asked when. Uren said by the next night. Hawke sensed a successful challenge was at hand; the party was moving towards him. He offered himself a cigar.

That evening Hawke deliberately increased the pressure several notches and took a public stand on the leadership which signalled the challenge. He was interviewed by the 'PM' programme, which was following up Cameron's interview that morning. The following exchange took place between Hawke and interviewer Huw Evans:

EVANS: Will you be taking [Cameron's] advice?

HAWKE: The only comment I've got to make, in any public way, is this. And it's very simple, uncomplicated. That the question of the leadership of the party and the electoral welfare of the party is a matter for the Caucus.

EVANS: Should the Caucus get the opportunity to express a view at the next meeting?

HAWKE: Well, that's, again, in the hands of the Caucus. I believe there are provisions under the standing orders if people want to do that. And it, it really is a matter, under the, what may be regarded as the peculiar constitution of the ALP, the question of leadership is entirely a matter for the Caucus . . .

From this point onwards the leadership became the burning issue, the only issue in the ALP. The National Conference would become, not a forum for policy, but for a clash over power. Hawke had positioned himself cleverly. His public comments fell short of explicit disloyalty while offering implicit confirmation of his challenge. Hawke had pointed to the mechanism by which the Caucus could change leaders.

Lionel Bowen declared himself for Hayden: 'There will be no support for any other candidate. It is clear that Hayden's parliamentary and party performance will get the support of the majority.' Wide sections of the Caucus watched these events in almost stunned disbelief. At this stage there was no hard lobbying. The Hawke camp had hardly confirmed many of its expected votes, let alone tried to persuade others. Many Caucus members were struck by the dichotomy between the fairly tranquil waters of the backbench and the tidal wave surging through the media. But the Hawke challenge was always destined to be a public one. It was still the strategy of the irresistible force building pressure on the Caucus.

After calling Hawke, Uren spoke to senior figures on the left—Gietzelt, Bruce Childs, Howe and Georges. Most were upset that he had acted unilaterally. Gietzelt said there were other issues of importance to the left apart from uranium. Georges told Uren that if Hawke had given a guarantee on uranium, the left should extract further guarantees. Uren and Howe agreed that the left should organise a national meeting and sort itself out on the leadership. Uren was determined to press ahead with his plan to make Hawke leader. He wanted to recruit to his cause Bob Hogg whom he considered to be the logical left negotiator with Hawke on the leadership issue. So Uren flew to Melbourne.

However before Uren left, he received a phone call from the Prime Minister. This phone discussion took place on either 28 or 29 June. The main issue on Fraser's mind was the manoeuvring over the Labor leadership and he raised this with Uren. Fraser wanted to know how strong was the move against Hayden and what were the prospects for a change of leader. Uren gave little away. But it appears he might have misled Fraser about his own position by suggesting the left was still with Hayden. It was an interesting phone call since Fraser and Uren could scarcely have been farther apart on the political spectrum. It also revealed that Fraser had a capacity to make contact with Labor people which most politicians would have scarcely thought possible.

In Melbourne Uren met Bob Hogg and Victorian left-wing organiser Gerry Hand, who had contested preselection against Hawke, on the evening of 29 June. Uren shocked them with his two items of political news. Firstly he explained the day's events, his approach to Hawke and his conviction that the left had to switch. However Hogg was left with the impression that uranium was just the peg on which Uren wanted to hang his future ministerial hat. Secondly Uren told them about Malcolm Fraser's approach to him. Hogg and Hand glanced at each other somewhat aghast. Uren's motive was to reveal Fraser's election ruminations. Hand told both men, in relation to the switch to Hawke, 'You're off your rocker.' Hand was convinced that the Victorian social-ist left would never move to Hawke no matter what inducements were offered.

The next day the national left-wing group comprising Uren, Hogg, Howe, Hand, Ray Hogan, Bruce Childs, Peter Duncan and Kevin Hardiman met in Melbourne. Uren argued for a leadership change and maintenance of the anti-uranium policy to guarantee the preferences of Australian Democrat voters. He said Hayden could no longer be trusted and was not likely to win an election. He warned that a Labor defeat would deliver the party into a Hawke–Keating leadership ticket in Opposition. Hogg said the ANOP research had revealed the weakness of Hayden's position; it was no better and perhaps worse than in 1980, and the party had failed because of this to make further electoral progress. Different opinions were expressed about the leadership. No firm decision was reached but there was an undercurrent that if the right wing moved to change leaders, then the left might follow. It was agreed that a contact man should be appointed to open dialogue with the Hawke camp; Hogg was the choice.

Hogg was already disillusioned and believed that Hayden was severely reducing Labor's chances of winning. Hogg's starting position was that the ALP had a leadership problem. He believed that in 1980 this had been overcome by use of the Hayden–Hawke–Wran troika. But the troika could not be resurrected, and Hayden had reverted to old and bad habits. Hogg was in a state of 'mild despair' at this stage and could not fathom a solution. He had discussed this only with a few close confidants in the party of whom John Button was one. Button and Hogg came from different factions in the Victorian party, but had a mutual respect. Button wanted to keep Hayden as leader. But in the weeks before the July conference he had considered the possibility that Hayden might not perform and felt, if this happened, that he would tell Hayden directly.

Hogg now became pivot of Labor politics—contact man between left and right on the leadership, and the left's representative on the uranium policy review subcommittee. When Hogg came to Canberra for the pre-conference National Executive meeting on 1 July, he carried this double responsibility. Hogg soon found that Hawke knew about his role. 'I believe you want to see me,' Hawke said grinning. But it was uranium which dominated the executive meeting.

The mood of the National Executive was for a change in uranium policy. Compelling arguments to this effect were put by Hayden, Hawke and Richardson. The more Hayden had studied the uranium policy, the more worried he had become by it. His fear was that Fraser would wage a scare campaign accusing Labor of being the 'funny money' party, since repudiation of big export contracts would damage Australia's international credit position. Hogg himself admitted that the policy was 'inadequate', but said the status quo should prevail at the conference and evolutionary change could come later. But the very fact that Hogg made this admission only encouraged Hayden to press ahead. The executive asked Hogg to draft an alternative policy; he declined, but wrote a brief and gave it to Keating.

Richardson would not let his fervent support for Hayden's bid to change the uranium platform detract from his equally fervent campaign to make Hawke leader. During the executive meeting Richardson, with a straight face, asked McMullan for a report on the latest ANOP research, knowing that this qualitative report from Rod Cameron was damaging to Hayden. McMullan was cautious. He wanted an executive decision before he read out the report, so Richardson moved a motion. That afternoon McMullan, intensely embarrassed, read the ANOP report, not lifting his head from the document. Hayden was even more embarrassed as his deficiencies as a leader were read out to his colleagues. The coming struggle would be a pitiless contest.

That evening Hogg went to Hawke's room at Canberra's Lakeside Hotel, venue for the conference, to parley on the leadership. Hogg kept uranium and the leadership quite separate. In acting for the left he had to establish the conditions on which Hawke was running for leader, how wide was his support, and whether Hawke would negotiate. While Hawke and Hogg were talking, Richardson rang and Hawke invited him up. The three men went through the numbers and Richardson learnt for the first time about the movement on the left. Hogg reported that Uren led the left break-out to Hawke but other left-wing support was uncertain. There was no collective decision so far and it might not come. Hogg was sympathetic to Hawke's position, but felt Hawke exaggerated his Caucus strength.

Hayden had grasped that the Hawke campaign would destroy him if it was allowed to run. No leader could tolerate the open denigration that was becoming commonplace. Hayden decided during this week before the conference that he would follow Fraser's tactics against Peacock and force the issue. Hayden believed Hawke had gone too far, that his judgement had fallen victim to his ambition. He sensed that the challenger had become intoxicated with the flow of opinion polls and media comment, thereby striking too early with his Caucus support still shaky and unsure.

The tactical problem for Hayden, as it was for Hawke, was the conference itself. As leader Hayden had most to gain by a successful conference and most to lose if it foundered. Consequently Hayden decided he would try to keep the conference separate from the leadership issue. He would not allow the Hawke threat to inhibit him from tackling policy changes like uranium simply because he might alienate votes he needed in a leadership ballot. Hayden knew that to make such a compromise would be an admission that his leadership was already demoralised. So he would occupy the high ground. He would treat the conference strictly on its own merits. Hayden calculated that his prestige would reach its zenith after a successful conference and then, when he addressed the National Press Club the following week, he would announce the special party meeting to determine the leadership. This approach had its ironies. It meant Hayden would be a conference ally of the NSW right, led by Keating and Richardson, upon whom Hawke relied for any challenge. It also meant Hayden ran a grave risk of alienating the left through campaigning against the uranium policy, when he desperately needed the left's backing for his leadership. So Hayden's approach was both courageous and tough-minded. At no stage in his five years as leader was the conflict between his policy dictates and power base more obvious or dangerous.

Over the weekend of 3 and 4 July 1982 delegates poured into the Canberra winter for the National Conference, Labor's supreme policy-making

163

body. The left met on Sunday and decided to resist any change to the uranium policy, rejecting the amendment drafted by Keating. Uren rallied the left; he insisted on a collective stance. Meanwhile the Hawke forces—Evans, Holding, Barry Cunningham and Crean—occupied the Lakeside bar, an assassination squad in leather and suede, studying the passing parade, refining their tactics. Observed in the foyer, Hogg had already assumed a worried frown that would deepen each day until his political martyrdom over uranium. That evening Hawke entertained Keating, Richardson and Hogg.

The conference had a split personality. Debate on the floor was ritualistic with occasional sparks, off the floor the drafts were discussed, the numbers counted, the muscles flexed. The 16-storey hotel became a living mass of political dialogue, all day, all night, meetings upstairs, downstairs, in the coffee shop, the restaurant, the bar; all the while television, radio and the print media provided the nation with an exhaustive coverage of the ALP's biennial visit to the psychiatrist's couch where the party would be pulled apart in public and then put back together again. This was the fascination of the National Conference. This forum, in its homage to rank and file participation, its battle over Labor's ideological soul and its clash between leadership personalities revealed the psyche of the ALP. The 1982 Canberra conference would maintain this reputation. Wran gave the presidential address appealing for unity but cognisant of a higher priority among delegates. Off-the-floor draft uranium platforms were as prevalent as multinational lobbyists. Keating, Hayden, John Dawkins and Bob Collins all had their offerings being scrutinised, amended, rejected. Uren handed out a poignant letter from novelist Patrick White which said one image from Hiroshima summed up the nuclear situation—the figure 'of a naked man reported standing on a dark plain which had been his city, holding his eye in the palm of his hand'. White said, 'In the light of this symbol of humankind reduced to disbelieving despair, let us not succumb to our own blindness. Let us not soften to gain votes or appease allies.' Hayden spoke to Uren and formed the impression that Uren was suggesting a 'linkage' between uranium and the leadership. Hayden did not inquire further. Meanwhile Hawke told journalists he wanted uranium policy changed and had a view similar to Hayden's.

On Monday afternoon Hogg, worried about the vortex into which the party was being sucked, made a final appeal to Hayden to pull back. Hogg believed the party now faced a crisis. The parliamentary wing led by Hayden had gone so far out on a limb to change the uranium policy that dire consequences threatened. If Hayden succeeded, the rank and file would be alienated from its own party. If Hayden failed, which Hogg believed was far more likely, then the parliamentary leadership would have been publicly repudiated by the movement while simultaneously giving Fraser all the arguments he needed to win an election. Fraser's new electoral asset would be the failed assault which the ALP leadership had launched against its own policy. Moreover, any victory by the rank and file anti-uranium forces would be phoney. They would know the leadership had no commitment to the policy and would never implement it. Hogg believed the situation had been reached where some shift in policy had to occur, but in this change he wanted 'to protect the movement from itself'.

Hogg discussed the situation with Hayden on the conference floor. He asked Hayden if he intended to proceed. Hayden did. Hogg said, 'You realise that we will be effectively voting on your own leadership?' Hayden admitted this. Hogg told Hayden he did not have the numbers, nothing like the numbers. He emphasised, 'You realise that if you lose, it will finish your leadership. You realise it will extend into areas that will destroy our capacity to run an election campaign. Fraser will only need to use our own words against us. People will be talking about the economic destabilisation of our policy.' Hayden admitted the force of Hogg's argument. He also accepted Hogg's point that if he failed, then it would be irrelevant who was Labor Party leader. Labor would have no chance of winning the election. For Hayden, it was crash through or crash. At this point Hogg began to prepare a fallback uranium position in a bid to reach a compromise between left and right.

On Tuesday 6 July Hayden had his first victory at conference when he led right-wing moves to limit an ALP Government's capital gains tax to a strengthening of the current law. Hawke, who had previously been on record supporting a stronger capital gains tax, voted with the left. During the tax debate Hogg wrote out his uranium policy amendment and lodged it. This amendment offered both Hayden and Keating the softer uranium policy which they needed but fell short of the more dramatic changes they had proposed themselves. That night the faction leaders of NSW and Victorian centre-unity met in Hawke's room. The Victorians, under pressure from the left, were reluctant to support a change in the uranium policy. Richardson said it was a 'fucking outrage' that the Victorians expected NSW to fall into line and ditch Hayden, yet on a fundamental policy like uranium they were prepared to leave NSW stranded without the numbers. Richardson said Victoria would need to reassess its attitude on uranium if it expected NSW backing on any leadership challenge.

Meanwhile the left was in uproar. People were asking why Hogg, one of their own, had circulated an amendment against them. Unfortunately Hogg had missed the left-wing meeting where his faction took a collective decision to reject his amendment. His choice now was to stick by his faction or move his amendment which he believed was necessary in the party's interest. Hogg knew Hayden would proceed; if Hogg did not move his amendment then somebody else might, or Hayden or Keating would sponsor one of the earlier drafts. Hogg was still explaining his position to his Victorian left colleagues at 2 a.m. on the day of the debate. When he finally got to bed Hogg had little sleep. He was about to break from the left, the cardinal sin for which he would not be easily forgiven by most and never forgiven by some. Hogg's role as a negotiator between the left and Hawke had been terminated.

The leadership issue moved to its crisis in tandem with the uranium debate. On the first two evenings of the National Conference the ABC's 'Nationwide' programme had featured profiles of Hayden and Hawke. Hayden had been stung by the portrayal of himself which was highly critical. But he faced a greater trial on Wednesday morning, 7 July, with the publication of *The Bulletin*, containing the latest Morgan survey which was taken when the warships issue was at its peak. In response to the question, 'Who would have made the better Prime Minister?' Fraser polled 50 per cent, Hayden 31 per cent. Fraser's rating had increased in two months from 46 per cent and Hayden's had fallen from 38 per cent. The conference forum magnified the damage to Hayden from this result. Hawke flourished in the climate of instability that he was generating. He gave interviews just off the conference floor, saying the results of the poll should be 'closely considered by members of the public and the Caucus'. He said he was 'disturbed' by the results and had no doubt that Labor would win under his own leadership.

Hayden's Press Secretary Alan Ramsey watched Hawke and was appalled at his exploitation of the poll. At lunchtime Ramsey went and told Hayden: 'You're bleeding to death. You've got no idea of the damage being done there. You must call this party meeting as fast as possible.' Hayden agreed; they decided on Friday week, 16 July. Then Hayden prepared for the uranium debate which he also needed to win to save his leadership.

As Hogg moved his amendment Hayden was more confident. The Victorian centre-unity group had decided 6–5 to vote as a bloc for the Hogg position. Hayden had given Button a special dispensation. Button's Victorian faction, the independents, relied on left-wing support for preselection for many of its candidates. Button's own Senate preselection was looming and without left-wing support he might not survive. Because Hayden and Richardson judged they had the numbers, Button and his factional colleague Victorian Premier John Cain were allowed the luxury of voting with the left. On a free vote they would have supported Hogg.

The uranium debate was the most dramatic seen at a National Conference in the 15 years since Whitlam had pioneered the opening of conferences to the public. The debate wrenched both the heart and ideology of the party. Hogg told the conference it was a tragedy that the debate was occurring but impossible to put off. He asserted that the long and complicated amendment he moved was still 'anti-mining'. But it was interpreted by the conference as allowing existing uranium export contracts running until 1996 to be honoured. It also contained a formula suggesting the South Australian Roxby Downs mine could proceed. Richardson, Hayden, Hawke and Keating gave powerful speeches in support of the Hogg amendment. Richardson summarised all the arguments the National Executive subcommittee on uranium had considered:

> In 1977 we designed a policy, a policy designed to scare the banks, to make sure that there was no investment in uranium mining in Australia. It would be pretty obvious to all of you that that policy has failed. Ranger and Nabarlek went ahead—a billion dollars worth of investment—and when you look at the banks from the international community who have invested in it, then what you are looking at basically is the lot—21 of the European and Japanese banks . . . What sort of retribution do you think these banks will take? Do we think they will take it lying down? The answer, of course, is no. Investment into Australia will just dry up. Our capital inflow will stop and we will be faced with a balance-of-payments crisis.

Richardson was followed by Hayden:

> We have legal advice that we have no legal obligation to compensate, but I put it to you that if you terminate the industry overnight you will, in the public view, have a moral, political responsibility to compensate those people.
>   The 'fair go' syndrome will be gravely offended and the community will react against us . . . We would almost become a banana republic in the standards of the condition of the economy . . . I am telling you, however, in my assessment you will not even get into that position because before election day the people who have got money here, are going to start hauling their money out.

Hawke argued that nobody could ignore the dangers associated with the nuclear fuel cycle. The amendment allowed existing contracts to be honoured but it did not open the way for new mining. Hawke said no other socialist party had adopted the ALP's anti-uranium stance and denied there was any socialist principle involved. He said that to reaffirm current policy meant 'no conservative Prime Minister in the history of this country will have been handed a more effective weapon to stop a Labor government'.

The left savaged both Hogg and the campaign against the policy. Stewart West launched the assault:

> Bob, it is an irresponsible document. It is not even credible, mate. It endorses the existing policy, and then goes on to repudiate that policy. Delegates, do not kid yourselves, it is a pro-mining amendment . . . There are more reasons now to continue with our policy against uranium than there were back in 1977. Have the proliferation problems been solved? No. Has the waste disposal problem been solved? No. Have the environmental problems here in Australia been solved? No.
>
> It is a pro-mining document. It is pro-nuclear. It says it will phase it out but you all know deep in your hearts that it will not phase it out. You know that the contracts will be filled . . . Let us not worry about the fact that the waste will be still around in half a million years . . . half a million years. In 20,000 years maybe the name of the great Australian Labor Party will be forgotten but this stuff will still be around. Don't you see? Don't you see the responsibility you have to mankind?
>
> Delegates, I want to conclude—why, why, why? Our leader says he is optimistic. Bill, who informed you of that? It is just not true. The reason why we want a change is because we are running scared; running scared of the electorate. We are running scared of the mining companies and of the Fraser Government and all the pressure that can be brought on.

Uren reinforced this line:

> Frankly, I believe this document is a tragedy. I believe itself that it will bring a lot of discredit to the movement and frankly I have told Bob [Hogg] himself that this document is a pro-mining document . . . In every case, proliferation, waste, the whole nuclear question has worsened since 1977, but expediency now wants to change it. As I say, it is a sad thing and I am asking delegates for your conscience vote . . .

Towards the end of the conference Gareth Evans revealed some of the back-door pressure on delegates:

> There has been an unprecedented degree in my experience of heaviness, bordering on occasions on thuggishness in the way threats have been bandied about. An extraordinary degree of pressure has been placed upon those of us— and I am one of them—who face preselection in this party in the very near future. Certainly that is true in Victoria. John Button—he may wish to speak for

himself, I don't know, he is probably more sensible to remain silent—has been faced with some very chill winds indeed in this respect. I have been faced with them. Clyde Holding has been faced with them.

After the Hogg amendment was carried 53–46, the vanquished left wing called for a division. Delegates milled about, bathed in TV lights, and anti-uranium demonstrators from the gallery hissed or applauded as each person crossed the floor. In a phone call to Hogg several days later Hayden said, 'I know why you did it. You did it for the party, not to save me.' Hogg explained his position later:

> It was nothing to do with saving individuals . . . They come and go whether they're leaders or not. It was really about the capacity for the Labor movement to survive and sustain a credible position in the community where, regardless of leadership, it could run the next federal election campaign with some chance of winning. I considered the actual amendment if carried, given its warts, a more than reasonable balancing act so that the contending interests could survive. In an electoral sense 5 March showed that. In an organisational sense I think the party has sustained what was a traumatic process, yet there is still capacity for an anti-nuclear and anti-uranium movement to operate in the party and achieve its goals.[2]

That evening Hayden turned his attention to the leadership. He spoke to his three closest colleagues in the party—John Button, Peter Walsh and John Dawkins. Hayden said he thought Hawke might defeat him but he had to force the showdown. Then Hayden told Bowen. The deputy's view on the Hawke challenge had been summed up in his quip to delegates: 'If we want a film star why not go the whole way and get Jane Fonda.' The next morning Hayden told left leader Brian Howe so the faction had prior warning. Just before 3 p.m. on 8 July Hayden walked across the conference floor to Hawke and told him of his intention. Then he issued a statement announcing a special Caucus meeting eight days hence, 16 July, to settle the leadership:

> I am seriously concerned that a deliberate campaign has been carried out in recent weeks to destabilise the cohesion of the federal parliamentary Labor Party. It has undermined the gains of this week's National Conference, and is doing serious damage to the morale and credibility of the party. It can only assist Labor's political opponents . . . this destructive exercise has gone on long enough. No leader can tolerate such insidious destabilisation of our team effort.

At a press conference two hours later Hayden, fired by his success on uranium and the declaration of war, was at his forceful best. It was an omen for Hawke.

The next morning Keating was having a shower in his room at the Lakeside Hotel when there was a knock at the door. Assuming it was breakfast, he got out of the shower and opened it. An ebullient Uren strode in. 'Come on, come on, get out, I want to talk to you,' Uren declared, pacing about Keating's room and opening the window, letting in some of the Canberra winter. Keating finished his shower, wrapped a towel around his waist and sat down, still soaking wet. Uren wanted support from the NSW right to save his urban and regional development policy to be debated that morning. Button was moving a succession of amendments. But Uren wanted Keating's help on the leadership and the rolling of Hayden. If Keating agreed to preserve the urban and regional policy it would also be a sign to the left of their capacity to co-operate to change the leadership. In the event Uren got help on his urban policy. But that morning he bent down on one knee, pounded his fist into his hand, slapped Keating and told him that they would work together to change Labor leaders.[3] Keating was wary about the leadership. Sensing that the week ahead would be one of changing fortunes, he wanted to begin by getting dressed.

12
Hawke on the brink

*I understand that what politics is about is communication and
persuasion of people to support you.*

Bob Hawke, 12 July 1982

During his challenge Bob Hawke had two identities—saviour and demon
of the Labor Party. His career had been like that of Mohammed: the mountain
always came to him: ACTU industrial advocacy, ACTU presidency, ALP presidency. Now the great test was at hand. Hawke's nomination for leader of the
ALP also confronted the party with a decision of historic significance.

Hawke himself brought clarity to the choice when he said that what he
offered Labor was popularity. He never actually campaigned for the leadership on grounds of superior judgement, policy grasp, parliamentary ability.
That is, he never campaigned as a better Prime Minister than Hayden.
Hawke's appeal was totally pragmatic: he promised to be a winner, thereby
making an appeal as timeless as politics itself. Winning. This was Hawke's
slogan. The candour with which Hawke put this proposition during the
challenge week was startling:

> Obviously, it is not the province of Bill Hayden or Bob Hawke to offer [Labor]
> new policies; it is a function of the conference to lay down policies. It is true
> that within the policy framework it is up to the parliamentary party to decide
> priorities and emphases. I think it is clear from the debates and our known
> positions, that there is not a great deal of difference between Bill and myself in
> any area of those policies . . . I understand that what politics is about is
> communication and persuasion of people to support you. I think that my record
> as a communicator and a persuader speaks for itself. So I offer the party,
> I believe, the best abilities as a communicator and a persuader.[1]

Hawke made it clear that his personal skills transcended any ALP policy defects. Asked on what issues or policies he thought he could best Fraser, Hawke replied:

> On any. Any issue that the Prime Minister wants to debate with me in the Parliament or outside. I will meet him. I have confidence in my capacity to best him.[2]

Hawke saw politics as a contest of men rather than a battle of ideas. In fact one of his tactical mistakes during the challenge was that he made too few concessions to the idealism of the ALP. Many Caucus members believed that Hayden, based on his record of performance, would make an able and dedicated Prime Minister where his strengths would be more obvious than as leader of the Opposition. When such members looked to Hawke to project his own prime ministerial concept, they found a man projecting only himself. By declaring policy as virtually irrelevant, Hawke was insensitive towards the party and failed to do justice to himself.

The key to the reactions of love and hate which Hawke engendered in the Labor Party lay in his duality. He was steeped in the Labor movement yet also beyond it, a man of ideals yet a political 'fixer', a believer yet an agnostic, the trade union boss with the mates in big business. Hawke became Labor's saviour because he could deliver the party to office when it began to fear it might lose, but he was a potential demon who might terminate Labor's identity as a party of reformist ideology and turn it into a party of cautious pragmatism.

To his supporters Hawke was the symbol of hope, the source of Labor's electoral revival, radiating a confidence uniquely his own, holding a patent on his own telepathic bond with the community which no other politician could reproduce or steal. His detractors saw a different reality. They saw a man unwilling to serve Labor unless allowed to make the party his own. The leader's closest supporters made this assertion: Hayden would win if Hawke got behind him and harnessed himself to the party's service.

The necessary condition for the challenge was Hawke's refusal truly to accept the status of a shadow Cabinet member: one of the team. He was awkward and unhappy in such a role. It was inconsistent with his messianic self-image. His critics said the party should demand of Hawke what it demanded of others. His supporters said that Hawke was not like others, that he was different. Ultimately the issue boiled down to whether the party accepted Hawke's view of himself. The power that exuded from Hawke originated not in his warmth of personality or quickness of mind but from an evangelical vocation to political leadership. Despite its disguise, the derivation of Hawke's sense of destiny was religious. That made it foreign to most of Hawke's colleagues, many of whom could never grasp the nature of the core force. Hawke carried his sense of destiny, sometimes with inspirational flair, other times with appalling indulgence. Consequently his personality provoked deeply conflicting emotional responses from those with whom he came in contact. At the extreme his friends saw him as endowed with a 'special quality' not given to others; his opponents saw him as a manic egoist identifying self-interest with morality.

The Hawke challenge defied the traditions of both the Labor Party and Australian politics. Malcolm Fraser served 20 years in Parliament before he became leader, Gough Whitlam 14 years and Bill Hayden 16 years; these were formidable men. Yet Hawke was asking the Labor Party to accept him after less than two years. There could be no more dramatic sign that the source of Hawke's authority was different from that of these leaders.

Prime Ministers cannot escape the demands and the dilemmas of office. The question put, although with declining force, by the 'parliamentary club' was whether Hawke had the experience, the administrative skills, the knowledge, the political depth and breadth, the grit—the basic capacity—to become a competent Prime Minister. Fraser and Whitlam had spent years refining these skills and mastering the challenge. A good Australian Prime Minister in the 1980s requires a diverse range of qualities of mind, body and spirit. A Prime Minister must handle Cabinet, the party, the Parliament, the public, the bureaucracy—all at one and the same time. He must have the physical and mental stamina to switch from one complex issue to another and back again. He needs to gauge which public service advice is suspect and which is sound; when to rely on his own instinct and when to repress it. Nobody outside the job could appreciate the huge pressures a Prime Minister endures. The question facing the ALP in mid-1982 was whether Hawke had the competence for the job. Certainly he lacked the experience. He was a plunge into the unknown.

Hawke's great appeal was that he represented the wave of the future; he symbolised the new politics in which the people would be the direct source of a leader's authority and television the instrument of that authority. He was riding to power on the modern trend which gave more emphasis to the leader's personality and less to party identity in determining voting intentions. Market research had verified this point. ANOP surveys had highlighted the growing role of leadership as a factor in swinging election results. It had also found that the party 'team', the senior group of frontbenchers supporting the leader, was almost irrelevant in contributing to the image. This added a new dimension to the traditional role of political leader. Hawke was a television personality in his own right, a major plus. So was US President Ronald Reagan. British Prime Minister Margaret Thatcher was not renowned for this ability in her early period of office; but she was able to use the Falklands War as a circuit-breaker and then project herself as the symbol of a strong Britain, revitalised by resort to traditional values. The extra dimension to leadership is not just a function of technology; it is also a function of recession. History reveals that during economic downturns people look towards decisive or strong leadership. Such choices are often far-reaching and sometimes dangerous.

The impact of this new leadership concept on a system of responsible government such as Australia's and a party system of democratic participation such as the Caucus had to be vast. Hawke was a presidential candidate. Yet a presidential leader must adhere to the dynamic that has generated his position. For a Labor leader whose authority originates with the people the temptation, even the necessity, for a unilateral declaration overruling the Caucus and the party platform is ever present. So, in a crisis, is the ultimate option: resort to the people to overrule the party's will. In his advice to the Liberal Party in 1972 David Kemp gave an analysis relevant to Hawke's position in 1982:

> It was not simply that Mr Gorton's electoral appeal was somewhat less than had been hoped . . . But rather that there was more to successful leadership of the Liberal Party than presenting a good image to the public . . . The leader's first task—as the very word implies—is to lead the party he heads. The first and most important relationship is between leader and followers, not between leader and the public. The experience of the last few years underlies the crucial point that the man who cannot unify and lead his colleagues in Parliament and in the organisation cannot make a successful appeal to the electorate . . .

The prospect of Hawke as Prime Minister would provide a new test of the validity of Kemp's thesis. The potential for tension between the Caucus and Hawke as leader would be immense because of Hawke's priority relationship with the public. It was obvious in 1982 that Hawke's relations with the party would depend upon whether they were shaped by his presidential instinct or his consensus yearnings. As ACTU President Hawke had transformed the factional divisions in the executive itself so that the ACTU ran along consensus lines. Could he, or would he, try to do the same in the Labor Party? Of course, it was always possible that Hawke might be a president when facing the Caucus and then a consensus chairman at the Cabinet table.

Since his entry into Parliament, Hawke had displayed a relaxed disregard for much of the Caucus—an unusual attitude for an aspiring leader. Hawke's personality had changed since he gave up drinking. He became less social, spending more time with very close friends and spurning the wide circle of Caucus colleagues. Many ALP members found after two years that Hawke had barely exchanged a word with them, some claimed never to have spoken to him. Graham Richardson later chided Hawke for being a recluse. In his first 18 months in Parliament, Hawke appeared far less frequently than most members in either the dining room or the bar. Often at lunchtime, certainly in summer, Hawke and his loyal staffer Jean Sinclair would return to his Kingston apartment where Hawke would change into shorts and grab an hour deepening his suntan. Hawke was determined that the Labor Party would have him on his own terms.

The backdrop to the Hawke challenge was the collapse of an intellectual position inside the Labor Party. The party had lacked either a clear sense of direction or working philosophy since the fall of Whitlam. Indeed this was one reason Fraser enjoyed such a decisive edge over the ALP. Fraser was a ruthless and pragmatic politician, but he understood the importance of theory and used it so much that for a time it was the Liberals who appeared the party of ideology. So comprehensive was Fraser's right-wing philosophical assault on the Labor Party and so credible was the position he enjoyed after the Whitlam debacle that Labor remained on the defensive for nearly six years. It was only in 1981 that Hayden took the fight back to Fraser in a series of speeches, arguing the relevance of democratic socialism and the necessity of a strong and viable public sector in Australia. But Hayden still failed to provide a conceptual framework for Labor's attack. Much of his leadership was spent in developing the 'family theme' argument, namely that Fraser was eroding family living standards. This was an accurate and sound position. Yet it hardly amounted to an alternative Labor vision of society.

By 1982 *The Age* of pragmatism had engulfed the Labor Party. Gough Whitlam appeared as a philosophical politician compared with Hayden and Hawke—yet in his own time Whitlam was often attacked as being too pragmatic. Whitlam had been both the architect and salesman of his own programme, which he marketed as a vision for Australia. By contrast Hayden was a policy man with no vision; Hawke displayed meagre interest in policy but had a vision of consensus. Hayden supporters recognised his policy grasp and communications weakness and argued that Hayden was more suited to Government and would therefore make a better Prime Minister than Opposition leader.

The reality is that Hayden was a good political technocrat. As opposition spokesman and a minister he had a wide policy experience: external territories, social welfare, health, treasury, foreign affairs and defence. Hayden's ability was to take an issue, master it, balance the economics and the politics, work through to a final position and then steer the policy through the party and the community. But in Opposition there was none of this. Opposition was only images, shadows and impressions. Hayden had no hard data, no actual policy to implement. As Opposition leader he was under incredible pressure to perform. But what did perform mean? One suspected that Hayden was never quite sure and kept changing his mind. Hayden's defect as Opposition leader was his failure to integrate policies into a package that could attract the nation.

John Button identified this flaw in a paper he wrote on 3 March 1982 for the shadow ministry. Button did not set out to criticise Hayden; he was discussing the ALP decision-making structure. But he offered insights into the failure of both Labor and its leader. Button said:

> The ALP is a party intent on promoting itself as the alternative government of Australia . . . A programme or 'blueprint' for a party of social and political reform necessarily involves an alternative vision (something different from an 'alternative programme') of the way in which society should develop . . . Since the Chifley Government went out of office, perhaps the nearest the ALP has got to establishing a perception of an alternative vision was in the early 1970s. In 1972 we won. That vision was perhaps too splendid—impossible to implement in haste by a Government of mortals . . . In the ALP all sorts of tensions and confusions arise as to how an alternative programme or vision is to be developed and articulated or even elements of it. (The recent capital gains tax issue is a case in point.) What we have is a series of disaggregated policies in various stages of development: plenty of trees, but no Burnham Wood to take us to Dunsinane . . .

It was Hayden who took the Labor Party far down the road towards the pragmatism which Hawke championed. It was Hayden in 1982 who so often radiated the determination to win at any cost. Now, if the ALP was only concerned about winning, there was no reason to keep Hayden leader; he should be replaced by Hawke at once.

For many members of the Labor Party Hawke was another step—the final step—on the road to super pragmatism and a new conservatism. For the first time the Labor Party had a potential leader whose close friends were drawn from both sides, from capital and labour. Over many years Hawke had enjoyed intimate friendships with men such as Sir Peter Abeles and George Rockey from TNT and prominent businessman Eddie Kornhauser. Such friendships were a test of Hawke's own identity and values. At another level they reflected Hawke's ability to treat all men as equals and select those he desired for his own company. Consequently Hawke moved from the members' stand to the outer, from the board room to the factory floor, with an ease that defied class divisions and mocked social pretension. But while Hawke moved from one arena to another, his own political outlook appeared to be shaped by the network of conservative business and union power in which he had dealt.

When Hawke's view of the world was translated into political theory, he stood for corporatism. Hawke did not actually call upon individuals to submerge their identity in the corporate state. He had instead a vaguer, general notion of power where unions, employers and Government worked together and focused on their common interests as opposed to their differences. At its extreme this stance repudiated the conflict between labour and capital, the precise reason for the existence of the ALP. The proposed National Summit often appeared as the first step, at least in theory, towards the corporate state. A few left-wing theorists within the ALP argued this proposition, but inside the party it was neither taken up nor taken seriously.

The reason is probably because Hawke, as a practical politician, was a 'fixer'. He always seemed committed to the existing system and its stability: the reassurance he offered was that change would be made only at the margin. In his polemical article supporting Hawke, Phillip Adams wrote:

> The English radical, Tony Benn, says there are only three types of political leaders (a) straight men, (b) fixers, and (c) maddies. In the English context Jim Callaghan's a straight man, Harold Wilson's a fixer and Margaret Thatcher is mad. The Australian context is full of straight men—John Cain, Lindsay Thompson, John Howard, with Wran as the archetypal fixer and Bjelke Petersen and Fraser as maddies (using 'maddies' in the sense of ideologues who actually want to drag society in one direction or pull it in another). Applying the Benn test, Hawke is clearly a fixer, someone who would seek to use his network of influential mates to sort out social problems. It is, after all, a technique he used for years in ACTU negotiations, ringing up Sir this or Sir that to sort things out.[3]

Hawke was a great negotiator; he knew how to fix a deal—get Frank Sinatra out of Australia, get Sir Peter Abeles into ACTU business, get the oil industry back to work. Hawke was inept in his handling of the Labor machine, but put at the head of a table of people he was incomparable. Hawke was a great chairman and always had been. What sort of Prime Minister would Hawke make? The logical answer is that he would be a negotiator and 'fixer' as he was in his capacity as President of the ACTU. Hawke would rely upon his mates and then find a compromise with his opponents. Hawke, the 'fixer', was the flip side of Hawke, the agent of consensus. The former was the private reality, the latter was the public persona.

Hawke appeared to be a conservative because, it was felt, he had no theoretical position from which to sustain his early radicalism which had been eroded in the backrooms of union and business power. His critics said he was likely to be vulnerable to the conservative whims and ideology of the federal public service. What position would he have from which to resist the bureaucracy? After more than two years of shadow cabinet meetings with Hawke some of his senior colleagues concluded that his diverse experience in public office had not generated any intellectual momentum. It is fair to say that at this time many senior shadow ministers including Hayden, Bowen, John Button, Don Grimes, Paul Keating, Peter Walsh, John Dawkins and Dr Neal Blewett—a sizeable portion of the 'brain cells' of the ALP—believed that Hawke was not delivering the intellectual performance expected from an alternative leader. His academic record proved he had the equipment; but the equipment was not functioning.

A balanced assessment of Hawke in mid-1982 is that he was likely to be the most cautious ALP leader for many years. He was determined to keep a solid standing with the business community, with Australian suburbia, and overseas with the United States. Indeed during his 1980 visit to America he had indicated to the US his support for Fraser's offer of Cockburn Sound near Perth as a home port for the US Navy.[4] This was one of the more radical right-wing stances Fraser adopted; but would Hawke also match Fraser's radical left-wing stands on race relations, Southern Africa and the North–South dialogue on international economic issues? His critics doubted it.

Hawke had turned the 1982 ALP National Conference, designed to strengthen Labor's sinews for Government, into a forum for his own ambition. On the floor of the conference Hayden dared and won, securing triumphs that would have confirmed the mantle of statecraft on any other leader. But the accolades which he deserved were muted. Off the floor of the conference Hawke manoeuvred and cajoled, gestured and smiled, sending shadows of doubt racing across Hayden's landscape. Hawke made the conference the communications centre for Australia's greatest communicator. This was a different Hawke from previous conferences; the recklessness of Perth and the rage of Adelaide had both been conquered, subsumed into a clarity of purpose.

Hawke's tactics infuriated the Hayden supporters. They pointed to all the challenger's faults: his arrogance, disloyalty, ego, lack of judgement. But much of the party merely accepted this as the price worth paying for Bob Hawke. This is exactly what most of the Australian public seemed to think.

Hawke had exposed both his strengths and his weaknesses to the people and, because of this, they were prepared to forgive his foibles. Hawke could commit atrocities yet be forgiven. It was part of his personality make-up. The challenger himself legitimised his tactics:

> I said to the people around me, and it was the truth, that if I believed Hayden could win the next election for the Labor Party, I would not make a challenge. That was the truth and it remains the truth. But I'd become more and more convinced that while there might be an outside chance of him winning, I didn't believe in my heart that he could. That was the basic reason why I proceeded. I'm not trying to imply from that that I didn't want the leadership. Of course I did.[5]

In essence Bob Hawke was offering the Labor Party a contract. His obligation under the contract was to win. Labor's obligation was to give Hawke the freedom to win. The left said Labor was selling its soul. The right merely asked, 'What soul?'

Hawke accentuated the clashing ethos represented by the left and right wings. The left often saw Hawke as an agent of betrayal whose allegiances lay outside the circle of Labor politics. Yet Hawke was really the most flamboyant exponent of the NSW right-wing approach to politics. The right saw Hawke as deeply entrenched in the moderate Labor mainstream. Graham Richardson believed Hawke would be the most committed ALP right-wing leader since Ben Chifley.

But Hawke's duality remained. It was bound to until, as Prime Minister, he would finally prove whether he was saviour or demon.

13
The challenge

We've got the numbers now. I've won.

Bob Hawke,
14 July 1982, two days before the ballot

Bill Hayden's decision to force the leadership issue to a crisis was vindicated in the opening skirmishes of the battle. Hayden had a longer experience of the flirtations of the Caucus and made a more rigorous appraisal of his colleagues than did Hawke. The week before the 16 July contest would prove to be one of the most dramatic in recent Labor Party history. The power balance moved suddenly one way and then another, like an orchestra changing pitch. On 9 July, the day after Hayden's announcement and within hours of Uren's bursting into Keating's shower, the march of the left towards Hawke was halted; by Sunday, 11 July, it was in retreat, and finally by Tuesday, 13 July, the left had returned to the fold and was parading behind Hayden's banner.

When the ALP National Conference broke on the Friday, Keating and Richardson drove back to Sydney together. These men, key figures in the NSW right and greet friends, were divided. Richardson wanted Hawke; Keating was ambivalent. Before leaving the Lakeside Hotel Keating, as State President, had articulated a position for his NSW group. He had told journalists that the NSW right would support Hayden as the incumbent. But if Hayden's natural power base, the centre-left, began to break up then NSW would reassess and, in those circumstances, would shift to Hawke. This position was based on the view that if Hayden kept his left-centre power base intact, then Hawke could not beat him. But Keating knew that defections from the left were predicted, that Uren wanted cooperation between left and right factions to depose Hayden. So Keating's formula really meant that the NSW

180

machine would go to Hawke, provided Uren stayed with Hawke, without incurring blame for initiating Hayden's removal. It meant that NSW would 'kingmake' Hawke as leader or, if Hayden's numbers held, then reinforce his leadership.[1] Keating's position also incorporated his own ambitions. Within the right there were doubts about Hawke, and Keating, who shared these doubts, was the alternative candidate. He would not hand the ALP leadership to Hawke; the challenger had to prove himself.

The left Caucus met to consider the leadership at Parliament House at 1.00 p.m. on 9 July with its convenor Brian Howe in the chair. Howe said the left had to consider the opinion polls, Hayden's actions on uranium and the capital gains tax, and Keating's declaration. Uren was definite, saying Hayden could not win an election and that 'we either support Hawke or live with more of Fraser'. If Hayden were re-elected, Fraser would call a September election; he would win and the ALP in Opposition would have a Hawke–Keating leadership. Stewart West backed Uren for similar reasons. George Georges said the left should withhold any decision until the day before the ballot; this delay would encourage Keating to declare for Hawke. Arthur Gietzelt argued that Hayden was 'a better human being with better values' but had been remiss and had taken the left for granted. Gietzelt reported that the previous night Hayden had said he wanted to talk to the left. Gietzelt suggested a committee be established to negotiate with both Hawke and Hayden. Don Grimes criticised the de-stabilisation of the party by the Hawke forces and leaned towards Hayden. Ken Fry, Pat Giles, Nick Bolkus and Peter Milton all supported Hayden. Bolkus said the divisions between Hawke and the left were long-standing. The left should make a decision and declare itself first. Giles said Hawke could never be sold to the rank and file in Western Australia. Andrew Theophaneous began, 'Women and children in my electorate are starving . . .' He made an emotional appeal for the left to ditch Hayden and support Hawke. As convenor Howe reaffirmed the need for left solidarity and by implication questioned Uren's unilateral approach to Hawke. Howe came down firmly for Hayden and this was the majority view of the meeting. It decided on a negotiating committee comprising Howe, Uren, Gietzelt, West and Georges. The issues it would negotiate included: an increase in the left's strength in the shadow ministry, its request for an economic portfolio, the protection of Ralph Willis as shadow Treasurer, guarantees on implementation of the new uranium policy, a continuation of wage indexation, an effective capital gains tax and more consultation between the leader and the left. Within minutes of this meeting breaking Hayden was given a detailed account of the challenge thrown down to Uren and the gathering support for his own leadership.

The insurmountable obstacle to left-wing support for Hawke was hostility towards him within left-influenced branches and left-wing unions. These sections of the party had always preferred Hayden to Hawke. Uren's defection to Hawke had no roots to sustain it in the forums of the left itself, although Uren would never have split the left. He sought a collective decision for Hawke. But he knew after the Friday meeting that he could never carry the left Caucus. On Sunday, 11 July, Uren rang Hayden and said he was returning to the fold. Uren's 14-day defection was over, but he did not bother to tell Hawke. While the left-wing breakout to Hawke had not provoked the challenge, it had given huge momentum to the Hawke surge and had convinced Hawke he would become leader. Now he was stranded, as Hayden's power base solidified.

Meanwhile a confident Hawke complained about the press gallery: 'First they said there wouldn't be a contest; then they said if there was one Hawke would win no more than 20 votes. Now they know they were wrong on both counts and don't know how to admit it. It's all vanity, all bloody vanity.'[2] Hawke and Hayden both appeared that morning on the 'Sunday' television programme. Subsequently Hawke branded Hayden's performance as 'dreadful'. He said that if he were leader, he would utilise Hayden's talent, but noted that the deputy leader had the right to choose his own portfolio. Since Bowen had Foreign Affairs, then, by implication, this job was ruled out for Hayden.

The day of critical dialogue in the contest was Monday 12 July. Hawke awoke at the Boulevard Hotel optimistic about his chances and excited about Italy's World Cup Soccer win. He had nearly 30,000 Italians in his electorate and Jean Sinclair was sending off congratulatory telegrams. During the day Hayden and Hawke held separate talks with Keating as spokesman for the NSW right and with the left-wing negotiating delegation. In the morning the two contenders breakfasted together with businessmen at the Wentworth Hotel. There was plenty of juvenile slapstick, a technique politicians use to overcome acute embarrassment. Hawke suggested they swap seats; Hayden put his arm around Hawke. Finally the serious business began. Hawke was encamped in the Persian Room on the 17th floor of the Wentworth. Hayden was directly opposite in his Chifley Square office. ALP politicians crossed the no-man's-land of Phillip Street to parley with the contenders.

Paul Keating entered the Persian Room with a detailed analysis of the Caucus in a slim brown file. For the purpose of his analysis he had assumed that Hayden's left-centre base would stay intact and all of the right wing would support Hawke. This gave him: Hayden 40, Hawke 38 with one undecided. The conclusion was that Hawke could only win with left-centre defections from Hayden; so Keating did not give Hawke any commitment of NSW right votes. Keating wanted to be on the winning side and his private position was the same as his public position. If sections of the left defected, then the NSW right would 'kingmake' Hawke. The challenger did not press Keating or seek a firm commitment. Hawke was utterly convinced that the left was moving and in four days' time he would be ALP leader. His ego betrayed his judgement. Hawke seemed unable to imagine that people, once they had 'seen the light', could slip back into the darkness.

An hour earlier, 18 floors below, Tom Uren breakfasted with George Georges in the downstairs Boulevard restaurant. The two men had been up most of the night badgering each other. Georges was unhappy about Uren coming back to Hayden. But Uren was adamant that across the country the left was closing ranks. Australia's biggest left-wing union, the Amalgamated Metal Workers' and Shipwrights' Union, was lobbying hard to keep Hawke out. 'I've come back to Billy and I'm going to make sure he wins,' Uren told a journalist in the Wentworth foyer at the very time Hawke was assuring Keating he had the left, or enough of the left to win.

Keating crossed Phillip Street and caught the lift to Hayden's office. He told Hayden, 'My position is that if you keep your natural support, then we will back you. If you don't and your own coalition starts to break up, then we'll move to Hawke.' During their talk Hayden put to Keating a proposition which he had previously floated: if Keating supported him, then Hayden in turn would support Keating as his own successor further down the track, thereby denying Hawke the succession. Hayden appealed to Keating's ambition and his scepticism about Hawke. The Opposition leader, ever suspicious, had taken his own soundings in NSW and concluded that it was probably moving to Hawke anyway. He believed Keating's control of the NSW right votes was diminishing. When Keating left Hayden's office he went to the men's room, and Hayden rang Lionel Bowen and relayed his talk with Keating. Unbeknown to Hayden Keating then stopped off to see Bowen. The deputy had some news; it was a double-barrelled shock for Keating.

Bowen said Hayden had just told him that Keating had been 'telling me a heap of lies'. Hayden had told Bowen on the phone that he did not believe Keating's claim that he had eight to 10 votes to deliver from NSW. He believed Keating could not hold his own troops from the drift to Hawke. The second message Bowen gave Keating was that Uren had turned at the weekend and come back to Hayden. Bowen's source was his former staffer Ted Wiltshire. Bowen had asked Wiltshire at the start of the contest to use any trade union influence he could to help Hayden. Wiltshire said the AMWSU had reported that Uren had returned to the fold. The left's movement towards Hawke had been checked. Keating left the Commonwealth Centre a worried man.

The political beauty of the Keating 'formula' suddenly evaporated. Keating was now confronted with a diabolical dilemma: if the left stayed with Hayden, then Keating would be breaking his own word if he switched his support to Hawke. Yet by opposing Hawke, he would risk repudiation by his own faction and friends. It was a choice between personal honour and Bob Hawke. Keating was angry that evening when he spoke to Richardson. The NSW Secretary was pushing hard for an early and firm commitment from NSW to Hawke. Both Keating and Richardson were alive to the exquisite difficulties the return of the left to Hayden had created for Keating. Keating told Richardson that Hawke was 'a mug'. He said, 'Our candidate is proving to be a clown. He can't count and I don't believe he can win with just NSW and Victorian centre-unity support. He entered this contest with a pledge of support from his enemy [Uren and the left] without proper consultation with us and now he wants NSW to bail him out.' Richardson's reply was basically, 'You can't let him down, mate; you can't let him be humiliated. As a faction we have no choice but to support him. Hawke will give us a loyalty we can never expect from Hayden. He'll win an election.' In his heart Keating knew Richardson was right. But he was also convinced there was much truth in his own analysis. Keating decided to wait. He would make Hawke come to NSW and plead for his political neck.

The left delegation saw Hayden for four hours from mid-morning right through lunch. The delegation had a distinctly less enjoyable two-hour meeting with Hawke from 2.00 p.m. onwards. Hayden was more adroit than Hawke in his handling of the left. Hayden knew how to flatter the left; he could harness years of experience for this task. He predicted that there would be no election budget and no 1982 election, but that he could win when the election came. He agreed to keep Willis as shadow Treasurer and, in the longer term, to give the left an economic portfolio. And he promised that the uranium policy would be implemented as an anti-uranium commitment. Hayden was sympathetic to public intervention in the marketplace, but he was not prepared to have proportional representation introduced as a new voting system for election to the shadow ministry. He promised instead to review the existing voting system in the face of the left's desire to improve its front bench representation. Hayden reacted positively to a capital gains tax in the context of the prices–incomes accord with the union movement. Hayden agreed to hold regular meetings with the left leadership. The left complained that in recent policy changes Keating was the key person Hayden had consulted—an obvious reference to uranium and capital gains tax. The left found Hayden anxious to discuss policy at length; the meeting continued through lunch at his initiative. Its significance was not just in rebuilding ties between Hayden and the left, but in the commitments Hayden made. However, ultimately he paid a price for left support which became apparent later in his failure to capitalise on his defeat of Hawke.

Hawke revealed his insensitivity during his own talk with the left. For an aspiring leader he was cavalier in his disregard of party tradition and inept in his feel for party dialogue. Hawke was not much interested in discussing policy. One delegation member said Hawke's stance was: 'What do you want from me? Now, can I get the numbers?' Hawke was convinced Fraser wanted a 1982 election and that Hayden could not win. He said it was 'inexcusable' for Labor to be in this position during such a deep recession. Hawke agreed there would be no new uranium mines, supported an economic portfolio for the left and said he would recognise the left according to its numerical strength in the Caucus. Uren later described Hawke's position towards the left as 'patronising'.

Hawke was more comfortable discussing numbers with the left, but he was dealt a cruel blow. The delegation told him that the left would probably make a decision in favour of Hayden. Hawke asked whether there would be defections, but he was told it was unlikely. He then appealed vigorously to the left to allow its members a free vote and not tie them to a collective decision. Suddenly the hopes Hawke had held out for Uren and the left were exploded and his grip on the leadership was fading. Hawke left the Wentworth Hotel to return to Melbourne a deeply despondent man:

> The energy had all drained away. He walked towards the Commonwealth car and, for the first time, brushed aside a television crew . . . His mood had changed dramatically. In the car on the way to the airport he sat low in his seat, his head on his chest, his overcoat collar drawn up around his ears. It was raining and the only sound in the car was the beating of the windscreen wipers. All he said during that 20-minute drive to the airport was that he was tired, that it had been a long day.[3]

Hawke's naivety had been exposed. A man who relies upon his enemies is susceptible to betrayal. But Hawke had failed to extract even a commitment from his friends, the NSW right. Hawke returned home to the bosom of his Victorian faction. That night, in a bid to point the direction to left-wing parliamentarians, both the NSW Steering Committee and the Victorian socialist left supported Hayden. The Hawke forces met at Simon Crean's house with the challenge at its nadir. Those present included Hawke, Clyde Holding, Gareth Evans, Peter Redlich, Bill Landeryou, Barry Cunningham and David Charles. With the left fading, it was imperative to consolidate the NSW right. The

Victorians had been anxious to establish a national alliance of right-wing forces to combat the left. But if NSW failed to support Hawke now, there was no prospect of closer cooperation between the two states against the left. Hawke's future hung in the balance, so a delegation was dispatched to Sydney. The Victorians, as Keating had anticipated, were coming.

Meanwhile Hayden's new danger was that the left's support for him, inspired by years of pent-up hostility towards Hawke, was too provocative. Two of the most prominent left-wing unionists in Australia—John Halfpenny and Laurie Carmichael—had gone public. Carmichael was probably the best-known member of the Communist Party in the country: Halfpenny had resigned only recently from the Communist Party. In the trenches of Labor politics these men were the murderous enemy of the right, particularly the NSW right. Halfpenny was interviewed on the 'AM' programme on 13 July and declared:

> We feel that Bill Hayden would make a better leader of the Labor Party because he has a deeper, a more honest commitment to the Labor movement and the policies of the Labor Party . . . I think it's pretty well common knowledge that Hawke decided to abandon the presidency of the ACTU to go into federal Parliament because he wanted to be Prime Minister. It wasn't because of any sense of commitment to the Labor movement generally . . .

Left-wing support for Hayden was formally agreed at a meeting of the left Caucus at Parliament House on the same day, 13 July. Brian Howe and Stewart West reported on the talks the negotiating committee had held with Hayden and Hawke the previous day. Arthur Gietzelt described Hayden as a 'centrist' who preferred to be seen as left of centre. Gietzelt said the meeting with Hayden was far warmer than that with Hawke. The feeling through the Labor movement was 'irresistible for Hayden'. Gietzelt said Hawke had pleaded for a break in left solidarity, but warned 'our strength is our solidarity'. Uren said that although Hayden was electorally the weaker of the candidates, the left should support him and maximise his vote. Uren denied that he had ever committed the left as a group to Hawke. He had spoken to Hawke on the uranium issue and to Bob Hogg about Hayden's electoral prospects. Hogg had advised, 'If I had to sell a winner, I couldn't sell Hayden'. Uren said it was 'bullshit' to claim that the left had approached and primed Hawke. Explaining his own change, Uren invoked the 'little people' who had made known their views. They were the people hurt by divisions in the left. Uren said the left's decision would give 'strength to Bill—we're not sitting on the fence like Keating'. The delegation had told Hawke that Hayden had the party's rank and file support. According to Uren Hawke had 'lost his cool' at this point. All other speakers with two exceptions, Andrew Theophaneous and George Georges, supported Hayden. Theophaneous warned that the pressures on him were intolerable and that the party would either win with Hawke or have to live with Fraser. The party faced a major problem if Hawke lost the challenge. The middle class loved him and the left would be blamed for defeating its hero. The danger facing the left, as Theophaneous saw it, was a centre-right coalition inside the party. He argued that if the left voted Hawke into the leadership, then it could expect to have some influence over him. While he wanted Hawke, he would, with great misgivings, support the majority view. Georges criticised Hawke, but said Hayden was a grave risk to the party and likely to fold under pressure. Finally, on a motion moved by John Scott and seconded by Peter Milton, the left endorsed Hayden.

A total of 19 members of the left Caucus attended the meeting. They were Howe, Uren, West, Scott, Milton, Theophaneous, Georges, Gietzelt, Ken Fry, Moss Cass, Ruth Coleman, Nick Bolkus, Bruce Childs, John Coates, Don Grimes, Cyril Primmer, John Kerin, Pat Giles and Jean Hearn. Absent overseas were six members who usually subscribed to the left: Harry Jenkins, Gordon McIntosh, Lewis Kent, Doug Everingham, Jim Keeffe and Charlie Jones. Messages of support for Hayden were received from most of this number. The exercise was the most blatant for many years in the left, caucusing and operating as a collective, in the words of its critics, as 'a party within a party'.

Meanwhile at 6.30 that same morning Hawke had shivered in shortie pyjamas outside his Sandringham home, waiting for the tidings of gloom in the morning papers. The street was deserted, dark and still awash from the torrential overnight downpour. Hawke read about the left wing firming for Hayden, but his spirits had improved. One of Hawke's abilities was to start each day anew, putting aside the setbacks of yesterday. He knew that John Halfpenny was going on 'AM' that morning to declare for Hayden. This time his political instincts were right. He sensed immediately that the prospect of extreme left-wing and Communist backing for Hayden was not just a potential liability in the electorate but would be repugnant to the Caucus itself. Hawke would exploit this issue and was already flirting with the idea of an ACTU statement deploring the intervention of trade unions in the affairs of the parliamentary party.

Hawke spent most of the day closeted with his Victorian 'numbers man' Senator Robert Ray, and the main focus of their attention was Graham Richardson. Sections of the NSW right were clamouring for action, notably Doug McClelland and Dick Klugman. McClelland, a fervent Hawke supporter, was ringing around NSW seeking a commitment to the challenger, demanding the Keating position be swept aside. Richardson was confident that NSW would declare for Hawke, but he warned that Keating was still holding out. Meanwhile Hawke was told about the Morgan poll to be published in *The Bulletin* the next day. The two-party preferred vote showed Labor leading the Government 52–48 per cent. But Hawke needed a poll showing the Government actually beating Labor to swing the waverers.

The challenger saw the media that evening to comment on the left Caucus decision. Hawke put on a brave front: 'I'm a punter and when I've often won I find that the bookmakers pay the same amount whether the horse wins by a short half head or the length of the straight.'

That night the Hawke delegation flew out of Melbourne for Sydney and an appointment with destiny. The meeting the next day between the Victorian and NSW centre-unity forces would be the most important of Hawke's political career. The task facing Hawke, Holding, Evans and Crean was to obtain an unequivocal public declaration of support from Keating as NSW President. Nothing less would suffice. The big left-wing domino had fallen Hayden's way; Hawke needed a counter-coup within 24 hours. If he failed, then the momentum for Hayden would intensify for the waverers would swim with the current. Hawke needed NSW support to win; without it he could be humiliated. The only concession Keating gave Richardson on Tuesday evening was his promise to attend the meeting and 'watch them grovel'. Richardson told him, 'We are going to vote for Hawke. You had better decide whether you're with your own troops or against them.' Richardson knew that some of the NSW right were personally committed to Hawke. He believed that John Brown, Barry Cohen and several others, along with McClelland and Klugman, were all Hawke voters and unlikely to be turned.

The meeting was held in Hawke's presidential suite at the Boulevard Hotel on Wednesday 14 July. The four Victorians met Keating, Richardson and Mick Young. Most of the debate centred on efforts by the other six to persuade Keating. The argument Keating advanced was that Hawke did not have the numbers and that NSW would attach itself to a losing cause. Keating told the Victorians they had not consulted properly before launching the challenge; NSW had made no prior commitment to Hawke. He said, 'You say you've got the numbers, but I don't believe you have.' Holding and Evans argued the Hawke case, producing their numbers, claiming a majority. They told Keating nobody else shared his assessment. Ultimately Keating had no choice but to submit. To do otherwise would have been a negation of his political career: Keating was a factional politician, and in recognition of his leadership of the dominant right-wing faction he was President of the NSW party. The essence of his political life was the struggle against the left inside the Labor Party and against the Liberals outside the party. The iron law of the right was that this battle was simultaneous; success against the left was an indispensable condition for the election of Labor governments. The right wing in Victoria and NSW was embracing Hawke. If Keating held out, he would be denying Hawke, denying his own faction and, in the process, be diminishing his standing with his power base. The Halfpenny-Carmichael issue influenced some right-wingers, others merely exploited it. The factional issue for the future was whether the right-wing forces would mobilise nationally to match the organisation of the left. The leadership was a litmus test of this proposition. If Hawke were humiliated and his vote kept to below 25, the left would enjoy a smashing victory. Finally the NSW right was divided. If its leadership declared for Hawke, the votes could be delivered. But if the leaders stood by Hayden, not all the 'bolters' to Hawke could be pulled back. So the need for unity dictated support for Hawke.

Keating faced a conflict between his personal ambition and factional loyalty. By going to Hawke he would finish his own hopes of succeeding Hayden and would recognise Hawke's superior claims as the candidate of the right. Keating's agreement was a vindication of Hawke's judgement and tactics. Hawke was never a numbers man; but he grasped the essential truth of his own position. Once he cast the die, the right wing would fall in behind him against Hayden. The decisive factor now, as always, was that Hawke offered power.

The Halfpenny–Carmichael comments were used as the rationale. They were a peg on which Keating could justify his switch. Evans drafted a statement which Keating amended. Then at 11.30 a.m. Keating stepped into the lift at the Boulevard Hotel, statement in one hand, factional solidarity concealing personal doubt, and pressed the ground-floor button. A few minutes later in the Boulevard foyer he publicly launched his assassination attempt on Hayden; it was the toughest decision of his political career:

> The left has now made it clear that it is resiling from any commitment tendered to Bob Hawke on its behalf . . . It made this decision after having been brought into line by interests outside the ALP. The centre-unity group in NSW finds the involvement by Messrs Carmichael and Halfpenny in the leadership of the Labor Party totally unacceptable.
>
> The centre-unity group was originally prepared to ensure, in the best interests of the party, that the successful candidate won by a decisive margin.
>
> In the circumstances it is no longer appropriate that NSW members be bound by their original attitude. The centre-unity group respects Bill Hayden's capacity and contribution to the Labor movement and will support him absolutely, without reservations, in the event that he wins Friday's ballot.

I believe, however, that the NSW members will take the view that the best interests of the Labor Party, and the millions of Australians who deserve and need a Labor victory and the end of Fraserism, will be best served by Bob Hawke now becoming leader.

Hawke was jubilant. Inside the VIP lounge at Sydney airport a journalist asked Hawke how he felt. He stood very close and smiled: 'We've got the numbers now. I've won.'[4]

Hawke received a second boost to his prospects the same day. ANOP had just completed its major quantitative 1982 survey for the Labor Party, conducted in 10 marginal seats in June–July with a total sample of 3,500 respondents. Rod Cameron had contacted Bob McMullan on the Tuesday and told him the preliminary figures were available. Would the figures be released and therefore used in the contest? McMullan rang Wran, putting the final responsibility on the National President. Wran asked what procedure was normally followed. McMullan replied that he would usually report to the next meeting of the National Campaign Committee, whose members were entitled to the results. Wran agreed that if these members asked for the figures, they should be provided. Consequently the ANOP material was widely circulated by the Hawke camp. Hawke used the results repeatedly when lobbying Caucus members throughout Wednesday and Thursday. When finally completed the ANOP report was in two volumes totalling nearly 100 pages. But Hawke used the raw data from only two answers. The material appeared in the final ANOP report in this form:

QUESTION: Thinking about who should be Prime Minister, of all the people prominent in political life at the moment, who do you think would make the best Prime Minister for Australia?

	TOTAL	POTENTIAL SWINGING VOTERS	LABOR VOTERS	L-NCP VOTERS	DEMOCRAT VOTERS
	%	%	%	%	%
HAWKE	43	42	63	19	46
FRASER	20	15	3	43	2
PEACOCK	11	15	5	17	16
HAYDEN	7	5	12	–	6
CHIPP	2	3	1	1	14
BJELKE-PETERSEN	2	2	1	2	3
WRAN	1	2	2	1	4

ANTHONY	1	1	–	2	1	
UNSURE & OTHERS	13	15	13	15	8	

QUESTION: In reality it is probable that either Mr Fraser or Mr Hayden will be the Prime Minister after the next election. Irrespective of which party you vote for, who do you think would make the better Prime Minister—Mr Fraser or Mr Hayden?

	TOTAL	SWINGING VOTERS					
		LOWLY COMMITTED	VOTE SWITCHERS	LABOR VOTERS	L-NCP VOTERS	DEMOCRAT VOTERS	SURVEY
	%	%	%	%	%	%	%
FRASER	53	58	47	21	88	43	34
HAYDEN	35	26	40	63	6	37	49
BOTH BAD	7	8	7	9	3	12	8
UNSURE	5	8	6	7	3	8	9

It is doubtful whether Hawke mentioned the main conclusion of the ANOP survey: that the average national swing to Labor was 3.5 to four per cent, far beyond the 1.4 per cent it needed to win Government. The conclusion was that despite Hayden's weak leadership profile Labor should still win.

Minutes before Hayden stood up to address the National Press Club lunch on 14 July, he got messages from Keating and McMullan. The former told him about the NSW decision, the latter that the ANOP survey was available. It was a double blow. In his speech Hayden defended the left, saying it was a legitimate and authentic section of the party whose votes both himself and Hawke had sought. He argued that there was no necessary relationship between the leader's popularity and the party's popularity. Hayden rejected the Fraser Government's attack that he was becoming hostage to the left: 'I can only remind you to look at my record. It is a record of a moderate reformer who has operated independently in the Caucus . . . [if] I believe I have got to fulfil certain tasks for the good of the party and the country, then I will pursue them even at considerable risk to myself.'

The main lobbying for Hayden was done by himself, Walsh and Dawkins. Button spoke to a handful of people, not so much to lobby but to influence. Lionel Bowen worked on those members with whom he had a special relationship to bind them to Hayden. But as the Labor Party polarised about left and right, the centre was torn. Both Button and Grimes came under intense pressure from the Hawke camp and Hawke himself. Richardson told Button: 'When I asked you to vote for Doug McClelland against Don Grimes after the

1980 election, you said you couldn't because Grimes was the superior candidate. Now I'm asking you to vote for Hawke against Hayden and the reason is because Hawke is a superior candidate.' Button replied, 'It's not that simple this time.' Neal Blewett took Susan Ryan to lunch in an effort to bring her back to Hayden. But when they sat down she said, 'Neal, the reason I'm voting for Bob is because I want to see you as Health Minister.'

Uren, stung by the attack on the left in the Keating declaration for Hawke, hit back. 'The situation is that Mr Keating has decided to publicly tear down the Labor leader and is trying to blame other people for his actions,' Uren said. He continued:

> I approached Bob Hawke on my own initiative in order to assess his intentions, especially in relation to the matter of Labor's uranium policy. At no time did I tell Mr Hawke that I would transfer or seek the transfer of a block of votes to him and I made no deals with him . . .

Thus provoked, Keating responded with speed and fury:

> Centre-unity denies all responsibility for this challenge. It was the responsibility solely of the people who wanted to get back at Bill Hayden over uranium, that's what started it. They started it and have not been prepared to finish it . . .[5]

Hawke was meticulous to the point of paranoia about his public stance. Leaving the Boulevard Hotel the previous day, he had been cheered by a passer-by who said, 'Go on Bob, kill 'em.' Hawke retorted, 'Yeah, we'll kill 'em.' Several moments later Hawke explained, 'That comment was made there by a passer-by about we'll kill 'em. That was not my comment. It was the passer-by's. So, when I say "Yeah, we'll kill 'em" , I am referring to the Libs and nothing else, and I want that made clear.'[6]

Under the shower on Thursday morning Hawke went through the mental exercise of putting himself in the position of a Caucus waiverer. Wouldn't he go for the man who had the momentum now? Hawke left his Melbourne office for the airport in the middle of the afternoon. It was an emotional departure, his last, Hawke believed, as a mere shadow minister. There were hugs and kisses. As he stepped into the car Hawke said, 'We've got it won, mate. Just, but we are there.' At the airport Hawke met Hazel and daughter Rosslyn, and they flew off to the expected victory the next day.

The major newspapers were divided over the contest. *The Age* was pro-Hawke with support for the challenger coming from its editorial and leading columnists. For instance, Claude Forell wrote, 'Bill Hayden would serve the best interests of the ALP and the nation if he were to resign from the leadership in favour of Bob Hawke and accept the position of deputy leader.' *The Australian* also supported Hawke. *The Australian Financial Review* criticised Hawke and supported Hayden. *The Sydney Morning Herald* also backed Hayden and its national columnist, Peter Bowers, declared on television:

> The presidency of the ACTU is not prime ministership of Australia. In my view he does not have the qualifications for that job . . . I mean, Menzies did his apprenticeship. Why can't Bob Hawke do his apprenticeship? He had one big victory in the Parliament. He called the Prime Minister a liar and got away with it. Well, hooray.

The major question facing Hayden, as it had Fraser two months earlier, was the margin of victory necessary to consolidate his leadership. This issue now became the obsession of the Hayden camp. On both the night before the ballot in Button's office and the next morning in Hayden's office, the key Hayden backers—Button, Walsh, Dawkins, Blewett, and John Kerin—canvassed this issue. Button argued that Hayden had to win with a margin of five votes, or secure 45 votes or more in the ballot. (That is, Hayden should poll 11 votes more than Hawke so that a switch of more than five Caucus members would be needed to reverse the result.) To Button this was the dividing line since a close result might only submerge but not sink the Hawke threat. Kerin thought this was nonsense and said, 'One is enough'. Walsh and Dawkins, however, tended to believe that the Hawke campaign would continue no matter what Hayden polled. Significantly Hayden agreed with Button. He believed he needed to win by at least 45–34 to avoid a Pyrrhic victory. This meant that a switch of six votes would be needed to reverse the outcome. Hayden, like Hawke, was over-optimistic and had hopes of getting 47 or 48.

An axiom of politics is that before a leadership ballot there are always more votes than members. Hawke and his Victorian backers believed that he would win by a similar margin to Hayden's own expectations of victory. The NSW side of Hawke's axis was much less confident. Keating and Richardson believed they had insufficient 'hard' votes finally to prevail. Keating's belief was that in any contest the 'pledged' votes had to be significantly higher than the victory majority to compensate for the inevitable defections.

Hayden arrived at Parliament House on Friday 16 July and observed with a smile, 'There are chilly winds on the plains of Philippi.' He held a final round of talks and then went to Button's office. Hayden sensed that Button felt that he would lose and Button confirmed this. Button was already a disillusioned Hayden supporter and lacked the ardour of Dawkins, Walsh and Kerin who were the real disciples. Button was loyal to Hayden because the complex emotional and personal bond between them gave him no option. Nor did his looming Senate preselection in which the Victorian left would be likely to retaliate against any defection by Button. Hayden and Button were bonded not just by politics; they were linked by tragedy. Hayden had lost one of his four children in a car accident years earlier. In 1982 Button lost his son, David. Bill and Dallas came down for the funeral. Afterwards Button went alone to the crematorium, while Bill and Dallas went back to the house and had been tremendous with the Button family, particularly with Button's other son, Nick. Hayden wrote Button a long letter after his son's death, drawing upon his own tragedy, helping to console his friend. During their meeting before the ballot, Button said, 'I want you to know that if you lose there will be one person in Australia who will be broken-hearted. That's my boy, Nick.' Hayden, momentarily, was overcome. Then he went out to the order of the Caucus battle.

The meeting started at 11.00 a.m. Hayden said there should be no debate. He believed the best course was simply to declare the leadership vacant. The Caucus concurred. Hayden and Hawke drew for lots on the ticket. The ballot was conducted, officially in secret, but semi-secret would be a better description. Some members showed their ballot paper to others to ensure their vote was known. The Caucus sat down for the announcement. Dawkins whispered urgently to Hayden, 'One is enough.' The result was announced: Hayden 42, Hawke 37. All eyes turned to Hayden. But Hayden hesitated; he leaned towards Button and asked, 'Is it enough?' Button shook his head and said no. But the clapping started; Hayden stood and made his victory speech.

He thanked the party and called upon it to unite and remember its great traditions upheld by its previous leaders, Fisher, Scullin, Curtin, Chifley and Whitlam. Hawke pledged his loyalty. He told the Caucus he would work to the utmost to ensure that at the next election there was a Hayden Labor Government.

Hayden returned to joy and tears in his office, and a cake. It came from the Parliament House chef, with the inscription 'Isaiah Chapter 57 Verse 18'. It read, 'I saw their doings but I will now heal them and guide them, repaying them with comfort—those of them who are sorry.' Hayden told a staffer, 'God, you've got no idea how close I came to resigning.'

The white heat of battle works in strange ways on the warriors. Hayden had undergone a cathartic experience; this was his own description. The magnitude of the event overwhelmed the reserve in the Hayden personality. The leader was inspired by his own victory and the conduct of the battle. For the first time since Hawke had entered Parliament, Hayden extended the hand of friendship. It was a genuine offer and it was accepted. After his defeat—a loss he never expected—Hawke produced a virtuoso performance, testimony to his emotional nature. He joined the Hayden office victory celebrations and stayed for most of the day. Hazel and Rosslyn with him. Hayden and Hawke had their most constructive and frank discussion for years. This day both men were purged of their obsessions about each other and the psychological barrier between them lifted spectacularly. It was an opportunity. Hayden made it clear that he saw Hawke, and nobody else, as his successor. He felt that Hawke had fought an honourable battle, but Hayden had no time for Keating or Uren. They were the men who had switched sides. The left had doublecrossed Hayden then Hawke. The NSW centre-unity had doublecrossed Hayden. This was the challenge of the triple doublecross. Hayden shrank when Uren entered his office later, kissed him on the forehead and said, 'I've been a bastard, Billy, please forgive me.'

The television event of the year then ensued. Hayden, Hawke and Bowen faced the media. Hayden was frank about the damage caused but the most memorable part of the programme was the following exchange:

QUESTION: Will you now appoint Mr Hawke to the Electoral Strategy
            Committee?
HAYDEN: (Laughter) Yes.
HAWKE: What a hell of a way to announce it!
HAYDEN: What a hell of a way to prove you've had to get there.[7]

A widespread view of the result was that Labor was left in the worst possible position to handle Malcolm Fraser. By re-electing Hayden with a small margin, Labor revealed its equivocation on the leadership and exposed its factional fractures. The result was interpreted by Fraser and his ministers as the optimum for their interests.

However the result did not doom Hayden's leadership. It gave him more of a fresh opportunity than an extra burden. It was precisely because the contest was an intense and drawn-out struggle that the positions adopted would not be easily reversed. That is, there was no easy way Hawke could secure the extra votes he needed. But there was a significant chance for Hayden to enhance his leadership, building upon this win both in the party and in the electorate. The post-climax reaction of the party was to close ranks. Because Hawke and his supporters had been beaten, they were under intense pressure to accept the result and fall in behind Hayden. It was true that the contest had created new personal animosities and ravaged old ones, but the overwhelming imperative was for a return to order. The initiative lay with

Hayden. It gave him a second chance, a chance to reassert his leadership, reshape his shadow ministry and refurbish his political armory. The test was whether Hayden could perform and seize his chance. The result had also reinforced the Hayden–Hawke power equation. Hayden, more than ever before, could not afford another major blunder. His margin for political error was further reduced. Hawke was 'on the brink', but he could only prevail through Hayden's own failure either on the political stage or in the opinion polls. So Hayden was under more pressure as well as having a new opportunity.

Hawke was also a winner. The significance of the July challenge was that Hawke had finally broken the opposition to him of the 'parliamentary club'; some of it still remained, but he was now a long way towards Caucus acceptance of himself and his claims. He had come within five votes of the leadership; a switch of only three members and Hawke would have been home. Despite the rancour he had generated in the party since his entry into Parliament, he displayed during the week of the challenge a firm personal discipline. Hawke emerged with a substance and standing in the ALP Caucus he had never previously enjoyed. His vote established him as the next leader. The ballot proved that when forced into a decision nearly half the party wanted him.

This was the significance of the July challenge for Hawke. It meant that when Hayden stumbled and fell later in the year, it was possible for the Labor power-brokers to 'manage' a leadership transition that was quick and smooth. Hawke could never have become leader in February 1983 when he did, the way he did, without this July result under his belt. At some stage or other there had to be a leadership contest and this was it. Hayden would never have resigned the leadership in February 1983 if Hawke had not come to the very brink of victory in the July ballot. Graham Richardson said later it had been at the Boulevard Hotel meeting on 14 July where Hawke really won the ALP leadership because this meeting had guaranteed him his 37 votes against Hayden.

After the challenge Hawke was left in an ambiguous position, both stronger and weaker. Stronger because his party position was buttressed by hard numbers; weaker because in the post-contest atmosphere he could no longer continue the politics of de-stabilisation. In August Hayden's personal popularity rating increased. Richardson sent him a telegram filled with black humour: 'Congratulations on the *Bulletin* poll. Your popularity now matches that of the National President [Neville Wran]. We really did you a favour.' Hayden replied, 'I had not quite looked at the matter from this point of view, but I suppose I will have to accept that your motivation was to do me a big favour. However was it necessary to try to take my balls away in the process?' Richardson put this exchange on his office wall. But it was not the last. Hayden described another conversation with Richardson:

> Some weeks later Max Walsh broadcast on his TV programme 'Sunday' that there was another challenge coming up. About the Tuesday after that I had to ring Graham Richardson about a totally unrelated matter. I got him on the phone, and as soon as he got on, he was defensive, and apologetic, and saying, 'Oh, mate, mate . . .'— everyone's a mate in NSW. It's a bit like the mafia presenting you with a bunch of flowers. Anyhow Graham said, 'Mate, mate, I know what you are ringing up about, that dreadful programme on Sunday. Max Walsh, oh, he's a dreadful bastard. Look, I've got nothing to do with it, mate, and I want to tell you, mate, we're behind you all the way.'
>
> I said, 'Well, Graham, that's not what I rang up about, but now that you've raised it, that's what you said last time there was a challenge.'
>
> And he said, 'Oh, mate, mate, this time I've got to tell you the truth; last time we told you a lie.'[8]

July was Hayden's victory. Afterwards he took Dallas on a well-deserved break to north Queensland. But Hayden lost his political momentum in the sands. He forgot that he didn't have a moment to lose. Fraser was planning to strike.

14
Fraser's election strategy

*I'll just wake up one morning and find an election coming on—and that
will be the day.*

Malcolm Fraser to the Liberal Party Federal Executive,
July 1982

While Labor fought, Malcolm Fraser embarked upon his latest audacity. He
moved the Government onto course for a 1982 early election rather than let
the Parliament run its full term until late 1983. By this decision Fraser showed
that he was true to his deepest political instinct—aggression. Fraser was a
compulsive initiator. This meant that as Prime Minister he usually set the
agenda of issues and the terms of their debate. It was one of his leadership
qualities. Fraser's 1982 election strategy was based upon the twin pillars of
political confidence and economic pessimism, upon Fraser's conviction that
he had Hayden's measure and upon his diagnosis that the world economy was
heading towards its greatest crisis since the 1930s.

The 1982–83 budget was finalised against the backdrop of the Hayden–
Hawke leadership struggle. The main week of Cabinet's budget talks was the
very week of the challenge which climaxed on 16 July. Fraser's belief, after
the challenge, was that Hayden would probably continue to prevail against
Hawke. But Fraser's nightmare was that if the Parliament went its full term
he might be confronted at the end with Hawke as his opponent and with no
means of escape. A 1982 election budget had the added advantage of denying
the ALP the chance to switch leaders before an election—but this was not the
chief motive.

Fraser's strategy defied the public opinion polls which suggested a defeat
for the Government, troubled many of his ministers and terrified much of his
backbench. It was a course of high risk to plan an election amid a deteriorating
economy. The election budget became a conventional wisdom only because

Fraser made it so. Fraser acted because he believed that the economy would get much worse before it got better and that, consequently, a 1982 election might be a safer proposition than a 1983 election. This was a far-reaching strategic decision which had the potential to make or break Fraser's own career as well as his Government. Above everything it revealed Fraser's assertion of his own right to determine his Government's political strategy on the 'life or death' issue of election timing.

The policy issue at stake was the economic philosophy that the Fraser Government had championed. The previous 1981–82 budget had represented a high tide of the Government's efforts to 'beat inflation first'. It slashed the deficit in a bid to ease interest rate pressures and create room for private sector growth. Fraser now argued that, as circumstances had changed, policy should, too. But the policy he wanted changed in the 1982–83 budget was essential to his Government's identity. The debate was about Fraserism itself.

The previous six budgets of the Fraser Government all contained a deficit below the previous year's outcome. Despite delays along the way, the march to deflation had continued. The watershed in economic policy reached by the Fraser Cabinet in July 1982 was the decision to reverse this trend, to retreat towards public sector economic expansion so as to stimulate activity while trying to hold down wages. Indeed this was a policy of identical nature, if not dimension, to that of the ALP. In broad terms it was a shift back to Keynesian economics and a casting-off of the monetarist garb in which Fraser sometimes presented himself.

The debate inside the Government over the budget was represented by three protagonists who had created the benchmark positions and whose personal links were put under great strain. They were Fraser himself, Treasurer John Howard and Secretary of the Treasury John Stone. Not only was the course of economic policy to be changed, but the cost in men and blood was high: relations between Stone and the Government reached their nadir, Howard came to the greatest crisis of his career and contemplated resignation, and tension within the Government between the pragmatists and ideologues reached a new peak.

The rock upon which Fraser's election strategy was based was his political strength. Fraser used the defeat of the Peacock challenge as the springboard for his assault on the ALP. The Prime Minister did not just defeat Peacock, he maintained the momentum of his internal victory to attack Hayden and the Cain Government and promote the de-stabilisation of Hayden's leadership. Within a few months Fraser had defied his critics and vindicated his supporters. It was a study in the importance of psychology in politics. Fraser had transformed his own role from defender to aggressor.

In the electorate little had altered and Labor stayed ahead in the polls. But inside the world of politics Fraser's radiating self-confidence contributed to another reality—the belief that he would still win an election. The creation of this subjective reality as opposed to the objective reality of economic hardship and public opinion polls enabled Fraser to force Labor onto the defensive. He did this first during May and June, the months that were the prelude to Hawke's challenge to Hayden. Now he would repeat the effort by bringing down an election budget.

In retrospect it is clear that Fraser's budget decision to override Stone and, to a lesser extent Howard, heralded a new phase of dominance. The Government's identity became inexorably tied to Fraser's personality and conviction, so that it almost ceased to have any identity of its own. Over the next six months Fraser reversed economic policy, confronted his own party on tax avoidance, pioneered a dramatic wage freeze, stormed Hayden's leadership and nearly pulled off his re-election. Fraser displayed qualities of genuine leadership in this June 1982 to early February 1983 period. Ultimately he dominated too much and in the 1983 campaign he was exposed, aloof and isolated from his troops.

In early 1982 the Government lost its confidence in the international economy. In March Fraser produced a new political text stating that his Government was the best equipped to carry Australia through a dangerous world depression. He had abandoned his guise of the prophet of prosperity. Fraser showed no embarrassment at the fading vision of his $29-billion resource boom. As usual he became preoccupied by the latest challenge. He reappeared as a pessimistic realist warning Australians to lower their expectations of future living standards. During a Cabinet meeting and round of engagements in Brisbane, including a dinner with the press, Fraser expressed in private an even deeper worry. He called the unfolding downturn a depression, not a recession, and his fear was that the social fabric and political stability of major European nations might soon be in danger. Fraser warned that unemployment was near 12 per cent in Britain, almost nine per cent in the United States and approaching eight per cent in West Germany.

The 1982 framework was established in Fraser's 'State of the Nation' address to Parliament on 9 March. His essential argument was that the world economic downturn was overtaking Australia at the same time that the impact of high wage rises was hitting local employers. It was a double-edged squeeze. As recently as the previous December, during Christmas drinks at The Lodge, Fraser had been relaxed with journalists about wages growth. Now he warned it was 'imperative' that wage rises be limited to economic capacity. It was already too late to halt the substantial flow-on through the work force of the

December 1981 metal trades agreement. But Fraser had become sensitive to the wages explosion which would bedevil him for the rest of his prime ministership.

Fraser was still able to argue that Australia was performing well relative to other OECD nations. But this reflected the delayed impact of the international recession on Australia. The delay suited Fraser's 1980 election campaign; but it would hit Australia with maximum force in late 1982 carrying through into 1983, which meant it would disrupt his re-election prospects. In his speech Fraser offered a prescription of continuing fiscal and monetary restraint. This meant his priority was still to control inflation rather than boost employment—but his priorities were about to be reversed. It was now obvious that Howard's 1981–82 budget strategy, designed to lower interest rates, had not worked. High interest rates overseas had taken their toll on Australia; but high interest rates at home were perceived by Howard as a continuing necessity. Australia's energy exports had suffered as a result of the fall in world oil prices in early 1982, and other exports were declining as wage levels reduced Australia's international competitiveness. Therefore high interest rates were needed to maintain capital inflow. The earlier downturn overseas meant that inflation among Australia's trading partners had fallen significantly. Fraser warned that with a weak balance of payments and strong domestic inflationary pressures coming from wages there could be no relaxation in monetary policy. This stance dictated high interest rates. Australia was facing the twin dangers of inflation and unemployment. Fraser, Howard and Stone would respond to this problem in different fashions.

The immediate burden fell upon John Howard, nicknamed 'flintface' by his colleagues. Economic rationality and political orthodoxy were the touchstones of Howard's career. He was the monetarist in the Fraser Cabinet, deeply influenced by Treasury despite his strained relations with his department. It was Howard's responsibility to pilot the economic direction, and the downturn would be his great test. Every budget is a measure of a Treasurer's economic nous and political power. In his five years as Treasurer Howard had grafted the free-market ideology onto the pragmatism of his NSW Liberal machine background. It was Howard not Fraser who held to a philosophic position on the nature of liberalism. Howard believed in small Government and, unlike Fraser, in market forces. He wanted to deregulate the financial system, float the dollar, lower tariffs, abandon centralised wage fixation for collective bargaining, insist that everybody pay tax and restrict welfare to the needy. These were revolutionary ideas in Australia. That such a straightforward suburban solicitor espoused them was a telling commentary on the characteristically Australian art of compromise. In 1981 Howard had used his philosophy as a political ladder which took him to the deputy leadership; now, in the budget, he had to implement it.

Howard's economic approach and political limitations were revealed in April, just after he became deputy leader, when he had to rebuff Liberal Party pressure for a change in economic policy. He said:

> Bad economics is normally bad politics, because it produces things that are politically disastrous, such as high inflation, economic stagnation, much higher interest rates . . . We're not going to change the basic thrust of [policy] because we believe that the essentials of our economic policy are still correct.
>
> And I get back to the point that you have to keep asking yourself: what is the alternative? Is there a rational, better alternative?[1]

The conventional Liberal Party wisdom, inside the ministry, on the backbench, and from Tony Eggleton, was for tax cuts in the budget. An extended Government party-room debate on economic policy conducted in April–May saw a powerful demand for tax relief. Howard tried to temper such demands with realism. His objective was to ensure that tax cuts were not given at the cost of the fight against inflation. The clearest exposition of Howard's stance and his proximity to the Treasury line came in his address to the June Premiers' Conference. This speech highlighted the extent to which expectations in the financial community had come to dominate the determinants of macro-economic policy. Howard rejected any notion of recovery through an expansionary policy stance by quoting the Mitterand example:

> The recent experience of France is particularly instructive in this regard. The resort by that country about a year ago to a major expansion of the budget deficit and other exceptional measures has, on current indications, proved counterproductive.

Howard then defined his paramount priority in budget Cabinet, which was only a few weeks away:

> It would be extremely damaging to inflationary expectations for there to be a relaxation of the Government's economic policy stance .
>
> The regrettable fact is that, whereas 18 months ago Australia could rightly claim that her inflation rate was below the average of the industrialised world, the reverse is now the case . . .
>
> Is it any wonder that we have had trouble with our exports and have lost sales to imports when in the 12 months to March 1981 wages in Australia grew

by over four per cent in real terms, whereas in the US and Germany wage rises for the same period were below the inflation rates of those countries . . .[2]

This summarised the Howard–Stone position which contained differences only in policy degree between the two men.

The architect, exponent and champion of the Treasury view was John Stone, whose blend of formidable intelligence, driving personality and persuasive advocacy made him the most remarkable public servant in Australia. Stone believed that the source of most economic evil was inflation. Nations might suffer economic decline, high unemployment and crippling interest rates—but these were only symptoms. The cause was inflation. This diagnosis permeated Stone's view of the world and his advice to politicians. Stone's objective was zero inflation, which meant, in the imperfect world of politics, that Stone's campaign against inflation was endless as well as aggressive.

When faced with rising unemployment and rising inflation Stone was uncompromising. It was inflation that caused unemployment so he refused to make concessions in the policies necessary to control inflation. If unemployment in the interim got worse, that was unfortunate; perhaps the politicians might learn a lesson this time. If they did then people would be saved unnecessary hardship next time. The Treasury approach had once been described in the Whitlam years as the 'short sharp shock'; during the Fraser years a more accurate label became the 'long hard grind'. John Stone had taken Fraserism, knocked it about, and produced a doctrine known as 'fight inflation first'. He saw his task as Treasury chief as ensuring that wayward politicians stuck by the doctrine. Stone soon realised that in Malcolm Fraser he had a Prime Minister whose chronic restlessness created a potential to lurch in another direction. At each budget Cabinet Stone's aim was to force down the deficit, thereby easing the Government's own demands in financial markets and giving the engine room of growth—the private sector—the confidence to expand.

Stone brought both a distinctive ideology and tactical dogmatism to his position as Secretary of the Treasury. He believed in individual freedom and private enterprise. He distrusted Governments and saw the growth of bureaucracy as one of the great dangers in modern society. Stone had a deeply ideological view of the world: he was champion of small Government and reliance on the market, an opponent of the arbitration system and, except in exchange rate policy, a critic of Government intervention. There are two types of public servants in Canberra: the pragmatists who bend with the Government of the day and the believers who stand committed to their own policy visions. Stone was the archetypal believer. He was a great anti-appeasement figure. Stone saw the recent history of economic policy as being dotted with little

Munichs, where politicians had walked the easy road to popularity only to retreat when confronted with economic reality. Stone prided himself on presenting politicians with tough decisions. Treasury itself was notorious for its monolithic outlook and its contempt for advice containing options. 'Give a politician options and you're asking him to take the soft one,' was a Treasury axiom.

At his best, Stone was a public service adviser of unrivalled persuasion, at his worst, he lapsed into puritanical irrelevance. Asked to analyse other departments or ministers' submissions, he applied a destructive logic without equal. One senior minister in the Fraser Cabinet declared: 'He's so forceful and so good that after a while, listening to him, you succumb almost naturally.' Stone had a bureaucratic sense of territorial imperative, for Treasury had been created as the central economic advising department and would not tolerate rivals. Stone himself as Secretary to the Treasury had become a public figure; Treasury's views on policy were normally known but Stone gave a number of major public addresses identifying the economics agenda.

For years Fraser and Stone had been both allies and rivals. When they agreed, policy was confirmed, when they disagreed, the sparks would fly. Since the 1980 election relations between Stone on the one hand and Howard and Fraser on the other had deteriorated sharply. Prior to mid-1982 this had been a product of personality and power factors. Howard believed that Treasury operated too much as an entity in its own right. It gave advice, then put pressure on Government to accept its advice. One example of Howard–Stone tension came in December 1980 when, on the eve of a Cabinet debate about interest rate increases, the Business Editor of *The Age*, Terry McCrann, wrote:

> John Howard faces one of the most important tests of his political career today when he goes to the monetary policy committee of Cabinet with a Treasury brief arguing for significant increases in politically sensitive interest rates. Mr Howard's performance in this Cabinet Committee, his persuasiveness, will go a long way to determine whether he has the strength and clout to climb higher in this Government's pecking order . . .

Angry at this report Howard asked Treasury for a list of its officers who had spoken to McCrann. The list came back with only one name on it—John Stone. Stone did not have a record or reputation for briefing journalists on Cabinet, but Howard believed Treasury, one way or another, would always get its view into the marketplace. The Treasurer once said of his department: 'They grunt, groan, smile and mutter to great effect.'

Another clash occurred in March 1981 after Stone's evidence to a Senate Committee in which he appeared to support a resources rent tax—a proposition which Treasury had earlier advocated and the Fraser Cabinet had rejected. While Stone's words were qualified in his evidence, they remained open to interpretation. Howard felt his ministerial authority would be undermined if he did not censure Stone and be seen to do so publicly. Howard rang Stone at home and queried his comments, and Stone replied that he had been misrepresented by the press in a number of respects. Howard then went public with an obvious but indirect rebuke of his Secretary. The Treasurer wanted people to know that he was 'on top' of Stone. The turning point in the Fraser–Stone relationship came with the publication in mid-1981 of Stone's stinging criticism of Fraser in a letter he wrote to the Prime Minister's Foreign Policy adviser Professor Owen Harries. Stone attacked Fraser's view that a major push was needed to develop the north-south dialogue on economic issues. This was the theme of Fraser's keynote speech at the University of South Carolina during his 1981 visit to the US. Stone made it clear he believed Fraser's approach to the Third World was fundamentally wrong:

> In my view half-baked proposals, based largely on political criteria and which do not pay due regard to economic rationality, are more likely to accentuate he problems to which the Prime Minister purports to be addressing himself—except, perhaps, in the very short-term context of appearing to be 'sympathetic' . . .
>
> At some stage, moreover, some developing countries are going to be so impolite as to ask Australia to put its policies where its mouth is. At that time, unless we can show considerably more 'political will' than has been evident until now (for example, in regard to the dismantling of our high protection regime), the Australian emperor is going to appear remarkably unclothed . . . Do you really want to have the Australian Prime Minister publicly criticising the Reagan Administration policies, particularly in the United States—and particularly, if I may say so, on such weak ground in doing so?[3]

Fraser was deeply angered by the leaking of this letter and felt that Stone was both too indulgent and patronising. Stone, in fact, was severely undermining his own position and influence with tactics that could ultimately cost him his job.

Howard believed another element in the strained relations between himself and Treasury was his own reliance on non-Treasury advice. Howard found himself with essentially three departments to run: Treasury, the Tax Office and the Reserve Bank. In April 1982 he became deputy leader with a consequent special party responsibility. After 1980 Howard came to rely far more on the Reserve Bank and would often speak to its senior officials in Sydney without Treasury officers being present. Howard and Reserve Bank Governor Harry Knight went to the same church.

The main implication of Stone's economic advice was often missed by politicians. Treasury never pretended to be able to solve Australia's economic problems. The essence of the Treasury position was summed up in the 1980–81 budget:

> Though progress in the strengthening of economic activity has been fairly slow in the years since 1975–76, the Government's strategy has achieved considerable success in reducing distortions, and thus in restoring the *preconditions* needed to allow stronger growth in private sector activity on a sustained basis. [my emphasis]

In other words, Treasury's aim was to establish the conditions for growth— low inflation, high profits, low budget deficit. It believed that, sooner or later, growth would take off in the private sector in this climate. Stone applied this strategy without regard to the depth of recession or level of unemployment. It was the only way out. As unemployment moved from one historic plateau to the next, the Treasury prescription never changed. Treasury repudiated the notion that in a recession the Government should maintain activity through its own spending. The reason was that Stone believed that when the upturn came it would take too many years to wind back the public sector once again.

Treasury might or might not have been right in its economic remedy. But this remedy could not suffice for politicians in a democratic society facing an historic increase in unemployment. In this situation the Government needed a growth strategy based on a mix of Government economic stimulation, manpower, re-training policies and industry restructuring.

The Government and Treasury brought a history of deep tension to the 1982 budget Cabinet table. It was accentuated by Fraser's suspicion of Treasury advice and his belief that in the current situation the Treasury philosophy was inappropriate. Relations between the Government and Stone disintegrated very early in the process. Stone, who refused to compromise and adopted a position on the high ground, was irrelevant, the conscience of Fraserism and a symbol of the extent to which Fraser had ditched his own philosophy.

But ultimately the most important figure in the budget process was Fraser himself. The 1982 budget is a window into the real nature of Fraser the politician. Unlike most politicians Fraser was able to form his own independent and fairly accurate assessment on many policy issues. The first of the two principal economic judgements Fraser made in the prelude to the budget was that the world depression and its effects on Australia would be much deeper than Treasury predicted. On this score, Fraser was right and Treasury was wrong. Secondly Fraser decided that such a downturn required a reversal in the policy of deflation. The Prime Minister entered budget Cabinet convinced that a new economic direction was necessary.

Fraser's economic pessimism was reinforced by his May 1982 US visit. In Washington Treasury Secretary Donald Regan predicted a US recovery in the second half of the year and said it would be 'moderately strong'. But in New York Fraser found that the financial community remained deeply sceptical. The Prime Minister attended a River Club lunch hosted by David Rockefeller and a dinner at the Brook Club hosted by Exxon Corporation Chairman Clifton Garbin. He concluded that the US deficit remained too high for any strong recovery and felt that the New York financiers had a better appreciation of this situation than did the Washington economists.

In June two significant pointers towards Fraser's economic policy reassessment were evident. The first came at a meeting of the Liberal Party Economic Advisory Committee on 4 June to discuss budget strategy. The key businessmen on this committee, Sir Robert Creighton-Brown and Sir John Wilson, led the charge for a higher deficit. Sir Robert said he would go as far as $3,000 million. This compared with the deficit outcome for 1981–82 of $550 million. The meeting, chaired by former Liberal Party President Sir John Atwill, agreed that personal income tax cuts were necessary on both economic and political grounds. Its significance was that it told Fraser wide sections of the business community also wanted the Government to abandon the Treasury line and move towards expansion. Howard entered the debate with a strong speech against a big deficit because of its impact on interest rates and inflation. But he was isolated in this view.

The proof of this came at the 24–25 June Premiers' Conference when the federal Government boosted loan funds and general revenue grants to the states. Total loan funds rose 11.5 per cent compared with 6.6 per cent in 1981–82. This figure excluded state electricity authorities which were given permission to borrow independently. General revenue grants rose 16 per cent compared with 11.3 per cent in 1981–82. The more generous treatment for the states was inspired by Fraser and his own department and was in conflict with the rhetoric of Howard's speech drafted by Treasury and Howard's office. The conference signalled a return of the Prime Minister's Department to policy influence, and the fading of the Treasury.

The climate was right for a change in policy. Tony Eggleton's advice to Fraser was that the Government must use the budget as a means of restoring its lost political credibility. Liberal surveys throughout 1982 had revealed that the ALP was the party which voters thought most likely to deliver tax cuts—a mortal blow for Fraser's credibility. This advice was reflected by other senior Liberals such as Creighton-Brown and Atwill.

The Country Party ministers were the first to see that Fraser was looking towards an election after the announcement of his budget. Fraser discussed this strategy with Nixon, who endorsed it wholeheartedly. Fraser told Nixon that he was confident he could prevail against Howard's arguments in Cabinet and take the ministry with him, but the Prime Minister was concerned about Howard's reluctance, as deputy leader, to embrace a 1982 election.

In early July there was a tripartite conference involving the Government, the ACTU and the Confederation of Australian Industry. The conference supported tax cuts, which was consistent with the argument from Employment and Industrial Relations Minister Ian Macphee, who wanted tax cuts as part of a wage restraint strategy with the unions. At the start of budget Cabinet a major meeting was held involving senior ministers, departmental heads from economic departments and ministerial advisers. Three main positions were expressed at this meeting which established the guidelines for the budget process: the views of Treasury, the Prime Minister's Department and Howard.

Stone began with a long exposition and concluded by advocating a balanced budget with a policy tolerance up to a $500-million deficit, which was about the previous year's outcome. Treasury wanted a severely deflationary budget.

The second position was put by the deputy Secretary of the Prime Minister's Department, Ed Visbord, who proposed a $1,900-million deficit. This was equivalent to a domestic balance. That morning Visbord and Fraser's economic advisers from his private office, Professor John Rose and Professor Cliff Walsh, had met and agreed on the $1,900-million position. A few days before this meeting Walsh had prepared options for Fraser and found that the Prime Minister had been anxious to explore an expansionary position beyond the $1,900-million deficit. Walsh and Rose argued for maximum spending control to maximise the scope for tax cuts. Visbord said he agreed in principle with much of Stone's exposition and that it would be fine—if Government did not have to concern itself with people.

The third position was put by Howard and his own adviser Professor John Hewson. Hewson argued for a deficit of $1,000 million, which would produce a significant domestic surplus and maintain a tight policy stance. Because the economy was moving into recession with the rate of revenue increase falling, a maintenance of the existing policy stance would see an automatic increase in the deficit anyway. It was estimated that the 'status quo' position was a 1982–83 deficit of slightly more than $1,000 million. That is, Howard and Hewson were advocating retention of the same degree of policy tightness, while Stone wanted an increase in the severity of policy and the Prime Minister's troika wanted to ease policy to a moderate extent. Fraser was leading the charge.

Fraser went public before the Cabinet talks to create a climate of opinion for a shift in Government policy. On 11 July Fraser told a Liberal Party meeting in Perth:

> We cannot prevent world conditions from affecting us, but there is much we can do to help ourselves. Certainly this will be very much in the Government's mind, faced as we are by circumstances which are both different and difficult. It is no longer necessarily a matter of the Government making way for private sector activity, for activity is falling and employment prospects are diminishing.

Budget Cabinet began on Monday 12 July—the same week as the ALP leadership challenge. Howard's submission, which repudiated his own department, was for a $1,000-million deficit, but it was swept aside right from the start. Fraser set the tone for his ministers and his own more relaxed attitude towards spending permeated the Cabinet. Social Security Minister Senator Fred Chaney wanted a significant boost to public works to encourage employment, and this line was accepted. Ministers were agreed on the need for a tax cut and on 15 July Fraser convened a full ministry meeting which gave in-principle endorsement to income tax cuts.

Howard's authority was flouted each day, until relations between himself and Fraser reached their nadir. The two men sat at the head of the Cabinet table engaging in brutal and bitter exchanges. Fraser said, 'I want the largest responsible deficit that can be brought down, so the Labor Party's position will be irresponsible.' The expansionary peak was reached on Friday 16 July, the day of the Labor leadership challenge. Howard's aide brought a note into him bearing the result of Hayden's win. Howard passed it to Fraser, who announced the Caucus decision: Cabinet burst into spontaneous applause. The election began to look more promising: Hayden remained in the chair and, with Fraser in such a buoyant mood and in the midst of preparing an election budget, there was hope left yet for the Liberal Government.

There was little hope left for John Howard when Cabinet broke on 16 July, and he was left facing the gravest crisis of his career. This would be his fifth budget and his first as deputy Liberal leader. Although a budget represents the collective Cabinet position, it is a very personal document for a Treasurer. Howard felt that this budget was turning into a document that he could not countenance. It was anathema to his personal and political philosophy; a repudiation of the stance which he had championed inside and outside the Government. The deficit was now somewhere in the vicinity of $2,500–$2,750 million compared with Howard's original $1,000-million target. For Howard the political consequences of bringing down a budget like this would be catastrophic. Howard considered his position with his main adviser John Hewson, and with his wife Janette. He examined his options, including resignation. Eventually Howard concluded that, even if he failed in Cabinet, there was no point in resignation. He had obligations to the party and did not believe in resignation threats; so his only recourse was to keep fighting—and that meant persuading Fraser.

Howard saw Fraser on the weekend of 17–18 July to put his case. He did not mention resignation, but he told Fraser that he would not be able to publicise and sell a budget in which he did not believe. Howard argued his case by taking the full-year effect of the revenue decisions being contemplated and projecting them into the 1983–84 year, which produced a deficit estimate in the range $4,000–$5,000 million. There was no dispute between Fraser and Howard; the Prime Minister readily agreed and it appears that he had independently reached the same conclusion as Howard. Fraser was an extraordinary politician to fathom. He would explore one avenue to the hilt and then retrace his steps to try another path. His final position was never settled until a public announcement was made. When budget Cabinet resumed the following week the cycle began all over again. Spending decisions were re-examined.

One revealing sign of the extent to which the Government had changed policy was the 18 July statement by Hayden calling for a budget deficit of $1,500 million. This was below any figure Fraser ever entertained. If Hayden had been Prime Minister and stuck by this policy, he would have introduced a more contractionary budget than Fraser. But it revealed the weakness of Hayden's position because, when the budget was brought down, he reverted to normal and proposed a moderate additional stimulus. As usual Hayden stood for a deficit of D + 1.

During the weekend of 17–18 July reports of Fraser's election budget filled the press. But there were deep fears on the Liberal backbench about the strategy. A survey of backbenchers that weekend condemned an early poll and any change in economic policy in order to win votes. John Hyde said that the Parliament should run its full term: 'If the Labor Party sticks together we would lose an election in October.' Jack Birney (NSW) warned: 'You must have a reason to go to the people with an early election. You can't go just because Hayden won the ALP leadership ballot.' Murray Sainsbury (NSW) said, 'My gut reaction is that the Government should get on and govern.' Jim Bradfield (NSW) opposed an early election for two reasons: 'First because we would have to be sufficiently in front to forgo public resentment, and second because the idea of elections is to get into Government. We're already in Government.' Senator Reg Withers remarked: 'The public is sick and tired of elections and I would think six elections in 10 years is a few too many.'[4] Fraser's optimism was not shared by his colleagues.

In late July the Prime Minister got a blank cheque for an election from the Liberal Party. By this stage Eggleton knew that the budget would contain not just tax cuts; it would create a powerful option for a late 1982 poll. At the Liberal Party federal Executive meeting on 23 July during budget Cabinet, state presidents agreed the election decision would be left with Fraser. The party would accept his judgement; it would remain in a 'state of readiness'. Fraser told the Executive he was confident that the Government could present itself as the party of economic management during difficult times. Fraser said the Hawke challenge may have de-stabilised the Opposition, but it was too early to know. He identified the Senate's attitude towards Government bills as a vital factor in shaping the outlook. Fraser never confided to the Liberal Executive his election intentions. He simply said: 'I'll just wake up one morning and find an election coming on—and that will be the day.' Asked about an election Tony Eggleton said, 'In view of the unpredictable times and speculation, we decided we ought to be advanced in our planning.'

In the second week of budget Cabinet Howard redoubled his efforts to cut back spending and was supported strongly by both Finance Minister Dame Margaret Guilfoyle and Peter Nixon. Howard got two senior Treasury officers, Ted Evans and David Morgan, to brief Cabinet. They put the case bluntly and forcefully and later got a pat on the back from Howard, who said it had been 'great stuff'. Significantly John Stone was not to be seen. He was conspicuously absent from many of the debriefing sessions Howard and Hewson gave during the long Cabinet process. Stone felt he was being excluded by Howard, but Howard denied this later, saying it was a matter for Stone's discretion to come to whatever briefing he wanted. At one stage Hewson proposed to Ted Evans a lunch with Howard to canvass sensitive issues. Evans subsequently suggested that Stone attend, only to find the idea withered on the vine. There was no lunch at all. The collapse in understanding between Howard and Stone permanently impaired their relations. Its enduring significance is that it made John Stone ripe for a change of Government.

The key to the 1982–83 budget was produced late in the day by the Taxation Office. It was the solution of the 'black holes'. Howard told Cabinet that the Taxation Office had two proposals which would raise over $800 million. The first was a new law to recover the tax evaded in bottom-of-the-harbour schemes, which would produce $225 million. The second was a higher penalty for the late payment of tax, expected to raise an estimated $615 million. The Fraser ministers felt both guilty and lucky; it was not supposed to be this easy. When these 'black holes' in revenue were filled the Government would be able to bring down the budget it wanted. It could combine big tax cuts with economic responsibility, and everybody would be satisfied—except Stone.

The origins of the bottom-of-the-harbour legislation lay in the work being done by the Taxation Office in the new political climate created by the McCabe–Lafranchi Report recently tabled in the Victorian Parliament. When Cabinet had met in Darwin in early June it discussed the failure of both the Taxation Office and Crown Solicitors to prosecute an important Perth test case which had been brought to Attorney-General Senator Durack's attention. (This was the 'bottom-of-the-drawer' case identified in the yet-to-be-received damo-clean Costigan Report.) The Government decided then to get an opinion from the Solicitor-General, Sir Maurice Byers, on whether a prosecution could be launched and the lost revenue regathered. The Byers opinion, given to Durack on the eve of budget Cabinet, suggested prosecution could be launched. It also went into detail about how the money could be recovered. Howard was getting similar information from the Taxation Office. The Fraser Cabinet, now under attack for allowing the bottom-of-the-harbour tax evaders to escape, decided to throw out a net and pull them in.

The Government had two motives for its decision. The first was that it desperately needed revenue. The second was that it also needed a weapon with which to strike back in the tax debate. Deputy Taxation Commissioner Trevor Boucher briefed Cabinet on the details. Stories circulating at the time claiming that the decision was taken in haste are false. Fraser insisted that ministers understand the full import of the decision and its far-reaching nature. The Prime Minister also quizzed Taxation Office officials about the revenue estimates, which were very large. But the Taxation Office insisted that they were the most reliable figures of the monies they expected to raise.

The result was that Malcolm Fraser got a budget with a $1,674-million deficit and the biggest personal income tax cut in history. The deficit was tighter than originally recommended by Fraser's troika comprising Visbord, Walsh and Rose. It was nearly $700 million higher than Howard's original position but, in view of the earlier march to expansion, was a satisfactory result for the Treasurer. When the benefits of the extra revenue were packaged into handouts this became the most election-oriented vote-buying budget of the Fraser years.

A minority of Liberal advisers believed that the so-called Thatcher approach should have been followed: if you have a monetarist philosophy, then stick to it. This requires extraordinary nerve during a downturn, with an election coming. It means a Government would not act to boost employment in the short-term, but rather would simply argue that its policies were right for the long-term. Fraser's former Press Secretary David Barnett believed the slide in the Government's fortunes began with this election budget, when Fraser abandoned his longer-term strategy. After Fraser lost office in 1983 Barnett provided this diagnosis:

> The answer, I believe, was a loss of faith in basic principles, and with that loss of faith a loss of direction. The Government delivered tax cuts, a soft budget and retrospective laws to collect additional company tax . . .
>
> The Prime Minister and the Government went into the election campaign without a philosophical direction. It was no longer free enterprise against socialism. The deliberate deficit and its consequent inflation destroyed the basis of the Government's economic arguments.
>
> There was no answer to the ALP on what had become the central question of unemployment. It was half-hearted Keynesianism against the wholehearted Keynesianism of the Labor Party. And the Labor Party won.[5]

John Stone was the champion of this school of thought. In a long letter he wrote to *The Bulletin*, marked 'confidential' but subsequently leaked, Stone drew a parallel between the fate of the Whitlam Government and the 1982 policies of the Fraser Government. Stone recalled the advice which Treasury gave the Whitlam Cabinet in 1974 and which it ignored. He continued:

> Having had some personal hand in the drafting of those words at the time, they revive in me a somewhat nostalgic sadness at the incapacity of Governments to discern the pits they dig for themselves when short-term political expediency comes to hold sway over longer-term economic principle . . .
>
> Of course what we all know is what happened to that Government when it stopped 'listening to Treasury'. Indeed less than 12 months later—with, meanwhile, the egregious Dr Cairns having come and gone formally as Treasurer—a new Treasurer was beginning to indicate a rather different view of

those matters. By that time, of course, it was too late not only for his party but also for the economic health of Australia, as the years since then have witnessed.

History, of course, never precisely repeats itself. Nevertheless, as has been remarked, those who will not learn from history will be doomed to repeat it.[6]

Stone's critique of the role of ministerial advisers such as Hewson and Walsh, both influential in the budget, was also in this letter: 'Public servants—perhaps because they have a continuing responsibility to provide advice and stay on to live with its consequences—have longer memories than the more meretricious players who flit across the private ministerial advisory stage.'[7] This reveals how jealously Stone and Treasury guarded their role as principal economic advisers to the Government. It also reveals that while the Fraser Government recognised Treasury's contribution, it was determined at both the Prime Ministerial and Treasurer level to have economic advisers able to criticise and counter such advice.

Barnett himself was deeply concerned over the rupture in relations between Treasury and the Government. He believed it would impair both the public standing and efficiency of the Fraser Government. Barnett sensed that Stone felt isolated and suggested to Howard that it was normal practice for the Secretary of the Treasury to be knighted. John Stone did not yet have his knighthood. But the Government appeared to have other priorities. However Fraser himself was worried about the rupture between Howard and Stone. After the budget he called Howard to a special meeting to discuss the matter with him. Fraser had been told by senior officers of his own department that Stone was very worried about the lack of contact between Howard and the department. But Howard told Fraser there was no problem, everything was fine. In fact dialogue between Howard and Treasury had broken down beyond repair.

The burning question is whether Fraser's 1982 budget strategy was the right one. This has both an economic and a political dimension. Events proved that Fraser's initial economic diagnosis was correct. Everybody misjudged the depth of the recession and the huge increase in unemployment, but Fraser got closer than his own advisers. The budget that Treasury and, to a lesser extent, Howard advocated was inappropriate to the times and would have only accentuated the recession. The notion that Fraser would have retained credibility in sticking by the 'fight inflation first' strategy has no evidence to sustain it. Eventually people will vote on results rather than ideology. By moving towards economic expansion Fraser's judgement was correct.

The real issue is whether Fraser's political strategy of a late-1982 election, which was implicit in his budget, was also correct. The Prime Minister's pessimism about the world economy had become such an article of faith that he wanted a 1982 election rather than face the full ravages of the economic recession in 1983. His decision to go to a 1982 election was, on balance, unsustained by economic factors. It is true that a delay until late 1983 would have been a gamble on recovery having arrived or, more likely, the upturn having begun. But the 1982 dash to the polls was a gamble in itself. Many of Fraser's senior ministers such as John Howard and Fred Chaney opposed his 1982 strategy, arguing that there was no rationale for an early election and that the Government should get on with governing. A less restless Prime Minister who lacked Fraser's electioneering compulsion might have chosen this 1983 course and steered the Government through it in an effective fashion. But the pugilist in Fraser led him to an election fight and his confidence always told him he could win. As 1983 unfolded the signs of economic recovery ripened with the most appealing fruit being falling interest rates, equivalent to a tax cut for most families, which provided further evidence that Fraser's economic pessimism was too exaggerated. If Fraser had been more patient and waited a year, then he could have pointed to genuine economic gain to justify his re-election.

The magnitude of Fraser's 1982 risk was documented by the opinion polls which showed that Hayden led the ALP in front of the Government throughout the whole year. Fraser would have been starting from a significant disadvantage in any 1982 poll. He had hoped that a generous budget combined with his own leadership strength and electoral doubts about Hayden might have given him an edge sufficient to make up the leeway. It was always a gamble and Fraser's chances were never better than even money. Yet Fraser's overall decision was right because of another unique factor.

Hawke's ambitions were given a numerical reality in the July challenge. Once Hawke became ALP leader he was certain to defeat Fraser whenever the election was held. Hawke would enjoy a long honeymoon as leader of the Opposition. Consequently the clinching argument which justifies Fraser's early election strategy is that it was best because it would have eliminated the danger of facing Hawke. Fraser took the decision on economics rather than the ALP leadership. The latter was always an ingredient, but not decisive. Although he thought Hayden would survive, Fraser wanted to be certain of facing him. In one sense Fraser was being cautious; he was calling an election against Hayden to avoid facing Hawke.

15

Costigan thwarts Fraser

Never have a Royal Commission unless you know the result.

Arthur Fadden,
many years ago

Malcolm Fraser's budget was dispatched to the Government printer in late July and Fraser embarked on his latest overseas trip, to Malaysia, China and New Zealand—a revitalising break before the likely election. The Prime Minister flew out on his VIP plane on 1 August oblivious to the document that had just arrived in his office with the political force of an exocet missile. It was a salutary lesson in the politics of unpredictability: even the best-laid plans of the most clever of Prime Ministers can go awry.

On 27 July the Governor-General received interim report No. 4 from the Royal Commission on the Activities of the Federated Ship Painters' and Dockers' Union. The commissioner was Frank Costigan, a Melbourne QC, a man of personal courage, Labor background and investigative zealousness. Government House dispatched the report to Fraser's office the same day. But it was not the highest priority for the Prime Minister; not on the eve of an overseas trip, and with the budget looming. The report lay dormant but it had a political fuse sufficient to blow the lid off the Liberal Party. When the Costigan Report exploded it would completely overshadow the budget and negate the immediate option of a September election which the budget had offered. The Costigan missile, which was not launched by accident and was indeed fired by Fraser's own hand from his own flagship and intended to deplete the ALP fleet, travelled in a complete circle and torpedoed its instigator.

The Costigan Report has a special place in the Fraser years. It succeeded where so many other efforts had failed, and made tax avoidance one of the big issues in politics; it provoked Fraser's greatest assault on his own party

216

and confronted the Liberals directly with the tough anti tax-avoidance line pioneered by John Howard; it ruined Fraser's September election option and, finally, it undermined Bill Hayden. Quite a report.

Fraser became interested in the Painters' and Dockers' after a series of articles in *The Bulletin* in 1980 which revealed murder and mayhem on a frightening scale. Alan Reid, veteran press gallery correspondent for *The Bulletin* and shrewd judge of political opportunity, discussed the articles with ministers, perhaps with Fraser. The Prime Minister got enthusiastic. Here was a union infiltrated by criminals that the Government had ignored.

Fraser had embarked on a political exercise—his senior ministers had no doubt of this. He wanted a full-scale inquiry, even a Royal Commission, and would not tolerate the powerful opposition to this proposal. It was Fraser who took this submission to Cabinet, not Attorney-General Peter Durack. Opposition came from the Hamer Liberal Government in Victoria, the Victorian police, the Australian federal police and the then Administrative Services Minister, John MacLeay, who had responsibility for the police. They argued that these were police matters and that a Royal Commission was superfluous, but Fraser prevailed.

It fell to Durack to find a Royal Commissioner and to Kevin Newman, the new Administrative Services Minister, to staff the commission. The judiciary was uninterested. Victorian judges had an established practice of declining Royal Commissions. Moreover the inquiry looked like a fairly limited one into some arcane and unsavoury cupboards of trade-union life. Durack struggled to find his commissioner. Finally his department suggested Costigan, an experienced QC who had the merit of wanting the job. Durack accepted. Costigan had been a member of The Participants, the Button group in the Victorian ALP, and he had stood unsuccessfully as a Labor candidate for federal Parliament in a 1970 by-election. His father Joe Costigan, a tax expert, fought tenaciously for the legitimate claims of his clients but refused to help cheats. This rigour and morality was instilled in Costigan at the family dinner table. Costigan had risen to the top of the pile at the Melbourne Bar.

It was Richard Searby who recommended to Durack that Douglas Meagher, QC, would be suitable as counsel assisting the Commission. It was to be a joint Royal Commission for both the federal and Victorian Governments and was finally set up in September 1980. Costigan and Meagher made a formidable combination. Intelligent and innovative, they pioneered a sophisticated approach analysing organised crime. They invited ministers and officials to Melbourne to inspect their operation. Significantly Costigan obtained vast resources from Kevin Newman: staff many more than that of a normal Royal Commission, as well as a computer. Newman examined the operation and was impressed. Durack was briefed in autumn 1982 and was also impressed. While the commission brought a vastly different approach to the job from traditional police methods, there were some reservations in the Attorney-General's Department as they detected in Costigan a sense of missionary zeal, a quality in scarce supply in the Canberra bureaucracy.

In Costigan's 3rd Interim Report of December 1981 he found the Painters' and Dockers' were being used by promoters in the tax-evasion industry and recommended that the income tax law be amended to allow his commission access to confidential tax records. After weighty consideration the Government agreed. It also issued fresh letters patent in April 1982 to supplement and strengthen the original terms of reference. At every point, Costigan received strong backing.

The commission was perceived as an exercise inspired by the Prime Minister; its views on taxation were in harmony with the tough stance taken by Howard—tough in terms of traditional Liberal politics. It was now obvious that the Royal Commission, originally established to investigate crime in the unions, had shifted its focus to tax crime. But few people in Government realised that when Costigan's zeal was brought to bear on this new field, littered with traps set by the tax-evasion industry, the inevitable explosion would occur under the very foundations of the Liberal Party.

Meantime ministers began to become more concerned about the need for a permanent body to continue the work Costigan had initiated. Durack told his department that the Government would soon examine whether a full-time Crimes Commission was needed. A little later Fraser rang Durack and put this very proposition to him with great enthusiasm. Costigan's influence permeated to the highest levels. It was mid-1982 and the Fraser Cabinet was polishing its election budget.

With the budget as his platform Fraser had two options for a late-1982 election. The first was the sudden death option, September, to be held as soon as possible after the budget. The second was the November–December period, more usual for general elections. But Fraser was interested in September. He never dismissed an option until absolutely necessary. September seemed attractive because it gave the Labor Party very little time to recover from the Hayden–Hawke crisis. Its other attraction was that it would precede the looming economic downturn which Fraser and his advisers correctly identified but underestimated.

The Prime Minister's office was guilty of a major political error in not alerting Fraser earlier to the implications of the Costigan Report. During the overseas trip senior officials of the Prime Minister's Department raised the issue with Fraser but it was not until after Fraser returned, on 10 August, that he understood its full import.

It is doubtful if a more gripping Royal Commission report has ever been presented to Government. The Costigan Report was well written, clear and concise with a story-line that carried the reader along with it like a crime-thriller. But it went one better; it was real life. Costigan was a journalist's delight. Shouts went through the press gallery the afternoon it was released. Those ministers who read it carefully felt a chilling sense of alarm.

The thrust of Costigan's argument was that dishonesty, negligence and incompetence in the Crown Solicitor's Office had allowed a 'major fraud' on federal revenue through tax evasion. Costigan argued that the notorious bottom-of-the-harbour tax scheme had flourished because of legal error and administrative incompetence by the Government's own advisers. This scheme was outlawed by John Howard's *Crimes (Taxation Offences) Act 1980* which introduced criminal penalties, but Costigan said that the scheme was first detected 'in a widespread manner' by the Taxation Office as early as 1973. Costigan stated:

> The amount of money likely to be lost to the revenue of the Commonwealth was of enormous amounts and even today I do not believe any sensible estimate can be made of its extent, save to say that it is measured in hundreds if not thousands of millions of dollars,[1]

In his analysis of the problem Costigan said the issues 'reflect upon the office of the Crown Solicitor'. His report documented the history of the bottom-of-the-harbour test case being handled in the Perth branch of the deputy Crown Solicitor's Office, the case identified by the Tax Department in 1973. He claimed there was dishonesty in the Perth office and incompetence in the Canberra office of the Crown Solicitor. His report was a severe embarrassment to the then Secretary of the Attorney-General's Department, Alan Neaves, who had been Crown Solicitor for much of the period covered by the report. Costigan said the principal legal officer in Perth had left instructions for prosecution of the case in a bottom drawer of the deputy Crown Solicitor's Office and it appeared that 'they had been deliberately placed there, away from the file, so that it would not be apparent that they had been prepared and ready for delivery to counsel'.[2] He alleged false statements had been made by the Perth office to Canberra, which further delayed action. An officer in the Perth branch, along with his wife, began a prostitution business under the name 'Kim's Introductions' through which he tried to avoid tax. His wife became involved in the bottom-of-the-harbour tax schemes. Costigan said of this public servant, 'His attitude was that he would break the law and defy those charged with its enforcement to prove his breach . . . he is a dishonest man.'[3]

Three officers of whom Costigan was particularly critical were the Perth deputy Crown Solicitor, Mr R. Massie, principal legal officer, Mr S. O'Sullivan, who left the instructions in the bottom drawer, and senior legal officer, Mr A. Bercove, whose wife was involved in the tax evasion schemes. But the report continued:

> An even more fundamental criticism to be made of the Canberra office is that it has a responsibility of supervising the discharge of duty in the states . . . Ultimately responsibility rests with the Crown Solicitor himself . . . this matter first came to [his] attention in early 1978. That it was at the instance of the Taxation Commissioner only gave added force to the responsibility to discharge the supervisory duty, yet notwithstanding that the Crown Solicitor was shortly thereafter himself in the very state where the matter was handled, and notwithstanding that the Crown Solicitor involved himself in the matter personally and directly early in 1979, no attempt was made to discharge the supervisory function . . . It, the office, has stood by and allowed the most appalling conduct to continue.[4]

Closing the circle of his argument, Costigan said the existing law in the 1970s was never tested:

> The consequences of the gross negligence in the Crown Solicitor's Office are difficult to understate. There have been many promoters of schemes similar to that which this case is about. With the lack of action in the courts confidence grew that the law could be broken with impunity. The Crown Solicitor's Office failed to discharge its primary duty, namely, to uphold the law. By its negligence it permitted the law to be disregarded and brought into contempt. The loss to the revenue is enormous.
>
> These consequences were bad enough. What was worse was that the Crown Solicitor's Office permitted the inference to arise that the existing law was not adequate and that new laws were needed. Thus the Parliament of the Commonwealth of Australia was induced to enact new criminal laws of great breadth and scope when all that was required was the enforcement of the existing laws.[5]

Costigan attacked the secrecy provisions of the tax law as a source of trouble. He recommended that secrecy be lifted, giving both the Treasurer and Attorney-General access to files in order to restore ministerial supervision.

The commissioner said that both the Crown Solicitor's Office as well as the Taxation Department had an erroneous view of the law and misunderstood the fundamentals in moving against bottom-of-the-harbour tax schemes.

The report dramatically opened a window on the process of Government in Australia. It revealed not just the power of the bureaucracy but its inertia. Above all it demonstrated that ministers were prisoners of bureaucratic advisers and the values, procedures and conventions which public servants devise. It was a vindication of an enduring truth about Australian politics: Royal Commissions have a life and an authority of their own. Equipped with a vigorous commissioner and able staff—both conditions satisfied in the Costigan Commission—their power to call witnesses and publish under Parliamentary privilege is formidable. Arthur Fadden once advised: 'Never have a Royal Commission unless you know the result.'[6]

When the report was released a classic debate on ministerial responsibility followed. The Labor Opposition invoked this principle and called upon both Durack and Howard, as the responsible ministers, to resign. Neither minister was aware of the events documented in the report. So the issue was the extent to which ministers were accountable for the grievous sins of their advisers. Durack and his department disputed Costigan's central argument: that the existing tax law of the 1970s was sufficiently strong to prosecute bottom-of-the-harbour offenders. Costigan's charge against the Government was, however, elaborate and spectacular. His report had the weight necessary to highlight the gravity of the issue, but it had the spice to transfix public attention. Reg Withers said:

> Funnily enough, I think it's that silly, stupid sort of escort agency running in Perth, because that's what the average Australian understands, and he will be totally puzzled as to why a well-paid public servant lawyer should be indulging in such an activity, and he will think to himself, if that's happening, there is something terribly wrong with Government administration.[7]

The real danger the Costigan Report presented to the Fraser Government was its central charge that huge amounts of revenue had been lost due to the Government's own incompetence and corruption. The charge was serious in its nature and potentially lethal in its political impact. It questioned the basic integrity of the Fraser Government and its ability to govern within the bounds of fairness demanded by the community. The issue was one that could destroy the Government.

Durack was on leave in a remote part of Western Australia in early August when he received an urgent call from his departmental head Alan Neaves. The

Attorney-General's Department had just read the report. Durack said later, 'They had their heads on fire.' Neaves wanted Durack to come to Canberra immediately. The Attorney refused. Ministers in the Fraser Cabinet always earned their holiday and Durack wanted to enjoy his. Cabinet considered the Costigan Report on 10 August, the day Fraser returned from his overseas trip. Neil Brown was acting Attorney-General. Fraser rang Durack the next day, by which stage the Attorney had returned to Perth. The Prime Minister was alarmed, as he wanted Durack to bring forward a series of recommendations the following week so that the Government could demonstrate its determination to act.

When Durack returned to Canberra he found his department demoralised. They had been condemned by Costigan, yet were now required to recommend what action to take arising from his report. Durack had great trouble getting either a statement or recommendations from them. The Attorney-General's Department was very reluctant to recommend action against the officers named in the Costigan Report. Durack later told a colleague, 'They behaved at their negative best'. Meanwhile ministers were sent copies of Chapter 3, the key section of the report.

Fraser spent a few hours at the Liberal Party Secretariat on 11 August while the party's advertising agency D'Arcy–MacManus and Masius gave a detailed presentation. Material was advanced for a campaign based on the budget against a Hayden-led Labor Party. Eggleton remained worried about the Government's low credibility on interest rates and taxation, but the budget was designed to counter this problem. The briefing was to assess whether Masius should be retained. Its former chairman Len Reason, the key agency figure in three previous Liberal federal campaigns, had left and was now only a consultant to Masius. Eggleton wanted to ensure that the Prime Minister still approved the Masius material. Fraser left satisfied.

The high point for the September option was the weekend of 14–15 August and newspaper reports, based on high-level briefings, appeared on 16 August. Fraser always resented election speculation, although he was never loath to generate it. When the Prime Minister arrived at Parliament House that morning, the day before the budget, his election message seemed clear:

QUESTION: Good morning, do you expect the Government to run its full term?

FRASER: I hope so. Yes, I do.

QUESTION: Is the speculation of an early election well informed?

FRASER: The speculation as far as I can see is totally and universally badly informed and I just wonder why so many people damage their reputations by continuing to promote it, and that, of course, includes the Australian Labor Party.[8]

That evening Fraser's Press Secretary, Eddie Dean, rang senior newspaper reporters and cautioned them not to interpret these comments as ruling out a September election.

Such was the climate surrounding the budget. The incident was an insight into Fraser's political operation. At the very time the Prime Minister publicly ridiculed suggestions of an early election his own office was informing journalists that this remained a possibility. Moreover there was nothing exceptional about this discrepancy. Senior reporters had for years experienced numerous instances of Fraser taking a course of action in private and claiming the opposite in public. It seemed to accompany many of the highly political decisions of the Prime Minister. Such behaviour generated a pervasive cynicism, not just between the press and the Prime Minister, but between Fraser and many of his own colleagues. Yet Fraser regularly became impatient and angry when the public and the press failed to take him at his word. He never betrayed an awareness or capacity for self-analysis which would have allowed him to understand why this happened.

Cabinet considered the Costigan Report in more detail that same day. Ministers examined follow-up Government action, the danger of the report leaking and the difficulty caused by the fact that the Cain Government also had the report since the Royal Commission had been a joint one. However the Victorian Government did not at that time have the damaging Chapter 3.

The first decision taken was that the report would need to be tabled. The Government decided to release it a week after the budget, 24 August, the day of Hayden's budget reply. Their strategy was to make a strong tabling statement with a view to neutralising Costigan's criticisms. But the vital political decision was whether the Government could have an election immediately after the tabling of the report, and that was most unlikely.

The Prime Minister was unhappy that the press had interpreted the budget as a prelude to elections. In fact an orgy of election speculation immediately broke out in its wake, but the difficulties in procuring an early election were increasing, not receding. The budget was the most intensely political of the entire Fraser period. Its motivation was politics not economics. This was obvious from an analysis of the Treasurer's speech which was devoid of an economic philosophy or argument. Howard labelled the document a 'family budget'—a political, not economic title.

The budget was clever because it gave many interest groups handouts, yet the overall deficit was a relatively modest $1,674 million. Income tax was cut for everyone. About 75 per cent of taxpayers, including average- and lower-income earners, were placed on a new and lower-standard tax rate (reduced from 32 per cent to 30 per cent). Two million families benefited from a 50 per cent increase in family allowances for the first and second child. About 430,000 pensioners with private incomes benefited from the decision to increase by one-third the amount of extra income entitlement without affecting the full pension rate. A new home-loan interest rebate supplemented the Government's existing housing scheme that had been announced in March. While the original was pitched to the needy the new scheme was not limited to first-home buyers, and allowed a rebate on mortgages up to $60,000, a major concession to the middle class. The Government gave significant assistance to business and industry, tertiary students, sole-parent families and private investors. These benefits overcame the budget 'sting'—a sales tax increase on all goods and a hefty excise increase on beer and tobacco.

Fraser followed the Menzies' practice. He raided both the political and economic larder of the Labor Party. He tried to steal from under Labor's nose its family living standards appeal on which Hayden almost won the 1980 election. In that campaign Hayden's magic figure was $16 a week—the extent to which the average Australian family was disadvantaged because of taxes, petrol, health, housing and the freeze on family allowances. Labor had pledged to restore family living standards. Significantly Howard said in his speech that the average family would be $16.84 a week better off due to the tax and other concessions. Fraser used the big tax cuts to argue the case for wage restraint. This was designed to neutralise the prices–incomes accord being negotiated between the ALP and ACTU. Although neither side would admit it, the budget was another example of convergence: both Government and Opposition were moving much closer together in policy terms. Fraser had turned from the economics of contraction and moved back towards expansion. A Hayden budget would not have been greatly different.

The day after the budget the Labor Party and the Australian Democrats hastened to deny Fraser his rationale of Senate obstruction. Neither party wanted an early election. Certainly the ALP was unprepared, still recovering from its leadership trauma. It had not formulated the policy with which to fight a campaign and wanted more time. ALP Senate leader John Button conferred with the Australian Democrats leader Don Chipp. Both men promised the budget itself would pass the Senate intact. They suggested that all 19 related bills would probably be passed as well, although no guarantee could be given until the bills had been examined. This assurance was highly unusual, both in its speed and firmness, and made the difficulties even greater for Fraser. The Prime Minister was being comprehensively denied any reason for an early election.

Fraser hit back at the media's depiction of his budget as an exercise in election cynicism:

If we brought in a hair-shirt budget, a hair-shirt made out of steel wool, I have got no doubt that it would have been branded as callous, unthinking, unfeeling and 'didn't we have any concern for the way the recession is affecting many average Australians'.

You bring in a budget that does show concern for these things. Instead of recognising that for what it is, people just want to attach the word 'election' to it.[9]

The Cabinet agreed that after the Costigan Report had been tabled the Government could not call an election. Fraser, Howard and Carrick all reached this conclusion. So did Peter Nixon, who had previously been an election 'hawk' but had changed because of Costigan. The only senior minister who held out for September was Doug Anthony. Fraser's other problem was that the Senate had not provided him with any political justification for calling an early election. The logic of Fraser's position was to follow an election budget with an election, but the political climate was changing yet again and the gamble was too great. The two possible dates were 18 and 25 September and an almost immediate choice was required. In the event the September election option withered.

Fraser travelled to Victoria and Tasmania at the end of budget week. *En route* to Launceston, sitting at the back of the VIP plane, Fraser criticised two political reporters, Anne Summers and Michelle Grattan, over the stories they had written that week about the September option. He attacked the journalists saying that there was no discussion of such an option. In fact the stories came from people close to the Prime Minister who were maintaining a 'state of readiness' until Fraser rejected the option. In Launceston on 20 August Fraser made it clear than an early election would depend upon the Senate, a formula which kept the option alive in name only. 'You never know when the Senate is going to twist or turn,' Fraser said. He observed that on the election issue 'everyone wants to back me into a corner'.

The final decision was taken late on the evening of 24 August after Cabinet had broken. Eggleton and newly elected Liberal President Dr Jim Forbes came to Parliament House and listened to Hayden's budget reply. They had a brief word with Fraser before Cabinet and then left. After Cabinet had broken Fraser conferred with a few senior ministers and they agreed to await a more opportune time. Fraser rang Eggleton at home late that night and told him that September was out, the main reason being the Costigan Report. Eggleton was baffled. As the Liberal campaign manager he had known nothing about Costigan until he noticed newspaper reports over the previous couple of days suggesting that the commissioner's report would be significant.

He wondered why such a politically important issue had not been considered earlier in an election context. The other reason Fraser gave Eggleton was the need, in the light of Costigan, to get the Government's special tax recoupment bill through Parliament before an election. This bill was the controversial retrospective measure to re-gather lost moneys through bottom-of-the-harbour tax schemes. Fraser feared that if he called an election before the bill became the law his critics could always argue he was not 'fair dinkum' in stamping out the rorts exposed by Costigan. Fraser was already aware of growing divisions inside his own party over the bill and was anxious to prevail there first. He knew that a sustained campaign against the bill was underway and that it must be defeated.

In telling Eggleton of the decision Fraser immediately said, 'Let's have a look at November or December.' This startled Eggleton. He and Forbes, along with the ministry, were prepared to accept Fraser's judgement on a September election; it was risky, but there was a strategy. Eggleton felt apprehensive about the end of the year.

One major defect with a September election scenario had always been the absence of any reason or justification for such a poll beyond that of electoral expediency. Simply because this factor might not have plagued Prime Ministers in recent early elections did not necessarily mean that it might not have become an issue this time. The fact is that, while the technical requirements existed for a double-dissolution election, there was no genuine political deadlock between the Houses. The Senate had provided the technical but not the political conditions for a sudden election, since the Government's capacity to govern was not being threatened. Indeed the speed with which the Opposition parties promised passage of the budget confirmed this. Fraser needed a good reason to call a sudden election in the opening fortnight of the budget session of Parliament before his budget had even been debated, let alone passed, by Parliament. Yet he had no such reason and would have faced concerted media criticism for calling an early poll. The charge would have been levelled at Fraser that he was running to the polls before the recession, predicted by the Prime Minister himself, had taken its fearful toll on the community. There was strong evidence to suggest that the calling of a September election would have become an issue in its own right.

Would Fraser have won a September election? It would have been a great gamble. Fraser adopted the obvious and sensible course at the time in sitting pat; suggestions to the contrary rely too much on the benefit of hindsight. Opinion polls conducted throughout August and September showed Labor maintaining its lead, although that lead fluctuated from a swing of 2.5 to six per cent. The Government had a lot of electoral ground to recover and its capacity to do so must have been doubted. Certainly the campaign period would have been critical and the Government would have relied upon its tax cut budget. But the electorate had been down that track before, and this time it would not have been so enthusiastic. Benefits given before elections tend to disappear after voting day. The danger for Fraser was that his budget was too cynical, and was perceived as such. It did not meet the emerging needs of the community. The public was looking for a political party which offered a new programme, a way out of the spiralling economic decline with its concomitant social debilitation. The Labor Party was ill-prepared, but its capacity to run a campaign from scratch remained a threat. Hayden's slide into demoralisation had not begun and it is possible that he would have responded to a campaign, fighting as effectively as he did in the 1980 election. In that case Fraser would have lost. At the time the Government could not have rated much better than even money—too great a risk.

The extent to which the Costigan Report would have become a campaign issue must have assisted the ALP. Given the divisions which subsequently rent the Liberal Party, the potential existed for a split within the Government during the campaign period itself. If Fraser had called an election in September it would have been wiser to suppress the Costigan Report—a risky ploy in itself. But the closing of the September option launched a new battle, an emotional and bruising brawl over tax evasion. It offered both Hayden and Fraser fresh opportunities and posed unusual dangers.

16
Election strategy foiled

We don't believe you're likely to win and we don't believe it's the right time to call an election . . .

Jim Forbes and Tony Eggleton to Malcolm Fraser,
October 1982

The Labor Party was now poised to exploit Fraser's election retreat and use the tax issue to take the political initiative. This was Labor's minimum expectation; its maximum was that the tax avoidance debate could destroy the Government's standing and seal Fraser's doom. Labor had two advantages: it remained significantly ahead of the Government in the polls and the tax scandal slotted exactly into its own election strategy.

The Prime Minister sought to use his bottom-of-the-harbour tax-recoupment legislation as a political tool to cleanse his Government of blame for the tax rorts documented by Costigan. The tax debate revealed Malcolm Fraser as a moral zealot, a scheming politician and a dogmatic leader. In the next few weeks Fraser would confront not only the Liberal Party but the snug certitudes of the 'new rich'.

Fraser was challenging one of the great undercover growth industries of the previous decade, legitimised by the Barwick High Court, fuelled by the 'fast buck' ethics of the professional class and dependent upon the inertia of Government. Fraser's tradition was 'old money' and he was ignorant of the styles and values of the 'new money'—Perth's mining-boom barons, property speculators and most significantly, the medical and legal fraternities who had spearheaded the attack on the Taxation Commissioner. In his challenge to 'new money' Fraser struck at both prominent Liberal Party figures and legions of Liberal supporters. His own background as a pastoralist-turned-politician imbued with a sense of public service was never more accentuated. Fraser now declared war on his own party. His political instincts told him it was a necessity; his morality told him it was his obligation. But the spectre of division did great harm to the Liberal Party.

Within a week of the Costigan Report being tabled, Fraser took his stand:

> I think those high-priced lawyers and accountants who have devised and promoted tax avoidance schemes do more damage to the basis of this society than a thousand BLFs in this world. That is why Governments have to act or react with vehemence and strength in eradicating this unmitigated evil from the body politic within Australia.[1]

The Fraser crusade had begun. The Prime Minister publicly warned that any members of the Liberal Party engaged in 'certain approaches in relation to tax avoidance' had better leave the party. They were not wanted. According to this definition the Liberal Party might as well sever one of its arms. When Fraser said in private that the disease should be cut out, he was referring to significant sections of the Western Australian and Queensland Liberal Parties which opposed him. However opposition to the tax recoupment bill was broadly based. It was led by wide sections of the legal and accountancy profession who believed that the Government was transgressing basic principles.

The Government had outlawed bottom-of-the-harbour schemes and imposed criminal penalties in its 1980 law. It now proposed retrospective legislation stretching back for many years prior to 1980 in order to regain the revenue lost. The Government proposed to regather the revenue from the 'vendor shareholders', not the actual promoters who evaded company tax and dispatched companies to the bottom-of-the-harbour. This was because it was not administratively feasible to regain monies from the promoters themselves. Therefore the Government was attacking an earlier stage in the process and making the sellers of the companies liable for the tax evaded by the buyers. The trouble was that under the existing law in the 1970s the sellers had practised only legal tax avoidance, unlike the promoters who were guilty of illegal tax evasion. So the legislation was not only retrospective, but transferred a tax liability from one group to another. To justify the bill Fraser argued that the sellers were not innocent parties and that they knew they were participating in a tax evasion arrangement. That is to say, he took a position on morality and not in law. Fraser's ethics were highlighted in the following exchange:

> QUESTION: By the same token, those loopholes were available to thos people [vendor shareholders] who took enough time to study them, though, weren't they?

FRASER: Oh, yes. But are we governed only by law? Is there not a question of ethics? Is there not a question of honour in the way in which people do their business? If every wrongful act has to be proscribed by law, then we're really going to be so circumscribed by laws that you'll need a couple of solicitors behind you at every step, and I don't particularly want to live in that kind of society.[2]

Fraser himself had negotiated the morality curve of tax avoidance. The Prime Minister and a number of his ministers had operated family trusts and thereby used a conventional legal loophole to minimise tax. Fraser disbanded his own family trust in early 1979 and went out of his way to brief the media on this decision.[3] But in earlier years Fraser had defended the use of such tax loopholes by saying it was the responsibility of the Government to formulate laws and that citizens could not be criticised for using a loophole that the Government tolerated. A sound principle.

When John Howard began his drive against tax avoiders in favour of the public interest, Fraser had been supportive but not always enthusiastic. He had been concerned about the political impact on the Liberal Party's own constituency. At one stage early in his Government, in an exchange with a staffer, Fraser laughed at the amount of tax his aide was paying. But the Prime Minister had now convinced himself about the morality of his own position. Tax avoidance was an evil and he would eradicate it.

Fraser's stance took a fearful toll inside the Liberal Party as he applied, in true Whitlam fashion, the technique of 'crash through or crash'. Within the Liberal Party the Western Australian division spearheaded the opposition; the Queensland division passed an ambiguous but essentially critical motion; and the NSW division voted initially, by a narrow margin, to condemn the legislation. It was opposed publicly by former Western Australian Premier Sir Charles Court, and openly questioned by the then South Australian Premier, David Tonkin. Fraser's own supporters enunciated the Whitlam tactic in defence of their boss: the greater the Liberal Party opposition, the bigger Fraser's ultimate victory, because the public would see him as a strong leader.

Fraser took the issue to the Liberal Party Federal Executive on 27 August, which finally agreed on a unanimous position after a grim debate. The chief protagonists were Fraser and the Western Australian Party President, Ian Warner, but concern about the tax bill was also vented by the NSW division and by the party's Federal Treasurer Sir Robert Creighton-Brown. Fraser made a number of impassioned statements during this debate and declared: 'I'd rather resign than back down on this tax law.' Eggleton was instrumental in negotiating a compromise which allowed both Fraser and Warner to read their own interpretation into the resolution.

A fortnight later the Western Australian party purchased newspaper space in which to attack Fraser. Under the heading 'Open Letter to Western Australians' Warner said:

> We believe that the lure of retrospective tax is too easy a temptation for expedient politicians to get out of self-inflicted troubles, in a delayed demonstration to the public that they are doing their job—eventually . . .
>
> We are solidly opposed to retrospective tax legislation because of the impossibility of turning the clock back some five to 10 years to put liability accurately on those citizens who deserve such liability. We are very concerned that such legislation will hit innocent parties.[4]

The Labor Party attacked the Fraser Government on two broad fronts. The first was that Attorney-General Durack and Treasurer Howard had presided for years over the rorts exposed by Costigan; the ALP said that the dictates of ministerial responsibility demanded their resignation. The second ground was that Liberal figures were identified as participants in tax schemes and, by attacking them, the ALP tried to taint the Government with impropriety. As the debate continued, Labor's tactics became an issue in itself.

Durack defended his refusal to resign because of Costigan's criticism on the grounds that he was ignorant of the bungling of his own department. The Attorney spent some time studying the literature on ministerial responsibility and then declared: 'I think it's been very rare indeed for ministers in Britain in recent decades to resign on a principle simply because there was a bungle in a department.' Reg Withers, Andrew Peacock and the anti-Fraser backbench chorus were crying for Durack's head just as much as was the Labor Party.

Documents released by the Government on 22 September, in response to ALP pressure, revealed that the Taxation Office had for several years been urging upon the Government the 1980 law against bottom-of-the-harbour tax schemes. They also showed that ministers had delayed the bill for more than a year. On 7 November 1979 Taxation Commissioner Bill O'Reilly had advised Howard:

> I am gravely concerned to hear that there may be some question about going ahead with the planned legislation on this matter, the nature and level of penalties proposed being, I understand, a source of difficulty for some of your colleagues . . . This activity is occurring on a large scale daily.

One promoter has stripped over 1,500 companies in Victoria which had income tax liabilities in the year prior to the strip totalling $14 million . . .

I repeat that the only way to curb white collar crime—of which these practices are an integral and costly part—is by imposing criminal penalties and the threat of gaol. Unless something effective is done along the lines proposed, we may almost as well not bother with anti-avoidance legislation. I say that advisedly.

The Labor Party savaged the Government for its delay, but Howard replied that the Government had first taken the necessary precautions for civil liberties and then acted decisively.

The sharpest dilemma for the Government in the tax debate centred around the Western Australian businessman, Denis Horgan, a former Chairman of the WA party's finance committee, who was named in the McCabe–Lafranchi Report on tax avoidance. Horgan became a focus of Labor's attack, an example of Liberal impropriety. Horgan denied that he had ever participated in illegal tax evasion practices, but his companies were named as the type of operation which Fraser was attacking. Hayden made great political capital from the moral absolutism that Fraser had espoused. He quoted back across the parliamentary chamber Fraser's own words on the bottom-of-the-harbour schemes: 'I do not believe anyone could have taken part without knowing they were wrong.' Fraser needed to cast a wide net to justify the scope of his tax recoupment bill, yet such a net was appearing to drag in many prominent Liberal supporters.

Some of the most rugged and exhausting Cabinet clashes of the Fraser years began during the week starting 13 September when Fraser told Cabinet he wanted Horgan to stand down from his many Government positions. The main ones included director of the AIDC, ABC Commissioner, member of the Australian–Japan Foundation and member of the Advisory Council of the CSIRO. One minister later estimated that Cabinet spent 20 to 30 hours that week fighting over Horgan. Fred Chaney, a friend, spoke to Horgan who said he had done nothing wrong and would not resign. Resignation would be an admission of guilt. As the Fraser campaign against Horgan intensified so did the opposition both of the Western Australian Party and senior ministers. Fraser tried to impose his will, but faced a wall of Cabinet opposition from Carrick, Howard, Chaney and Jim Carlton, who said that people invited to serve on Government boards should not be stood down simply because unproven accusations were made against them in Parliament or in public. During this long week the tax issue exhausted the Government's stamina and compromised its political standing. Relations between Fraser and his closest ministers plummeted; backbenchers openly savaged ministers. The Liberal organisation was at war with the Prime Minister. Finally backbenchers signalled their determination to oppose much of the recoupment bill. The tax issue was consuming the Liberal Party and the normal business of Government had long since been forgotten.

In its early stages the tax issue began to take shape as the 'loans affair' of the Fraser Government. It was big, uncontrollable and prone to sensational media treatment. The Costigan Report danced a forensic path through petty criminals, trade-union murderers and Liberal Party tax avoiders. Rumours swirled through the financial and political communities about the names mentioned in the confidential sections of the Costigan Report. The Wran Government hastened to the fray; its Attorney-General Frank Walker said that the NSW Corporate Affairs Commission had uncovered tax evasion on an unimagined scale, with 4,000 companies involved. He predicted the loss to revenue would be measured in 'thousands of millions of dollars'. Fraser was thereby put on notice that whenever he called an election the Wran Government might drop its own time bomb. Suddenly the strategic advantage of ALP Governments in Sydney and Melbourne appeared lethal.

The chief reason that the Labor attack was so damaging was that it threatened the early-election priority on which Fraser had staked so much. By mid-September it appeared that Fraser had probably made the most vital miscalculation of his prime ministership. He was caught in an economic and political squeeze. Only a fortnight after the budget the deficit began to blow out. Cabinet approved significant funds to farmers as drought compensation; the slide towards a deep recession was soon evident and that meant more welfare payments and less revenue. The political appeal of Howard's 'family budget' with its extra $16 a week for the average family was almost forgotten. The fiscal realities, as Fraser perceived them, were that he could not wait for another budget. The full-year cost in 1983–84 of his 1982 tax cuts would leave no scope for further generosity. Fraser knew that as each day went by unemployment and inflation would both escalate. Time was running out. So he fought the tax issue not just to defend his Government or himself, but to salvage and then implement his 1982 election strategy.

During September Hayden decided to shift his attack more towards prominent Liberals. He was supported by his two closest Caucus colleagues, John Dawkins and Peter Walsh, whose natural parliamentary aggression was suited to this type of assault. There was uproar nearly every day in the House of Representatives and the Senate as the Labor Party, spearheaded by the Hayden–Dawkins–Walsh troika, gunned for prominent Liberals. Dawkins named both Horgan and another former Chairman of the WA Liberal Party finance committee, Syd Corsor. He said: 'They were the bag men and they were also crooks. They knew what was at stake . . .' The Australian High Commissioner to London, Sir Victor Garland, was 'in tax avoidance up to his neck'. Dawkins said Western Australian Liberal Senator Noel Crichton-Browne was 'another crook'. He further claimed that Durack was a victim of 'pressure and preselection threats' from the tax avoiders.

The tax issue was not just a parliamentary struggle but, more significantly, a struggle for the mind of the electorate. It was a golden opportunity for Hayden, but one which, if squandered, would bring retribution. Hayden began the August session in the ascendancy and the issue should have allowed him to turn his hold on Government into a tight grasp. But Hayden failed. He reverted to populist attack rather than scientific and systematic destruction of Fraser despite the fact that the strategy needed had been explained for him in the major ANOP research for 1982.

In August Rod Cameron gave the ALP the results of his quantitative research from June–July together with a recommended election strategy. On the first page of this report Cameron concluded: 'The theoretical swing to Labor in mid-1982 is between 3.5 to four per cent and, provided Labor can hold this figure, it will win the next federal election.'[5] Cameron's sample comprised 3,500 voters, taking 350 from each of the ten marginal seats. The ALP two-party preferred vote was as follows: Canning (WA) 54 per cent, Perth (WA) 54 per cent, Barton (NSW) 54.5 per cent, Herbert (Qld) 53.5 per cent, Bowman (Qld) 52.5 per cent, Calare (NSW) 51 per cent, Franklin (Tas) 49.5 per cent, Wilmot (Tas) 52 per cent, Casey (Vic) 50 per cent and Kingston (SA) 51 per cent. This gave the ALP an estimated national vote of 52.5 to 53 per cent.

Cameron said economic conditions suggested that 'Labor should have achieved a bigger swing' and that the ALP must expect to lose ground to the Government during the campaign. But the survey showed that Fraser's weak states were Western Australia and Queensland, the states where the Liberal Party divisions on tax were just being exposed. It is important to note that this ANOP survey was completed *before* the tabling of the Costigan Royal Commission, but *after* the release of the McCabe–Lafranchi Report in the Victorian Parliament. The latter was very much a prelude to the Costigan Report which had brought the tax debate to its peak.

Cameron had extracted a communications strategy for the ALP. He said:

An underlying theme running through most of the specific reasons for vote-switching is a reference to or a call for a fairer system. In many instances specific reference to interest rates or taxation levels or a misallocation of financial resources is phrased in terms of what ANOP has previously described as the growing preoccupation by middle-income earners with a lack of fairness in the system and with a perceived lack of competence in the economic management of Australia . . . Labor's central theme position might be along the following lines:

A fairer (lucky) country through better economic management.

There is a strongly held view amongst swinging voters that the institutional system on which Australia is based is becoming unfair at a rapid rate . . . While the mood amongst swinging voters still has it that Australia is the lucky country, there is a growing suspicion that this lucky country is under threat by virtue of the fact that the system is becoming more unfair for middle Australia . . .

In a rank ordering of priority an overview of all the research in 1982 would suggest that at present the key individual issues for campaign inclusion would be:

(i)   interest rates
(ii) taxation—levels, fairness, tax avoidance
(iii) inflation and the cost of living
(iv) unemployment, job security and youth unemployment
(v)   pensions and other welfare benefits.

Cameron found that the overtones of Whitlamism—economic irresponsibility and overspending—were fading, with seven years having elapsed since 1975, but financial irresponsibility remained an ALP image weakness. Yet Labor was slowly moving to a position where it could run a positive campaign on the notion of 'doing it better' than Fraser. The Government's overall satisfaction rating had improved on the 1979 ANOP survey—a tribute to Fraser. But 'in every specific economic judgement the Government is deemed to be less competent than before the last election—and at levels which can be described as condemnatory'.

The tax issue was integral to the community view that the system was unfair. Cameron said, 'The perceived unfairness is expressed in terms of the average Australian bearing the brunt of the tax burden and the rich getting richer and the poor getting poorer.' Nearly two-thirds of the community felt that the Government was not tough enough in handling tax avoidance. Support was evident for punitive legal action against the big offenders. But the majority view was that 'there would not be much difference in the amount of tax paid under a coalition Government or a Labor Government'.

A careful reading of these results by Hayden and his senior shadow ministers should have made their approach to the tax debate obvious. The issue fitted their strategy like a hand into a glove. They could argue that during the entire Fraser period ordinary Australians had paid far more tax than they would have otherwise because the Government had failed to stamp out the tax rort. But Hayden went off at a tangent: he attacked personalities and became infatuated by image. Hayden was convinced that he knew better than the party professionals.

The turning point in the tax debate came on 23 September when Fraser announced that industrialist John Reid would head the Government's review of the Commonwealth public service. Later that day Hayden, using information from NSW Attorney-General Frank Walker, accused Reid of being associated with bottom-of-the-harbour tax evasion.

The previous day Fraser had written to Horgan asking him to stand down from Government boards while his financial affairs were investigated. Suddenly Fraser was confronted with the implications of this action. Should he now ask Reid to stand down as well? Fraser and Reid were closeted together for much of the day and Reid eventually made a statement denying any involvement in tax avoidance.

Hayden's charge was a bombshell, but immediately placed him under pressure to substantiate it. That night in the Caucus lobbies there were murmurings that Hayden had 'gone too far'. Dawkins later told him: 'You should have let me to do that; it was too much of a risk for you.'

Fraser asked Taxation Commissioner O'Reilly to investigate Reid's involvement in companies named by Hayden. Within the day O'Reilly concluded, on the basis of the facts available to him, that Reid had not been involved in bottom-of-the-harbour activities. Fraser, after waiting so long, finally had a line of attack to use against the ALP. He called on Hayden to issue an 'immediate apology', saying it was required if Hayden had 'a sense of decency, a sense of honour'.

Fraser henceforth turned the debate with Hayden into a slanging match of claim and counter-claim. Hayden continued to criticise Reid; Fraser defended him. While the electorate, no doubt, got bored by the political squabble, Labor lost its momentum in its fury and Fraser eventually emerged into daylight out of the great tax evasion tunnel.

Before Fraser's release he faced the biggest backbench revolt of his prime ministership. The party meeting on 23 September to consider the tax legislation became a forum of bitterness. Western Australian backbencher Peter Shack raised the Horgan issue and protested against the use of Commonwealth power against an individual who should be considered innocent until proven guilty. Shack declared: 'If this is what the Liberal Party has come to, I don't want any part of it.' Reg Withers turned on Fraser: 'Prime Minister you are doing exactly what Richard Milhous Nixon did to his political enemies. He got the Internal Revenue Service to have a tax audit of them.' Shack declared later the Government had forgotten about basic principles: 'I was brought up on John Stuart Mill.'

Later that day 14 Liberal backbenchers issued a statement saying they wanted to make it 'crystal clear' that they disagreed with Fraser's request to Horgan to stand down while his affairs were investigated. Howard and Chaney spent most of the day negotiating with Fraser—using the Reid example—to force him to rethink. It was the grimmest and toughest personal encounter Fraser and Howard had ever had, but eventually Fraser relented and the Howard–Chaney cot promise was accepted. Howard announced later that night that Horgan would not be standing down from his posts during the inquiry.

From late September onwards the main issue became the legislation itself and the Government was negotiated into a series of backdowns by a knowledgeable and determined backbench. However by this stage recriminations had begun to mount inside the ALP. The shadow Cabinet had never settled on a strategy at the start for handling the tax issue. Labor's reply had developed as a matter of course, spearheaded by Hayden and his supporters. Hawke had always dissented from this approach and his own speeches were noticeable for their lack of personality attack and their focus on the economic and equity issues. As the debate evolved Hayden's performance deteriorated and his strategic mistake was revealed.

It soon became an article of faith among the party professionals—Hogg, Richardson, Cameron and McMullan—that Labor had lost its opportunity. Hogg called the Costigan Report 'a lost chance to dismantle the Fraser Government'. He was upset about Hayden's tactics and challenged the leader on two occasions. At the National Executive meeting where the disaffiliation of the Painters' and Dockers' from the ALP was discussed, Hogg accused Hayden of being too interested in personalities and not sufficiently in the issue. He also complained about Hayden's unilateral announcement regarding the disaffiliation of the union. Hogg said this was trial by Royal Commission. He had in fact gone to the Painters' and Dockers' himself and persuaded them to withdraw ALP affiliation, otherwise there could have been an open row between the party and an affiliated union. Looking at Hayden, Hogg told the National Executive that the union showed 'a greater sense of solidarity than some people in this room'. He warned Hayden at a 28 October campaign-planning meeting in Parliament House that the tax strategy had not worked, but Hayden defended himself and pointed to a recent improvement in his ratings.

It gradually became clear that Hayden's failure was much wider—he had not built upon his July victory over Hawke. He had taken that result as confirmation of his leadership, not the chance to renew that leadership. The proof of this was Hayden's agony of indecision about the necessary shadow ministry reshuffle. Hayden wanted to move Ralph Willis from his position as shadow Treasurer but was too worried about the political implications. Willis had the best technical grasp of economics on the ALP frontbench, but he had no clout against the Government or persuasiveness with the public. Hayden told Willis at the start of the budget session that he was on probation; unless he performed better, he would be moved at the end of the year. Hayden told colleagues he was not going to let a poor performance by Willis stop him becoming Prime Minister. Yet Hayden's dilemma was that he had promised the left during the leadership contest that he would retain Willis. Moreover Willis had strong ties to the Hawke camp and Hayden feared that a move against him might alienate both the left and elements of the right. Willis was the centrepiece of any reshuffle; without moving him, a reshuffle made no sense.

Hayden eventually pondered on this reshuffle for five months, rather than imposing it early in the budget session. He knew the basic changes required in any reshuffle as he had contemplated moving Keating into the shadow Treasury job and discussed this with him. Keating had been reluctant and Hayden did not press it. He had even flirted with promoting Dawkins to shadow Treasurer and it was in this period that Hayden and Button formed the view that Dawkins was a future leadership candidate from the Caucus centre group. Some of Hayden's advisers said he should put the onus on Hawke by giving him the Treasury job—a position to which Hawke had never aspired. But Hayden did nothing, a lack of action which his critics later used against him. His refusal to impose the reshuffle was the first sign that political paralysis and indecision was taking hold of him.

The final verdict on Hayden's effectiveness during the tax debate was produced when Rod Cameron conducted qualitative research over 16–18 November. He gave a report to the campaign committee a fortnight later which said in part:

> There is, in late 1982, not the slightest hint that Labor has positioned itself as the more honest and ethical political party. The upshot of the tax avoidance debate has not left Labor enjoying a position related to honesty, equity or a more ethical approach to government.[6]

Despite the trauma, Malcolm Fraser had achieved his electoral objectives on the tax issue. But Fraser had paid a big price and during late 1982 the Liberals became the party of internal division, an electoral liability.

Fraser's election plan received a jolt in mid-October when his former deputy Sir Phillip Lynch fell ill and was advised by his doctors to quit politics. It would prove to be a fateful illness. During the Liberal leadership crisis in April Fraser had told Lynch he could have 'whatever he wanted'. A fortnight later they reached the tentative agreement that Lynch would become Australia's next Ambassador to the United States. But as months went by this plan fell apart, one reason being Fraser's reluctance to have a by-election in Flinders, the other the political backlash that the appointment would generate. Fraser put pressure on Lynch and asked him to reconsider.

Lynch's sickness swept these doubts aside and on 11 October he announced his intention to resign. He had to settle for a seat on the Reserve Bank Board rather than Washington. Fraser declared: 'If there is a by-election, we will win it.' Fraser later moved to quash the general election speculation which this line had generated by asserting that talk of an early election was 'indecent'. But Fraser arranged with Lynch that his formal resignation be delayed a few weeks. This prevented an early by-election and gave Fraser the chance to coordinate the Flinders by-election with his planned general election.

In mid-October Fraser's fortunes seemed to revive. He used the retirement of Lynch to heal the breach with Andrew Peacock and recall him to the Cabinet. Peacock had spent six months since April proving that he would not buck the party-room decision after his unsuccessful challenge. Fraser now managed to present himself as healer as well as victor. Then the Prime Minister flew north to spend a week in Brisbane amid sunshine, Australian athletes, an obsessive display of nationalism and plenty of 'gold, gold, gold' at the Commonwealth Games. Fraser was pictured frequently with Australia's sporting heroes. He flew south with his batteries recharged; it was the prelude to the campaign.

Towards late October Fraser had settled on December as his optimum election date and was determined to press ahead despite the battered condition of the Liberal Party. The Prime Minister's obsession with a late 1982 election now led him into another head-to-head clash with the Liberal Party organisation. As Federal Director of the Liberal Party it was Eggleton's job not just to advise Fraser but to relay the views of the six state divisions of the party. The opposition to a December election was unanimous. Eggleton asked Fraser for a meeting at which Party President Jim Forbes and himself could put the party's view. A few days before this meeting Eggleton convened in Canberra on Monday 25 October a Liberal Party State Directors meeting. Each director outlined his state's position and gave an estimate of the likely number of seats to be lost.

After this meeting Eggleton wrote Fraser a memorandum summarising the conclusions. He said the federal secretariat opposed an election and was influenced in this position by the Liberal Party as a whole. Eggleton continued:

> We are cognisant of the fact that professional research over the 18 months has shown the ALP consistently polling better than the 1.4 per cent it needs to win Government. We are concerned about the state of the party in Western Australia and Queensland and fear the loss of up to four Government seats in each of these states.
> This would leave a safety margin of only three seats through the rest of Australia. At staff planning committee in Canberra yesterday the directors forecast the loss of four seats in NSW, five in Queensland, one in South Australia, one in Tasmania, one in Victoria and four in Western Australia; a total of sixteen seats.

Eggleton listed the 16 seats, describing them as 'probable losses' in an early election. They were, in NSW, Barton, Philip, Riverina, Macarthur; in Queensland, Bowman, Fadden, Herbert, Petrie, Leichhardt; in Western Australia, Canning, Moore, Perth, Stirling; in South Australia, Kingston; in Tasmania, Wilmot; and in Victoria, Bendigo.

The next day, 26 October, Eggleton flew to Sydney and had lunch with Forbes, NSW president John Valder, and former Federal President Sir John Atwill. They said NSW opposed an early election. Valder said later the party still faced financial difficulty and had problems with fund-raising. Eggleton and Forbes returned to Canberra for an historic confrontation with the Prime Minister.

The meeting which Eggleton had requested began in the Cabinet Room about 9 p.m. on the evening of 27 October and was conducted while Government rebels in the House of Representatives tore into the Government's tax legislation. Eleven backbenchers would vote against the Bill that night and then 13 the next day. But nothing could deter Fraser. He had made a virtue out of crashing through his own party. Those present in the Cabinet room were Fraser, Howard, Carrick, Chaney, Macphee, Nixon, Fife, John Hodges (representing Queensland) and Kevin Newman (representing Tasmania); Eggleton and Forbes represented the party organisation. Fraser quizzed his ministers about the trade-off between going in 1982 versus 1983. He was contemplating the announcement of an election the next day, 28 October.

Eggleton gave the meeting a detailed exposition of the pros and cons of an early poll. He outlined recent Liberal Party surveys which showed the Government's major plus was the perception of Fraser by swinging voters as a man of strength. Its big minus was its diminished record as economic managers. Fraser said little, but his views were obvious. He had the support of the National Country Party. Doug Anthony was overseas but he had relayed a message to Nixon: 'Go now'. Anthony had wanted to go in September; now he favoured December. This time there was no Costigan report to restrain Nixon and he urged Fraser to go, confident he would win. Nixon felt that party organisations always opposed elections. It was the job of politicians to push them into it.

Fraser faced a troika of ministerial opposition—deputy Howard, Senate leader Carrick and Chaney—the same group which had opposed him in Cabinet on the Horgan issue so long and so effectively. Both Howard and Chaney were sceptical about Fraser's prospects of winning. Beyond that they had a fundamental dispute with the way he was conducting the Government. They felt there were moral and political obligations on the Fraser Government to face the challenge of the economic recession rather than expend its energies in opportunism and a probably futile dash to the polls. Both Chaney and Howard believed that Fraser's electioneering obsession was becoming a Government liability.

Macphee was ambivalent. He asked Fraser whether the election specu-lation could be categorically ended. Could he announce a full-term Parliament with a 1983 election? If not, then the Government should go now and avoid the damage involved in continued speculation which, by its very nature, was destabilising. The strongest election opponent was Forbes and, as Liberal President, he told Fraser that the party across all states was opposed to any early poll. The meeting broke up not having made any firm decision, but the anti-election camp had declared itself more forcefully than Fraser expected. A few minutes later there was a second and more important meeting of three people—Fraser, Forbes and Eggleton.

Fraser felt that Anthony and himself could pull his ministers into line. But the opposition of the Liberal Party was of a dimension different from usual. The second meeting was tough and much franker. Forbes and Eggleton went through the arguments again. They told Fraser 'an early election is opposed by the community, the media and the Liberal Party'. They predicted that, if Fraser proceeded, then there would be 'tremendous anger and resentment at the calling of an early poll' for which there was no justification. The Government no longer held the political initiative. The Liberal officials said there had been a significant loss of confidence and credibility in the Government; the choice between the coalition and the Labor Party was no longer so clear to the electorate. They warned that the voters were more inclined than ever to give the ALP a try.

Forbes told Fraser that he had a full 12 months of his three-year term still to run. He said: 'This risk should only be taken if it is certain the Government can win. If it is not sure, then the party organisation is asking you to wait until later.' Forbes said the risk was too big to take. The political climate was unpredictable. Could anyone really be certain that the climate would be worse next year? Eggleton supported this argument by reference to polls and research which showed that, while the Government might win, it was still a risk. One of the arguments Fraser used for an early election was the Labor leadership. He said: 'If you don't let me go now, I could be facing Hawke at the next election.' But Eggleton's assessment was that Hayden would survive until polling day. Fraser himself tended to this view.

The Prime Minister became testy and resentful. Fraser said: 'I want this election and I believe I should have it, yet the Liberal organisation won't support me.' Forbes and Eggleton protested. 'That's not right,' they said. 'We're reporting the views of the party; they're not just our own views. We don't believe you're likely to win. And we don't believe it's the right time to call an election.' Finally Fraser drew back. Eggleton ventured to clarify the position to confirm that Fraser was saying he would not go in December. Fraser replied: 'Of course that's what I'm saying. How can I have an election if you won't support me?' Eggleton replied: 'That's not entirely fair . . .' But Fraser cut back: 'Well, it is really. You must see the situation in these terms. I just can't go in these circumstances.'

The three men had a drink to repair their differences and Forbes and Eggleton left Fraser's office at 1 a.m. Eggleton, taking Fraser at his word, believed the possibility of a December election had now passed and the next day he went public in a bid to kill the speculation: 'It has always been my understanding and remains my belief that the Government will run its full course unless the Senate impedes the work of Government.'

Fraser was like a wild buffalo with the smell of water in its nostrils. As he wandered about the lobbies of Parliament House or paced his office, the election mood would grab him. Fraser told Nixon the Liberal organisation had 'jacked up'. Both men agreed to make another assessment before the last day for such a decision. Howard spoke to Eggleton later and warned that Fraser might reopen the issue in a serious way. But Fraser never had that chance.

Malcolm Fraser, like Gough Whitlam before him, possessed a mammoth constitution on which he shouldered the burdens of the prime ministership. But unexpectedly that constitution buckled at this time. Before the expiry-hour was reached for his December election a sciatic back virtually crippled him. He went to hospital rather than to the hustings.

His close colleagues were aware of the problem but underrated its potential danger. A few days earlier Nixon had told Fraser to stop pacing about. 'I can't, my back's crook,' Fraser replied. Obviously his back was a greater worry than Fraser let on. He was admitted to hospital in Melbourne on the following Sunday, 31 October. Doug Anthony became Acting Prime Minister, and the 1982 election was a lost cause.

Lying in his hospital bed Fraser's feelings of self-righteousness and resentment fused over the election issue and were directed towards the media. The Prime Minister wrote to *The Age* on 5 November denying that he had been the author of early election speculation:

> This speculation has been the creature of the press and the ALP for a period of several months . . . Your journalists and others have attempted to keep that speculation up by showing a morbid curiosity in a subject which should have been left alone. It is totally dishonest and false to put the continuing speculation into my mouth when it has been in their pens.
>
> I have said consistently that I am in favour of Parliaments running their full term. But I do not control the Senate . . .

These comments exposed Fraser's credibility gap between words and intent. The Prime Minister had given very serious consideration in both August and October to calling a September and December election respectively. But in public Fraser would scarcely admit he had ever dreamt of it. The reason the Labor Party and the media were election 'hawks' with Fraser was that they knew his record; it was also known that Fraser wanted a late-1982 poll.

In Fraser's letter a resentment could be detected; a resentment because events had conspired against him. Fraser's obsession was to control and manipulate events, to reconcile the course of history with his own aspirations. His record proved it: 1975, 1977 and 1980. But in 1982 Fraser's audacity overreached itself.

The irony of the tax debate is that, while Fraser imposed his will on the Liberal Party, he subsequently paid a high price for it. The Liberal organisation was in the front line of the tax brawl and it finished so bruised and apprehensive that it simply refused to countenance a December election. Liberal surveys in late 1982 revealed the Liberals were perceived as divided as the ALP, thereby losing one of their traditional assets.

Would Fraser have changed his mind if his back had held up? The most opportune time to announce a 4 December election was in Parliament on 28 October, but Fraser let that pass. He would have reassessed this decision later, but the array of Liberal opposition and its force would probably have proved too much. A Prime Minister likes to have an enthusiastic party backing his election decision.

Would Fraser have won in December? His chances were probably a little less than his even-money prospect in September because the Labor Party would have been far more prepared. The Morgan gallup poll was consistent over its two surveys conducted on 27 November–4 December and 11–18 December. The first result had Labor 53.5 per cent and the second 53 per cent on the two-party preferred vote. Election analyst Malcolm Mackerras pointed to these figures and said: 'Fraser would have lost any election held in 1982 . . . If he had called the early election Fraser would have gone down in history as a turkey who had called on an early Christmas.'[7]

But there was another contest coming a month before Christmas. Lynch's retirement from politics was about to produce a whirlwind.

17
The curse of Flinders

Flinders has much to answer for.

Tony Eggleton,
March 1983

The Victorian seat of Flinders occupies a special place in Australia's political history. It was in Flinders in 1929 that Stanley Melbourne Bruce became the first Prime Minister to lose his seat at a general election. But in 1982 the voters of Flinders excelled this earlier performance and produced a by-election result of such perversity that the course of history was changed. The 1982 Flinders by-election was the most important since Bass in 1975—but its impact was different. Bass confirmed an emerging trend: Gough Whitlam's decline and Malcolm Fraser's rise. Flinders reversed the trend of politics. It dealt Bill Hayden a cruel blow from which he never recovered, but it also deceived Malcolm Fraser into exaggerating his strength. Flinders cast a profound and insidious spell over Australian politics, with the Labor Party sinking into pessimism and the Liberal Party becoming dizzy with optimism. This spell destroyed Hayden and then Fraser.

The great beneficiary of Flinders was Bob Hawke and it is possible that without this by-election he would not have succeeded Hayden as leader before the next election; it is certain that he would not have replaced Hayden as early as February 1983. Flinders weakened Hayden against Hawke and gave Fraser a false confidence to confront Hawke. The by-election changed the terrain on which the three men fought in a peculiar fashion which only Hawke began to understand. Tony Eggleton declared later: 'Flinders has much to answer for.'

The Flinders and Lowe by-elections gave 1982 a remarkable political symmetry. But the results defied logic. Throughout 1982 the Fraser Government had moved from one crisis to another, plagued by division, excess and

245

upheaval. Yet at the close of the year, in Flinders, the Government finished on top while at the start it had suffered an abject defeat in Lowe. How could this be? The answer lies in an unusual mix of events which produced a very bad Labor result in Flinders. In this by-election Fraser stole a political march on Hayden through a faster response to community concern about unemployment; he sensed the people's need for leadership and a new direction.

Fraser never got his 4 December general election, but the Flinders by-election on the same day was the final political test between Fraser and Hayden. It was because Fraser had wanted to call the general election that day that Flinders assumed such significance. It became a litmus test for a federal election.

Flinders proved to be a great strategic victory for Fraser, who was bed-ridden for most of the campaign and in acute pain at its start. While the Prime Minister did not appear on the hustings he still defined the terms of the political debate. Flinders is one of the best examples of Fraser as a restless and impatient Prime Minister searching for the new idea. This time the idea was the wage pause, an experiment which had been tried in 1977 and failed, but which Fraser resurrected in a new guise. The translation of the wage pause from idea into actuality by the Fraser Government in late 1982 was a genuine achievement but nobody, not even Fraser, could have envisaged the confusion and convulsion it would generate inside the Labor Party. It led to Hayden's humiliation as ALP leader and it compromised the relationship between the ALP and the ACTU, on which so much of Labor's campaign thrust depended. The story of Flinders is tied to the politics of the wage pause.

The idea came from former Western Australian Premier Sir Charles Court, who saw Fraser for two hours on the afternoon of 28 October—the day after Fraser's late night retreat from the early election. Despite his defects Court was a politician of vision and action and he briefed Fraser on a speech he was giving in Canberra that night titled 'What Are We Waiting For?' The spirit of Court's approach was captured when he quoted the SAS motto: 'Who dares, wins.' Court explained his economic idea and gave Fraser a lecture on leadership. Their discussion had a seminal influence on subsequent events. Court said later:

> I believed that leadership had to be shown at the national political level to get the public to respond to the crisis facing the nation. I decided to see the Prime Minister, to put to him my considered view that the time had come for him to bypass the employers, the trade unions and the industrial tribunals. It was time for him to talk to the public about the crisis. The work force was crying out for leadership. He was the one man who had the capacity and strength to get the idea moving on the basis that it would revive the country.

The two objectives were to save existing jobs and create new jobs. I realised it would be difficult to actually cut wages. I believed if you could hold the situation, with no wages catch-up then you would have more progress. Every dollar saved had to go into meaningful works to get the infrastructure of the nation developed.

As a result of our discussions I postponed my return to Perth and we decided I would go to Melbourne with Fraser the next day. But when I got to the RAAF base Fraser was in agony. They had to rearrange the seating in the plane. He was in terrible, excruciating pain and was in no condition to be discussing my idea.[1]

Court told Fraser that Australia wanted a leadership appeal to the employed to make a sacrifice to create jobs for the unemployed. He branded this an appeal to mateship. Within minutes of Court's departure, on 28 October, Fraser had called several senior ministers to his office: Howard, Macphee, Carrick, Sinclair and others. Fraser paced up and down the room thinking aloud; he fired questions at ministers as he went: 'How much money would be saved if all Governments, including Labor Governments, had a freeze on wages for 12 months?' Quick sums were done; someone suggested $2,000 million, an inflated figure. Fraser kept pacing. He continued: 'If all Governments could agree, then employees could make a sacrifice for the unemployed.' Public works programmes could be established with the revenue saved. 'How many jobs could be created?' Fraser asked Macphee. He replied that for every million dollars spent only about 20 to 30 extra people could be employed. But in areas such as welfare housing the figure was higher.

Fraser said the idea could capture the idealism of the community and reflect the mateship ethic. Ministers were cautious; many suspected he was trying to return to the early-election argument. Carrick said the idea had 'merit' and alluded to the previous night's session. Fraser smiled and said: 'John, you know I've given up that particular proposal.' The upshot was that Macphee and Howard began work to turn the concept into a proposal. Macphee warned that it could only work in a non-election atmosphere in order to get cooperation from the three Labor states. Ministers were digesting it slowly, but Fraser was pushing. He was already a convert.

Six days later Macphee and his Departmental Head Mike Codd visited Fraser in Melbourne's Freemasons' Hospital to develop the plan. The Prime Minister was alone in a small room, in terrible pain from the pressure on the sciatic nerve in his lower back. He was resting following spinal manipulation which had revealed the need for a major operation. Fraser was spitting out political ideas: a boost to the Commonwealth Employment Service, job counselling for all school leavers, the wage pause, job-creation schemes. Fraser said a Cabinet decision was needed as soon as possible to cement the proposal. The next day Fraser went 'under the knife'.

There were three main stages in the saga of the wage pause. The first was the full Cabinet approval on Monday 15 November with Acting Prime Minister Doug Anthony in the chair. This was followed by the special Premiers' Conference of 7 December in which a compromise between the Commonwealth and the states was reached for a six-month wage pause with a review towards the end of the period. Finally on 23 December the Arbitration Commission endorsed the six-month pause. The essence of the Government proposal was that the wage freeze would cover both public and private sectors. The pause became the Government's most dramatic response to the deepening employment crisis. While a useful economic idea, its political utility was greater.

The Government had identified three major causes of the growing recession. They were the world downturn, the drought, and the domestic wage explosion. The Government could not be blamed for the first two factors but it had to share responsibility for the wage explosion. The value of the wage freeze concept was that it enabled the Fraser ministers to argue that they were confronting the real issue. It gave the Government a new appeal for the Flinders by-election: it was responding to the crisis with decisive action.

During November both Fraser and Hayden were apprehensive about Flinders and it became the by-election which neither side wanted. Fraser worried that an adverse result would send his Government into a spiral of decline; Hayden feared that, unless he won, it would be used as proof of his election inadequacies.

Flinders was an urban-rural mix on Victoria's Mornington peninsula, flanked by Port Phillip Bay and Westernport, and it had been a Liberal seat almost continuously for 50 years. Labor won Flinders in a 1952 by-election but lost it at the 1954 general election. The swing Labor now needed was 5.5 per cent—almost exactly the average swing against Governments in Government-held seats at by-elections over the past 30 years.

Political leaders always need their slice of luck but in Flinders every factor conspired to work against Hayden. There were three problems with the Labor campaign. Firstly the ALP had an unattractive candidate who was well-known, a dangerous combination. Secondly Labor ran its campaign on negatives which contrasted with Fraser's positive proposal for a wage pause to boost employment. Thirdly in the last week of the campaign the Labor movement was racked by spectacular division over the wage pause, which reinforced Hayden's image as a weak leader.

Lynch's retirement in mid-October caught the ALP totally by surprise. Only a week earlier Labor had conducted its preselection for Flinders with the successful candidate being a local real-estate agent, Rogan Ward, who had a Prince Valiant haircut and a stature similar to Mickie Rooney. Labor never expected a by-election and assumed its candidate would face the people of Flinders submerged in the publicity of a national election. Ward had served a term as mayor of Frankston, the biggest town in the seat, during which he and his wife Diana had attended 700 functions, an average of two a day. The national press arrived in Flinders having heard about Ward's popularity. But a local journalist warned: 'Rogan sells politics like he sells real estate—very hard. I would list his political assets as his hide, his persistence and his wife— though not necessarily in that order.'[2] When Lynch retired, Ward announced there were 40,000 homes in Flinders and he would try to doorknock all of them. But as national ALP politicians joined Ward on the campaign trail they found that, like a fox terrier in search of an ankle, he never knew when to close his mouth.

Labor's campaign strategy was finalised at its 28 October meeting of senior politicians and party officers. Rod Cameron reported on an ANOP survey of 400 people which showed an exact dead heat, a 5050 result, with a 5.5 per cent swing to Labor. The survey revealed that Rogan Ward was a liability. But ALP officials thought a good campaign should deliver victory in a close contest. Labor decided to slam the Government rather than promote the Opposition and agreed that its theme should be 'Send a message to Canberra'. In hindsight this negative campaign was a mistake, but it was a normal by-election tactic. The irony for Labor is that the very day it took this decision the Prime Minister was embracing the wage pause.

The irony for Bob Hawke is that at the start of the Flinders campaign, when logic dictated loyalty, he publicly reopened the leadership issue. The reaction was not just sharp; it was electric. Hawke's fortunes inside the ALP nosedived in early November and he was forced to write to all Caucus members pledging his loyalty to Hayden. The man who enforced this penance was John Button.

The incident stemmed from Hawke's comments on 5 November on the ABC's 'Midday with Schildberger' programme. He said that recent polls suggested that people 'don't seem to be thoroughly approving of the perform-ance and the style and the priorities' of the Opposition. 'I am not making any challenge. What the party may want to do or not to do is a matter for the party,' Hawke said. 'I can't and don't control my colleagues.' Hawke added, 'I think it is a pity that we are not further ahead nationally . . . there is no doubt that concern is being expressed . . . it's pretty widespread concern . . .' Fraser had just gone into hospital. Hawke seemed to be cultivating the ground for a fresh leadership bid before any 1983 poll.

It was just four weeks before Flinders and the ALP was in no mood to tolerate Hawke's indiscretion. He was immediately put down by Keating, who wanted to kill the momentum for another Hawke move before it began. Keating said: 'Bill Hayden has our confidence and our support.'

Button had more lethal retaliation in mind. The more he reflected on Hawke's comments, the more angry he became. Over the weekend Button spoke to several party figures including Hayden and decided on Sunday, 7 November to challenge Hawke on his remarks. Button wrote out for himself the arguments against Hawke and had these notes with him for the Caucus meeting the next day. Firstly Button believed that Labor politicians were wasting their efforts if Hawke was allowed to continue to undermine the party. Secondly he noted that Hawke had given a pledge to the party just over three months ago of no further challenge. Consequently Hawke's honesty was at stake. What had happened in the interim? Had Hawke heard voices? Thirdly the principle to be followed is that doubts should be raised, as a first step, inside the party. But Hawke had said nothing in party forums before he went public. Fourth if Hawke believed events had changed, then let him move a motion against the leader in Caucus. Button would say that in these circumstances he reserved his own right to move a spill of all frontbench positions. Such a statement in the Caucus would have been tantamount to a retreat to Hawke, made with a view to diminishing Hawke's vote in any Caucus ballot.

Before the meeting began Button pulled Hawke out and told him as a matter of courtesy that he intended to open a debate on Hawke's comments. Hawke immediately replied that the media had blown the whole thing up. Button said that was wrong, the media had got it dead right. Then Hawke appealed to Button to defer his action; he had an appointment to see Hayden later and he would sort it out then. He would have a long talk to Hayden; in fact, he wanted to have a long talk to Button as well. He claimed that people had misconstrued his remarks. Button agreed not to raise the matter then; the implication was that he might raise it later but it was up to Hawke.

At lunch the same day, 8 November, Hawke and two of his closest supporters, Gareth Evans and Clyde Holding, drafted a letter from Hawke to all Caucus members promising there would be no challenge before the next election. Evans and Holding argued that an unequivocal statement was needed. It was required not just to pacify Button but Caucus itself. The party wanted a sacrificial offering from Hawke. That morning Hayden had confirmed to the press that he had rung Hawke on the Friday and told him that his comments 'would inject extraordinary de-stabilising influences into the party, especially with the by-election in Flinders and general talk of an election'. Hayden exploited Hawke's comments as evidence of disloyalty, not just to himself, but to the party. That afternoon Hawke's staff delivered a letter to Caucus members. It read:

> I stand by absolutely the commitment I made at the joint press conference on 16 July where—in answer to the question: 'Can you guarantee that there will be no further challenge before the next election?'—I answered 'yes' . . . I hope, together with Bill Hayden, to play a major role in ensuring a decisive victory for the party in the Flinders by-election and the general election whenever it is held.

With the Hawke issue clarified, yet again, Labor returned to its by-election.

In mid-November John Howard and Bill Hayden opened the campaigns for both the Government and the Opposition. While both sides escalated their rhetoric the voters of Flinders were not interested. In the sleepy towns throughout the Mornington Peninsula, past the leafy streets, along the rolling beaches, through the acres of 'grey power' and young home buyers, neither Howard nor Hayden offered hope or relevance. As Howard's commitment to monetarism grew during his years as Treasurer, his political popularity declined accordingly. The wage pause was a potentially popular idea but Howard could not give it the touch of life. The Liberal candidate, Peter Reith, a tall and sleepy-looking solicitor, came from outside the electorate. Phillip Lynch did his best to help, but candidly admitted the mood of the public was elusive.

Hayden's campaign opening was notable for its lack of professionalism. The Opposition leader had no prepared text; his staff could not advise television which 'grabs' to feature. His speech had no news story and it possessed coherence only as an assault on the Fraser Government. It revealed Hayden more suspicious than ever, now distrustful of his own press staff. He had become stubborn to the stage of folly in his refusal to accept advice on public relations. Wran's staff, who accompanied the Premier to the opening, could scarcely believe their eyes. The political professionals concluded that Hayden still had no idea how to present himself as a leader to the people. Hayden made several visits to Flinders, realising that he must make a maximum effort, and some of his staff, along with the ALP officials, worked full-time in Flinders during the by-election. But the voters remained curiously aloof, unresponsive.

On 15 November Doug Anthony, flanked by Howard, Macphee and Peacock in Fraser's office, announced the special Premiers' Conference to seek a national 12-month public and private sector wage freeze. Anthony said an estimated $700 million should be 'saved' by federal and state Governments to plough back into employment. He ruled out price control since the Government believed the need was for profit restoration; only control of wages, not prices would facilitate this. Putting the onus squarely on the Premiers Anthony said: 'The support of the state governments is absolutely critical.' All senior ministers were committed to the proposal. Macphee told Parliament a few days earlier:

> I cannot understand how anyone who knows the faintest thing about the economy can imagine that we who are so uncompetitive in everything that we manufacture and everything that we extract from the ground or grow can go on in this lotus-land increasing wage costs and not worsening our unemployment situation. I want the employers of this country also to understand it.[3]

While Howard and Macphee wanted a pause they had conflicting views on how to achieve it. This was a clash of both ideology and tactics, with long-term significance for the Liberal Party. Macphee was a champion of the Arbitration Commission and centralised wage fixation and believed the cause of wage restraint could be successfully negotiated in this framework. Howard was a right-wing radical and wanted to move away from arbitration to the marketplace in a new system of collective bargaining. He saw this as the viable means of ensuring that wage rates actually reflected capacity to pay rather than abstracted legalisms.

The federal Government intended to pass legislation to freeze the wages of its own workers for 12 months; it wanted state Governments to do likewise. Macphee proposed that the Government then approach the Arbitration Commission and request it to extend the pause into the private sector. Howard's alternative was for legislation to cover the private sector by preventing tribunals handing down pay rises during the pause. Howard saw the pause as a means of eliminating the influence of industrial tribunals so the pause would become a transition to a decentralised wages system. Macphee wanted to have the Arbitration Commission legitimise the pause thereby paving the way for a return to centralised wage fixation. This battle between Howard and Macphee still continues inside the Liberal Party in Opposition and represents an issue of fundamental importance for its future.

The state Premiers responded cautiously to Anthony's announcement but it contained significant inducement for them. State budgets varied only according to their degree of financial crisis. A freeze in the wages of state employees would be of major assistance to all Premiers. The Premiers themselves recognised that the Commonwealth offer opened the field for negotiations. They wanted more money and greater loan funds and were prepared to negotiate on this basis.

Three out of six Premiers were now Labor—Wran, Cain, and John Bannon, newly elected Premier of South Australia. In one sense the South Australian election on 6 November, which Labor won with a strong seven per cent swing, only created further problems for Fraser and Hayden. The Liberal Government had lost on the state of the national economy and the defeated Liberal leader, David Tonkin, had warned that it was 'a very salutory lesson' for the Prime Minister. Hayden, with the Lowe by-election and Victorian and South Australian election wins all behind him, faced greater pressure than ever to perform well in Flinders.

Significant differences soon emerged inside the Labor movement in its response to the wage pause. The first rift was between the troika of Labor Premiers and the federal ALP. At a Melbourne summit on 18 November Wran, Cain and Bannon signalled they would negotiate and not reject the freeze outright. The Premiers wanted a significant rise in federal spending on capital works and an easing in monetary policy. There were differences between the Premiers, with Wran far more prepared to reach a compromise than Cain and Bannon. Their response was pragmatic; it was geared to their own needs, those of practical politicians running state budgets, and not of federal Opposition leaders fighting by-elections.

For five years Bill Hayden and the federal Labor Party had been working towards an accord with the union movement to establish a basis for sustained economic growth. The aim was to develop a framework so that during a downturn wages would be higher than usually expected, while during an upturn a wage explosion would be contained. Hayden wanted to condemn the wage pause as a gimmick, as an inadequate substitute for a long-term prices–incomes accord. Hayden wanted to demonstrate that the ALP could work with the trade unions to secure wage restraint and that Malcolm Fraser could not.

On 22 November the shadow Cabinet rejected Fraser's wage freeze as 'totally unfair'—but admitted the need for wage moderation. Hayden said: 'A freeze is not an answer. In fact a freeze will only worsen the economic collapse we see about us.' The Opposition leader said that he was speaking 'only for myself and my colleagues'—not for the ALP Premiers. But he had consulted Wran the previous night and knew that he had 'no problems' with the federal ALP position. Having condemned the freeze, Hayden then looked to the ACTU to forge a joint stance against the Fraser initiative.

It is possible only in hindsight to understand the profound confusion which Fraser's pause generated inside the Labor movement. The ALP had up until then been negotiating with the ACTU to reach an agreed formula for wage restraint which meant some diminution in real wage maintenance (the adjustment of wages to the same level as price rises). However Fraser's wage pause proposal, which was now due to go to the Arbitration Commission, had forced the ACTU to formulate a position in response to the Fraser Government. This ACTU position overtook its negotiations with the ALP. The result was that the concessions which Hayden hoped to extract from the ACTU for the benefit of the Labor Party were delivered, in the first place, to Malcolm Fraser.

The fact is that the first time the ACTU made the concession that it would accept real wage adjustment 'over time' rather than sooner was in its response to Fraser's wage pause. For a brief period of weeks the Fraser Government had actually got from the ACTU the big wage restraint concession which Hayden and the federal Labor Party had been working towards for so long. The result was a political explosion inside the Labor movement and a poisoning in personal relations between Hayden and the ACTU elite.

As early as 20 August, three days after the budget, the ALP had met the ACTU in a bid to seal the accord. Hayden had precipitated this meeting, anxious to reach agreement in case Fraser called a September poll on the budget. There was nearly a major eruption between Hayden and ACTU President Cliff Dolan at this meeting, at which the Labor Party was represented by Hayden, Hawke, Bowen and Willis. Hayden had arrived with a draft press release which began with the words 'The ACTU and ALP today agreed . . .', but Dolan could not agree. Hayden was stunned. There had been significant differences earlier that day inside the ACTU executive over the rate of progress on the accord but the situation was saved when ACTU Vice-President Simon Crean and Research Officer Bill Kelty persuaded Dolan that a statement expressing 'in principle' endorsement of the accord could be made. The sticking point was the ACTU commitment that: 'The wage system must provide for full indexation in line with rises in the CPI.' The ALP wanted this commitment qualified in the accord, thereby opening the way for wage restraint.

It was the ravage of the recession which forced the ACTU to reassess its wages strategy. It knew that economic activity was so low there was already a de facto wage pause because employers could not afford to pay. In late October Hayden had phone discussions with both Crean and Kelty. They told him that a new ACTU policy was 'in the pipeline'. Their message was that the ACTU needed a wages strategy based, not on abandonment of real wage maintenance, but on the idea that real wages could be maintained only over a period of time. This allowed the ACTU to come to grips with the reality of the present economic downturn. Hayden understood that it would be only a short time until the tortuous machinery of the trade union movement reconciled its theoretical position to economic reality.

After Anthony announced the wage pause initiative the ACTU Executive met on 29–30 November to finalise its response. Kelty, now ACTU Secretary, was anxious to ensure a joint ACTU–ALP position to counter Fraser. So was Hayden. Kelty suggested that the senior ALP politicians meet the ACTU officers late on 29 November to begin this process. This meeting was attended again by Hayden, Hawke, Bowen and Willis. It was only five days before the Flinders by-election and Hayden was already worried by the significant differences between the ALP and the Labor Premiers over the pause. The ACTU officers briefed the ALP men in detail on the type of resolution the union movement would finalise the next day. They said they opposed the wage freeze but had to accept market realities. Their aim was to put Fraser on the defensive by specifying the conditions needed for a viable wages policy and for a wages pause.

The ACTU Executive decision the next day, 30 November, was a landmark. For the first time the ACTU embraced the proposition that the objective of real wage maintenance was to be achieved 'over time' . The way was now open for the ALP and the ACTU to proceed to finalise their prices–incomes accord. The ACTU did not reject the wage freeze outright. The resolution said the ACTU would 'recommend to unions that they give serious consideration' to a wage pause provided that the Government met certain conditions. The conditions were that the pause be limited to six months, that the Government agree to some form of catch-up, that all parties agreed to return to centralised wage fixation and that the Government would move towards a more expansionist economic policy which would create jobs. The ACTU said that if the federal Government did not accept its package then it would continue its current campaign for a six per cent wage rise. In many ways the ACTU conditions were a neat summary of the core of the February 1983 ALP–ACTU accord. Kelty, who drafted the resolution, believed it offered a viable ALP–ACTU stance against Fraser. That is, it established a political position short of an outright rejection of the freeze around which the Labor movement could base its counteroffensive against Fraser.

However Hayden was furious. Headlines the next day emphasised the willingness of the ACTU to negotiate with the federal Government on a wage pause. The federal ALP was becoming more isolated as the Premiers on one hand, and the union movement on the other, showed they were receptive. By this stage Malcolm Fraser, recuperating at Nareen, was watching enthusiastically the groundswell of support for his initiative.

The split between the ALP and the ACTU came on Thursday 2 December just two days before Flinders. The ACTU had had a long and painful executive meeting at which the full story of the financial chaos surrounding its new Swanston Street headquarters was documented. When the meeting broke up about 6.00 p.m., there was little spirit left for reconciliation and the ACTU officers went straight to a meeting with the same four ALP leaders. Hayden began with an aggressive attack, accusing the officers of a misleading briefing the previous Monday. He said the ACTU resolution was much more accommodating towards the Government than he had expected. He made the issue a breach of trust.

Crean, Kelty and Charlie Fitzgibbon hit back. Hayden had made the mistake of impugning their integrity—a grave charge to level against competent trade union leaders whose life is negotiation and whose negotiations depend on their word being accepted as their bond. They denied having misled Hayden. The ACTU kept pointing to the resolution, arguing that it was a far-reaching wages compromise for the union movement. But Hayden was upset because the ACTU had offered Fraser a concession on real wages which they had not yet finalised with the Labor Party.

The meeting degenerated even further. Bowen said he had been campaigning all day in Flinders and it was obvious that nobody wanted a wage freeze. He said the ACTU should come out and oppose it. Hawke went off at a tangent. He floated his old idea of wage restraint through a return to the basic wage concept plus margin. The ACTU dismissed this at once. The affiliation of major white-collar unions with the ACTU meant that it was now committed to full wage indexation and could never shift back to the old formula. Bowen then suggested that the meeting the next day between the ACTU and the three Labor Premiers should be widened to allow the federal ALP to be represented. He was afraid the Premiers were likely to be induced into accepting a wage pause to help their state budgets.

But the ACTU declined; it saw no point as it had already seen the federal ALP twice this week on the wage pause issue. At this stage Bowen leaned across to Hayden and whispered, 'These boys and the Premiers have done a deal on the freeze; it's a bloody outrage.' When Hayden refused to accept the ACTU position on the pause the meeting reached total deadlock. As they broke up Crean said to Hayden, 'Let's ensure this doesn't become a PR disaster. Let's keep quiet about it.' Hayden replied, 'You can be certain that's what we'll be doing.'

Dolan came out and told the waiting media there would be no press conference from the ACTU side, but the hints of a major row were soon in the air. A few minutes later Hayden held a press conference and revealed that the parties could not reach agreement. Hayden continued to answer press questions on the disagreement; next to him Hawke smoked a cigar, blowing rings into the air, and catching the glance of journalists, rolled his eyes towards his head. Hawke was amazed at Hayden's behaviour and the damage it was causing. Towards the end of the press conference, a Canberra journalist said to a senior Hayden staffer, 'What the hell is he saying this for?' The reply was: 'What's wrong? This is great stuff.'

The newspaper headlines the next day, the Friday before the by-election, were devastating for Hayden; nearly every paper highlighted the ALP–ACTU split. These stories appeared when the television blackout for Flinders was already underway. Consequently they were very difficult to counter. The ACTU was rocked by Hayden's comments and the open schism they created between the political and industrial wings. The divisions in the Labor movement only served to give the stamp of legitimacy to Fraser's wage pause. For five years Hayden had championed ALP–ACTU cooperation. Now the crucial test had come this unity lay broken, a victim of Fraser's policy.

On 3 December the three Labor Premiers met with the ACTU and reached a joint position. The federal ALP under Bill Hayden was isolated within the Labor movement. As Neville Wran left Melbourne that night he told a colleague: 'I think this could be the end of Hayden. These blokes will never forgive the way he spoke to them.' Lionel Bowen regarded 2 December, the day of the ALP–ACTU fall-out, as the turning point for Hayden's leadership. Bowen said later that it had made genuine cooperation between Hayden and the ACTU unlikely and that, in the post-Flinders climate, the ACTU would mark time and wait for Hawke.

The source of the problem was the lack of consultation and trust between the ALP and ACTU leaderships. Dolan and Kelty believed their position had been sabotaged by the political wing. Hayden believed that the ACTU had made concessions to Fraser it had never made to himself at the very time of Labor's greatest electoral need. In fact neither Hayden nor Bowen was fully familiar with ACTU thinking; neither was closely involved in the 1982 nego-tiations over the prices–incomes accord. Incredibly Hayden had left this matter to Hawke and Willis.

Hayden distrusted Hawke and was always wary of the ACTU, knowing it was Hawke's political homeland. Years earlier Hayden had wanted to bypass the ACTU and negotiate for the accord between the ALP and individual unions. But this was too difficult a process. The accord necessitated dealing through the ACTU, Hawke's personal network. The ACTU officials felt after their talks that Hayden was not sufficiently briefed on the details. The con-clusion to be drawn from this is that Hayden should have had a senior member of his personal staff concentrating on this ACTU dialogue, a member known to the ACTU itself, who could have prepared the ground and removed the potential for division.

In the week after Flinders the special Premiers' Conference agreed on a wage pause for six months with $300 million 'savings' from the Commonwealth budget to be directed into job creation. The two key figures who put the deal together were Doug Anthony and Ian Macphee. During the course of the previous three weeks Macphee had worked to undermine Howard's insistence that the pause be implemented through legislation covering the private sector. After lunch at the Premiers' Conference, Macphee, at Anthony's request, did the deal with Wran, Cain and Bannon. There would be no legislation; the avenue would be industrial tribunals. Federal Cabinet finally agreed to the compromise late in the day after another Howard–Macphee clash.

Two days later on 9 December the ACTU came to Canberra to see the Government about details of the pause. Then they adjourned to Hayden's office in a bid to re-establish a working relationship. This was an important meeting because it hammered out the basis for the ALP–ACTU accord. Kelty later reviewed the saga of the ALP–ACTU split and argued convincingly that the ACTU had not had ulterior motives:

> Nothing we did was influenced by the Labor leadership question . . . Our basic assumption was that Bill Hayden was leader of the party and would continue to lead it. If we wanted to undermine Hayden, then why would we have spoken to him before our 30 November Executive meeting, foreshadowing our decision? Why would we have interrupted our Executive meeting of 2 December to speak with him in an effort to get a joint position? Why would we have tried the next week to organise another meeting in Canberra to sort out the disaster of the previous Thursday?[4]

However the real damage had been done on 4 December on the Mornington Peninsula and nothing would undo it. Alan Ramsey rang Hayden at home that night and put it simply: 'Bill, it's a disaster. It's just a disaster.' Labor had a swing of just under three per cent when it needed 5.5 per cent to win. That is, Labor polled just over half the average by-election swing against Governments in Government-held seats—yet the economic climate was very bad; far worse than normal. In such a climate against a Government of such longevity, a big swing could have been expected. If Cameron's research was correct—it was only a small sample—then Labor lost ground during the campaign.

Rogan Ward was a major liability for Labor. *The Age* ran a front-page story in the last week of the campaign saying that his real-estate business had been involved in artificially inflating the prices of houses. The story was lethal and must have severely damaged the Labor vote since the candidate is more important in a by-election than in a general election. But the 'candidate factor' in Flinders is only one part of the story.

The first lesson of Flinders was that the mood of the electorate had changed. This was initially revealed on the morning of the by-election in an excellent survey of the seat published in *The Age*. It showed that people were now starting to worry about unemployment because they feared that it posed a threat to their middle-class security. Suburbia felt at risk. The people saw no relevance for themselves in the Flinders vote since they were disillusioned with Fraser but held no faith in Hayden as an alternative. Only one politician could inspire any hope: Bob Hawke. There was a touching naivety in the way people believed that Hawke could succeed where Fraser had failed and that Hayden was not even worth a try.

This assessment was verified by an ANOP report Cameron gave the Labor Party in early December based on qualitative research on 16–18 November. The report identified the return of unemployment to the political agenda of the campaign professionals:

> It is our judgement that unemployment will be a major vote-switching issue in Australia in 1983, but the issue is really better thought of as involving personal financial security. While the hardline, anti-dole-bludger response appears to be on the decline, there is little evidence to suggest that unemployment is an issue because of sympathy for the person out of work. Rather unemployment is a growing issue because ordinary suburban, middle-class swinging voters are becoming personally more concerned about their own security.[5]

Flinders revealed that Fraser's wage pause, despite its defects, typified the yearning for action within the electorate. Hayden, who attacked the pause throughout the by-election, admitted on 5 December:

> There is a good reason to believe that the Government's 12-month wage freeze significantly influenced the campaign. The Labor Party cannot ignore this clear likelihood, nor the implications of it for the entire Labor movement.

By these words Hayden condemned his own strategic misjudgement in the campaign period.

The ALP strategists had always believed their chances of winning the next election depended upon whether the electorate's hostility to Fraser over the economy was sufficient to overcome Hayden's perceived leadership weakness. Flinders suggested that it was not. The outstanding feature of the campaign was the collapse of the ALP effort. Flinders was the most damaging blow Hayden had sustained as ALP leader. It highlighted his vulnerability—his incapacity as a vote winner. In Flinders the ALP fell into a heap when it should have been surging to the tape. Flinders injected a deep sense of worry, then urgency, into the Labor Party because it suggested there was a pent-up hostility towards Fraser but that Labor had lost the key to unlock it.

The divisions inside the Labor movement on the eve of Flinders revealed Hayden's lack of strength and judgement. The failure of Labor to communicate its message reinforced Hayden's other deficiencies. Hayden had failed to provide a framework in which to sell Labor's policies to the people. Flinders proved that Hayden had comprehensively lost the opportunity afforded to him by the tax debate. The party professionals, Bob McMullan, Rod Cameron, Bob Hogg and Graham Richardson, felt Labor now faced an election defeat. The Caucus and shadow Cabinet were so worried by the result that they began saying the reason lay beyond either Rogan Ward or Bill Hayden; it must be Labor policy as well.

The curse of Flinders was the fear that Labor might not win the next election with Hayden. It spread gradually but relentlessly through the ALP like a disease systematically destroying its victim. After Flinders the Labor Party slid into a pessimism so deep that it became convinced that Hayden could never beat Fraser.

This was an understandable reaction. Flinders left Hayden's greatest advocates without an argument. Realists in the ALP had to conclude at this point that the probability of defeat with Hayden was too high. In terms of personal power Fraser had beaten Hayden. It has to be judged this way because that was the conclusion the Labor Party itself had drawn.

The three-way power struggle had now changed suddenly. Fraser's assumed dominance over Hayden even from his sick bed gave Hawke a chance—but that depended upon the ruthlessness of the ALP itself.

Finally Flinders created an exaggerated optimism inside the Liberal Party. The by-election featured a bad ALP candidate, a misconceived Labor strategy and a spectacular ALP split—three ingredients not likely to be simultaneously reproduced again in the near future. Malcolm Fraser had always believed he had the measure of the Hayden Labor Party, now he felt he had established command over the Opposition itself. Fraser saw Flinders as evidence that he would have probably won a December 1982 election. But there is no reason to assume this or to suppose the ALP would have performed nearly as badly in a general election as it did in the unique circumstances that produced Flinders.

18
Recovery, reconstruction and reconciliation

The reconciliation strategy is right, it represents what the electorate wants; in itself it is cost-free.

Bob Hawke, January 1983

For Bill Hayden the irony of the Flinders by-election was that the Fraser Government won on a positive programme at the very time Hayden was shaping a new response to the economic crisis. That response was the recovery and reconstruction programme which, by the time of the Flinders by-election, had been canvassed by ALP strategists, tested by ANOP and found to be electorally viable. The programme was the political tool Hayden had needed for so long. It was a framework in which Labor policies could be presented to the people as a philosophical whole.

In September 1982 more than two months before Flinders, Hayden decided to use recovery and reconstruction as the central idea in his campaign for Prime Minister. The programme was not developed sufficiently to be used in the Flinders campaign. The result was that Fraser's wage freeze, an effective but narrower concept, beat Hayden's recovery and reconstruction into the marketplace. This triumph of timing would prove to be decisive. Because he lost the Flinders by-election Hayden lost the leadership—only weeks before he was scheduled to release his new economic policy.

When Hawke assumed the leadership on 3 February he inherited the Hayden concept, But all new leaders must stamp the party in their own image. Hawke kept many of the Hayden policies, even retained the R and R phraseology, but his thrust was always reconciliation and consensus; thus recovery and reconstruction withered before it was formally launched. In practice it became a bridge to the Hawke policy of reconciliation.

The stimulus for the new strategy came from the August research report

262

ANOP had produced for the Labor party. In this report Rod Cameron had identified 'fairness' as the key theme which Labor should use as its message. But Cameron had gone one step further. He also advised the ALP to move towards what he called a 'new directions' strategy. The ANOP report said:

> In 1982 the ALP's credibility is sufficiently better as would enable it confidently to propose a different and better (and more ideologically founded) approach to the economic problems facing Australia. Thus a theme which implies a fresh approach, a better way, a new direction is suggested. Moreover this position appears to be vacant in communication terms in 1982, following the Government's budget strategy which gives scant regard to a new-direction strategy in favour of a blatant attempt at buying-off the swinging voter.[1]

The need for a 'new directions' strategy was even more obvious after the tax debate since Fraser's tough line pre-empted the 'fairness' theme. Cameron said the party which properly seized the 'new directions' position would gain a major advantage. This challenge was faced by a new ALP campaign strategy committee. In August–September a five-man committee was set up comprising McMullan, Richardson, Hogg, Hayden's Private Secretary Mike Costello and his former Private Secretary Clem Lloyd from the Australian National University. Cameron attended most meetings. Labor had found big campaign committees were unworkable and this smaller committee soon produced an election strategy.

Richardson, with the help of Wran's Press Secretary Peter Barron, had suggested the campaign slogan 'Australia Deserves Better', designed to exploit the tax debate and 'fairness' theme. This remained the official ALP marketing position until late November. But the turning point towards a new position began with Lloyd's paper to the 14 September meeting of the committee. He gave the 'new directions' a political content. Lloyd wrote:

> The impression comes across overwhelmingly from the swinging voters of mounting unfairness and inequality in the Australian society . . . All of these evils can be painted as un-Australian, as totally opposed to our national traditions, our long-accepted notions of patriotism, of dinkum Aussie conduct . . . Would the Anzacs or the Man from Snowy River or Don Bradman or Phar Lap have rorted their taxes through bottom-of-the-harbour schemes? . . .
>
>   In the presentation of economic competence, there seem to me to be limitations to a 'new directions' or a 'doing things differently' kind of approach. Such a campaign would be based largely on assertion, coupled perhaps with some lingering perceptions of Hayden as a successful Treasurer. (On the

evidence of research, this is no longer a major strength.) . . .

There are two possible themes which might assist us here:

a   the notion of reconstruction,

b   the notion of restoring national prosperity.

The first seems to me to be much the more promising. Reconstruction as opposed to straight construction or development logic has always exercised a strong appeal in Australia: reconstruction after war; reconstruction after depression; reconstruction after national disaster. One of the great things the Chifley Labor Government had going for it was post-war reconstruction symbolised in a great national project—the Snowy Mountains Scheme. In a similar vein, why can't we come up with a programme of national reconstruction after the Fraser recession?

The strategy committee took up Lloyd's reconstruction concept and began to refine it. Hayden read Lloyd's paper and was immediately enthusiastic, fired by the idea. At the full campaign committee meeting on 28 October Hayden asked Lloyd to provide a brief on the reconstruction theme. Hayden then gave his own views on the meaning of reconstruction and how it could be harnessed for Labor's use. Hawke joined in the discussion and spoke of the need for revival and reconciliation, using the phrase 'national healing' to encapsulate the message. Cameron saw merit in reconstruction as a political tool and agreed to test it. Cameron conducted qualitative research in Perth with six discussion groups over 16–18 November and produced two significant results. Firstly unemployment was emerging as a genuine issue, and secondly reconstruction, assisted by this new mood, tested well.

Cameron's report to a strategy committee meeting in either late November or early December said, 'The extent to which unemployment is becoming a "real", rather than survey or media issue, is increasing quickly in Australia . . . The emphasis with which swinging voters regard unemployment has certainly changed in late 1982.' Cameron warned:

We should not be lulled into repeating past campaign errors by assuming that the unemployment issue implies electoral sympathy for the unemployed. There is very little in the way of a humane response from selfish swinging voters on this issue or any other . . .

There is little evidence that the federal Government is being heavily blamed at this point for Australia's growing unemployment. Importantly there is very little suggestion that the ALP is credited with much greater abilities at solving the problem . . . However there is a clarion call by swinging voters for

positive, understandable, simply explained, constructive and real action by
Government at all levels to ease the unemployment situation.

Cameron reported on the response to reconstruction:

> Reconstruction as a concept tested remarkably well . . . The concept of a
> 'Snowy River Project' has real and genuine appeal to swinging voters. It is a
> worthwhile project for Australia . . . But to work the reconstruction idea needs
> real symbols. It will not be a credible position should there be no accompanying
> reality. The idea of a major project in each state had great appeal as it brought
> the concept closer to the ordinary person.[2]

In this report Cameron said there was no sign that Labor had emerged from the
tax debate perceived as a more honest or equitable party, and that as a result
the 'Australia Deserves Better' slogan was inappropriate. This meeting of the
strategy committee rejected the slogan. It endorsed reconstruction as Labor's
campaign position.

Hayden went back to two of the great surviving figures of the post-war
reconstruction era: former Director-General of Post-War Reconstruction Dr
H. C. Coombs and Ben Chifley's adviser and biographer Professor L. F. Crisp.
He read Coombs' autobiography *Trial Balance* and wrote to Crisp asking what
was applicable now from the post-war experience. Crisp's reply was sobering:
'Not as much as I had expected.' He explained that circumstances now were
very different. The community, including business and industry, had emerged
from the war more acquiescent about public planning; Labor had enjoyed in
1944–49 control of both Houses of Parliament and there had been a pent-up
demand for development. Crisp recommended that Hayden and Gareth
Evans plan a referendum in the first six months of office to expand the
Commonwealth's economic powers. But he warned, 'This little exercise I am
suggesting for you should not be made public before being launched . . .' Crisp
suggested that two organising structures from the immediate post-war period
were still relevant. One was a National Works Council to plan priorities, on
which the Commonwealth and states were represented. The other was a
National Training and Retraining Authority, which Crisp described as 'a pretty
crucial element in a general national up-turn . . . the sort of dual-purpose agency
essential in bad times, one to effect both real and psychological benefits'.[3]

Through December and early January, Hayden, Lloyd, Costello and the
economist on Hayden's staff, Michael Roche, pulled a new policy together. It
was divided into recovery, then reconstruction. Recovery was the immediate
expansionist, job-creation boost a Hayden Government would give in its first

budget, while reconstruction would extend over six years. Lloyd and an ANU colleague Dr Pat Troy proposed a job-creation programme for the recovery phase with the bulk of investment being provided by the private sector. Hayden's staff drew heavily on the draft industry policy coming from the shadow minister, Chris Hurford, and the draft science and technology policy which was the inspiration of Barry Jones identifying 'sunrise' industries based on technological advances which a Labor Government should support and, in the long term, rely upon as a vital employment base. Another arm of recovery and reconstruction was the housing policy drafted by Tom Uren and modified by the shadow Cabinet.

Originally Hayden wanted to release the recovery programme as soon as possible after the Flinders by-election, but the dismal result prompted a rethink. It was decided that a single major economic policy launch, involving both recovery and reconstruction, would have maximum impact and this was timed for early 1983. But problems remained, some of them identified by Costello in an 11 January note to Hayden:

> There is the question of identifying a 'Snowy River' type project. We have not yet been able to do so. One way around this might be to make the size of the programme ($2,500 million) the symbol, rather than any specific project. Another is to identify a grand project, such as the 'turn the rivers back' idea of Chifley, as something we want to undertake, but commit ourselves to no more than investigating its feasibility, cost, etc. There are a lot of unresolved costings issues. Further we are going to have to answer the inevitable 'where's the money coming from' questions, especially in relation to capital works . . .
>
> Two points on this. First, Ralph [Willis] has mentioned a specific amount as being additional budgetary stimulus ($1,600 million). I wonder if we should lock ourselves into a precise figure like this? Second, in 1975 Fraser steadfastly refused repeated questioning from the press about the size of the deficit he had in mind, and about many of the specific costings of his proposals, arguing that this was a matter which could only be settled in Government. He got away with it.

In early January Lloyd took all the available material and wrote a draft recovery and reconstruction document which was subsequently endorsed by the campaign committee at its 20 January meeting. Hawke's concept of reconciliation was added as a third leg. Lloyd's paper began:

> Seven years of Fraser Government have shattered the Australian economy and deeply scarred Australian society. The evidence of economic malaise is

everywhere. Unemployment has soared to the highest levels since the great depression. It is now 10 per cent of the Australian work force; it will be 12 per cent by the end of 1983. Great traditional regions of Australia such as the iron triangle of South Australia, the Hunter Valley and the Illawarra in NSW, much of Tasmania, have been denuded of jobs and investment. The way we are going now we will have lower per capita income levels than Singapore by 1990 and Iceland by the year 2000 . . .

Labor would establish a National Works Council made up of the Prime Minister, Treasurer, federal Minister for Recovery and Reconstruction, the six state Premiers and the Northern Territory Chief Minister. The Council would plan and implement a National Works Programme that would pump an extra $2,300 million a year into the economy and create up to 135,000 new jobs in its first full year. Two-thirds of the funds would come from private-sector investment and one-third from Government. Possible projects included the Melbourne–Adelaide standard gauge, the Alice Springs–Darwin railway, Goulburn–Canberra rail upgrading, construction of the second Port Kembla coal loader. An Australian Government office programme would be initiated to accommodate public servants, financed and built by the private sector under leaseback arrangements. Labor would also create a major housing programme and a community works scheme with the latter receiving $350 million in a full year for job creation.

Under the reconstruction heading Labor pledged to establish an Industry Reconstruction Finance Corporation to operate in the capital market to encourage the revitalisation of industry. The corporation would be empowered to make necessary investments by share purchase or loans and guarantees of loans. Its assistance would be dependent on certain criteria such as the adoption of new technology and job security. The Australian Industry Development Corporation would be converted into a bank to enable broader investment participation by small investors in new development projects. Labor would aim to double funding for research and development over ten years. A priority would be the channelling of investment to new 'sunrise' industries. Biotechnology was seen as Australia's best prospect and the objective was to make Australia a world leader in the field. Other areas listed included computer software, scientific instrumentation (an area of lost opportunity with the Interscan aircraft guidance system designed in Australia but manufactured overseas), medical and solar technology.

Once the campaign committee endorsed the package, it was to be circulated more widely inside the ALP for further advice and clarification. The Lloyd paper remained very much a draft document, but the 20 January meeting was given another document prepared by Hawke, which revealed that he had a very different idea to Hayden on how Labor should approach the campaign and present itself as an alternative Government. It turned out to be a prophetic document and outlined the exact strategy that Hawke would subsequently apply so successfully as ALP leader in less than two months' time.

In marketing terms Hawke saw little role for recovery and reconstruction as a concept. He wrote an historic analysis:

> The essential malaise to be identified with the period of the Fraser Government is the increasing erosion of any sense of common national purpose. Individuals and groups have been encouraged, explicitly and implicitly, to perceive and pursue their own self-interest . . . The rupturing of Australian society, which characterised the circumstances of Fraser coming to power at the end of 1975, was therefore not a one-off aberration. The application of this philosophy and the qualifications applied to it have inevitably intensified this rupturing process.
>
> While the electorate still believed that the basic economic mould of the past had not been broken—that continued growth and expanding employment opportunities would characterise our community—the espousal and practical reflection of this philosophy was not found objectionable . . . There is now an understanding that the mould has been broken. The fact and fear of high and growing unemployment—coexisting with high inflation and interest rates and flat or declining economic growth paths—has created a new environment . . .
>
> There is a desire for healing, for a sense of common purpose. We have a harder, longer job to sell our economic policies—indeed it is arguable just how far the electorate wants to be sold policies as such. However, it should be, and I believe is, very much easier emphasising that Fraser cannot change his spots—to show positively that we are much better equipped and more likely to undertake this task of national reconciliation.
>
> Anthony Sampson's observations in his recent *The Changing Anatomy of Britain* are relevant in this respect: 'Behind the cross-purposes lay the basic fact that the British in this post-imperial phase were still confused and divided; they still could not mobilise the sense of national purpose or unity, which had been so evident in wartime, to the more contemporary challenge of industrial survival.'
>
> Ours is the party which very effectively provided that 'sense of national purpose or unity' in war. One of the reasons the Labor Party was able to do this was its special relations with the trade unions—which demonstrably, however, was not one of automatic endorsement by the (then) Government of the industrial movement's platform or programme. Properly handled we can establish precisely that sort of perception in the mind of the electorate again.

The desire for this sense of national purpose or unity is undoubtedly present and strongly felt—it reflects, as well as economic concerns, an apprehension of increasing social disintegration.

The sense of danger is not as dramatically obvious as it was in war, but the implications are not dissimilar. I believe we should make this central to our strategy. In these terms we should be significantly more credible than Fraser. Most of our important, and somewhat esoteric, policies can be placed squarely within the framework of this approach—most obviously the prices and incomes policy, but similarly others as, for example, health and housing.

As well as making for easier comprehension of some particular policies, the theme of reconciliation can indeed provide an integrating theme for virtually all our policy proposals. It sits well with, and can in fact provide an underpinning for, any associated theme of reconstruction . . .

A final observation. Whereas the individual elements of our policy can, and will, be subject to the dessicated costing calculations of our opponents, and may give rise to some areas of electoral backlash, the concept of the reconciliation strategy has these advantages:

a   It is right,

b   It represents what the electorate wants,

c   In itself, it is cost-free.

This paper applied Hawke's personal philosophy to the circumstances rather than analysed the circumstances to produce a prescription. Hawke could have drawn the same conclusions about national division almost any time in the last seven to eight years. Significantly Hawke believed it was 'arguable' whether the community wanted to be sold policies and concluded that it was better for Labor to market an image. The image was national reconciliation as a substitute for Fraser's national confrontation. The reality was that only a Hawke-led Labor party could have waged such a campaign. The paper was a strategy for a Hawke-led Labor party that was inoperative for a Hayden-led Labor party.

In many ways recovery and reconstruction would have given Hayden a philosophical cloak to enhance his leadership. Yet in order to find this cloak Hayden had retreated into Labor tradition, rummaging through the cupboard of Labor history. It was an idea from a period of great Labor innovation and success. However it is difficult to judge whether the reconstruction concept, with its high degree of Government planning, its necessarily high degree of public and private sector cooperation and its huge investment in projects of dubious economic merit, would have worked in the 1980s. It is doubtful whether Hayden himself could have sold the concept without major projects to spark the public's imagination.

The significance of reconstruction is that Hayden had decided to turn his back on orthodoxy and find a better way. It was a move towards a greater role for Government and a bigger public sector as part of a new strategy for growth. Significantly Fraser had gone through the same process and reached a similar conclusion, although not as grandiose. In essence the conclusion was that Government could not allow economic growth to be a function of private enterprise activity. The crisis was severe and that meant that Government had to devise a reconstruction or growth strategy.

Hayden's recovery and reconstruction programme never proceeded beyond the document approved by the 20 January campaign committee. The obsession of the Labor Party from the Flinders by-election onwards was not with policy but with power. Hayden would be the victim of that obsession.

PART 3

THE CLIMAX

19

The Button defection

I'm not going to stand down for a bastard like Hawke.

Bill Hayden to John Button,
January 1983

Labor Senate leader John Button was the psychological and arithmetic key to the Hayden leadership. Button was Hayden's peer, not his acolyte; he had an independence which Hayden shared and an intelligence which Hayden respected. Button's political skill was concealed behind his guise as diminutive comedian. He was a clever politician committed to the creation of a Caucus centre group, to give more intellectual weight and political clout to the ALP. The centre was tied together through a common policy outlook and personal associations. Hayden was its leader and Button its strategist. The two men had risen together in friendship and power and this had provided a deep psychological bond.

The results of the July ballot had made Button the critical factor in the ongoing Hayden–Hawke struggle. The intensity of the July contest meant that neither individuals nor factions would easily switch sides. The left would stay with Hayden; the right would stick by Hawke in any new challenge. The centre stayed with Hayden, although partly disillusioned. While a net defection of only three was needed to change leaders, the Hawke forces knew they could not move until the numbers were guaranteed. For this reason, the Hawke camp looked to Button.

He was the most influential centre figure behind Hayden, yet he was known to harbour grave doubts. He was a figure of standing—the party's Senate leader—and receptive to argument. Button did not control votes as did the faction leaders, but he influenced them. If Button would defect, then Hawke must eventually prevail because he would have penetrated Hayden's inner sanctum and the ALP leadership group. Thus Button became the pivot around which the leadership would fluctuate. He was the target of the Hawke forces.

The Flinders by-election had changed the mood of the Labor Party as swiftly and completely as a drawn curtain turns day into night. Hawke's transgression in appearing to open up the leadership question a month earlier had become irrelevant, overwhelmed by Labor's introspective pessimism which, as it developed a focus, created the need to change leaders. Hayden had been tried and he had failed. Yet Button himself had always been anti-Hawke; his long-nourished 'parliamentary club' scepticism about Hawke had been confirmed since Hawke entered Parliament. He had assessed Hawke as intellectually arid and emotionally uninspiring. Yet as faith in Hayden declined, a worthier assessment of Hawke began to form. This was inevitable. Hawke did not change as a man or politician, but Flinders gave validity to his claim that only he could win power for the Labor Party. Flinders broke the bolts on the door of the 'parliamentary club' opposition to Hawke; it completed the process which the July challenge had begun. The 'parliamentary club' now began its move towards Hawke, and in the vanguard were his longstanding opponents, John Button and Lionel Bowen.

The day after the Flinders by-election both Button and Bowen issued statements to *The Sydney Morning Herald* to head off a move on the leadership. Bowen said, 'The result is very disappointing. I think local factors did some damage . . . The party makes its decision on the leadership after each election. There's no point in doing anything in the meantime.' Button, deeply depressed by the loss, warned, 'I might disagree with Bill Hayden sometimes, but I think it's sheer intellectual cowardice to blame everything on the leader. It's the collective responsibility of the shadow Cabinet.' Both men were merely rationalising a political dilemma from which they could not escape. Within the next week Button and Bowen had both moved a long way down the path from Hayden to Hawke.

The challenger was very cautious in his response to the Flinders defeat, determined not to repeat the events of early November. Asked on television whether Hayden would remain as leader for the election campaign, Hawke said, 'As far as I know he will. I've made my position clear just a few weeks ago that I will not be challenging him. That was clear in the statement and I intend to adhere to it.' When the reporter kept pressing, Hawke told him angrily, 'Grab hold of yourself. I've said it three times. Now you're just being a bloody pest. I made it quite clear.'

The day after the by-election, 5 December, Hawke flew to Sydney and had lunch with Richardson at the Boulevard Hotel. He was convinced that the Flinders by-election was the turning point, but the political task was to turn

Labor's pessimism into political action. Richardson said there was no purpose in a challenge unless they had Button's support. Hawke concurred. The tactics became private pressure and public silence. Hawke disciplined himself and made no provocative public comments.

That afternoon Hawke and Richardson attended a 'Young Turks' meeting for new recruits to the NSW right-wing machine. Richardson addressed this gathering at Sydney University and bluntly declared that Labor had to change leaders to win. Then, looking at Hawke, he said, 'But next time we'll be counting the numbers first so we know how many votes we've got and how many our opponents have got.' One Labor candidate, Garry Punch, from Barton, spoke up urging a change of leadership. Someone at the meeting later briefed Bowen, and the deputy in turn told Hayden.

On Monday 6 December Richardson rang Button in Perth. They agreed the party must reassess. Both felt big changes were needed in Hayden's staff. Labor would need to rethink its attitude to the wage freeze and relations with the ACTU had to be improved. Perhaps there should be a reshuffle. Richardson never mentioned the leadership.

The ALP Strategy Committee and shadow Cabinet met on Tuesday 7 December. Hayden offered to accept the bulk of responsibility for 'what apparently went wrong' in the Flinders by-election, but it was agreed that Labor's efforts to develop and project policies was the responsibility of the frontbench team, notably the economic spokesmen Ralph Willis and Bob Hawke. The Caucus conducted a lengthy post mortem which was remarkably free of criticism of Hayden. Senator George Georges was the sole voice asking Hayden to resign if he could not perform better. The party review was filled with fine words but no action.

Meanwhile the Flinders by-election had confirmed Bob Hogg's view that Hayden had squandered the taxation issue. Hogg moved into the Hawke orbit. On Friday 10 December Hogg reported to the Victorian administrative committee on why Labor had lost Flinders. He said that if the committee wanted an honest assessment, then he was forced to say that while Hayden stayed leader and performed badly the ALP faced the prospect of losing—not winning—seats at the next election. He believed Hayden had three choices: he could resign the leadership, he could improve his performance, or he could stay on to fight a leadership spill against Hawke's supporters.

Hogg's analysis was chillingly accurate. His personal view was that Hayden's recent efforts suggested he would not lift his game. Hogg also believed that another blood-letting through a leadership battle would be catastrophic for Labor. Hogg's prestige in the party as a national organiser meant that his views would be significant.

The next day, 11 December, at a meeting of ALP State Secretaries in Adelaide, Hogg broke the ice on the leadership question. He told the meeting that the party was avoiding the main lesson of Flinders, which was that the leadership problem had to be resolved. Hogg did not say how this should occur. However Hayden's aide Michael Costello defended the Opposition leader's performance at length. An adversary situation was established and the Hayden camp assumed Hogg was lost.

By Monday 13 December Hayden had received sufficient reports to know trouble was brewing. Bowen had told him earlier: 'Watch it, there's movement at the station.' Hayden's instinct was to solidify his base and that evening he hosted a dinner for the leaders of the left and centre in the Caucus— the alliance which underpinned his leadership. Those attending were, from the centre, Button, Dawkins and Blewett, and from the left, Uren, Howe, Gietzelt and West. Hayden also asked Lionel Bowen.

The dinner was held at Charlie's Restaurant, a haunt of politicians and journalists, which made the function semi-public. Hayden was happy to advertise this centre-left festivity. He discussed the revitalisation of the Labor attack and floated again the idea of a reshuffle, in which Keating would become shadow Treasurer. The left resisted this, but it was even more hostile to having Hawke as shadow Treasurer, which was the alternative. The left, in a spirit of collectivism, suggested instead that an economic team be fashioned as Labor's spearhead. Hayden knew that this was impractical. The other proposal Hayden made was that Dawkins move into the Industry shadow portfolio, a significant promotion. One participant later described the dinner as 'friendly but aimless'. But it provided an insight into Hayden. The Flinders by-election had made him wary and indecisive.

On 14 December, Richardson made his play for Button. They met at Parliament House about 3.00 p.m. Button and Richardson bore a mutual respect typical of men who manipulate others. As rivals they had admired each other's surgical precision. Richardson used power; Button applied guile.

Richardson delivered a dual message. The Labor Party was sinking under Hayden, who could not win an election; if Button was not prepared to make a peaceful change, then others would make a violent one. The message was both diagnosis and prescription. It was also an ultimatum delivered in good faith. Richardson did not threaten Button; he merely tried to persuade him by appeal and pressure. Button asked, 'Are you Bob's campaign director?' Richardson replied, 'There's no campaign yet, but there will be.' Richardson told Button there was no point in his being leader of the Opposition in the Senate if he did not become a minister at the next election. Button's job as shadow Communications Minister was ludicrous, he should be in a more senior post.

Richardson argued that the better shadow ministers were not in the top jobs. But every problem led back to Hayden. 'We've run into an impasse, the leadership is stalled,' Richardson said. Button told him, 'That's the phrase I've just used to Hayden.' Button said he had told Hayden in July he had to win by a significant margin and told him after the ballot that five was not enough. Richardson said NSW candidates were ringing Head Office saying they had no chance of winning with Hayden. Party morale could never recover while he stayed leader. Richardson said that there would be bloodshed. Button was the key. With Button's support there could be a smooth change of leadership before an early 1983 election.

Both men felt sure that Fraser would call an early poll, given the political transformation which the Flinders by-election both symbolised and generated. Button believed Richardson was right about party morale, but he would not condone a new challenge. He took Richardson's message on notice. As he was leaving, Richardson stood in the doorway and said to Button, 'I hesitate to say this to you, but if we go into the election with Hayden as the leader and lose, then you will be blamed.' Richardson placed the party's fortunes on Button's shoulders, and Button was to remember that line.

The Hawke forces were not marshalling numbers. Indeed they were doing the opposite. It was not a time for lobbying, it was a time for highly selective persuasion. Button and his centre-group colleagues would never be won over by Hawke, but they would respond to the argument that Hawke was the only viable leader. Hayden's mistakes, the Flinders debacle and the demoralisation of the party presented irrefutable evidence that Hayden's leadership was beyond revival. Button was now moving towards this conclusion, which was buttressed by the soundings he had taken after seeing Richardson.

Button spoke to two of his closest colleagues: Victorian Premier John Cain, who was a member of Button's own 'independents' group in that state, and Bob Hogg. Cain felt Hayden would not win an election. Although he held doubts about Hawke, Cain further encouraged Button to change sides. So did Hogg whose personal view, as distinct from the left position, was that the most viable of the three options was for Hayden to resign.

Button examined the position from every point of view. He believed that Labor had to win the next election. Given the depth of the economic recession and the sense of national crisis, if the ALP failed to win office now it would lurch into irrelevance. The consequences of such a defeat would be crippling. Hayden would be finished in politics, his reputation discredited. The centre group would also be weakened. Hawke would take over, while Labor squabbled in despair during another period of apparently permanent opposition. Button knew that if Labor lost the 1983 election then, by the end of that three-year term, it would have spent 11 years in Opposition since the 1975 defeat. Another generation of ALP politicians would be facing the demoralisation of Opposition, their talents squandered, their ambitions thwarted and their political lives wasted.

On Wednesday 15 December Labor's National Campaign Committee met in Canberra. Before this meeting Hogg went to see Hayden. He warned of the paralysis in the party and gave the leader his assessment of the options facing him. Hogg told him that if he did not resign, then he faced the prospect of another challenge. He also discussed with Hayden the growing criticism of his senior staff, notably Ramsey and Costello.

Later, at the campaign committee meeting, both Richardson and Hogg assailed Labor's shadow Cabinet, claiming they had failed individually and collectively to nail the Government. The significance of this criticism is that Richardson and Hogg were the secretaries from NSW and Victoria, the two biggest states, with a record of electoral success symbolised in the Wran and Cain Governments. Bowen made a strong appeal for a shadow ministry reshuffle. He wanted changes in the economic portfolios, an obvious but not explicit call to replace Ralph Willis as shadow Treasurer.

Parliament adjourned for the summer recess that same day and most Labor members began the trek back home, heavy with despondency. The only hope on Labor's horizon was Bob Hawke. It was at this time that Hayden had two conversations with Button which revealed that the accumulated impact of the previous weeks' events was starting to undermine the leader's confidence. Hayden asked about a reshuffle but Button advised against it, arguing that it would appear to come too late and so would be dictated by weakness. Yet Hayden knew he was under great pressure to act decisively and regain lost ground. He commented wryly: 'If I have a reshuffle, I'm gone; but if I don't have a reshuffle, I'm gone as well.' Button replied, 'Look, Bill, if you think you're gone, then perhaps we'd better have a talk about it.' In another exchange Hayden's self-doubt became transparent. He said to Button, 'Dallas and I were talking about the position the other night. We think it would be better for me to be a minister than a defeated Opposition leader. I might have a look at how the opinion polls are shaping up in January and see then.'

All this had a profound impact on Button. He saw right through Hayden's veneer of cockiness to his core. Hayden was anxious, almost desperate, trapped between his instinct to fight and his foreboding of doom. He was losing conviction in himself. The self-doubt in Hayden's nature had been given fresh licence by the Flinders by-election. When Button saw this he started to think it was about time for Hayden to step aside. Meanwhile Hayden decided, yet again, to avoid a reshuffle.

Richardson remained in contact with Button after his initial approach to the Senate leader on the leadership question. He had a standard, almost automatic drill. After speaking with Button he would put down the phone and then dial Hawke. The challenger was kept informed of every move, each nuance. During this period Hawke rang Richardson almost nightly; sometimes he rang twice a night, his eagerness balancing on a knife edge. Finally, Richardson had good news: Button had agreed to approach Hayden on the leadership. Richardson was jubilant. He had always been confident that Button would see the inexorable political logic of the situation. Hawke was told immediately. Richardson, knowing how elusive Button could prove, wanted to tie him down to a definite time for the approach.

On 21–22 December the Labor Party restructured its campaign committee during a two-day session. The old committee, which had devised the recovery and reconstruction programme, was disbanded. The new campaign committee comprised: Young (Chairman), Hayden, Button, McMullan, Hogg and Richardson. Just before the meeting Hayden, anxious to counter leadership speculation, declared: 'I can assure you I'll be leading the party to victory at the next election, and we'll be rolling up our sleeves and getting down to the task of getting the country working again.' At the meeting Richardson said, 'Flinders taught me a lot of things. Everyone knows what my solution to our problem is, but we can't do anything about that here.'

By now such campaign meetings had farcical overtones. People sat around tables discussing policy and strategy, yet Hawke's supporters were trying to depose Hayden and Hayden knew it. A few days before this meeting the Opposition leader had called Richardson and asked him about criticisms he had made of his staff. Richardson confirmed them. Hayden had replied that he hoped Richardson would have the courage to raise them at the National Campaign Committee meeting. So Richardson did. He criticised Hayden's staff, saying they gave Hayden poor advice and inadequate support.

At the end of the meeting Richardson had a quiet word with Button, who agreed that, as soon as he returned from his holiday in Fiji with his family, he would fly to Brisbane and discuss the leadership with Hayden. Button did not commit himself to asking Hayden to resign, but he led Richardson to believe that he would make such a request. Richardson left confident that Hayden's days were numbered. After the meeting several shadow ministers had drinks at the Wentworth Hotel and on this occasion Button signalled his intentions to Keating. Then Button flew out to Fiji for a physical rest, but little respite from mental tension.

A small group in the NSW right knew about Button's intentions— Richardson, Keating, Wran's Press Secretary Peter Barron and NSW Assistant

Secretary Steve Loosely. But there was a leak when this circle was widened to include others during pre-Christmas celebrations in Sydney. On Christmas eve, *The Financial Review* published a page-one story about the final decision Button faced in Fiji and his likely trip to Queensland on his return. Hayden was alerted immediately. He spoke about this story to the Editor of *The Financial Review*, Paddy McGuiness, his former staffer. Hayden waited for Button.

On Christmas Day Uren rang Hayden and gave him some advice. Uren knew that the anti-Hayden alliance was formidable and closing fast. He advised Hayden as a friend, not as a left-wing leader: don't trust Button; give Keating Treasury and do it soon; keep Willis in an economic portfolio and promote West.

In Fiji Button was incommunicado. He saw no papers. Returning in the plane a steward recognised him and invited him onto the flight deck to meet the captain. The captain startled Button by saying, 'I know what you've been doing in Fiji. You've been lying on the beach working out who should be the leader of the Labor Party. It's in all the papers.' Button slumped into his seat and felt like he needed a holiday.

On returning he went immediately to his Melbourne office to read the papers. While there he received a call from *The Financial Review*, which put a formal question to Button: Did he support Hayden's continued leadership of the ALP? Button's reply was published the next morning, 30 December, in another major story: 'I talk to my colleagues—and that includes Bill Hayden—before I talk to *The Financial Review*.'

The headline read 'Button coy on Hayden' and the story said that Button could ask Hayden to stand down within days. Its publication was too much for Hayden. He rang Button after reading the story. Button was able to read out a telegram he had just sent to Hayden. It played down any suggestion that Button would be a messenger of doom, but Button said he wanted to discuss the party situation with Hayden during his pending trip to Queensland and suggested a meal with Bill and Dallas.

Button travelled Melbourne–Sydney–Coolangatta–Brisbane and was careful to avoid the press. He was meticulous about preparing the ground. Button went to Sydney to see Lionel Bowen who, Richardson had told him, had undergone a similar conversion.

Bowen did not have to push his nose far into NSW politics to find that the demand for Hawke filled the air. He told Button that NSW wanted a leadership change. He said, 'I just tell them I'm deputy leader and the people who handle this sort of thing are those "independents" in Victoria—they know how to do it.' Bowen thought this crack about Button's faction was a great joke.

Button told Bowen he intended to ask Hayden to resign and that he believed Hawke should be leader. Bowen agreed. He endorsed Button's assessment that Hayden could not win an election.

So Button was dispatched to Queensland. He went and spent a day with his close friends Michael and Caroline Duffy, who were renting a beach house at Kirra. The next day Button went to Brisbane to have lunch with Hayden.

This lunch on 6 January was the turning point in Hayden's leadership. The significance of this meeting was not just that Button asked Hayden to stand down as leader and was rebuffed. It provided the final confirmation for Button that Hayden had to resign the leadership in the interests of the Labor Party. It left Button with the conviction there was no other option and that, despite Hayden's refusal, he had to try again. Before this lunch there had always been an element of doubt in Button's mind. More than most Labor members, Button was in a fairly desperate mood, aware of the sinking morale of the party. People would say to his face that 'It's the bloke you're keeping as leader who's our problem'. But while moving to the view that Hayden should resign, Button had not finally dismissed the prospect of Hayden taking a decisive step politically and psychologically to break out of the circle of defeat. Not until this lunch.

Hayden's mood was one of embattled introspection; he was aggressive and paranoid. It was a lunch that left the heart hungry with regret, yet the brain unrepentant. Button told Hayden he believed there would be an early election, that Hayden could not win and that he should resign.

They argued about the early election. Hayden disagreed; he said the signs were indicating an economic upturn in late 1983 and that Fraser was likely to wait. This was a complete misreading of Fraser's outlook. Button said he believed there would be a March election; he thought the party was in a very bad condition, that morale was low and defeatism was rampant. He told Hayden, 'If you don't win now when the Labor Party has to win, you'll be the one blamed, and I don't want to see that happen.' This was a transposition of the Richardson argument. Richardson had told Button that if he did not change sides then he, Button, would be responsible for any defeat. Now Button was transferring this burden to Hayden.

Hayden refused to stand down. Button reminded Hayden of their December conversation, in which Hayden said he would assess the position in January. Hayden replied, 'That was before the stuff in the papers. If they're going to do that to me, then I'm not shifting.' Hayden added, 'I'm not going to stand down for a bastard like Hawke.' Hayden was furious about the two stories in *The Financial Review*; he was digging in. He told Button these stories must have been inspired by Hawke. Button disagreed and defended Hawke.

Hayden was bitter. He said Button had said things in the past which he could make public. He reminded Button that in 1977 he had written to him saying Hayden should be leader of the party. Button said he would be happy for Hayden to publish any letter he had written him. 'I wanted you to become leader, Bill,' Button said. 'And in the past five years as leader I've supported you on every fundamental issue you've fought.'

Hayden saw demons everywhere. His dilemma was that Button's defection only accentuated his natural insecurity. If he was losing a colleague like Button, who had been so close to him for so long, then nobody could be trusted. He began displaying the signs of deep paranoia, about almost everybody, that would mark his final weeks as leader.

Button told Hayden that he remained personally loyal to him. He gave the impression he would support him against Hawke in any contest and told Hayden he did not want to see him defeated at an election. Button said he had no brief for Hawke; he was not Hawke's emissary. In many ways Hawke was a risk for the party to embrace. But, whatever reservations people had about Hawke, they knew that he was a great communicator and that Hayden could not communicate. Button then advanced a novel proposition. If Hawke won an election as leader, then Hayden should stand for the deputy leadership—an idea that owed more to Button's search for arguments than it did to sound political judgement. Hayden dismissed this. But Button rammed home the point with the provocation that 'in the long run, this might be your best chance of becoming Prime Minister rather than staying on now as Opposition leader to face an election'.

Hayden rejected this as nonsense. Yet he wondered. It was an obvious hint that if Hawke became Prime Minister, and proved inadequate to the task, a widely held view in many sections of the Labor Party, then Button would turn back to Hayden and give him the kiss of political life in a bid to assassinate Hawke.

Hayden said that Button did not understand him. 'I'm an existentialist,' he said. 'Things happen to you and I'm prepared to accept responsibility for my actions. It's like Coriolanus and Macbeth.' Button confessed he was unfamiliar with Coriolanus but knew Macbeth well. Hayden described Coriolanus as a Whitlam figure; he himself was like Macbeth. Macbeth was involved in crises arising from his ambition but, when he came to fight his final battle with Macduff, he never asked for mercy; he accepted the consequences. Hayden said, 'If I lose the election, I won't be asking anyone for mercy.'

Button at this stage became angry. He said that that was beaut for Hayden, but there were hundreds of thousands of people who wanted a Labor

Government. Not many of them were existentialists and if Labor lost they would not be interested in Hayden's views about the quality of mercy.

The two men briefly canvassed how Hayden could improve his performance. Button said Hayden's staff had let him down. They were criticised even by some of Hayden's closest Caucus supporters. Hayden was defensive. Hayden discussed the pros and cons of a shadow ministry reshuffle. The key issue here was whether Paul Keating should be appointed shadow Treasurer— the centre-piece in any portfolio changes.

Button left Brisbane deeply pessimistic. His view of Hayden had been shaken. Button's determination to change leaders hardened. He believed Hayden was in a bad mental and emotional condition, and concluded that Hayden was obsessed about himself and his own ambition rather than the fate of the party.

Perhaps Button was too harsh. After all Hayden, who had spent the past five years in the high-pressured and doubly destructive job of leader of the Labor Party and leader of the Opposition, was being told now, with his final test at hand, that one of his best friends and closest colleagues throughout this long struggle no longer had confidence in him. Worse, he wanted him to fly the surrender flag in submission to his arch rival, Hawke, a man who many believed had displayed throughout his career a penchant for putting his own self-interests ahead of the party.

When Button flew out of Brisbane that afternoon he was determined to pursue the leadership issue; he would speak to Hayden again. Button had ignited the fire in the party which so many had wanted him to set for so long. It would burn fiercely until Hayden submitted.

20
Race for power

The Labor Party is, however, desperate to win the coming election.

John Button to Bill Hayden,
28 January 1983

From mid-January politics assumed a new urgency as the race for power moved to a climax. The three-way nature of this struggle made it one of the most dramatic yet complex contests in Australia's short but brutally rich political history. As January unfolded the rivalry of Fraser, Hayden and Hawke, which had gathered intensity throughout 1982, now assumed its own force. It ceased to be a mere factor in politics and soon became politics itself. Every move was shaped increasingly by its dynamic. Yet no individual could control the force and the outcome always defied prediction.

Fraser moved with confident spirit and sure judgement towards a sudden, sharp election strike against the Labor Party. Fraser's nerves were inured to the tension involved which merely refined his instincts and steeled his will. Hayden was in an agony of ambivalence between ambition and self-doubt, resolution and surrender. He directed himself to the rescue of his political fortunes, which required shutting off the valve to the psychological and emotional trauma which the Button defection had released. Hawke was anxiety-ridden yet controlled, immeasurably confident within himself that once the call came—and surely it would come—his appeal to the nation against Fraser would be irresistible. Essentially it was a race between Fraser's bid for an early election and the drive of the Hawke supporters to switch leaders.

Fraser flew into Canberra on 11 January after ten weeks' convalescence and declared himself 'in better form than Ian Botham' who, incidentally, was having one of his worst seasons. Fraser was sun-tanned and kilos lighter. The

Prime Minister told the press that election talk was 'old stuff' and declared he was more interested in issues of substance. That night he attended a 'welcome back' dinner hosted by the ministry. By coincidence Fraser and Hayden both started work in their Parliament House offices on the same day, 12 January.

Eggleton had a long session with Fraser on 13 January to discover as quickly as possible his election thinking. But Fraser was more interested in exploring options than identifying priorities. Fraser even asked Eggleton if it was possible to have an early-1984 poll. They agreed this was impracticable. There was no sense of urgency about Fraser, no suggestion of a March election. Perhaps Fraser declined to tell Eggleton his preferences after their October differences; more likely Fraser was still getting his 'feel' for the political climate.

Eggleton left this briefing and rang Alan Pilkington, the chairman of Masius, the party's advertising agency, in Sydney. Pilkington's overseas trip depended on Fraser's election plans. Eggleton told him to go overseas as he felt the election would not be until the end of the year. So Pilkington went abroad and Eggleton breathed easier. But it was a false complacency. Within days Fraser was reassessing; within the fortnight he was dashing towards March.

Hayden's most important meeting after his 6 January lunch with Button was his visit to the Sydney office of his deputy Lionel Bowen. 'I believe you've been talking to Button and think I should step aside,' Hayden said. Bowen replied, 'Yes, I have, and that's right, Bill. I think you should stand down because you'll get beaten.' Hayden was unimpressed. He was not going to accept this advice either, although Bowen knew anyhow that he would never be able to influence Hayden. Hayden joked, 'Perhaps I could have your job.' Bowen retorted, 'No you can't. Go to buggery. You'll have to fight to get my job.' Bowen let Hayden know that the leader's position was at issue—not the deputy's.

So Hayden returned to work in January with an immense political and psychological burden. Both his deputy and his Senate leader were against him. They were not conspiring to organise the numbers but they simply shared the view that he should quit for the party's sake.

Bowen bumped into Keating a few days later. 'The boy has come to see me,' he said. Bowen told Keating he had reinforced Button's request, which Keating had in fact been pressing him to do.

Hayden kept a brave public front. Interviewed on his return to Canberra he was asked whether there would be another challenge. Hayden replied: 'I have no idea. Bob Hawke says no such thing. It's not on as far as he's concerned. John Button, who's been mentioned in this matter, has repudiated it. Tom Uren, whose name has been mentioned at one stage, has denied any such thing to me . . .'[1] Hayden was tough enough to fight and smart enough to have a strategy. He had three objectives. The first was to effect the long-discussed shadow ministry reshuffle and bring Keating into Treasury. The second was to finalise and release the new recovery and reconstruction economic policy—a policy which Hayden believed would revitalise the ALP. The third was to repair the pre-Flinders damage by concluding the ALP–ACTU prices–incomes accord as soon as possible. In short, Hayden had some big cards left to play.

In this crisis Hayden's instincts led him towards a tougher economic management position. He warned: 'Our first priority must be to improve economic growth. We can't eat up investable resources in welfare programmes because that will guarantee that the current economic decline only accelerates.' Growth was essential 'if Australia is to avert its fate as the white coolie nation of the South Pacific'.[2] On 13 January the December unemployment figures were released showing unemployment rising to 9.5 per cent. The nation belonged to the political leader with the programme to show there was a better way and the ability to communicate that programme.

The irony of Hayden's shadow ministry reshuffle is that, after waiting so long, he bungled in his haste. He sprang it on a bunch of surprised shadow ministers—evidence of the secrecy he now used as a defence. He had virtually decided on the reshuffle about two weeks earlier, but had kept it tight. The reshuffle had two purposes: to keep Hayden as ALP leader and to boost the party's election prospects. As the first stage of the 'save Hayden' programme, the reshuffle created uproar in the party and terrified Hawke.

Hayden planned the announcement for Friday 14 January but only made the necessary phone calls the previous evening. Willis was devastated; Hayden had confirmed him as shadow Treasurer in late November, but this 10 p.m. call was a nocturnal *volte face*. Willis would now have charge of the national reconstruction programme. He had been Hayden's personal choice as shadow Treasurer in 1977 and had stayed in this job during the five years of Hayden's leadership. Now as the crisis approached he was being executed. A bitterly disappointed Willis contained himself to telling journalists: 'I'm most disappointed . . .'

Hayden had left messages for Keating that afternoon but Keating had been in the city. He rang Hayden back when he got home, just after 11 p.m. Hayden told Keating of his appointment and said he was confident Keating would do a good job. Keating was stunned, then angry. After all, Hayden had told him in November that Willis would stay in the job. Why had he changed his mind now? Keating knew. Hayden was trying to save his own throat, which Button and Bowen had asked him to slit.

Keating was caught amid swirling emotions. The job which he had secretly feared, yet always assumed to be his fate, had now been thrust upon him. It was the worst possible time. Keating said later that if Hayden wanted him, then the change should have been made the previous July. Of course he was right, but that was Hayden's failure. Keating saw that Hayden was trying to hitch Keating's star to his own leadership and drive a wedge between Keating and Hawke. This was fine politics; but it was too late.

Keating and Willis both spoke to Hawke that night. Hawke was worried and resentful, and fearful that Hayden may have outmanoeuvred him. Hawke told Keating: 'He's fucked us all. He's fucked you by giving you the job. He's fucked Ralph and he's fucked me.' Hawke suggested that Keating call Willis.

Keating saw both himself and Willis as victims of Hayden's personal war but, now facing the great test of his political career, he needed Willis badly. Willis had all the expertise but no wham. Keating had wham but little expertise. Moreover Keating knew he might have no chance to learn with the election looming. He was particularly worried about the technical grasp needed to handle taxation legislation.

In the event he and Willis made a deal. The economic portfolio would be split and Willis, in addition to national reconstruction, would keep taxation, commonwealth–state financial relations and the ALP–ACTU prices–incomes accord—a big slice of the portfolio. Keating rang Hayden back after midnight. Hayden was in bed and his daughter answered the phone. He got up, spoke to Keating and agreed to these arrangements. He rang Willis the next morning to confirm it.

Hayden's two closest allies got big promotions: Peter Walsh from Finance to Resources, John Dawkins from Education to Industry and Commerce. Stewart West was promoted to Finance, thereby appeasing the left for the loss of Willis in Treasury. Barry Jones, a member of Button's group, was elevated to Science and Technology. Two Hawke supporters, Willis and Hurford, were demoted. Hurford told colleagues that Hayden's days as leader were numbered.

Hayden called a press conference just before noon on 14 January to announce the reshuffle. But he was forced on to the defensive and had to explain why a reshuffle was needed now but not before Christmas and how he could have a shadow Treasurer not responsible for taxation.

The reshuffle was a significant improvement in the shadow Cabinet—but too late. Six months earlier Hayden could have reshuffled from authority; this reorganisation was inspired by weakness, almost desperation. The historic role of this reshuffle would be not to save Hayden but to shape the portfolios in

Hawke's Government. In particular it ensured that Keating would emerge as Treasurer.

The same day, 14 January, Malcolm Fraser delivered a new political message to the nation, which would become his early election theme. During Fraser's long convalescence he had reassessed his strategy. Hitherto the Government had used the world recession as its excuse for Australia's declining economy and many people had accepted this argument. Now Fraser declared: 'It is no good Australians sitting down and waiting for America to move. It is our task to move this country ourselves by our own efforts.' This was the prelude to the Liberal Party campaign slogan: 'We're not waiting for the world.'

In early January Fraser and Howard had held talks in the coastal village of Peterborough in Fraser's Wannon electorate. At this meeting Fraser agreed with Howard that the Government should authorise foreign-bank entry. They also agreed that the federal Government should not override Tasmania and stop the Gordon-below-Franklin dam—that would have been clearly contrary to the Liberal philosophy on state rights—but Fraser was giving consideration to a generous offer to Tasmania for an alternative power project. Finally Fraser outlined his view that Australia should press ahead with its own development and not wait for the world. In this he was taking his stance on the previous budget one step further. The downturn had deepened, so the Government should increase its own spending and investment. It should couple this action with a political appeal to optimism and getting things done. Howard was sceptical, opposed to the economics and dubious about the politics, but Fraser was boss.

In his 14 January address to the Young Liberals, Fraser said:

> When private investment is down, it is appropriate for Governments to examine the levels of their own investment . . . Governments can do a great deal, operating in partnership, to build the basic infrastructure for the future and assist private enterprise when opportunities occur . . .
>
> If you were going to apply a cost-benefit analysis to any of the railways that have been built in Australia I suggest that none of them would have qualified and the inland of Australia would never have been developed. The railways preceded development and made it possible. I don't believe it is possible to put an economic rule over this kind of development of a nation.

Fraser cloaked his Keynesian economics in nationalistic fervour, but his new strategy was obvious. ANOP's Rod Cameron was aghast. He believed Fraser had clearly identified the theme on which the ALP was trying to base its campaign—a new direction. Fraser did not restrict himself to rhetoric: the Government announced the same day a 15 per cent cut in the Australian savings bond rate and renewed its commitment to the $545 million Darwin–Alice Springs railway—a national project of the type for which Labor had been searching for its reconstruction programme. Significantly Fraser foreshadowed action to promote more technologically advanced industries, thereby matching Labor's unreleased sunrise industry concept in its reconstruction theme. Senior ALP figures seriously began to fear that the Government had obtained copies of Labor's research. As the week closed the election climate intensified.

By the weekend of 15–16 January John Button believed he must see Hawke. Up to this stage his exercise had been conducted without reference to the challenger, although Hawke had in fact been kept informed through intermediaries. The only exception to this pattern had been an extraordinary incident before Christmas. At this time Phillip Adams had approached Button, informing him that Hawke wanted a talk and asking Button to ring Hawke. Button had made this phone call and said: 'The fat man has asked me to ring.' Hawke had started talking about the leadership, but Button had cut him off. 'I don't want to talk about it,' Button had replied. 'I'm not involved in a conspiracy and I don't want to start one.' But on 16 January Button went to Hawke's Sandringham home for a low key meeting. Button detailed his efforts to persuade Hayden to resign; his assessment was 50–50 that Hayden would submit in the near future. Button was reasonably confident, provided the matter was handled the right way, but he did not want to hold out false hopes to Hawke. The pretender said he bore no malice towards Hayden. He assured Button that he had a regard for Hayden's capacity and that Hayden would be looked after in any leadership transition. Button then began to widen his circle of confidants.

Two days later on Tuesday, 18 January, Button saw both his Senate deputy Don Grimes and shadow Health Minister, Neal Blewett, to tie them into the movement. Blewett sat stunned while Button outlined the amazing tale of the previous weeks and his request to Hayden to quit. Button argued not just that Hawke gave the ALP a better winning chance; if Labor lost, it would be better to lose with Hawke than with Hayden. Button asserted that if the Caucus centre maintained Hayden as leader and lost, then Hawke's right-wing alliance would dominate the party and the centre group would be severely weakened. But if Hayden resigned in a transition, then guarantees could be given to the centre group to maintain its influence in a Hawke-led ALP and ensure that there were restraints on Hawke's power, which is in fact exactly what happened with Hayden, Button, Walsh and Dawkins, all holding key Cabinet portfolios in Hawke's Government.

Button said he would not vote against Hayden in a ballot and, because Hayden knew this, he was in a position to influence and persuade Hayden. Grimes was noncommittal. Blewett said he would support Hayden in a ballot but accept any resignation decision. He felt Labor must avoid an early election and that a leadership contest would guarantee one.

At the start of this week, about 17–18 January, Hayden flew to Sydney for what he suspected was another personal confrontation. A week earlier Neville Wran, in his capacity as ALP National President, had rung Hayden and asked the federal leader to see him. This had overtones of a summons from an older and more successful politician. Hayden was apprehensive. He thought: first Button, then Bowen, now Wran. Hayden steeled himself for a request from Wran that he stand down. He decided that he would deny Wran such an opportunity.

When they met, Hayden said quickly and bluntly: 'I want to make clear that I won't resign as leader.' But Wran had no intention of making such a request. He interpreted his responsibilities as being to the party, not as arbitrating on the Hawke–Hayden issue. Since the Flinders by-election he had been deeply worried about the fate of the federal party and Hayden's performance as leader. He felt that Hayden ignored many of the requirements for successful political leadership.

Wran gave Hayden a stiff lecture, a pep talk. He wanted him to 'lift his game'. He told Hayden the party needed fresh ideas and a better image, and criticised Hayden's approach to the media, his style, his presentation. He referred to a photograph which had appeared in the newspapers over the holiday period of Hayden tiling his Ipswich bathroom. Wran said this was the opposite of the image Hayden should be projecting. It was a friendly but tough conversation.

It was on 17 January that Fraser began his election rethink and started sending signals indicating March. The next day, 18 January, Eggleton held a full strategy session at Liberal headquarters to discuss options and policy. The meeting had been organised before Christmas and it involved Fraser's staff, the Liberal secretariat staff and outside advisers. March was discussed as an option and it had some strong advocates, but nothing was definite. Eggleton said that the Western Australian party would have some problems with March, because of its own state election. The Liberal Premier, Ray O'Connor, had called a 19 February poll. This meant that the West would prefer a 12 March election or later, rather than 5 March. This would prevent any overlap and allow the state election to be completed before Fraser's policy speech.

This same day the Prime Minister obtained a bonus he had been carefully waiting for. The ACTU Executive now reverted to its fallback position and withdrew its cooperation from the wage pause. Furthermore it initiated an industrial campaign against the pause with the oil industry as its target. The union movement was now ranged against Fraser's one major policy plus. Fraser saw this not only as an election trigger but possibly an election winner. The March option had received an important boost.

On 23 December 1982 the Arbitration Commission, after introducing the six-month wage pause, had refused to ratify the second stage of the oil industry rise, which was eight per cent less a deduction, effective from 1 January. The Government argued, and the bench accepted, that this 1 January rise was part of a new wage round and therefore should be disallowed. The ACTU said the oil rise could be quarantined without flow-on. Fraser knew the oil industry held the key to the wage pause and that a Government–union confrontation of great political significance was likely. But so too did Bob Hawke.

On the eve of Christmas, as Simon Crean and his wife had been about to leave on an overseas holiday, Hawke had called in to their home. He had virtually asked Crean to cancel the trip and stay in Australia. He had predicted that Fraser would aim for an early-New Year election on the looming oil dispute and hinted at the moves afoot in the ALP over the leadership. He had made Crean aware that January would be a critical month.

In this, Hawke's political judgement had been superb. Clearly he had wanted to ensure that, if he became ALP leader, this dispute could be contained in any campaign. So Crean had stayed. Hawke had been a step ahead of Fraser.

The Prime Minister moved in exactly the direction Hawke had anticipated. Fraser contacted oil industry chief executives to ensure that they maintained a united front against the unions. The oil chiefs gave their word. They would stand behind the pause, the Arbitration Commission and the Government. Then Fraser moved to make this stance ironclad. He asked Government departments to draw up plans to assist the oil companies to withstand industrial action. Flying to Adelaide on 14 January, Fraser told journalists about his agreement with the oil companies. He was ready for the showdown.

ACTU officers Bill Kelty and Simon Crean knew they were walking a delicate tightrope. Under the ACTU's 18 January resolution they had kept industrial action under their control. They suspected Fraser wanted an election on the dispute and Ian Macphee had confirmed these impressions. On the one hand the oil industry unions were pressing for the pay rise; on the other Fraser stood ready to exploit the strife.

The ACTU and Macphee, the Government negotiator, were in the middle. Macphee's position was very different from Fraser's. He was committed to maintaining the integrity of the pause, but he wanted to deny Fraser an election on a divisive confrontationalist issue—a fascinating stance. Kelty believed Fraser would wait until there was widespread impact from the overtime bans the oil unions had imposed and then call an election. He was determined to prevent this through the ACTU's management of the issue. Crean, very close to the dispute, later recollected the situation this way:

> There is no doubt that the oil companies were deliberately creating the dispute because the limitations we had imposed affected no supplies to the public . . . We'd heard rumours that the Government had put pressure on. It was hard to confirm. But the example of unnecessary exacerbation can't be refuted. We had people being asked to unload tankers on overtime when those tankers weren't due for a couple of days. The oil industry bosses wanted to bring the dispute to a head.[3]

The same day that the ACTU initiated their campaign against the pause Hayden made a keynote speech taking the opposite tack. This was the first sure sign that Hayden's judgement was suffering under the great personal pressure he was enduring and it involved an enormous paradox. The ALP–ACTU pre-Flinders by-election rift occurred because Hayden took a tough line against the pause and the ACTU a softer position. Now the ACTU had moved to a much harder position, but Hayden had shifted in the opposite direction. Their positions had crossed *en route* as they established a new contradiction. The failure to consult, which had led Hayden and the ACTU to fall out pre-Flinders, was occurring all over again. Hayden, in his Ipswich isolation, had decided to get tougher with the unions. He reasoned that if Fraser had extracted concessions from them in November–December, then so should the ALP. Hayden's keynote speech was to the Australian Workers' Union Annual Convention in Sydney on 18 January. He signalled that he wanted a new dimension to the prices–incomes accord, which was supposed to be near finalisation. The unstated assumption of the Hayden speech was that the harsher the Fraser Government's wage freeze became, the more scope there was for Labor in its own negotiations with the union movement. Hayden warned bluntly that there had to be a shift from wages to profits to sustain the economy. He said that not only should the timing of indexation pay rises be a function of economic conditions, but so should the level of the adjustment.

This was a radical departure from his earlier stance. Hayden was suggesting not only that real wages should be adjusted over time, but that the unions might have to accept less than real wages. Bill Kelty later said: 'At no stage did Hayden consult with the ACTU on this new position. We didn't know what he was saying or why he was developing this line. It was incomprehensible to us. We didn't say anything. I got dozens of calls from people seeking our comment, but we just kept quiet.'[4]

The issue was pursued further the next day, Wednesday 19 January, when the ALP shadow Cabinet met in Canberra. It was the first shadow Cabinet meeting since Hayden's discussions with Button and Bowen, and since the reshuffle. Hurford was bitter; Willis disguised hostility with irony. Hayden was under great pressure. All the tension in the ALP focused at this shadow Cabinet table.

Hawke and Willis reported on progress with the prices–incomes accord. Hawke said he had good news and bad news. The good news was that the accord was proceeding well and should be finalised in late February or March. The bad news was that terrible trouble loomed in the oil industry. Hawke gave an excellent summary of the position, but no recommendations. One astute shadow minister said later: 'Hawke was so clever. He always understood the wage pause issue but remained elusive about it, reluctant to take a stand.' This time Hawke was asked to bring a firm recommendation back after lunch.

The shadow Cabinet decided that Hayden's economic policy—recovery and reconstruction—should be released as soon as possible rather than be delayed until the prices–incomes accord was announced. This was a sensible move. The Opposition badly needed to project itself. The policy was near completion and Hayden saw it as a vehicle to restore party morale and salvage his own leadership.

Mick Young then raised Hayden's supportive comments on the wage pause and sought an explanation for them. Hayden was defensive. He said one reason for his caution was 'the role taken by the party's industrial relations spokesman'. There was some shadow boxing at this time between Hayden and Hawke but the real flare-up was to come after lunch.

During the meal break Hayden examined Hawke's comments on the pause both in the printed word and on the electronic media. After the break Hawke came back with his recommendation: support for the ACTU campaign against the freeze but not necessarily the ACTU tactics. During the ensuing debate Hayden lost his self-control. He said he had taken a softer line because Hawke had refused to adopt the anti-wage-pause line in public. He had studied Hawke's comments, there was no doubt about it. Hayden said he didn't want to be in disagreement with Hawke and it was obvious that Hawke, as spokesman, refused to condemn the freeze. He was the one who had failed to adhere to policy.

Hayden's performance was a sad display of paranoia and failing authority. Hawke sat back and let Hayden go. The challenger glanced up and down the table and read dismay in the faces of Hayden's closest supporters. Hawke replied calmly and with dignity, cleverly establishing the contrast with Hayden. He said he was perfectly capable of defending his comments on the wage pause, but that was not the issue. He told Hayden it was not valid for him as leader to explain his own statement by reference to a shadow minister's comments. Hawke's point was effectively understated. Bowen at this junction calmed the Hayden–Hawke spat down. It was the first and only brawl between them in the shadow ministry in front of their colleagues.

The meeting then endorsed Hawke's recommendation as policy. It tied the ALP into the ACTU opposition to the wage freeze and support for the oil claim. But when Hayden brought the decision to his office and asked Alan Ramsey to turn it into a press release, Ramsey was dismayed. He complained to Hayden that the statement was political dynamite and that Fraser would have a field day with an ALP pledge to back the oil workers. Ramsey also felt that Hawke should be making the statement, not Hayden. After all Hawke was the spokesman and this statement was an apparent contradiction of what Hayden had said the previous day. But Hayden insisted the release be in his name. Presumably he thought anything less would be a sign of weakness. With Hayden's approval Ramsey wrote the statement to minimise the damage.

Hayden's dilemma was that he needed to cooperate with the ACTU to secure the prices–incomes accord for the campaign. But, by joining the ACTU drive against the wage pause, he would put his electoral position at risk. Hayden now concluded that he had little choice but to stick by the ACTU despite the risks. His statement that evening said the freeze was 'unworkable' and that the eight per cent oil workers' claim should be given. Lionel Bowen, who argued against the freeze in the shadow Cabinet meeting, made an even tougher public statement condemning the freeze outright. Ramsey's instincts were right, but Hayden's political disaster was delayed. The media played down Hayden's statement that night because Fraser was making much bigger news.

Fraser announced on 19 January his $500 million thermal power station offer to Tasmania as an alternative to the Gordon-below-Franklin dam. Given the 'states rights' parameters accepted by the Prime Minister, this was an excellent tactical move. Fraser was hoping to transform the focus of the dam debate from the environment to federalism. The offer was intended to demonstrate his *bona fides*; certainly it was generous. The $500 million was the biggest grant ever offered by any federal government to Tasmania for a single project and one of the largest offers for a project anywhere in Australia.

Tasmanian Premier Robin Gray rejected the offer the same day, just as Fraser had expected. In fact Fraser had made the offer to Gray the previous Thursday after federal Cabinet met and there had never been any sign it would be accepted. But in a sense this all worked to Fraser's advantage. The offer was designed to show Fraser's concern; it was hoped Gray's rejection would leave Tasmania, not Fraser, with the political backlash. The offer was now meant to prove to Tasmania that the Fraser Government would not override Tasmania's decision and it was thereby intended to confirm that state's support for Fraser in the forthcoming federal election.

Bob Hawke played his trade union card against Hayden on Thursday 20 January—a decisive day in the battle of wills for the leadership. So far Hawke had been an anxious onlooker and talker; now he played a direct role himself in the assassination of Hayden. At 8.30 a.m. four men had breakfast in Hawke's presidential suite at Sydney's Boulevard Hotel—Hawke, Mick Young, Graham Richardson and the new NSW Secretary, Stephen Loosley. One man absent, but present in spirit, was shadow Treasurer Paul Keating. Convinced that Fraser would call an early election, all their efforts were now bent on achieving Hayden's resignation before Fraser struck.

Keating and Richardson had already discussed the previous day's decision by the shadow Cabinet to proceed immediately to release the party's new economic policy. The details of this release were to be finalised later that day when the ALP National Campaign Committee, chaired by Young, met at the NSW party headquarters. Keating and Richardson had agreed that this release had to be thwarted. At the breakfast Richardson put the issue bluntly: 'We can't let the leader we intend to ditch announce the economic policy to save Australia.'

There was only one effective way to halt the release and only one man able to insist that Hayden wait. That was ACTU President Cliff Dolan, upon whom Hayden was relying to seal the ALP–ACTU prices–incomes accord. After breakfast Hawke rang Dolan, a man who had been his ally and opponent in countless union battles for years. Hawke told Dolan that he wanted Hayden's economic policy delayed. He put the leadership issue and its imperatives on the line. Hawke knew Hayden would have to listen if Dolan said the trade unions wanted Labor's economic policy postponed until after the special unions conference on 21–22 February, which the ACTU had called to approve the prices–incomes accord. The ALP and ACTU had worked towards the accord for years and Hayden would not want it prejudiced. Dolan agreed to Hawke's request. In fact there was already strong ACTU pressure for exactly this kind of timing.

Later that morning the campaign committee met on the ninth floor of

Labor's Sussex Street headquarters. Dolan's office was only a few floors below. Young told Hayden that the ACTU wanted the release of his new economic policy deferred. He asked Hayden to speak to Dolan. Hayden left for ten minutes and returned, resigned to Dolan's position. He told the campaign committee there would need to be a readjustment in the timetable because the economic policy would have to be delayed until after the special unions conference on 21–22 February.

Richardson winked at Young. The ploy had worked like a dream. The Hawke camp had more time to twist Hayden in the wind while denying him the weapon he desperately needed to fight back. The weight of the ACTU had been deployed for Hawke against Hayden in a brutally effective fashion. In fact after Hawke became leader there was no longer any difficulty and the ALP's new economic policy was launched in mid-February before the special unions conference.

Bill Hayden, who had championed the accord for so long, was sacrificed in its name by its negotiators, Hawke and Dolan. Once again Hawke's experience in industrial relations and with the ACTU had paid tremendous dividends. Dolan was able to explain the decision to defer the release in terms of legitimate union needs. After all, Kelty had advised him along similar lines to Hawke. But Hayden had lost the chance to launch his recovery and reconstruction vision. He was a leader played for a mug.

A fortnight later, when Hayden resigned, Hawke was quizzed about his own role. He replied indignantly: 'My integrity is recognised . . . and I'm telling you the facts. I was not involved in the discussions which Bill Hayden's fellow leaders had with him and which led to the decision that he made. That is clear and unequivocal.'[5] This was true but it cannot disguise the role he played in the events which undermined Hayden.

The campaign committee set 14 March as the tentative date for the economic policy launch—the first week in which there was a parliamentary recess after the special unions conference. Hayden's staff were horrified when told about the postponement. They instinctively felt a sense of betrayal but were unable to pinpoint it. The fact is that the National Campaign Committee was now taking decisions not to boost Hayden's position but to facilitate Hawke's ascension.

Perhaps sensing this, Hayden later decided he wanted to reverse the decision and went back to McMullan to ask the National Secretary to contact all committee members. McMullan asked them all: Young, Button, Hogg and Richardson. Not one wanted to change the arrangement. McMullan reported back to Hayden that the committee could not envisage the ACTU changing its mind on the timing and therefore felt the ALP must concur. Each member of the committee had a priority commitment to see Hawke as leader. Bill Hayden was losing his own party.

When the National Campaign Committee had broken for lunch on 20 January Hawke had met Richardson and Loosley at the Iliad Restaurant to get a report on the morning's successful work. Meanwhile down the road in Hawke's presidential suite, Button, Keating and Young met to review Button's progress. At various times Hawke and Young had wanted a delegation to ask Hayden to stand down. Young floated the idea again, volunteered to join it and said the left should be represented. But Keating was opposed to any delegation and refused to join one. He was determined to take a low personal profile this time; the events of the previous July had done him much harm. Keating's view was that 'Button got Hayden elected, so he can get him unelected.'

Button concurred with this approach. More than anybody, he knew the delicacy of this operation, given Hayden's personality. If Hayden were confronted by a delegation and threatened, then he would assuredly dig in. Button appeared confident. He told Richardson that Hayden seemed to realise he could not win an election.

That evening Young addressed a meeting of NSW marginal-seat candidates at the Sussex Street office. Young had been given this task to fulfil around the nation by the campaign committee. Young told Loosley, as they walked into the room, that it was the 'ultimate hypocrisy' to be lecturing candidates on why they should win. He attempted to give them a pep talk but found it was hopeless. He then asked the candidates and their managers about the mood in the electorate and received complaints about the lack of leadership. It was shadow boxing. The candidates knew that Young wanted Hawke and Young knew that the candidates wanted Hawke.

Eventually the candidate for Eden–Monaro, Jim Snow, laid it on the line. Snow gave an emotional speech: 'My conscience dictates that I should say this,' he began. 'What we are really talking about is the need for a change of leader and if somebody else won't come out and say it, then I will. The Labor Party is faced with a unique situation. We have a person in Parliament in Bob Hawke that everyone wants to vote for but we won't make him leader.' Snow said that if the ALP was 'fair dinkum' about winning, then it had to make Hawke leader, and he compared Hawke to 'the King of the Jews'. At first Loosley, as chairman, thought he should close Snow off, but he let him go. Loosley watched the left-wing candidates and saw no sign of dissension.

After the meeting Young and some NSW right-wing candidates went to dinner at a fish restaurant. There was much disputation. The candidates believed their chances of election to Parliament depended upon Hawke becoming leader. This was the view put most vigorously by three of the marginal seat contenders: Garry Punch in Barton, David Simmonds in Calare and Michael Addison in Cook. But at the end of the evening the message went out: stay cool, there was a plan of action underway.

Hayden and Bowen had the occasional telephone discussion in mid to late January. Bowen, finding Hayden more and more worried, warned him: 'If there's a challenge, then you'll get beaten.' Bowen did not ask Hayden to step aside, but he tried to nudge him by suggesting that Hayden talk to the backbench. At one point, Bowen proposed Hayden talk to 28 people—the most marginal 14 Labor backbenchers and the first 14 Labor candidates awaiting election—to sample their views. But, as Labor agonised, Fraser made his fateful move.

The Prime Minister spent the weekend of 22–23 January at Kirribilli House and after taking soundings decided on a March election. He asked Eggleton to see him on 24 January, then he gave his Federal Director the word. The next day Eggleton flew to Melbourne to see the Managing Director of Elders–IXL, John Elliott, a prominent Liberal who was providing space in his Melbourne building for the Liberal Party campaign headquarters. Eggleton put his own Liberal Party Secretariat on an election footing.

Fraser relied on sound judgement and immense self-confidence. He had wanted an election since last August, but had been thwarted successively by the Costigan Report, the Liberal Party and his own back. Now these obstacles seemed fortuitous. In December–January the Government's standing had risen higher than in the earlier September–November period when Fraser had been so anxious to go. The Flinders by-election proved that. All the signs suggested that the Government was enjoying a temporary popularity high, the product of the wage pause, disaffection with the ALP, falling interest rates and a particularly assertive demonstration of prime ministerial strength since Fraser's return from illness. The challenge to the wage pause from the union movement and the Labor Party had been a golden opportunity for a conservative Prime Minister and had fitted Fraser's style like a glove.

Finally, Fraser believed he needed an election before June since he could not bring down another election budget and this time unlike late 1982, Fraser found that neither the Liberal Party, his ministers nor business had any doubts. The soundings were positive and that in itself reflected the changed political climate since 1982. But there was another factor in Fraser's move.

Fraser was a student of Labor politics and leadership psychology. He had rung Uren about the ALP leadership during the 1982 mid-year crisis. Politicians like to pride themselves on their knowledge of the other side. Some rely upon instinct, others information. For instance, at a December 1982 party in John Howard's office, Doug Anthony told journalists he believed Hawke would soon become Labor leader. Nixon held the same opinion. This was the shrewd Country Party view of politics.

In mid to late January Fraser took several steps to penetrate the ALP manoeuvrings. One was to ring his former press secretary, Alistar Drysdale, and ask what he could find. Drysdale did some leg work and reported that there were rumours but nothing definite. 'Thanks,' Fraser replied, 'but I don't think you're right.' Fraser believed the situation was more serious and consequently the need to keep Hawke out was an extra factor in his decision to call the March election. But it was not *the* reason. Fraser's decision was based on a range of arguments and it would have been the same if Hawke had not been a Member of Parliament. However once Fraser was embarked on the road to March, the Hawke factor became more important in determining the date of the election.

Fraser stayed in close touch with Macphee about the oil dispute and rang him on 22 January to rake over the prospects. Macphee reported that the unions were saying they would break the wage pause by March; but he did not believe this. Macphee warned Fraser to be wary of Hawke: 'if he becomes leader, don't challenge him on an industrial relations issue.' This was significant advice as events subsequently proved. Macphee knew that much of Fraser's election planning hinged on the wage pause but he was convinced that Hawke would neutralise this if he became leader.

Fraser rang Macphee again about 24 January to refine further the Government's tactics on the oil dispute. Macphee had arranged a second meeting between the oil industry parties for 27 January and Fraser wanted to ensure that Macphee would stick by the wage pause. Although Macphee warned that a very big dispute could erupt, Fraser was not worried. The Prime Minister said he would not mind an attempt by the unions to crack the pause and asked Macphee to bring forward his second meeting, saying: 'It is very much in the Government's interests to have that meeting as soon as possible. Every day counts.' Macphee assumed the urgency was because of moves within the ALP. He brought the meeting forward two days, certain that Fraser had decided that if there was to be an industrial blow-up, then it should come quickly. But Fraser had misjudged the ACTU's ability to control this dispute. Kelty commented later: 'The ACTU had a fair measure of authority in the oil industry. We were on top of the dispute. We were always confident that once Fraser had gone all the way and called the election, then the very next day we would be able to have a meeting and call off the dispute. By and large the workers were prepared to accept our leadership on this issue.'[6]

Federal Cabinet met in Sydney on Tuesday, 25 January, another vital day in Fraser's election planning. The Prime Minister hosted a business lunch at the Sydney Hilton and ensured there was a minister strategically placed on each table to maximise his feedback. That afternoon ministers reported to Fraser that business was keen for an election and confident of Fraser's victory. Just after 3.00 p.m. Fraser and Carrick held a joint press conference to announce a far-reaching national water resources programme which had been endorsed by Cabinet on submission from Carrick. The concept which Carrick had produced was perfect for Fraser's appeal to national development. It was a $640-million five-year programme, a response to the drought and the recession. Fraser sounded exactly as Bill Hayden had hoped to when he drew a parallel with the Snowy Mountains project. He could have been reading from the ALP national reconstruction policy—which was still awaiting release.

The Fraser–Carrick performance had the false euphoria that pumping adrenalin creates in politicians. Asked when the projects could start, Carrick replied with nervous gusto: 'Immediately, literally.' Fraser romanticised about turning the northern rivers inland—an idea Hayden had grabbed from Bjelke-Petersen a few days earlier—saying his aim was to 'test the age-old dream that these rivers should be turned inland and put to better use instead of being allowed to run out to sea and be wasted.'

In the previous 10 days Fraser had offered Tasmania $500 million, pledged water conservation another $640 million and renewed the $545-million Darwin–Alice Springs railway promise—although the programmes would be spread over many years. Fraser, the supreme pragmatist, had hung up one identity and put on another. Small Government had surrendered to Greater Australia. The echo of Rex Connor, which had been so resonant in Fraser so often in the past, returned once more. That evening Fraser went to a Union Club dinner and received more election encouragement from business.

The next morning, 26 January, Australia Day, Eggleton rang all state directors of the Liberal Party and put them on a 'most advanced alert' election warning. Fraser was at a 7.15 a.m. Advance Australia Champagne Breakfast delivering his exhortation that Australia must not just 'sit around and wait for the rest of the world'. Then he held a Kirribilli House press conference to announce programmes costing $166 million for the 1988 Bicentenary celebrations.

It was a day of dazzling summer stillness around the sloping lawns of the harbour foreshores, a spectacle that transcended dreary politics and the plans of mere mortals. Fraser predicted Australia would win the America's Cup and regain the cricket Ashes. He droned on about the need to preserve the Australian flag and celebrate Australia Day on the 'real' day—26 January—and not some other day; nearby an old-fashioned sailing ship drifted past

Kirribilli moving from one world to another, untouched and uncaring about the race for power on shore.

Fraser and the press drank orange juice on the stone verandah of Kirribilli House and the Prime Minister revealed that arrangements were finalised for his short trip to America in March to see President Reagan. Reagan would meet him in San Francisco in early March and they would fly to Washington together on Air Force One. This was Fraser's political professionalism in action, an example of why it was so difficult to interpret his actions. He was organising a March election, but also conducting business as usual and planning to meet the US President. Fraser knew that one of these events would need to be cancelled. But he was meticulous in his planning for both. Fraser went to the cricket that night and accepted Kim Hughes' invitation to drinks in the dressing room. But England thrashed Australia and there was little to celebrate.

Meanwhile Bill Hayden committed his latest and his last blunder on the wage pause. A politician is entitled to make mistakes, but the wage pause saga was now assuming in Hayden's fate the proportions of a Kafkaesque nightmare. Hayden had been adhering to the tack set by the shadow Cabinet on 19 January when it decided, on Hawke's recommendation, to support the oil workers in their campaign against the pause. Hayden's statement that day had received little publicity for two reasons: the way Ramsey wrote it and Fraser's Tasmanian power offer.

Hayden now wanted to reaffirm and sharpen his position. His aim was to support the unions to the hilt, attack the pause and argue that the only constructive wages policy was a long-term one as provided in the planned ALP–ACTU accord. The irony of Hayden diligently trying to tie himself to the unions and support their cause, after they had already joined with Hawke to overthrow him, is exquisite.

Hayden was in Ipswich and this time the statement issued on 26 January was not re-written by Ramsey. The press contrasted it with Hayden's earlier and softer line on the wage pause taken on 13 January and 18 January. The headlines the next morning, 27 January, were devastating. *The Age* featured 'Hayden Rejects Freeze', *The Sydney Morning Herald* 'Hayden's Second Switch on Wages', and *The Financial Review* 'Hayden's Pause Backdown'.

There had been no need for Hayden to say anything about the pause or the oil dispute. Nobody asked him to speak. It was a difficult issue for the ALP and it would have been better to say nothing. But Hayden was trying to cement his position with the unions. It was a futile misjudgement. Hayden was isolated and embattled in Ipswich.

The next day Macphee effectively rebutted the argument upon which Hayden had relied in his latest oil dispute statement. Hayden had claimed that the Government had dishonoured its promise in refusing to permit the oil rise. Macphee explained that this was incorrect because the rise was part of the next wage round, not the present round, and the Arbitration Commission had endorsed this view. Finally Hayden phoned Simon Crean and said: 'You probably realise we're supporting you people on the oil dispute very strongly. Macphee is saying that if this wage rise goes through, then it's the start of a new wage round. What do I say to that?' Crean briefed Hayden on the ACTU argument.

Fraser read the morning papers of 27 January and went for the jugular during a series of morning interviews: 'It is quite clear that Mr Dolan and the ACTU have told Mr Hayden what to do and that, of course, is disastrous for any political leader.' Fraser dismissed the ALP and, with his mind's eye on the election, moved to reinforce the image of himself as Australia's natural Prime Minister: 'The Labor Party over recent months has demonstrated a total lack of understanding of what Australia is about . . . and we have been getting on with the business of Government. We have been making decisions that are important. We have been making decisions that will enable us to build for the future . . .'

By this stage even a Liberal Prime Minister determined to avoid a March election would have lost his resolution. Hayden's political incompetence, as he battled to save himself, sucked Fraser towards a poll like iron to a magnet. Fraser flew to Melbourne for talks with John Howard, Peter Nixon and Tony Eggleton; this was the quartet vital in planning the March election. Nixon broke the news to Fraser of his intention to retire, having told Doug Anthony two years earlier that this Parliament would be his last. Anthony was overseas and Nixon, although not a candidate, would become Fraser's closest confidant over the next week.

Fraser and Howard both saw the ALP–ACTU campaign against the pause as a genuine election issue. Its extra attractiveness was its exposure of Hayden's leadership weakness and the propaganda opportunity it provided to depict him as subjugated by the unions. The Government believed that the spirit of the Flinders by-election was still alive; its intention was to turn this successful by-election foray into a general election victory.

Hayden's hold on the ALP leadership was assumed by the Government to be eroding quickly. Eggleton had been told by what he judged to be a good NSW source that Hayden was in trouble. Fraser agreed with this assessment and said it accorded with his own intelligence. The Hawke factor was becoming more important in generating the election momentum. It reinforced

Fraser's inclination to go to the polls as early as possible and this made 5 March a likely date. But Fraser, always alive to every difficulty, knew that the Western Australian party had problems with this date because of the 19 February state election. So 5 March and 12 March remained the two real options. Ministers had given consideration to 19 March, but this date was discarded as the political climate intensified and the ALP leadership issue became more pressing.

While Fraser prepared to strike, a worried John Button made the second of his three visits to Queensland in his dual role as Hayden's conscience and executioner. Button attended the launch of the Queensland Senate ticket on 27 January and encountered Hayden there. Before the launch Hayden said to Button he wanted a talk afterwards. Button reciprocated; he wanted to talk to Hayden too. Button prepared for another session on the leadership and Hayden suggested they retire to his Brisbane office. The leader then proceeded with the Senate launch. He spoke; the television cameras rolled; the journalists asked questions of Bill Hayden, Opposition leader, alternative Prime Minister. And somewhere in this process Hayden's mind began turning in another direction.

With the launch completed, Hayden told Button he had first to go to the State Parliament building to see the new Labor leader, Keith Wright. Button went with him to the Parliament and waited. Button waited and waited. Finally when he inquired of a passing attendant he was told that Hayden was inspecting the new building. When Hayden returned he was with his close friend and biographer, Dennis Murphy, President of the Queensland Labor Party.

The three men went to Hayden's office. Hayden's family were there and they all chatted for some time. Then Hayden motioned Button into a room for their talk but, to Button's surprise, invited Murphy as well. Button had no intention of discussing the leadership, which was acutely personal, in front of Murphy. Instead they had a rambling talk about the Queensland ALP and the state of politics in the deep north. It was a bizarre conversation which did not demand Button's participation; it seemed clumsily contrived to avoid the burning issue of the leadership. Button left and flew back to Melbourne empty-handed. His strategy of persuasion was apparently unproductive. While Fraser was refuelling his election locomotive, Labor remained stalled at the station.

Hayden's emotions were taut and his temper frayed by the media coverage of his previous day's statement on the wage pause. He released, later on the same day, 27 January, a highly personalised reply through his Canberra office: 'I won't cop the rubbish that either I, or the Labor Party, is backtracking on the Government's one-sided wages freeze. I opposed this political stunt from the outset. The Labor Party opposed the enforcing legislation in both Houses of the Parliament. I have opposed it throughout as unfair and discriminatory against wage and salary earners.'

Bowen went further than Hayden in a statement of extraordinary provocation: 'There will be industrial action. The unions always foreshadowed it and are entitled to foreshadow it in certain industries . . .' Asked whether the ALP would support such action, Bowen replied: 'Yes. You have got to do that . . . This is an election ploy. Malcolm Fraser wants industrial trouble so he can have an election. It's probably programmed for March.'

By the evening of 27 January the ALP, through sheer dint of perseverance, had reached the nadir of its fortunes. Hayden and Bowen had tied the party into an electorally unacceptable stance on the wage pause, thereby repeating the mistake made in the Flinders by-election. Labor's learning curve was as flat as the horizon. Because of its trade union connection, some form of opposition to the wage pause was a political necessity for Labor, but Hayden and Bowen tried to make it a publicity virtue. In the process they encouraged Fraser's dash to the polls.

At about this time Hayden told Bowen: 'You're right, there's a fair bit of movement against me in the party.' In the meantime Bowen had continued to provide Hayden with his gloomy diagnosis, but had never detected any signs that Hayden would fold under pressure. Keating had previously mentioned to Bowen that if Hayden quit, the leader would expect to become Foreign Minister. A surprised Bowen had replied: 'Well, if that's what he wants to stand down . . .' During a subsequent phone call with Bowen, when Hayden raised this in a joking fashion, Bowen had replied: 'You can have my job; Keating tells me that you want to be Foreign Minister.' When Hayden expressed surprise that Keating had told Bowen, the deputy shrugged; he did not take it terribly seriously. Progress in shifting Hayden seemed to have stalled.

Towards the end of this week, probably on 28 January, Eggleton showed Fraser charts of electoral support for Government and Opposition. The ALP was plotted in red, the Government in blue. The red line had been above the blue for two years and it remained so now. Not even the August 1982 budget, with its huge tax cuts, had bridged the gap. Despite universal criticism of Hayden, the ALP remained, on paper, poised to win the election.

Eggleton's argument was that the charts showed the need for a powerful Government start to the campaign. The gap would not be easy to bridge. Eggleton wanted to be certain that Fraser understood, but the Prime Minister was confident that he could beat Hayden. Fraser and Eggleton sifted through the Liberal research on Hayden and found confirmation for Fraser's confidence. It was damning. It suggested that voters had no faith or belief in him.

Hayden was perceived as a weak leader who would be manipulated by others, notably the unions. The Government's strength lay in the Fraser versus Hayden leadership profile. The election would be close; this factor could clinch it.

On the morning of 28 January Button visited the dentist, thereby establishing the necessary mood for his main task that day. Button felt he had only one resort left concerning Hayden—the pen. He wrote a letter to Hayden and dispatched it that afternoon. It was an appeal to Hayden's idealism and a dispatch of death for his ambition.

In his letter Button recalled their discussion of 6 January. He said there were other points he would have made the previous day if not for Murphy's presence. He remained personally loyal to Hayden; he had supported him in his five years as leader on every major difficulty Hayden had faced. But Button believed that Hayden would not win the election. Button's ultimate loyalty was to the ALP and he believed Hayden should stand down as party leader. Button argued that Hayden's performance had 'declined considerably' since the July leadership challenge. While Hayden relied upon the polls, which showed Labor four per cent ahead, it was Button's view that, in the light of the Government's economic performance, Labor should have been 10–15 per cent ahead.

Button also said that morale within the ALP was 'very bad' and told Hayden that he could not win an election without the support of the rank and file. He said that while the ALP was divided in July over the leadership, the majority view now was for a change. Four of the state ALP leaders and five of the six State Secretaries, as well as the National Secretariat and a majority of the Caucus (Button could have also added the ACTU), wanted a change. He referred to Hayden's comment that he would not stand down 'for a bastard like Hawke'. Button said that being a bastard had never been a disqualification for ALP leadership. The party would have a much better chance under Hawke; if Labor was to be defeated, he would prefer Hawke rather than Hayden to be the leader.

Button said he was approaching Hayden not as an emissary but as an individual. The concerns he expressed were coming from Hayden's friends, not just his enemies. Although Hayden had difficulties in working with his colleagues, he still had their respect. He would retain it if he stepped aside. Button argued that some of Hawke's closest supporters had reservations about his capacity to lead Labor successfully. Button then moved to the clinching argument, the sentence which captured the ultimate reason for the party's flight to Hawke: 'The Labor Party is, however, desperate to win the coming election.'

Button told Hayden that the 'Macbeth stuff', which Hayden had given him in Brisbane, was 'bullshit'. His wish was to see the election of a Labor Government, in which Hayden played an influential and prominent role.

Over the holiday weekend, 29–31 January, events in the ALP moved towards their climax. The NSW right had acquiesced in Button's tactics but to no avail. It was totally committed to a change of leaders and had crossed the Rubicon for Hawke. The NSW machine was now getting feedback from the printing unions and the Electoral Office that an election was imminent. Keating and Richardson had both decided to go for power. If Hayden would not quit, then he must be axed, even if the exercise was bloody. Richardson rang Button and indicated to him that if his technique of persuasion did not prevail in the near future then a more violent means would replace it.

Meanwhile Hayden received a tip from a public service source in Canberra that the Cabinet decisions of the previous week meant an early election, with 19 March the favoured date. The source was good and Hayden began checking. He called Young, who said he would make his own inquiries. Hayden said: 'I hear you think that things aren't too good.' Young replied: 'It's not just me, Bill, it's what the candidates are saying.'

The anti-Hayden forces in the Labor Party were now in the ascendancy, but Hayden still had options. However he had never sought power just for power's sake; in the mind of the man himself his leadership had always been legitimised by the support he enjoyed in the Caucus. Hayden was a tenacious fighter, but the justification for his fight was thrown into doubt when his own friends turned against him. The overwhelming message Hayden got from all quarters—Button, Young, Hawke, the party professionals—was that he could not win. Now it was coming from the grass roots. How could Hayden sustain himself and believe he could win in the teeth of such opinion?

After reading the letter Hayden rang Button on Monday 31 January. He told Button that the next day was former ALP Prime Minister Frank Forde's funeral. Button should come to the funeral and they would talk afterwards. Hayden signalled his intentions; he was giving consideration to the matters Button had raised. But if he was to act, there were important issues he wanted to clarify. That night Button flew to Brisbane; he knew that Forde's funeral would be a cathartic day for the Labor Party.

The same day Fraser and Eggleton reviewed their election plans. Eggleton was amazed the election story had not leaked, since an ever-widening circle of people had known for some time. Eggleton was assuming 12 March would be the likely date, but Fraser favoured 5 March. The Prime Minister got ready to pull the plug.

Frank Forde was buried on 1 February at his local church, St Thomas

Aquinas, Brisbane, with the honours befitting a former Labor Prime Minister. The pallbearers included Whitlam, Bjelke-Petersen, Hayden and Killen. A cross-section of family, friends and politicians filled the church. Button knelt in a pew behind Hayden. After the funeral they retreated to Hayden's office for a two-and-a-half hour talk—the most agonising in the political torture of Bill Hayden.

Hayden could see the election rushing towards him and with it the prospects of death or glory. He was trapped in an agony of ambivalence. Hayden spent the first hour arguing why he should stay ALP leader, an argument valid at any time in the past, but now obsolete given the virtual collapse of Labor's faith in its leader.

As their dialogue continued Hayden's defence mechanisms were systematically stripped away. Hayden knew he needed Button to keep the numbers in the Caucus, but Button effectively told Hayden that he could no longer support him. Button named a dozen Caucus members who had supported Hayden in July and had now defected. Hayden argued that several others had crossed in the opposite direction, but did not name them. Hayden's trauma exposed his psychological dependence upon Button. He was appealing to Button, he wanted Button to change his mind and reaffirm his belief in him. If Button did this, then Hayden would draw support from Button's faith. He would vindicate Button's decision. But Button refused.

The second stage of this dialogue began when Hayden accepted that Button could not be turned. Hayden revealed the toughness of a professional politician who faces defeat by starting to negotiate the best conditions. Hayden specified five conditions. Firstly, he wanted his staff retained in jobs. Secondly, he insisted that his most prominent supporters be saved from victimisation, and named Walsh, Dawkins and Blewett. Thirdly, Hayden wanted letters from the other two ALP leaders Bowen and Grimes, repeating Button's request that he stand down as leader. Fourthly, Hayden wanted a guarantee that he would become shadow Foreign Minister and Foreign Minister if Hawke won the election. Fifthly, Hayden wanted an assurance in case he had to leave politics; he wanted the option of becoming Australian High Commissioner to London. This was a 'backstop' and reflected Hayden's concern about financial security for himself and his family. Button wrote down the conditions.

Hayden now accepted that Fraser would probably go to a March election and that he might call it any day. Hayden was most anxious to avoid a situation where he would have to resign after an election announcement and therefore appear frightened of Fraser. Hayden did not fear Fraser, indeed he wanted to fight Fraser, but the Labor Party refused to allow it. Button understood. Hayden was worried about the impact on his family, particularly his daughters. One of the factors that had plagued Hayden throughout January was concern for his family. Finally Hayden stressed that he must be seen to be standing down at the behest of the party and its collective leadership. It was agreed that Hayden would resign the following weekend. Button left exhausted.

It had been a meeting of personal trauma and tough bargaining. Both men had wept. Ultimately Hayden had lacked the ego or amorality to assume that his personal ambition was identical with Labor interests. The spasms of self-doubt which had flickered across his five-year leadership had turned into a final convulsion. It is true that Hayden put the interests of the ALP before his own. It is also true that he lost faith in his own ability to win the election and therefore, quite sensibly, could not countenance the consequences of a defeat for either himself or the ALP. He was not a great enough leader to draw upon reserves of confidence within himself and use this radiating force to convert pessimism into optimism inside his party.

Button flew to Sydney and rang Bowen from the TAA terminal. The deputy came straight to the airport and both men spent nearly two hours in discussion. Button said that two of Hayden's conditions affected Bowen. Hayden wanted to be Foreign Minister and he wanted a letter from Bowen as well. Button told Bowen how dreadful it had been: the trauma, the tears. Bowen was unhappy about the conditions. 'He can have my job,' Bowen said. 'But I'm going to make him fight for it. I'm not going to lie down and agree to this.' Bowen had set his heart on becoming Foreign Minister, but he was a realist and resigned himself to forgoing this ambition in the transition. He agreed to the letter. Bowen said Fraser was certain to call an election and that Hayden should resign the following Friday.

This long and dramatic day, the events of which were known only to the key participants, swung the race for power in Labor's favour. During the previous fortnight Fraser's relentless push towards a March election had possessed a logic which suggested he would strike before the ALP switched leaders. Now the balance was altered. Hayden had made his decision; the delicate details of its implementation lay ahead. Fraser intensified his election drive ignorant that the Labor leadership crisis had reached its climax.

Then a new urgency arose inside the Government. On that very morning, 1 February, the papers broke the news on the ALP leadership story and reported ever-mounting pressures on Hayden. It had in fact been an almost miraculous feat by the ALP to conceal the story for so long.

While Hayden and Button had wept, Eggleton had rung Liberal Party state directors warning that the election was a 'very high probability'. Then he contacted staff for the Melbourne headquarters and told them to 'start immediately'. Fraser's instincts told him to go now and go quickly; it was obvious that Hayden was bleeding to death. But Fraser did not know that Hayden had already shed tears of surrender.

21
The climax

I believe that a drover's dog could lead the Labor Party to victory the way the country is and the way the opinion polls are showing up.

Bill Hayden, 3 February 1983,
announcing his resignation as Labor Party leader

Just before lunch on Wednesday 2 February Bob Hawke knew that the gateway to his destiny lay open, when John Button briefed him about the previous day. Hawke was quiet, almost subdued, tranquil in the knowledge of his vindication. Yet he was steeling himself for the contest against Malcolm Fraser which he had sought so aggressively for so long. Unlike December 1975, that day long ago when Whitlam offered him the leadership, Hawke betrayed no frenetic agitation. This time he was a more mature man, better equipped for the task.

Button outlined Hayden's conditions—guarantees for staff, the Foreign Ministry, the London option, the letters from the other leaders, the protection for Walsh, Dawkins and Blewett—and Hawke agreed. The two men had a quick lunch before Button flew to Sydney to see his own Senate deputy Don Grimes.

The key participants had all eluded the press—until the ABC caught Lionel Bowen that afternoon. Bowen had given a speech on trade to a Sydney lunch and the ABC asked him for an interview. Bowen was reluctant but agreed on the basis that it stuck to the speech. But he was asked about the leadership anyway. Asked if he was still a strong Hayden supporter, Bowen said: 'I don't answer those questions.' Lionel Bowen, the straight man, the loyal deputy, the good mate, could not reaffirm confidence in Hayden. Bowen knew Hayden was gone. He returned to his office disgusted with the media and fearful of the television news that night.

Meanwhile in the Prime Minister's Parliament House office Fraser, Howard, Nixon and Eggleton were trying to finalise the election date. Fraser's staff were assuming it would be 5 March—the Prime Minister's preference. The obstacle to 5 March remained the Western Australian election. The main argument for 5 March, as opposed to 12 or 19 March, was the need to 'lock in' Hayden.

Fraser called his two senior Western Australian Liberals Fred Chaney and Peter Durack in a bid to mesh his strategy with that of the West. Then the Prime Minister rang WA Premier Ray O'Connor. The Premier was more relaxed than before about a federal election on 5 March; he had no problem with 12 March. O'Connor's election was on 19 February and his concern about a 5 March federal election was that Fraser's policy speech would need to be given before polling day in the West.

Fraser had watched the Labor Party in Canberra and in Melbourne for nearly thirty years. He knew its moods and understood its character. Fraser sensed a Labor leadership crisis was looming with a major blood-letting. The only difference it made to his plans was to reinforce their urgency.

The meeting broke with agreement for either 5 or 12 March but no decisions between these dates. Eggleton flew to Melbourne to brief the Liberal agency, Masius, the next day. Howard gave Fraser one piece of advice: 'Contact every Cabinet minister and make it a joint decision.' This was the voice of caution. Howard, who had come down for the day for talks with Fraser and bank executives, then returned to his family who were holidaying near Port Stephens.

Nixon stayed talking to Fraser. The late-afternoon light poured through the windows as Fraser and Nixon assessed, reassessed, contacted the Electoral Office, checked that every contingency was covered. Then Fraser was told about Bowen's comments, which had been broadcast on the 7 p.m. ABC television news. Bowen had watched them, furious. These comments were to damage unfairly his party reputation since most people drew the conclusion that he was trying to undermine Hayden.

Fraser's long and bloody road to power told him that when a deputy distanced himself the way Bowen had done then axes were being sharpened in back rooms. Eggleton had just got to the Windsor Hotel in time to see Bowen's television appearance. He spoke to Fraser at about 7.30 p.m. They discussed the Bowen remarks but there was no change in their tactics. Eggleton prepared to brief the advertising agency the next day. He was planning to cover the contingency of a 5 March election; but he still thought 12 March would be the date and that Fraser would put it to Cabinet for approval early the following week. But in Parliament House Fraser's personal staff were assuming the election would be 5 March and the announcement would be on Friday—two days away.

As dusk settled over Ipswich on 2 February Bill Hayden made the final reconciliation with his heart, his conscience and his identity which the resignation involved. The next day Dallas apologised to a Hayden aide who had rung that night: 'I'm sorry. I knew but couldn't tell you.' Hayden's staff believed it was not until that evening that he finally closed the book on his five-year Labor leadership.

At a Sydney motel John Button briefed Don Grimes about Hayden's conditions. Grimes' preference was to talk to Hayden rather than write him a letter, but Button felt there would be no problem. Then Button repaired to the home of Jim McClelland after an emotionally taxing few days of negotiating personal lives and political power. From there he rang Hayden and told him that the conditions he had set would be met. A despondent Hayden said they would discuss matters in Brisbane the next day. The Labor shadow ministry was meeting there and all senior ALP politicians were flying to Hayden's home state. That night Button and McClelland ruminated on the leadership. McClelland, like Button, had always admired Hayden rather than Hawke, but of late he had harboured great doubts.

That night in Brisbane the authentic Haydenites gathered at the Gazebo Motel not just to commiserate but to plan a strategic retreat. The strategy they devised for Bill Hayden is still operative and merely awaits the course of events. Its architects were Peter Walsh and John Dawkins, both of whom wanted Hayden to fight. Dawkins was in London and spoke to Hayden by phone. 'It's all over,' Hayden told him. Dawkins replied, 'I hope that's not right, but if it is right, you'd better demand the deputy's job.' Walsh and Dawkins agreed on this approach.

Late into the night Walsh, Blewett, Stewart West and Peter Morris caucused. Walsh told them that Hayden was about to resign; he was very depressed and did not believe it was worth fighting. They discussed Button's scenario that it was best to make Hawke leader, win or lose. They decided to support any Hayden resignation decision, but that, if Hayden resigned, he should ask for the deputy's job—and they believed that he would be strong enough in Caucus to get it. If there was a ballot between Hawke and Hayden, then they would support Hayden. Walsh conveyed these views to Hayden.

That night Fraser spoke to Macphee about Hawke and the Labor leadership. Macphee pointed out that the next meeting of the Labor Caucus would not be until 21 February. He predicted: 'Hawke will win.' Macphee said he had travelled to Canberra with Hawke on the Australia Day weekend and Hawke had been both restive and confident.

Fraser took another important phone call that evening which warned him the ALP crisis would come to a head quickly. His source said this information was reliable; it had come from the mouth of a member of Hayden's own staff. The Prime Minister now realised that the Labor crisis might overlap his election announcement. He pressed ahead.

When Fraser went to bed that night, 2 February, he had all but decided to start his dash to the polls the next morning. The Prime Minister saw that events in the Labor Party were overtaking him. But he believed he had a big advantage. If the ALP crisis came, then it would be a bloody affair that would take some days to resolve. While the Labor Party fought in public, Fraser would steal an election march on them.

The smell of big events had attracted interest in the shadow Cabinet meeting in Brisbane. That evening a number of senior press gallery reporters had flown north. They had made repeated efforts to find out what might happen the next day, but to no avail. When the press heard about Bowen's comments they knew it was big.

Australia's most lethal political reporter Laurie Oakes got up just before 6 a.m. on Thursday 3 February to confirm a story. Oakes was in Adelaide for a defamation case against himself and was staying with prominent South Australian Liberal Steele Hall and his wife Joan Bullock. Oakes had information from a lunch the previous day that Fraser would announce the election on Friday. He made a few calls and felt the story was firm. Then he rang his Canberra colleague, Ian McMinn, to compare notes. McMinn had the same story himself; he was putting it to air for 'Good Morning Australia' in a few minutes.

Oakes filed for the 7 a.m. news bulletins in the east—2UE Sydney and 3UZ Melbourne. Then he rang Bill Hayden to ask whether he'd fight for the Labor leadership. Hayden said nothing about his intentions. He listened to Oakes and commented about Fraser: 'So that's what he's up to.' Oakes hung up; Steele Hall and his wife were still in bed.

Meanwhile at The Lodge, Canberra, Malcolm Fraser was up and on the prowl. Fraser's first call was at 7.20 a.m. to his Private Secretary, Ron Harvey, already at work. The Prime Minister wanted Harvey to get him a list of contact points and phone numbers that day for all ministers—and to get it quick. It took Harvey 20 minutes. Fraser began calling ministers from The Lodge through his office switchboard before he came to work.

Hayden concluded from Oakes' information that he had one day's grace. His fear was that Fraser might announce an election before he had resigned the Labor leadership, and that he would then be depicted as a coward when he did resign. So Hayden decided to bring his resignation forward; get in first and beat Fraser. In other words, to do it properly. At 8 a.m. Hayden rang Button at McClelland's Sydney home. He told Button to see him as soon as he got to

313

Brisbane. He had information that the election was coming very quickly. Button sensed that Hayden wanted to resign at once. He told McClelland about the conversation. McClelland rammed home his advice to Button as he left: 'Don't delay any longer—get it done fast.'

Fraser phoned Eggleton at the Windsor just after 8 a.m. and told him he would call the election that day. It would be 5 March; he would go to Government House with election arrangements before lunch. Eggleton realised there was a new urgency in Fraser; the explanation was obvious. Fraser told him: 'It's moving very, very quickly, it's getting very serious.' Fraser said he had some 'well-informed information from a source inside the ALP'. Hayden's position was fading fast, and Fraser told Eggleton he had inside knowledge. Eggleton concurred; Fraser obviously knew exactly what he was doing. Eggleton left for his agency briefing thinking it was far better to go to the polls now than delay until later with the danger of facing Hawke.

At Masius headquarters Eggleton sat down with the advertising brains who would attempt to sell Malcolm Fraser to the people for the fourth time. Rick Otten and Col Curnow were the two key figures. Eggleton began: 'This is a very timely meeting. I expect the Prime Minister to announce an election today. I regret to inform you it's a very short period. It's 5 March.' The Liberal experts then had a long session on how to market the Fraser Government. They referred to Hayden several times: his leadership weakness and the potential it offered as a highlight to Fraser's strength.

Fraser got to Parliament House just after 8.30 a.m. He spoke to his Departmental Head Sir Geoffrey Yeend. There still seemed to be problems with 5 March, Yeend told him. The deadline was very tight. Fraser was alarmed. Eventually the problems were sorted out with the Electoral Office. Fraser rang Ray O'Connor and he endorsed the 5 March date. The Prime Minister called in his Office Director Dennis White and political staffer David Bloom. He told them he had information from within the Labor Party that Hayden was in deep trouble and could be challenged that very day. He had confirmed his information that morning. He was going for an immediate election.

Fraser rang Howard just after 9.00 a.m. and told him that 5 March was to be the date. 'He's going to be dead very soon, quicker than we think,' Fraser said of Hayden. Howard, like Eggleton, bowed to Fraser's judgement. He assumed Fraser had to hit immediately, otherwise Hawke would become leader.

Four girls now manned the switchboard in Fraser's office. The Prime Minister systematically contacted minister after minister. Most of the conversations were very short, only one or two minutes. Fraser was basically informing his ministry, not seeking their advice. Nobody dissented. Just before mid-morning, Peter Nixon arrived and joined the Prime Minister.

Button flew to Brisbane and went straight to the Commonwealth Offices at Ann Street. He joined Hayden on the twelfth floor. The Labor leader began by saying that he would stand down, and together they made plans for this. Button and Hayden went through the conditions once again. At 9.15 a.m. (Brisbane time) Bob Hawke arrived in a cream suit, a white-collared blue shirt and a blue tie patterned with the tiny stars of the Southern Cross. He went to the twelfth floor and Button told him that Hayden would stand aside; he would be leader elect of the ALP before lunch.

Labor shadow ministers were gathering in the downstairs conference room for the normal Executive meeting. As they arrived they were surrounded by a horde of cameras, microphones and journalists. Speculation was rife amongst the media that Hayden's crisis was upon him. In Canberra, at about mid-morning, the Prime Minister began to take account of a possible leadership change. Fraser asked Bloom to look at the ALP Caucus rules about the notice needed for a special party meeting, which he knew would be necessary for any challenge to the ALP leadership. He wanted details of Hawke's attitude towards the wage pause and the 35-hour week, and also his ACTU record. Meanwhile the letters which the Governor-General would require to dissolve Parliament were being prepared as quickly as possible.

Fraser's priorities seemed obvious. He wanted to lock-in Hayden and thought there was a chance he could do it. If that failed, he was prepared to face Hawke. Fraser told Nixon, 'The challenge will come today.' Nixon replied, 'Hawke will win'—but Fraser seemed a little sceptical. Fraser reasoned that if Hawke was going to be ALP leader, then it was best to confront him now and not in a few months time. Nobody believed the ALP was capable of a smooth leadership transition. Fraser had often told his colleagues: 'When Hayden's cornered, he'll fight like a cat.'

Meanwhile at the Melbourne headquarters of the Australian Security Intelligence Organisation, its Director General Harvey Barnett was briefing Attorney-General Peter Durack on a major security issue. It concerned Soviet diplomat Valeriy Ivanov. ASIO had identified him as KGB and believed action against him might be needed. But Barnett did not mention former ALP National Secretary David Combe, whose links with Ivanov were ASIO's chief worry. So Fraser knew nothing about the Ivanov–Combe connection; if he had waited until May, he would have got the whole story.

The ALP Executive meeting started about 10.10 a.m. Brisbane time (11.10 a.m. in Canberra, which operated on Australian Eastern Summer Time). Incredibly Hayden took the chair for a normal meeting. He whispered to

Bowen: 'I'm going to stand down after the morning tea-break.' This was news to Bowen. Hayden gave him some party cheques to countersign.

An air of unreality hung over the meeting; everybody suspected Hayden was going. Hawke whispered to Keating, 'He's quitting today.' Button left the meeting briefly and the press caught him. 'We're going very badly at the moment in my view,' Button declared. At 10.40 a.m. (Brisbane time) the Executive broke for morning tea. Hayden, Bowen, Button and Hawke went upstairs. Grimes followed later. They did not know Fraser would call an election within hours.

At this morning tea break the conditions for Hayden's resignation were finalised. The guarantees were ironclad, but a brawl erupted between Hayden and Bowen. 'I don't want to give you Foreign Affairs, but I won't stand in your way,' Bowen said. Bowen told Hayden he had been advised long ago by the Australian Secret Intelligence Service (ASIS) that Hayden had assured them Bowen would not be Labor's Foreign Minister. Hayden replied he knew nothing about that.

Finally the business was settled. The others left and Hawke and Hayden remained. Hayden, overwhelmed by the events, broke down; Hawke wept with him. The tensions between them dissolved as their seven-year power struggle was resolved; but their relationship would continue. This time Hayden would be Hawke's minister, rather than Hawke being Hayden's minister. So their tears were shed for different reasons.

Soon after the Labor leaders met upstairs Fraser read and signed the final version of his letter for Sir Ninian Stephen. Just before he left for Yarralumla his Press Secretaries Eddie Dean and Owen Lloyd brought down copy from the AAP wire-service machine in their office. It reported that Hayden was in trouble, with speculation that Hawke might succeed him. But Fraser did not appear concerned. He said: 'It makes no difference.' Fraser left for Yarralumla at 12.15 p.m., about 25 minutes before Hayden announced his resignation to the shadow Cabinet. The Prime Minister was in a hurry. His staff made plans for a 1.00 p.m. press conference in his office to announce the election. But in the rush nobody told the Governor-General.

The Yarralumla guards, the Government House 'frontline', first sighted the Prime Minister's car as it sped towards them down Dunrossil Drive past the green of Royal Canberra. All systems functioned as they should. The gate guard rang the office warning-bell; then Fraser's arrival was announced on the intercom system. Sir Ninian's staff began rushing about. The gates were flung open and the Prime Minister was properly met, but only just. He had arrived unannounced and unexpected to ask Sir Ninian Stephen to approve Australia's fifth double dissolution election since Federation.

But Sir Ninian was in a mood to deliberate on this matter. Moreover he was having the Polish Ambassador to lunch at 12.30. The Governor-General would need to eat, read, digest, and then approve. Fraser left just after 12.25 p.m. empty-handed; he spent most of the afternoon cooling his heels at Parliament House.

About 15 minutes after Fraser had left Yarralumla, the ALP Executive reconvened at 11.40 a.m. (12.40 p.m. Canberra time) and Hayden announced his intention to resign. He said there was a widespread belief he couldn't win the impending election; if there was another challenge to him, the damage would be too great. He believed he could win but had to bow to the party's mood. Hayden referred to Button's letter; he had made up his mind after reading it. It was 'brutal but fair'. Uren moved a tribute to Hayden; Hawke praised him as courageous. The shadow ministry response was relief tinged with guilt. Someone reported a radio news flash—Fraser had been to Government House. The relief was redoubled.

Fraser returned to Parliament House to find the media actually waiting in his office. They were ushered out very smartly. The press encamped outside the Prime Minister's office and at about 1.00 p.m. he came out to say he had discussed 'a number of subjects' with Sir Ninian; the press conference would be a bit later. Fraser went to The Lodge for a quick lunch and to pack his bags for Melbourne. He was still hoping to see Masius with Eggleton that afternoon. But at Yarralumla Sir Ninian was studying things meticulously. This was his first dissolution as Governor-General.

Hayden announced his resignation to the press at 12.25 p.m. (Brisbane time). Five minutes later, the news flash went around the nation. Hayden's resignation had beaten Fraser's election. It was the vital psychological blow from which Fraser never recovered; Labor had seized the initiative. The indelible impression was left: Fraser had been caught with his pants down. The Prime Minister who had outsmarted Whitlam in Parliament and at Yarralumla in 1975 had been out-gunned in 1983.

Displaying great self-control, Hayden made a short statement to the media:

> I didn't take this decision with any sense of joy; but it did seem to me as a matter of responsibility to my party, a party in which I have great faith and which really has an historic mission, that the situation confronting us was that an inevitable conflict was coming up in Caucus. At best I could win by only a very narrow margin. I don't rule out the possibility that I could have won such a contest by a narrow margin. It would have been unconvincing to the community and it would have resolved nothing . . .

I had to weigh up which was in the best interests of the party. There are
some occasions where people have to be prepared to make sacrifices, no matter
how fair or unfair, right or wrong, they are. One must do what one thinks is best
. . . The circumstances as I saw them had developed to the point where there
was only one way to resolve the problem . . .

I want to say this. I am not convinced that the Labor Party would not win
under my leadership. I believe that a drover's dog could lead the Labor Party to
victory the way the country is and the way the opinion polls are showing up for
the Labor Party. In that respect I have every confidence about the party's
prospects . . . I'm sure you'd understand it's created a great deal of heartburn
for me. It's not a decision that I would have preferred. In fact as recently as
Sunday I was still determined to fight the matter out, but it was increasingly
clear to me that if I did I would be guaranteeing great damage to my own party
and the return of the Fraser Government at the cost of my own personal interest;
and I'm afraid my motivation goes beyond that.

Hayden walked away from the press conference, joined his staff and
wept again. Button declared: 'I'm sorry to see him go personally. I'm happy
professionally.'

The ALP leaders had decided on a special Caucus meeting the following
Tuesday, 8 February, for the sole purpose of formally electing Hawke as
leader. Uren, speaking for the left, had told the shadow Cabinet that Hawke
would not be opposed. It was the consensus view. Labor had achieved a feat
which defied its history. It had risen above itself, its self-image and the expectations of others, notably Fraser: it had swapped leaders, smoothly, ruthlessly,
emotionally. But there was no blood, no public uproar, no disunity to alienate
the voters. The magnitude of Hayden's sacrifice was so great that the party
folded as one behind Hawke. He became the beneficiary of the emotional and
political release which Labor felt on 3 February.

Tony Eggleton and the Masius executives had done a good morning's
work and Eggleton flicked on the radio at lunchtime to see if Fraser had been
to Yarralumla. The advertising people crowded around. The first news item
was that Hayden had stood aside for Hawke, the second that Fraser had gone
to Government House. Eggleton was agog; the executives were rivetted. What
was Fraser up to? Why had Eggleton not told them about Hawke? Suddenly
the terrible truth dawned. Eggleton smiled weakly. Somebody exclaimed:
'God, Tony, this is better than one-day cricket.' But Eggleton sensed it was a
disaster. Much of the Liberal hopes had rested upon Hayden, and now he was
gone. After lunch Eggleton and Masius went through the entire campaign plan
again—this time with Hawke as leader.

In the early afternoon Eggleton spoke to Fraser: 'Well, this is all a bit of a surprise.' Fraser shot back: 'Oh, that was always a possibility, Tony.' Eggleton reflected that it was a pity nobody had told him.

John Howard had been driving his family towards the Myall Lakes when his wife Janette said: 'Are you sure they won't switch leaders on you?' Howard, the experienced politician, said it was very unlikely. A while later they turned on the radio. The unlikely had materialised. Howard suspected his days as Treasurer might be numbered.

Fraser and Nixon discussed the outlook during the afternoon hiatus. Nixon told Fraser he always believed that Hawke would prevail inside the ALP. He saw no sign of regret, worry or panic in Fraser. Nixon said later: 'I was there with him for an hour or so. The game went on although the players had changed. He was a man with a mission and there was no sign of alarm or concern.' But Fraser would have realised his hopes for a Labor bloodbath had disappeared. This was an ALP foreign to his long observation. Fraser spoke to Macphee in mid-afternoon and still seemed relaxed. 'I'm still waiting for the Governor-General's approval,' he said. Macphee asked, 'Is there any risk?' Fraser replied, 'No. He's just thinking about history and how his actions are seen.'

Hawke met the press while Fraser waited on the Governor-General. It was an omen of the next month, during which Hawke would make the news and Fraser would react to it. Hawke announced his campaign theme by pledging a Labor Government to 'national reconciliation'. He began Labor's election campaign before Fraser had even got the Governor-General's consent. Attacking Fraser Hawke declared: 'Australians have been deliberately set against Australians and group against group.' A Labor Government 'will be doing those things necessary to bring Australians together'. Hawke had begun his run to victory.

Fraser was a student of Menzies, but he failed to adopt his predecessor's attitude towards the vice-regal office. When Menzies had obtained the 1951 double dissolution from Sir William McKell he had made a point of calling upon the Governor-General a few days before to alert him and smooth the way. In the first three double dissolutions, 1914, 1951 and 1974, legal opinions from either the Attorney-General or Solicitor-General were provided in addition to the Prime Minister's letter. This time, there was just the letter. It was an important oversight.

Fraser sought his double dissolution on 13 bills, all of which met the requirements of Section 57 of the Constitution. All were rejected by the Senate twice with an interval of at least three months between rejections. The bills covered the extension of sales tax at 2.5 per cent to essential items such as clothing and footwear, reimposition of tertiary fees for higher level students and a measure to prevent the spouses of striking workers claiming unemployment benefits. None were matters of current dispute; the most recent rejections had been in autumn 1982. That is, the constitutional requirements for a double dissolution were satisfied yet, in political terms, the House of Representatives and the Senate were not in conflict over substantive issues. Parliament was neither deadlocked nor unworkable.

Fraser was really exploiting a previous dispute for a present election. Under the Constitution he had every right to do so. But a Governor-General with a wide interpretation of the reserve powers could note that Section 57 says the Governor-General 'may dissolve', not 'shall dissolve'. This could be interpreted as room for discretion. Former Clerk of the House of Representatives J. A. Pettifer says in his standard work that in granting a double dissolution the Governor-General 'should satisfy himself that there is in reality a deadlock'. Fraser should have been more careful.

Sir Ninian Stephen rang Fraser at about 3.30 p.m. and wanted more information. It seems clear from this request that Sir Ninian believed that the Governor-General did have a discretionary role in the exercise of Section 57. He wanted advice from Fraser on the importance of the 13 Bills and the 'workability' of Parliament. So Fraser drafted a second, shorter letter in which he formally advised Sir Ninian that he regarded 'a double dissolution as critical to the workings of the Government and of the Parliament'.

Sir Geoffrey Yeend arrived at Yarralumla at 4.45 p.m. with the second letter. Ten minutes later he telephoned Fraser to convey Sir Ninian's approval. Fraser held his press conference at 5.00 p.m.—four hours later than he had originally intended. The Labor Party had moved far too quickly for him. It had seized the psychological advantage.

Fraser was more nervous than usual. He based the rationale for his election on the wage pause and the opposition to it from the ALP and the ACTU. He had forgotten Macphee's advice about avoiding a battle with Hawke on the wage pause. Fraser was challenging Australia's greatest negotiator to an election campaign on an industrial issue. He was playing to Hawke's strength. Since before Christmas, when Hawke had gone to see Crean and then held long talks with Kelty, this move had been checkmated. 'I challenge the union movement . . .' Fraser declared about the pause and the oil dispute. But Fraser was already outmanoeuvred.

Asked if the Hayden–Hawke switch had caught him with his pants down, Fraser said: 'No. It makes no difference who the leader may be. The policies of the Labor Party are the same . . . The policies of the Labor Party are not altered by altering the shopfront window.' Asked whether he had had second thoughts about calling the election after learning of the Hawke ascendancy, Fraser replied: 'On the contrary. I had a little more relish. It will be the first election in which two Labor leaders have been knocked off in one go.'

Some critics said later that Fraser should have pulled back during the afternoon by calling Sir Ninian and withdrawing his election request. The best comment on this delusion comes from David Barnett:

> All that would have been required was the absolute humiliation involved in telephoning Government House to inform Sir Ninian that there had been a change of mind. Followed by gales of media laughter and a month of acute embarrassment. But Malcolm Fraser, with his impatience for action, and his great pride, would be about the last man to follow such a servile course.
> I hope we never get a Prime Minister who would.[1]

Did Fraser miscalculate? The Prime Minister's instincts were right in going for a March election. His Government enjoyed a temporary increase in its standing in the December–February period, which was dominated by the wage pause and confusion in the ALP. Fraser was also right in hastening the election in a bid to catch Hayden before Hawke ran him down. He almost succeeded. It is a measure of Fraser's strength that at this period of economic decline the Labor Party came to the conclusion that Fraser would probably beat Hayden. In this sense the turning point was the Flinders by-election, after which Labor lost its faith in Hayden.

In fact Fraser almost succeeded; if he had moved just a little faster, then Hayden would have been his opponent. There is no certainty that Fraser would have defeated Hayden, but the collapse in ALP morale, from the shadow Cabinet to the rank and file level, would have made an ALP revival more difficult and given Fraser a better chance of winning than he had in late 1982.

When he decided in January on a March election Fraser was influenced by the economy and the wage pause. The ALP leadership was always a factor but not decisive. However as Fraser's decision moved towards its climax, so did the ALP crisis, and Fraser then moved to lock-in Hayden. When he saw that events were overtaking him Fraser stuck by his plans on the basis that if Hawke did become leader, then a sudden-death encounter was best. It is difficult to dispute this judgement. Hawke would have enjoyed a long honeymoon as leader of the Opposition. Neither Fraser nor anyone else in the Government was able to predict that Labor would make such a smooth leadership transition.

Peter Nixon later summed it up this way:

> Fraser decided on March. The reason he called the election was not because of the Labor leadership. Anyone who says we called the election because we were scared Hawke might replace Hayden, doesn't understand the realities. There were a series of reasons. The fact that Hayden might be locked in as leader was an extra bonus. We looked at the possibility of Hawke becoming leader. Fraser's view was that he would be in no better situation against Hawke in May than he was immediately. He had the prospect of the Labor Party being seen to be in disarray if he went immediately.
>
> We talked it through. We were going whether they had Hayden, Hawke or God in the chair. We were going.[2]

However events had conspired against Fraser. Tony Eggleton had always insisted on two conditions for the Government campaign. Firstly there had to be concessions or tax cuts. Secondly if Hawke became leader, the election would have to be delayed as long as possible to tarnish his image. But Fraser called the election with the budget tax cuts forgotten and Hawke in his leadership flush.

Asked later if he harboured any doubts on 3 February that he could beat Fraser, Hawke replied:

> No. That unequivocal 'no' is not arrogance. It was calculated thinking on my part. I knew it was very bad dishonest Government with a bad and dishonest Prime Minister. I knew he could not match me in debate. I was certain of the sort of campaign he would run and my judgement was that it would not be acceptable to the people of Australia. I believed they would respond to the positive campaign I would run. I'd written out a campaign strategy. The Labor Party talked about reconstruction; I'd said reconciliation is the prerequisite. I knew I could run the campaign I thought was necessary. I was certain we would win.[3]

The irony of Bill Hayden's career is that by his resignation he finally sealed Fraser's doom.

22
The flight to Hawke

This is a fight for the future of Australia, for the true heart and soul of Australia.

Bob Hawke opening the ALP campaign,
16 February 1983

The 1983 election campaign was a triumph for Bob Hawke, who made a successful transition from folk hero to prime ministerial candidate. In the four-week campaign Hawke offered the voters hope and the prospect of moderate but firm leadership. His specific pledge to create more jobs was seen as credible; his vision of reconciliation offered a clean break from the politics of Malcolm Fraser and tapped an undercurrent in the nation which was looking for a better way. The ALP had surrendered itself to Hawke at the start of the campaign like an army that had lost its nerve on the edge of the mine-field. Hawke displayed a deft political touch, immense self-confidence and unparalleled media skills in steering his party through the campaign.

Labor's leadership switch was audacity itself—but it was not without risk. From the start Fraser waited for the untested Hawke to falter in his new role somewhere, somehow, sometime, so that mistake could be made the central issue of the campaign. But Hawke never gave Fraser a chance. Equipped with a temperament that rose to the occasion and a new grey suit that projected his calm resolve, Hawke stole Fraser's prime ministerial mantle during the campaign itself.

As the Government's campaign unfolded, the intellectual exhaustion and political collapse of the Fraser regime was inexorably revealed. The Government was out-gunned on almost every issue every day. It had lived for too long on Labor's negatives—Whitlam's economic extravagance, Hayden's so-called wealth tax, the trade union bogy. Fraser's only recourse was to continue his attack on the Labor Party but, when faced with a politically adroit and personally acceptable Bob Hawke, the Government scare campaign degenerated into irrelevancy. As Fraser became more urgent his greatest asset—his perceived strength—drifted into menacing intimidation and became a negative.

The ALP and Hawke ran an excellent defensive campaign systematically denying Fraser the peg on which to hang the big scare. Once this was accomplished the sterility of Fraser's record was exposed. Unlike either 1977 or 1980, the Government, caught amid the world economic downturn, had no achievements to market. By early 1983 Australia's annual inflation was 11 per cent compared with less than seven per cent for the OECD average. Unemployment was 10.1 per cent compared with 10.8 per cent in the United States, nine per cent in France, 12.7 per cent in Britain and 2.4 per cent in Japan. The Fraser Government's record did not entitle it to re-election and the Prime Minister could find no means to disguise this reality.

Both sides immediately identified the 1983 campaign as a political watershed. It would either end the Fraser years or deliver a profound psychological blow to the federal ALP. The unthinkable possibility for the ALP was its own defeat. Labor's ruthless pragmatism had precipitated the execution of Hayden and the elevation of Hawke so as to maximise the chances of victory. If Fraser had bested Hawke at the polls then the ALP would have lost its two spearheads within the one month, the first by its own hand and the second by Fraser's.

The defeat of Hawke would have unleashed within the ALP an inevitable backlash by Hayden and his own supporters, since the entire rationale for the leadership switch would have foundered. It is naive to believe that the Hayden group would not have demanded retribution. The Labor Party, by its embrace of Hawke, had worshipped at the altar of pragmatism. But if this had failed then Labor would have sunk into introspective postmortems of a bloody nature. Hawke's golden asset had always been the unshakeable confidence that he would win. If Fraser had destroyed this asset in Hawke's initial weeks, then his capacity to defeat Fraser at a subsequent election would have been severely reduced.

There were two separate stages in Labor's 5 March victory. The first was the consistent effort from mid-1979 to position Labor in the middle ground of politics and to win swinging voters through the projection of moderate policies aimed at helping the family while Fraser's economic problems compounded. By 1982 this approach had given Labor a theoretical four per cent swing, of which ANOP estimated two per cent was solid with another two per cent wobbly. The second stage was the Hawke ascension and his campaign, which turned some of the wobbly two per cent into hard votes and also attracted some entirely new swingers to the ALP cause. In retrospect the Labor campaign can be seen as providing the perfect mix: a long lead time to establish the middle ground position, followed by a new surge due to Hawke's leadership ascension at the start of the campaign proper.

The first week of the campaign literally belonged to Hawke who, as a new leader, enjoyed a honeymoon with the media and laid the basis for his win. Hawke charmed, joked and cajoled the media as only Hawke could. The opening days saw a breathtaking display of public confidence and private consolidation. Hawke took over an ALP machine ready for an early election; he merely settled behind the controls and readjusted the direction. It was a cooperative effort.

Within 24 hours the Hawke bandwagon was rolling. For the leader's personal staff Neville Wran provided Peter Barron, Victoria offered Bob Hogg, and the National Secretariat Geoff Walsh, while John Button provided his senior staffer Geoff Evans. Graham Freudenberg was recruited to write the policy speech. In Sydney Bob McMullan and Richard Farmer ran the campaign headquarters and drew up Hawke's daily schedule. Rod Cameron managed the research and his assistant Margaret Gibbs conducted a qualitative session almost each night to pilot the progress. Malcolm McFie from Forbes, McFie and Hansen continued his long-standing role as Labor's key advertising man. Senator Kerry Sibraa and Kate Moore from the National Secretariat became a successful advance team travelling a few days ahead of Hawke.

Fraser's expectation that the Labor Party would be bathed in blood became a mammoth miscalculation. Labor's morale was immediately boosted. The rank and file responded, the trade unions cooperated, the campaign professionalism of the ALP furnished Hawke's needs and the parliamentary party closed behind him. Labor was united and confident.

The party's campaign strategists met in Sydney on Friday 4 February. They decided on the slogan, 'Bob Hawke—Bringing Australia Together', on a campaign opening at the Sydney Opera House, and on a comprehensive pitch to both the idealism and greed of the voters. Hawke's reconciliation provided an appeal to the former; the offer of big concessions and tax cuts catered for the latter elements. Neville Wran told the campaign meeting that reconciliation was fine but 'if the greedy bastards wanted spiritualism they'd join the fucking Hare Krishna'. Wran said there was no substitute for a tax cut.

Hawke then met the press and delivered a mortal blow to Fraser's great election hope. Within 24 hours of the Governor-General approving the election, Hawke announced the ACTU would meet his request and call off its industrial campaign inside the oil industry against the wages pause. Hawke said the ACTU wanted the voters on 5 March to 'consider the real issues undiverted by any disturbances in the oil industry'. Once again the

Hawke–ACTU connection had triumphed—this time against Fraser. Hawke also predicted that the trade union movement would endorse the ALP–ACTU prices–incomes accord 'absolutely and overwhelmingly' at its 21–22 February unions conference. Finally Hawke revealed that Labor's campaign emphasis would shift from reconstruction to reconciliation.

Hawke's background was indispensable in clearing away the political–industrial situation which had plagued Hayden at the Flinders by-election so cruelly. The new leader negotiated successfully with his own ACTU network to eliminate Fraser's hopes for industrial disruption and then concluded the prices–incomes accord, which would provide the basis for Hawke's own positive appeal to national consensus. Hawke's ascension transformed wages policy from an ALP minus to a plus—a far-reaching achievement. He had Fraser outmanoeuvred from the start.

Hawke's reputation as political fixer was never better demonstrated than when he used his ACTU links against Hayden in January and then against Fraser in February. It minimised Labor's weakness and reinforced its strength. Within two days of Hawke becoming leader and Fraser calling the election, Cliff Dolan was able to declare that the unions fully agreed with the prices–incomes policy; no longer did the ACTU insist that the ALP economic policy be delayed until after the special unions conference.

Two important events, which affected both the campaign and its aftermath, occurred within hours of Fraser's election announcement. The first was Hawke's appearance on 'Nationwide' on the evening of 3 February when he clashed bitterly with Richard Carleton and rebuked him in a personal way, claiming Carleton's questions were 'perverted' and that his reputation was one of 'impertinence'. Hawke appeared to lose his cool. The Fraser camp was delighted. Both parties found an electoral backlash against Hawke in their subsequent research. The Liberals began preparing their campaign to combat Hawke: a man everyone liked but whose temper and incapacity to handle pressure made him unacceptable as a Prime Minister.

At this stage Hawke's great ability to listen to his professional handlers and take their advice came to the fore. He was told bluntly that his outburst was counterproductive; his weakness was his temper, which led some voters to fear him and others to the conclusion that he lacked the self-control needed for the job. This message was drummed into Hawke, particularly by Peter Barron, and it produced a new Hawke style. He became relaxed, well mannered and calm to the point of tranquillity. The natural Hawke aggression was repressed; he was surrounded by muted colours. Hawke became a benevolent prophet radiating peace. It was a consummate acting performance conducted by an actor of great skill who knew his part. The Carleton outburst was the last Hawke made and the Government waited in vain for another. So quickly did he learn.

The second incident revealed the private Hawke, still active and working behind the scenes to manipulate events. Hawke tried—in the opinion of the then ABC Chairman Dame Leonie Kramer—to influence the ABC's coverage during the election period. His intervention was provoked by the 'AM' programme on 4 February, which falsely implied that Hawke himself might have been named in the secret volumes of the Costigan Report on tax avoidance. John Button subsequently provided Hawke with a memo complaining about other aspects of the ABC's election coverage. The most notable complaint was about a warning given to reporter Helen O'Neil by a senior officer in connection with her interview with Fraser on 4 February. O'Neil had responded to Fraser's comment that 'many movie stars who've got a great image' would not necessarily be good Prime Ministers with the words 'I must ask President Reagan that . . .'

Hawke rang Dame Leonie on 8 February with Button present and 'proceeded to register his displeasure at certain aspects' of the ABC coverage. He referred to the warning which O'Neil had received and remarked that a member of the 'AM' staff 'had ties with the Liberal Party'. Hawke criticised the senior officer who spoke to O'Neil adding 'This warrants a change'. According to Dame Leonie, Hawke then said 'I'm damned if I'm going to put up with this sort of situation'. Dame Leonie said she would investigate the complaints.

She rang Button three days later. In this conversation Dame Leonie said the reference to the Costigan Report was fair in the context of political reporting. Button dissented strongly. She said the officer who warned O'Neil for her aside had behaved properly and that it was the duty of reporters to be objective. Again Button dissented. He asked what this meant, in particular whether it meant Fraser should not be asked questions he disliked. The incident revealed that Hawke was prepared to use his new position to apply pressure on the ABC chairman—a more private glimpse of the champion of reconciliation.

On Tuesday 8 February the ALP Caucus met and elected Hawke unopposed as leader, thereby formalising the arrangement of the previous Thursday. Fraser had assumed that seven days' notice was needed for a meeting with a leadership contest, but he was proved wrong because there was no contest. Hawke and his two aides occupied Hayden's office just before lunch while the former leader's staff were still packing and Dallas wept in the outer office. On 9 February Hawke unveiled Labor's machinery of Government policy, on which an ALP task force under Gareth Evans had been working for many months. Then on 10 February at Sydney's Wentworth Hotel Hawke, Keating and Willis unveiled the ALP economic policy. The cumulative impact of these events was that Hawke dominated the news and the Liberal Party began to nurse deep worries.

The new leader was also working to deny Fraser the political wedge he needed to drive into any ALP weakness. Hawke ruled out any new capital gains tax under Labor; he organised a trip to Tasmania to explain Labor's opposition to the dam and then spoke to Catholic education authorities in an effort to allay their fears about funding cuts to the better-off private schools. But it was the ALP economic policy which gave Fraser his only real chance during the campaign—a chance he blew.

Paul Keating was unhappy with the draft recovery and reconstruction document he had inherited and it was substantially redrafted in consultation with Hawke. The result reflected the determination of the ALP to 'go for broke' on winning. Hawke presented the voters with a $2,750-million programme of spending promises and tax cuts to break the cycle of recession. He claimed, somewhat optimistically, that with the extra revenue from tax avoidance and economic growth the increase in the budget deficit for 1983–84 would be only $1,500 million. The ALP programme meant big spending to create jobs. Its tax cuts were concentrated at the lower end but extended to income earners on $60,000 a year. Hawke and Keating argued that the 'principal thrust of Labor's strategy will be to reject the policies of contraction and embrace the policies of expansion'.

In retrospect it is obvious that Labor never needed such extravagant promises. They were really a legacy of Fraserism, since Labor had absorbed the Liberal belief that tax cuts were a vital ingredient of campaign success. Despite the clouds of idealism that swirled mystically around Hawke's bid for power, both Labor's economic policy and Hawke's own policy speech were heavy with cynicism. Labor revealed its hand first; it wanted to ensure it had outbid anything that Fraser might offer.

So Labor went into the campaign offering tax cuts for 99 per cent of income earners, petrol price reductions, increased welfare benefits for pensioners, families and the unemployed and a major public works programme. It promised to create another 500,000 jobs over the next three years. No avenue of vote-buying or economic expansion was left untouched. The ALP only provided consolidated costings of its programme and refused throughout the campaign to give an item-by-item breakdown. The media scarcely ever asked it for such a breakdown. Yet the ALP figures for its job creation programme were obviously dubious and meant the workers employed could be paid even below award rates. There was once a time when Fraser could have turned this ALP bonanza of extravagance to his own advantage. But in the 1983 campaign Fraser lost his judgement and finally ran out of luck.

The tone for the Government campaign which would be dominated by Fraser was set on 4 February when Liberal strategists met Masius in Melbourne. The agency suggested several campaign slogans but Fraser was not interested and insisted on the slogan 'We're not waiting for the world'. Prime Ministers do not make good advertising men and in the past they have normally left this task to the professionals. But Malcolm Fraser now dominated his Government at the cost of sound alternative advice. John Howard held reservations about the slogan. It contradicted the message which Howard had been selling for 12 months—that Australia's economic problems were a function of the world depression. The slogan, however, captured the new direction which Fraser had pioneered in recent weeks as he moved towards a more expansionary and development-orientated economic policy.

The slogan was a 'soft sell'. The flagship advertisement was a song of the same title written by Mike Brady of 'Up There Cazaly' fame and sung by Colleen Hewett. Cabinet ministers who heard the track on Sunday 6 February liked it. But the Liberals were drifting off on a tide of false reality. The truth is that their campaign lacked a hard centre. Obviously Fraser wanted to run on something positive, but the Government's performance simply denied it this opportunity. The upshot is that 'We're not waiting for the world' became a piece of advertising flimflam. The jingle was catchy and the television clip featured Australia's sporting heroes in action. Yet within days Greg Chappell said he had asked not to be featured in the advertisement and swimmer Lisa Forrest said she resented being used for political purposes.

The paradox of the campaign is that neither Fraser nor the Liberals were adequately prepared for the election which the Prime Minister had called. On the weekend of 5–6 February, when ministers gathered in Melbourne to chart their course, the sterility of the Liberal campaign was exposed. Hawke's elevation had put extra pressure on the Government. Yet neither Fraser nor his ministers knew what line of attack to use. When Fraser left the Cabinet room to meet the press on Sunday 6 February he attacked Labor for being 'a divisive party'—a theme which Hawke would easily repudiate—and finished by saying that Labor would 'tear up our flag'. From the start Fraser was lapsing into irrelevancy.

During this press conference Fraser was forced on to the defensive over the 13 bills on which he had obtained the double dissolution, most of which involved sales tax increases. The following exchange occurred:

QUESTION: If you win, will you put all the double dissolution bills through
Parliament?

FRASER: That's a matter we'd have to consider.

QUESTION: But surely you stand by them, don't you, seeing you sought the
double dissolution on them?

FRASER: I said that's a matter we'd have to consider.

When Fraser returned to the Cabinet after this encounter, he was a
worried man. The Government immediately interrupted its debate on campaign promises to devise a strategy to handle the sales tax issue. Eventually
Cabinet accepted Howard's recommendation that any rise in sales tax would
be offset by cuts in personal income tax. Fraser had failed to realise that
his use of Section 57 of the Constitution to obtain the double dissolution,
involving bills which imposed a rise in sales tax, might itself become an
election issue. This was a telling sign of both Fraser's arrogance and his
inadequate political advice.

The next day, 7 February, Fraser released the full text of his exchange
with the Governor-General while he retreated from his own advice to Sir
Ninian. The Prime Minister told Sir Ninian in his first letter of 3 February that
the 13 bills 'are of importance to the Government's budgetary, education and
welfare policies'. But Fraser now said that the Government, if re-elected,
would submit immediately only one of the 13 bills. The main bills, the sales
tax measures, would be considered only in a budget context. Asked if it could
be assumed that a new Fraser Government would act soon to broaden the tax
base the Prime Minister said: 'No. You can't.'

Meanwhile Hawke moved to exploit Fraser's embarrassment and
declared, 'The question now becomes a very simple one: Did Mr Fraser
deceive the Governor-General?' As the campaign progressed Fraser abandoned the Cabinet position that any rise in sales tax would be offset by a cut
in income tax. He categorically ruled out a sales tax rise. Howard, who devised
this Cabinet position, watched Fraser break it.

Fraser's campaign opening at the Malvern Town Hall lacked the enthusiasm of previous Liberal launchings. His policy speech was cautious and
without any shred of inspiration. He avoided the big ticket items of tax cuts or
pension rises and surrendered the election-promise stakes to the ALP. Fraser
sprinkled his speech with pledges to promote innovation in industry, to boost
education and welfare funding and to hold a referendum to give both the
Arbitration Commission and the federal Government power to protect the
public during industrial disputes. His employment initiative was the creation
of another 10,000 places in the armed forces. In his opening sentences he tried

to explain the reasons for Australia's economic recession, blaming the world, the drought and the unions—never his own Government. He declared that 'Australians have never had a clearer choice'. But his speech lacked vision or a unifying theme and late that evening, 15 February, it was obvious that the Liberals had only one tactic left—an assault on the Labor Party.

The next day Eggleton received polling results showing that the Government had fallen 11 per cent behind the ALP. Moreover the qualitative research suggested that the voters believed Labor would do a better job and saw few if any positives from Fraser's seven-year rule. The ANOP survey over the same weekend 12–13 February showed Labor leading in the capital cities with 55.5 per cent compared to the Coalition with 45.5 per cent (in two-party preferred terms). Labor had increased its lead in the 10 days since Fraser called the election and Hawke took over the ALP.

ANOP's qualitative research showed three doubts about Hawke, which the Liberals identified and would try to develop. They were his leadership inexperience, his potential emotional instability and the doubts about his statesmanship, notably, how he would conduct himself overseas. Relying on Rod Cameron's advice, Labor's strategists successfully neutralised these potential negatives.

Cameron's post-election report said: 'ANOP recommended that Hawke should adopt a subdued, calm, statesmanlike manner and approach throughout the campaign, that his language and natural aggressiveness should be muted . . . that he should be seen in prime ministerial garb and surroundings so that swinging voters would not be worried about his "meeting the Queen".' Cameron also identified the major Labor image weaknesses—the fear of Labor's ties with the unions and doubts about 'where the money is coming from'.

In his post-election report Cameron said that 'unions are a potentially volatile emotional issue among swinging voters'. But Hawke's consensus position was satisfactory to such voters. ANOP found that Hawke had produced an answer to one of Labor's traditional electoral weaknesses and that he had neutralised the hardline union approach espoused by the Liberals.

Cameron's early analysis had shown that Hawke would have to distance himself from the unions to maintain a viable position. It was for this reason that Hawke used the following declaration on 21 February when he hailed the ALP–ACTU prices–incomes accord: 'We as a Government will certainly not be your handmaiden and this historic document makes it clear that you do not expect that . . .' In his report Cameron noted that the 'Liberals were not able to exploit Labor's potentially damaging union links and that Labor was able to minimise these negatives. Less than one in ten (eight per cent) raised Labor's links with the union movement as being one of the negative aspects of the ALP campaign.'

Hawke's achievement was considerable. He exploited the accord as the basis for reconciliation, yet minimised the damage from such a close association with the union movement. No other figure in the ALP could have accomplished this so successfully.

Hawke's Opera House opening was brilliant theatre. He stood alone on the stage, the symbol of the new moderate Labor Party, and gave a highly personalised speech. Freudenberg revealed his professionalism; he had written many speeches for Whitlam and Wran—but this was a Hawke speech. Hawke began, 'This is a fight for the future of Australia, for the true heart and soul of Australia'. He called for an end to 'the politics of division, the politics of confrontation' and then made 'a commitment which embraces every other undertaking'. This was 'to reunite this great community of ours, to bring out the best that we are truly capable of, as a nation . . .'. Hawke finished by invoking John Curtin; then he embraced his 84-year-old father, Clem, who was hoisted onto the stage. Hawke's eyes were moist with emotion.

The Government campaign now moved to its decisive state—the bid to discredit Labor. This was the tactic which had saved Fraser in his battle against Hayden in 1980; it was an assault for which Labor had prepared. But this time Fraser was a victim of the searing bushfires which ravaged Victoria and South Australia on Ash Wednesday. He lost four days, during which he travelled to the destroyed locations and then observed a mini campaign-moratorium. The significance of this pause is not that Fraser disappeared, for in fact he was able to respond to this national crisis in his prime ministerial capacity. But Fraser was forced to postpone for four days his counterattack which, by its nature, would be savage and virulent and hence needed to be distanced from the mood of national concern generated by the fires. All the omens were running against Fraser. The Western Australian state election that Saturday saw a sweeping ALP win—and Labor expected to poll better in the West in the federal election.

When Fraser returned to the fray he was more urgent than ever. He knew time was running out; he had to hit Labor very quickly and hurt it badly. Fraser lunged for the jugular—but he went too far. Instead of making Hawke the issue, Fraser made himself the issue.

The turning point of the campaign—the stage at which it became clear that Fraser could never recover—was Tuesday 22 February. Fraser had already attacked the ALP–ACTU accord; now he was trying to nail Labor as the party of economic irresponsibility. The day before, Howard had replied to Labor's costings estimating them at $4,200 million, not $2,750 million—but this attack should have been made by Fraser to get maximum impact. Then at a

Melbourne lunchtime rally Fraser screamed into a microphone that people should not assume their savings were safe in the bank. He warned: 'Under Labor it'd be safer under your bed than it would be in the banks. They would be robbing the savings of the people to pay for their mad and extravagant promises.' (Hawke riposted with devastating mockery: 'They can't put them under the bed because that's where the Commies are!')

The banks were concerned, some of their depositors became anxious and senior Liberals began to retreat from their own leader. Howard rang a senior Fraser aide asking: 'What the fuck is this money under the beds line?' Later on television Howard said that it was a 'colourful' description—but refused to endorse it. The anti-Fraser backbenchers, Senators Kathy Martin and Don Jessop, criticised Fraser. So did Premier Bjelke-Petersen, obviously sensing Fraser's defeat. The newspapers heavily criticised the Prime Minister, and then the Executive Director of the Australian Bankers Association Research Directorate, Ron Cameron, deplored the comments. The latter guaranteed a damaging news story for Fraser.

Having made one mistake Fraser then made another. Instead of retreating he sought to justify his damaging assertion. That evening Fraser spoke to Ron Cameron and the next day released the transcript of their discussion, during which he talked Cameron round to his own point of view. The transcript was studded with Fraser comments such as 'you would agree, Mr Cameron, wouldn't you' and finished with Fraser saying: 'Thank you very much. I think that clarifies it from my point of view.'

The next day, 23 February, Fraser flew from Melbourne to Perth via Adelaide and the bankruptcy of the Fraser regime was exposed. In Adelaide Fraser repeated his remarks and told journalists 'before most of you were born the Labor Party tried to grab all the institutions and nationalise them'. In Perth the Prime Minister told a rally that Labor wanted to 'paint the whole of Australia red'. Then, referring to the 'money under the beds' line, he informed a press conference that, 'I will use it again, again and again because certainly the word "rob" is correct and it is graphic.'

Here was a most vivid demonstration that there was only one strategy in the Government campaign—that devised by Malcolm Fraser. The Prime Minister completely lacked Hawke's ability to listen to his own professionals and in this campaign Labor's professionalism outmatched that of the Government in most departments. ANOP chief Rod Cameron wrote in his post-election report: 'It was clear that only a small minority (about 10 per cent) had any worries about Fraser's statement . . . Research confirmed that the Liberal's scattergun scare tactics damaged Fraser's credibility . . . Hawke's lead in terms of being the best Prime Minister increased. In the qualitative research towards the end of the campaign, the impact on Fraser's image was clearly apparent. He was described as being "rattled", "under pressure", "lost his confidence", "he thinks he's going to lose", "he's aged, he's not well".'

In Cameron's separate post-election survey he found the worst feature of the Government campaign was the mudslinging (27 per cent) and the second worst feature was Fraser's leadership (12 per cent). Hawke had comprehensively outmanoeuvred Fraser; Hawke's moderation contrasted with Fraser's recklessness. Suddenly their roles were reversed. Hawke appeared as the reliable statesman while Fraser appeared strident and irritable.

ANOP research revealed that this second week—the critical period for Fraser's fightback—guaranteed Hawke's win. Its 27–28 February survey showed that the ALP lead had risen to 56.5 per cent of the two-party preferred capital city vote compared with 43.5 per cent for the Government. There was a small swing back to the Liberals in the last week, but they had lost their chance.

Given Hawke's performance Fraser could not have won, but his own failures contributed to the size of his defeat. Fraser waged an incompetent campaign and let the ALP off the hook. At almost no stage did the Prime Minister try systematically and seriously to take apart the ALP economic programme. Fraser's difficulties were compounded by the lack of any adequate campaign strategy. His Government had been moving tentatively but surely towards economic expansion. He had watched in late 1982 and early 1983 as interest rates fell and the budget deficit blew out, and had become in the process even more sceptical about Treasury advice. Yet Fraser could never match the full-blooded economic expansion and fresh hopes offered by Hawke. On the other hand many Liberals such as Howard argued that the Government should have stuck by its hard line and made no concessions. Yet it is naive to believe this course would have substantially improved its vote. Fraser's trouble was his inadequate record which could not be concealed.

As the campaign progressed Fraser became more alienated from his senior ministers. The split between Fraser and Howard over economic policy widened dramatically; a re-elected Fraser Government would have become quickly involved in a deep brawl over economic direction. Both Andrew Peacock and Ian Macphee made statements that contrasted with those of Fraser. The Prime Minister's staff reported that Fraser noticed an absence of inward calls from his colleagues and responded in kind: he declined to call his ministers.

Fraser's effort to nail the Labor Party over its prices–incomes policy caused deep heartburn inside the Hawke camp. Fraser seized upon comments made by shadow Treasurer Paul Keating that he was 'not sure' if the prices–incomes accord could work. The remarks were a tiny part of a long interview Keating gave John Laws on 24 February on 2UE. They were innocuous but, in the context of a campaign against Fraser, certain to be used against the ALP. Hawke defended Keating, saying he was merely being honest. But Hawke also began to reassess Keating's capacity for the Treasury job. These doubts were short-lived but were fed on Keating's struggle to handle the Treasury portfolio—a battle which continued during the initial months of the Hawke Government. Keating's crisis was a necessary and vital stage of his political development. For the first time many of his colleagues saw him tentative and deeply unsure of himself, fighting to overcome his lack of economic training.

As Labor's campaign progressed it became clear that Hawke was not marketing the $630-million tax cut or the ALP job-creation programme. The specifics were unimportant. Hawke was marketing the personal vision that he had devised years before and had brought to a peak the previous month. Hawke's message of hope had a spiritual dimension. National reconciliation gave the Labor campaign a unity of purpose which Fraser's campaign lacked. Hawke exposed as never before the confrontationalist style, the emotional deficiency and the sheer woodenness of Malcolm Fraser. No other politician in recent years could have run a campaign on reconciliation because the concept refers essentially to the emotional condition of the nation. Only a leader like Hawke, whose relationship with the electorate was deeply emotional, could make such a pitch. It was an approach foreign to Fraser's own experience and one with which he was ill-equipped to deal.

However Hawke's campaign reflected the duality, the ambivalence in his nature. It was both idealistic and cynical. During the campaign, reconciliation was used as a tool with which Hawke could keep open his election options; it was a subtle instrument that would allow him to shift from one policy to another. Reconciliation would be invoked to legitimise such changes. But few people realised that reconciliation would later be used to cancel much of the economic policy on which Hawke went to the nation.

The economic reality of the 1983 campaign is that Fraser had largely embarked on the policy of economic expansion which Hawke and Keating championed. Fraser was always reluctant to admit this because he could never ditch his rhetoric of responsibility and Labor had a vested interest in denying it. Yet it was public knowledge during the campaign that the Government's estimated 1982–83 deficit had risen from the budget figure of $1,674 million to about $4,000 million. This was the result of post-budget spending decisions taken by the Fraser Cabinet and the revenue depressing effects of the recession. On 19 January Treasury wrote Howard a memo critical of the long-proposed National Economic Summit concept but also warning that the deficit for 1983-84 might be double that of 1982–83, that is, about $8,000 million. John Stone, meticulous with memos, and Ted Evans its author certainly remembered this one. But it escaped Howard's attention and he took no action on it.

During the campaign, on 21 February, Howard suggested in a qualified fashion that the deficit for the following year might be about $6,000 million. The significance of any such estimate was that Labor's expansionary programme—with its great danger of inflation—would have to be built on top of such a figure. In retrospect, it is clear that from the campaign start the Government should have promised nothing itself and then released the Treasury $8,000-million figure to destroy the ALP policy.

However it was only on Monday 28 February that Stone met Howard and gave him firm advice that the projected 1983–84 deficit was about $9,000 million. At this meeting the 19 January memo was recalled to Howard's attention. Howard rang Fraser the same day and said the figure should be released; he wanted the Government to 'come clean' and reveal the extent of the economic problem. Howard wanted Fraser to abandon the Government's election promises because of the gravity of the situation. Fraser had no intention of doing anything of the sort. He told his economic adviser Professor Cliff Walsh to convey his refusal to Howard. The Treasurer tried a second time at staff level to persuade Fraser. Again he was rebuffed.

Hawke appeared at the National Press Club just two days later and positioned himself perfectly to exploit the blown-out deficit projections. They were still secret but the Hawke camp had received an excellent tip-off. Hawke specifically warned that if the Fraser Government's budget deficit proved bigger than expected then he reserved the right for an incoming ALP Government to modify its policy. This would be done 'in the light of consensus and understanding reached at the National Economic Summit Conference . . .'.

On Friday 4 March, the day before the election, Stone rang Howard to inform him that the projected 1983–84 deficit was $9,600 million. On the Sunday Stone gave this same figure to Hawke and Keating after their election win the previous day. The outgoing Fraser Government had worked itself into an impossible situation. By saying nothing about the deficit throughout the campaign the Government allowed Hawke to use his vote-buying election promises; but it also gave Hawke the political justification he needed to cancel these promises because he could claim, once elected, that Fraser had covered up the true deficit. Finally by not using the estimated $8,000 million at the start, the Government denied itself the big weapon it needed to nail Hawke as irresponsible, and to transform the political climate. Howard's unsure handling of the issue must rate as one of his greatest mistakes.

The truth about the 1983 campaign is that beneath the contrasting images both Fraser and Hawke were offering very similar policies. Once you adjusted the ALP policy for the deficit 'gap'—as Hawke did post-election—then the differences dramatically diminished. The shift to the right which Hayden had initiated was carried on by Hawke. Probably the sharpest policy difference lay in wages and industrial relations and stemmed from the accord with the unions towards which the ALP had been striving for years. But the intangible factors of hope and optimism cannot be dismissed; Hawke engendered them and Fraser had lost them.

When Eggleton went to Fraser's room the weekend before polling day with survey results showing Hawke still far ahead, the two men had their first and only discussion about defeat. Fraser concluded by saying: 'No matter what happens, I'll never give anybody any impression other than that I expect to win.' He kept his word. When Fraser arrived at the Southern Cross Hotel on election night the magnitude of Hawke's win was just emerging. Fraser was like an old general. He accepted full responsibility for the defeat; he kept back the great chokes of emotion welling up. But after his television statement, walking out with Tamie, Fraser saw his son Mark crying and burst into tears himself. Perhaps he should have wept much earlier in his political life and let the public see more of the man—but that would not have been Fraser.

Hawke's win was of far greater magnitude and likely to prove more enduring than Whitlam's 1972 'It's Time' victory. It was one of the most comprehensive wins for the ALP since Federation. It was a vindication for Hawke himself and also for John Button, whose stance in January was instrumental in Hawke assuming the leadership when he did. The final figures gave Labor a 25-seat majority. In the new House of Representatives Labor held 75 seats compared with 50 for the Coalition. The swing to Labor was an estimated 3.9 per cent on a two-party preferred basis with the ALP polling 53.5 per cent and the Coalition 46.5 per cent. The nationwide result was as follows:

STATE	LABOR	COALITION	SWING TO ALP
NSW	54.4	45.6	4.0
VIC	54.7	45.3	4.0
QLD	49.7	50.3	2.8
SA	53.0	47.0	3.4
WA	55.1	44.9	8.4
TAS	43.0	57.0	−4.1
ACT	66.0	34.0	7.4
NT	51.9	48.1	3.1
TOTAL	53.5	46.5	3.9

Apart from its magnitude the feature of Labor's win was that the swing extended right across the mainland, from Cairns to Melbourne, from Sydney to Perth, in both city and country, among young and old voters. Only Tasmania stood out, isolated against the trend and moving in the opposite direction. The comprehensive nature of this win was also different from 1972, when Whitlam owed his victory to the big city suburbs. Hawke genuinely won Australia and inherited a mandate to govern in the national interest, not for one section only. His superior position, compared with Whitlam in 1972, is revealed below:

ELECTION	LABOR	COALITION	MARGIN
1983	53.5	46.5	Labor 25
1980	49.6	50.4	Coalition 23
1977	45.4	54.6	Coalition 48
1975	44.3	55.7	Coalition 55
1974	51.7	48.3	Labor 5
1972	52.7	47.3	Labor 9

Labor won not just on Hawke's 1983 effort but on Hayden's 1980 success as well. At the last three elections in 1977, 1980 and 1983 the national swing to the ALP was 1.1 per cent, 4.4 per cent and 3.9 per cent which reveals in the 1980–83 period a sustained recovery. Hawke's 1983 swing was the most outstanding because it was built upon a higher plateau of initial support. In 1983, unlike 1980, Labor's gains were at the direct expense of the Liberals as revealed in the table of first preference votes:

	1980	1983
LABOR	45.2	49.5
LIBERAL	37.4	34.4
NATIONAL	8.9	9.2
AUSTRALIAN DEMOCRATS	6.6	5.0
OTHER	1.9	1.2

Labor was very strong in the cities, polling 52.5 per cent of the primary vote compared with 44.4 per cent in the rural seats. Its overall 49.5 per cent primary vote was the highest for the ALP since the election of the Fisher Government in 1914. It is true that, according to the post-election analysis of Malcolm Mackerras, the Coalition needed only a uniform 2.3 per cent swing to regain office but this understates Labor's 53.5 per cent two-party preferred vote and reflects a bias in the electoral system against the ALP. A redistribution is needed before the next election and after that the swing the coalition will need is likely to be very close to four per cent. For a superb campaigner like Bob Hawke, this margin provides a lot of electoral fat and should guarantee Labor a long period of office. There can be no doubt that Hawke's aim is to establish a Labor hegemony at both federal and state level across the nation.

Labor won five seats in NSW, Western Australia and Queensland, six in Victoria, and one in South Australia as well as the Northern Territory seat. Seven of its victories were in rural provincial seats—Calare, Eden–Monaro and Macarthur in NSW, Herbert and Leichhardt in Queensland, Bendigo in Victoria and the Northern Territory seat. Labor came very close to winning Riverina in NSW and turned a number of other rural seats into marginals. All election observers were surprised by the magnitude of Labor's victory in Flinders, where a swing of 6.6 per cent far excelled the meagre by-election result of the previous December. This was a powerful vindication of Hawke's vote-pulling capacity measured against that of Hayden.

The outgoing Fraser Government lost four ministers—Ian Viner, John Hodges, Neil Brown and David Thomson. It also lost many of the members that made up the free-market lobby—John Hyde, Peter Shack, Murray Sainsbury and Ross MacLean. The election terminated not just the Fraser era but many potential ministerial careers. It also guaranteed that Fraser's old rival Andrew Peacock would inherit the mantle. Howard was only ever an outside chance; but Howard lost far more of his supporters at the election than did Peacock. Fraser's demise meant Peacock's rise.

Labor failed to win control of the Senate but significantly increased its position in the Upper House. In the 64-strong chamber Labor's numbers went from 27 to 30. The Coalition fell from 31 to 28 and the Australian Democrats maintained their position at five. Senator Harradine (Tasmania) remained the sole independent. This gave the Australian Democrats the balance of power. However Hawke's position *vis à vis* the Senate was fundamentally different from Whitlam's in 1972. Whitlam faced a hostile Senate prepared to block supply. The Australian Democrats have pledged never to block supply and their leader, Senator Don Chipp, is an open admirer of Hawke. So the Senate will not pose the danger to Hawke that it did to Whitlam—another advantage for Hawke over the 1972 result.

The 1983 election outcome reflected the great resilience of the ALP and its underlying strength. Labor's capacity to run an effective campaign had improved immensely at both state-branch and national level. There is no doubt that Labor's election professionalism exceeded that of the Coalition. The earlier victories in the state elections in Victoria, Western Australia and South Australia were further proof of this. When Hawke won office, the ALP governed in Canberra and four of the six states. The party had recovered in every sense from the debacle of 1975, which had destroyed its electoral standing.

Labor had conducted the most research-orientated campaign in its history. In his post-election report Bob McMullan reported that 'the strategic success of the campaign was largely due to the competent and comprehensive research programme conducted by ANOP'. There is no doubt that Labor's approach was more scientific than that of the Liberals.

In his post-election report, Rod Cameron of ANOP said:

> The survey results suggest that the campaign added a crucial percent to the swing to Labor. They do not suggest, however, that the 1983 campaign was the reason for the ALP victory . . . What emerges as being the campaign's real value is that the campaign represented a concise—albeit frantic—summation of the ALP's communications and marketing strategy and direction since 1979.

The target groups which Labor had identified for so long swung significantly towards the ALP. For the first time in history as many women as men voted for the Labor party. ANOP estimated that 69 per cent of the population aged under 20 and 63 per cent of those aged under 25 voted for the ALP. But Cameron said:

> The real demographic trend that Labor capitalised upon in its victory concerned the much more numerically large middle-aged segment . . . In 1983 the average ALP support in primary terms amongst the 25–44-year-old aged group was 53 per cent—exactly the same as the overall average ALP support in the capital cities . . . In a two-stage process (1980 and 1983) the ALP, federally and in most states, virtually 'owned' middle Australia in political terms.

Cameron estimated that Hawke added one per cent to the ALP vote and the campaign another one per cent. But, viewed in a different light, the Hawke elevation and the campaign merely turned the long-standing theoretical four per cent swing to the ALP into a certainty. Hawke gave the ALP acceptability. He gave the voters the confidence to turn to Labor, to forget its hazards, its ties with the unions and the memories of Whitlam, and gave them the courage to embark upon a new experiment. The electorate had lost its own naivety since the heady days of 1972. It was now worried about its personal security and the nation's future. Hawke offered hope, but reassurance too. The voters saw him as a leader who would make improvements at the margin, but never provoke an upheaval. The messiah was a conservative.

Hawke's win was the final victory for him in the three-way contest involving himself, Fraser and Hayden. In fact, the ghosts of ambition and weakness had haunted the ALP in this 1980–83 period. The party had wanted power, but had known that its lead in the polls had been due to Fraser's negatives, rather than Labor's positives. The Hawke challenge had always danced amongst these doubts. Hawke prevailed against Hayden because the party had lost faith in its ability to win with Hayden. Ambition was ripe, not just because Labor had been in the wilderness for seven years but because the Fraser Government was so obviously exhausted. It had run its course and deserved to be thrown out. The Liberal backbenchers admitted it, the journalists affirmed it and, after the election defeat, so did many of the former Fraser ministers. But Fraser had not been told. The Prime Minister was always utterly confident that he was going to win. So during 1982 Labor was gnashing the teeth of its ambition on the Fraser edifice. Thwarted ambition breeds on itself. The more formidable Fraser loomed, the more he provoked Labor's ambition. The ALP was a hungry party in 1982 and 1983, filled with hungry people. Beneath the ambition lay the central reality: if Labor failed to win the election then what relevance did it possess as a political force? At stake was the validity of the party and the careers of the people in it.

As Fraser's political revival proceeded during 1982 it breathed new life into the Hawke bandwagon. The more Labor worried about Fraser, the more likely it was to take flight to Hawke. Consequently Fraser's strength tended to be directly proportional to that of Hawke. Hayden was stranded in the middle, with Fraser in front of him and Hawke behind, and finally he fell.

The Labor Party's spectacular flight to Hawke was the precursor of the public's embrace of Hawke. By purging the ALP of its self-doubts Hawke gave the party the belief in itself for which it had been searching since Whitlam's departure. This belief grew strong with the party's confidence in electoral victory. In the new Labor Party it was victory not ideas, pragmatism not principle, that were paramount. Fraser was never going to match Hawke on the hustings.

The people were worried about their future, but stubborn in clinging to the notion of the lucky country. Looking upwards they saw in Hawke's idealism the light on the hill which Labor politicians had tried to ignite so often; then, looking even further, beyond the market researchers, they saw themselves reflected in Hawke's caution, and perhaps his cynicism, and knew instinctively they were right. With their home mortgage safe in one hand, Australians moved forward, their money ready in the other hand, to gamble on a winner. They had nothing to lose.

PART 4

EPILOGUE

23

The vanquished

There were seven years and four months between Malcolm Fraser's November 1975 assumption of power and the return of Labor to office under Bob Hawke in March 1983. That period, which began with the eclipse of Whitlam, saw the rise and fall of Fraser and the denial of Bill Hayden by the Labor Party itself. Whitlam, Fraser and Hayden were all vanquished as leaders and each decline closed off a political possibility.

In the 1980s the achievements of the Whitlam Government are easy to forget, even for the Labor Party. This is because policies so controversial before 1972 have been absorbed into the social status quo. In fact the early phase of the Whitlam years evokes nostalgia precisely because it is the most recent and successful period of genuine reform. That Government abolished conscription, terminated the Vietnam commitment, spearheaded equal pay, laid the basis for Aboriginal land rights, moved to apply the needs principle to school funding, created a new consciousness about urban issues, abolished the sales tax on contraceptives, gave a fresh impetus to the arts and cultural expression and signalled to the world a more independent and nationalistic Australia by opening the door to China and closing it on South Africa.

However the Whitlam Government failed—primarily for three reasons, each of which exercised a profound influence upon the post-1975 Labor Party dominated by Hayden and Hawke. The first reason was that the old-generation Whitlam ministers, raised in the stable Menzian age, suddenly had to confront a new world of oil price rises, declining manufacturing industry and stag-flation. The golden programme of Whitlam—equality of opportunity, more power and spending by the federal Government on education, welfare and cities—was overtaken by world recession. It became impossible to give the programme priority over the paramount challenge of economic management, a reality Whitlam recognised but a transition he failed to make. Both Hayden and Hawke were determined to cross this bridge which had defeated Whitlam.

The second reason was that the Labor ministers, the old generation, lacked the professionalism and the skills to handle contemporary Government. Whitlam was the best of them, yet he launched a frenetic reformist rush into terrain so difficult that it ended in electoral oblivion. As leader he failed to weld his ministers into a disciplined team. As a strategist he made fundamental misjudgements—the loans affair, his faith in Sir John Kerr and the Bass by-election being the best examples. Consequently Whitlam's imperiousness and impetuousness established a style which the Hayden–Hawke generation was determined to avoid at all costs.

The third reason was that the Whitlam Government was subjected to a political attack rarely seen before. While Whitlam fumbled with funny money, his opponents responded with constitutional steel. Labor was broken by the Senate, once, then twice. The chilling reality is that in three years the Whitlam Government sought supply six times and on only one of those occasions, autumn 1973, did the Opposition parties not speculate about blocking it. The lesson learnt by the Hayden–Hawke generation was that only a new ruthlessness and professionalism within the ALP could combat the conservatives.

So the 1970s became the broken decade, broken first in 1974 by the world economic downturn, which changed the agenda, style and priorities of politics. But it was broken also by a new temper of anger and turbulence on Australia's political stage, symbolised by the Governor-General's use of the dismissal powers on 11 November 1975. The economic crisis of 1974 was a frontal assault upon Labor ideology, its belief in the full-employment economy and the welfare state. Then the political crisis of 1975 left Labor demoralised, cancelled much of its faith in itself and created a malaise still evident as recently as early 1983.

Yet the origins of the new Hawke Labor Party lie in Whitlam's demise. The Hayden–Hawke generation concluded that Labor must become the party of economic management, fashion a new discipline and professionalism and, finally, aspire to become the majority party in office rather than reformers waiting in the wings.

It was during Whitlam's own Government that the great transition had begun. Eventually one generation surrendered to another. Whitlam, Crean, Cairns, Connor and Cameron were replaced by Hawke, Hayden, Keating,

Button and Dawkins. The forces which moulded these generations bore little similarity to each other. The old Labor leadership was far more influenced by ideology and class struggle; it was riddled with the rancour of Labor's factional warfare in the 1950s and 1960s. Yet it was complacent as a result of the steady economic growth of the post-war years, which it assumed to be automatic. Ultimately this generation lacked political sophistication because of its isolation from the power centres of Australian life and its inadequate understanding of the forces that shaped the nation: the bureaucracy, business and industry, international capital, the media, the opinion-making elites and the basic middle-class yearnings, dominated by aspirations for personal security and opposition to sudden unexplained change. In one sense Neville Wran became the first new-generation Labor leader as he pioneered the politics of recantation just six months after Whitlam's fall. The more Fraser tried to brand the Labor Party with the Whitlam insignia, the more Labor politicians tried to disprove the claim.

The second great influence on the Hayden–Hawke generation was the Fraser Government. Fraser's electoral wins taught the ALP that it had to beat Fraser at his own game, that there was no substitute for policies to control inflation, contain wages, hold down interest rates and thereby create jobs. It was Fraser whose destructive ruthlessness finally put steel into the heart of the Labor Party.

The 1974–83 period, which saw the collapse of Whitlam and the dominance of Fraser, is more likely to be remembered for the destructive energy and Shakespearian drama of its power struggles than for the creative output and policy advances of its Governments. The decade became an orgy of spectator satisfaction; it was manna for the media, the political reporters and the Canberra lobbyists. The media, notably television, dominated and manipulated the politicians, creating false images and phoney realities for the public, thereby ensuring that only politicians who were media manipulators themselves would survive. The irony of the decade is that so much blood was spilt, so many conventions were torn up, so many institutions were damaged for personal advancement, so many promising careers were prematurely checked or terminated, so many leadership challenges were launched, so many resignations and sackings were forced. There was such political excess for so little genuine policy gain. Towards the end of the Fraser years Canberra was an exhausted city. The political system was run down. The parliamentary system, its flaws exposed in 1975, remained compromised. The public service was more demoralised and disheartened than it had been for many years. Consequently, the Hayden–Hawke generation grew more worldy and cynical and Labor lost much of its reformist naivety.

The magnitude of the failure during the decade is great because the two dominant figures of the time—Whitlam and Fraser—were convinced that their leadership could make the system work for the people. Fraser's words in January 1975, when he was plotting for the Liberal leadership, captured this apparently unquenchable confidence: 'I do not believe that men and women are governed by inexorable events beyond their control. When political leaders say the present situation cannot be helped, it is part of a world situation, they are expressing the futility of their own leadership when, if they were men of real stature, they would be saying "We can overcome".' Sadly neither Whitlam nor Fraser *did* overcome in this sense. These men, so different in style, temperament and substance, were united in their concept of the leadership ethic, in their conviction that they would build monuments and change history, and finally, in their defeat by social and economic forces.

Nonetheless Australia was transformed during this period. But the real change took place outside and around Canberra. Australia became a more confident, tolerant, multicultural society, more internationally aware, self-critical and energetic. Sometimes post-1974, always too fleetingly, the politicians captured the public mood or moulded it, and turned popular feeling into executive or legislative form. More often the politicians were uncertain of where to go, and then, when they knew, frightened to take the bold action and tough options the crisis demanded.

There are two almost inevitable judgements on the Fraser Government. The first is that it was successful in terms of conventional achievement. The second is that Fraser squandered his immense political opportunities. Fraser was a very good Prime Minister, much better than people would have suspected in 1975. He ran a Government of above-average competence, by Australian standards, with acumen, dedication and professionalism. He learnt enormously as his Government ran its course and he made many genuine achievements and much steady progress in the fields of foreign affairs, defence, the environment and national development. His economic policy was remarkably consistent over the first six difficult years with moderate economic growth in the 1977–81 period when inflation was significantly lowered, more than 500,000 jobs were created and confidence was restored to the community.

He was never a monetarist, never a Margaret Thatcher. When Thatcher became British Prime Minister he advised her to tackle the big issues and take the tough decisions at the start—advice he had not followed himself. In fact Fraser brought a blend of ideology and realism to bear on almost every issue. When Fraser had to be pragmatic, he normally was and where dogmatism was required, he could provide it. He was a complicated man and applied his complicated personality to the issues of Government. But throughout he displayed a political nous and reading of the electorate second to none. Despite his rhetoric of sacrifice, Fraser did not take many unpopular decisions.

Fraser was both a traditionalist and a radical in terms of Liberal Party orthodoxy. His radicalism was significant and, in certain areas, carried the party some of the way from reaction towards enlightenment. Fraser supported Aboriginal land rights in the Northern Territory. He showed a commitment to the preservation of the environment in protecting Fraser Island by use of the Commonwealth export powers. Overseas Fraser supported the South in the North–South dialogue over international economic issues, assisted significantly in the creation of an independent Zimbabwe under a Marxist leader and became a comrade with black African leaders against South Africa's apartheid. But Fraser's most significant stand for the Liberal Party was his final embrace of John Howard's policies on the bottom-of-the-harbour tax legislation. This was a confrontation which went to the core of the party's identity. It juxtaposed Fraser's conception of the Liberals as the party of national interest against its 'new money' wing, which defended its sectional interest.

As a Liberal traditionalist Fraser's two most historic decisions were his off-shore constitutional settlement, and his refusal to interfere in the Gordon-below-Franklin dam dispute. Both were actions in support of state's rights. Fraser turned the clock back from the High Court seabed decision to re-establish state power and ownership over the territorial sea. But because the High Court upheld the Hawke Government's use of its power to stop the Franklin dam, history will record Fraser's refusal to act in this matter as a failure of will and a subjugation to tradition for tradition's sake. Finally Fraser tried to implement his 'new federalism' and hand taxation powers back to the states, but the states were not interested.

Fraser made no secret of the fact that Menzies was his chief influence, but he shunned Menzies' obsequious attitude to the British. Fraser's Oxford experience turned him into an Australian nationalist. He saw Britain as part of the decaying old world while Australia was the new world. Overseas Fraser was always the nationalist. He believed in America, not just to help Australia, but in a global sense as the rock upon which the Western alliance inevitably rested.

The second judgement of Fraser is rooted in the pessimism of the Australian people and the profound nature of the problems that are his legacy. Australia was in a deeper crisis in March 1983, when Fraser lost office, than it was in November 1975, when he assumed office. In 1983 the long-term employment crisis facing Australian youth and breadwinners, the lack of any economic growth, strategy, the growing inefficiency of industry caught between technological change overseas and an obsolete cost structure at home, the rapid change in world trading patterns, the decline of our educational institutions, the deepening inequalities in the nation, were problems of a greater dimension than before. Ultimately the problems lay in the structural obstacles to change and the social attitudes underpinning those obstacles. In the meantime nations rise and fall more quickly than ever as economic entities—but Australia is a ship without a course on the ocean of the world economy, relying upon periodic waves for its ride and becalmed without them. The question becomes: what fundamental change did Fraser bring? Or, to what purpose did he use the power which he acquired in 1975 so ruthlessly, with such righteous justification?

The answer is that very little has changed fundamentally and the reason is that Fraser, for all his radicalism, was a conventional politician. He fell victim to his own political skills. Fraser was too clever a political animal, too shrewd a judge of the electorate and too smart to alienate the voters. The first major weakness in Fraser as Prime Minister was his caution. At first this claim seems absurd, since Fraser appeared the companion of audacity and sometimes the cousin to recklessness. But stumbling through Fraser's record is like a stroll through a mirror maze. Things are not what they first appear, just as Fraser was rarely as radical in practice as he pretended to be in rhetoric. Fraser's caution was integral to his political and electoral success. But the gap between what he did and what he could have done is a yawning chasm on the political landscape. Fraser had a political mandate in 1975 so comprehensive it is not likely to be reproduced in Australia for decades.

Fraser's other major weakness was that he misperceived the essence of the economic problem and, when this was corrected, he avoided tackling the causes, preferring to concentrate on the symptoms. Fraser's failures lie in most areas of major public policy. Fraser was elected as possibly the most protectionist Prime Minister for a generation and only in the second half of his prime ministership did he realise the damage his protectionist approach had done in his first half. But it was never rectified because politics came first. In the area of industrial relations Fraser's energies overflowed into futile dramas as he strove to transfer power from unions back to employers through a network of repressive laws and regulations, apparently forgetting that these legalisms would flounder on marketplace power. On the critical issue of wages policy, Fraser's compulsion to confrontation made any viable trade-off or accord with the trade union movement impossible. The Government relied instead upon kicking the Arbitration Commission to get partial wage indexation; then it used high unemployment as a disincentive for unions to claim higher wages.

Fraser's deficit reduction was achieved more through tax rises than spending cuts. The increase in the tax burden fell almost entirely on personal income-tax payers—the very people Fraser was going to liberate in his 1975 programme. In the period from 1972–73 to 1981–82 personal income-tax collections as a proportion of GDP rose from 9.5 per cent to 14.3 per cent. The other significant boost to revenue came from the Fraser Government's crude-oil levy. In the Fraser years total federal tax receipts rose from 25.1 per cent of GDP in 1975–76 to an estimated 27.5 per cent in 1981–82.

Fraser learnt that there is only scope for permanent tax cuts according to the spending reductions Government is prepared to make. Moreover, contrary to conventional wisdom, in the early Fraser years the Government was not confident that there would be political support for the ruthless cuts in spending needed to finance such tax cuts. People will object when public services and Government infrastructure, upon which they depend, are slashed. If economic growth had been greater in the Fraser years then, given the restraint it achieved in Government spending, there would have been a surplus for genuine tax cuts. But growth was not great enough.

Fraser was neither an innovator nor an inspirational leader. Only after losing office did he bemoan Australia's failure to keep pace with technologi-cal advances and the information revolution. He never seemed to realise the extent of the rundown in public sector resources and manpower over which he presided. Fraser's own limited personality meant he could never persuade the nation against its prejudices. He was a social conservative who had little understanding of and no sympathy for the new social forces changing the traditional family structure.

The one great idea which Fraser conveyed—by rote rather than gripping oratory—was the need to 'fight inflation first'. Assisted by the Whitlam legacy Fraser secured public support for at least some belt-tightening policies. This was a significant achievement and for a time inflation was reduced as private sector growth took off. For the first six years Fraser kept the growth of public spending to under an average annual increase in real terms of 1.5 per cent. This was a considerable, probably a great managerial achievement as Fraser's successors will discover. But Fraser failed to keep monetary policy sufficiently tight to achieve his anti-inflationary objectives. He was always prepared to compromise the fight against inflation for other political goals such as tax relief, resources development or lower interest rates. Squeezing the public sector to promote private sector recovery eventually foundered because Fraser was not prepared to adhere to the strategy when unemployment reached a new plateau in 1982. Fraser's lurch towards Keynesian economics and an expanded public sector at this time merely revealed his lack of a long-term viable growth strategy.

It is difficult not to conclude that Fraser ran from the big structural issues that shaped Australian politics and society because he feared they were just too hard to handle. He preferred to shelter behind his House of Representatives and Senate majorities, deceiving himself into thinking he was a man of action and history when all the time he was a very clever, pragmatic but ultimately conventional politician. For too long his rhetoric of sacrifice and his reputation as a political giant-killer of men obscured his immersion in the problems of today and not tomorrow. At a policy level his was merely a shadow of the audacity displayed by Whitlam; but where Whitlam was cavalier, Fraser was careful. Hence Fraser survived for far longer. The Fraser years were a unique opportunity for Government to grapple with the big issues, but the judgement of time is likely to be that of an opportunity lost.

The feature of the Hayden–Hawke generation is that it responded to Fraser, not by lapsing into introspection and clinging to its ideology, but by looking outward to the community and adapting itself to the demands of the electorate.

Labor maintained itself as a broad coalition keeping its union base and its left wing, but moving decisively to the right. Finding its ideology under attack, Labor cloaked itself in pragmatism. Responding to the ruthlessness of Fraser Labor became more ruthless. Labor parties around the nation deposed old leaders and voted in new ones—in NSW, Victoria, Queensland, Western Australia and, finally, Canberra. The party's factions, once seen as bulwarks of old-fashioned politics, were the instrument used to tie Labor to moderate policies and to promote new leaders. The centre-right forces established a dominance inside the party. A new breed of party professionals brought to the Labor organisation political and campaign skills superior to those of their Liberal counterparts. All this took Labor in early 1983 to the brink of victory. Yet the very nature of the new ALP demanded success against Fraser and Labor knew that the essence of success in Australia's media-dominated political system was leadership. When Hayden faltered, Labor went to Hawke.

The source of Hayden's dilemmas as a leader lay in his own personality. Hayden eventually failed because he could not overcome the habits of suspicion, distrust and stubborn loneliness which he had absorbed as a youth. These lost him the support of friends, turned potential allies into enemies and led him to make fatal misjudgements. Many reasons have been advanced for Hayden's failure, but the ultimate cause was not either of his chief antagonists, Fraser and Hawke, but Hayden himself.

Hayden failed to sustain his best performances and build upon them. His inner flaw would always reassert itself. The man who distrusts everybody does so because of his own lack of confidence. Suspicion becomes a conduit for self-doubt; and self-doubt is a plague on the authority of any leader.

The tragedy is that Hayden was an admirable man with many qualities unusual in politics. He was a leader who never lost his humility, an economic rationalist who remembered that the statistics represented people and a realist who believed in the labyrinthine maze of Caucus committees and techniques of party dialogue. He was an ordinary bloke with a contempt for pretension who dressed like a former Queensland policeman and helped his kids with their homework, a politician who stayed receptive to new ideas and, finally, a man whose deficient ego would never permit him to identify irrevocably his personal ambitions with Labor's interests. Hayden had the combination of intelligence and integrity which attracted many of the 'new breed' of ALP politicians. His vulnerabilities were so exposed that his friends felt compelled to become his protectors. Hayden's fragility inspired advocates everywhere.

Parallels between Hayden and John Curtin, frequently drawn in the 1979–81 period, originated in this curious package of characteristics. Both men were subject to the accusation that they lacked the toughness to lead; both suffered self-doubt when facing the challenge of reconciling Labor principles to a harsh reality. Curtin prevailed and became sanctified in Labor's annals. Hayden would have prevailed had not the external pressures on him from Fraser and Hawke been so great. But at the top level of political leadership one must expect great pressures. Hayden failed in the personal sense in that he did not become Prime Minister; but his five-year leadership was a success, not a failure, for the Labor Party.

Hayden's leadership record shows he was a great servant of the Labor Party. All the major decisions he took about the party's direction and shape were the right ones: federal intervention in Queensland and Tasmania, the ALP–ACTU prices–incomes accord, the broadening of the National Conference, insistence on the doctrine of economic responsibility and then realism in Labor's uranium platform. It is easy to underestimate Hayden's achievements and to forget that he was the principal architect and builder of the bridge that spanned the river of Opposition between the Governments of Whitlam and Hawke. His mistakes lay not in what he did but in what he failed to do.

In a personal sense Hayden's tragedy is that he became a victim of the quest for power. Leadership comes from the core of a man. Hayden read books about power hoping to discern its secret; but power was more elusive than the theory of international economics. It was not to be found within the pages of *The Economist*, *The Guardian Weekly*, *The New York Review of Books* or *The Kennedy Imprisonment* by Gary Willis. Hayden surrendered much in his own make-up to the search for power but found his goal too elusive.

The Hayden–Hawke generation prevailed and returned to office a very different Labor Party from that which had failed under Whitlam. But Hayden fell victim to the very changes he had championed. Out of the broken decade of the 1970s and the public's disillusionment with the political process Hawke emerged as a saviour for the disenchanted. The vanquished leaderships of Whitlam, Fraser and Hayden provided a foundation for the Hawke ascendancy.

24
The victor

As 1983 unfolded, Bob Hawke demonstrated that he was a Prime Minister of both longevity and substance. The untested leader graduated to become a formidable Prime Minister. The expectation that the magnitude of Hawke's election victory would guarantee at least a two-term ALP Government was reinforced by the authority and skill Hawke displayed in office. When John Button switched his leadership support in January 1983 it was because he had always been confident that Hawke would deliver office. But Button wrote in his famous letter to Hayden that 'even some of Bob's closest supporters have doubts about his capacities to lead the party successfully'. After six months of Government Button was the first to admit that Hawke's prime ministerial performance was better than most of his closest colleagues had ever imagined.

Hawke set the political tone and strategic direction of his Government. In office he established a presidential one-to-one communication with the electorate. Other ministers, of course, were seen. But Hawke became THE symbol and communicator. From the start Hawke was a very political Prime Minister, since his tastes were for salesmanship despite his long hours at both administration and the desk. Six months after winning power his personal approval rating hit 70 per cent; in 1984 it stabilised above this level—an unprecedented result. Hawke appeared as both a strong leader and an ordinary bloke. He impressed the Prince of Wales and President Reagan and then went to football grand finals and the Royal Perth Yacht Club to celebrate Australia's win in the America's Cup.

Bob and Hazel settled easily into The Lodge and repudiated Fraser's remark that it was an inadequate residence. The Secretary of the Prime Minister's Department, Sir Geoffrey Yeend, was retained and he became a subtle tutor in the art of prime ministership. Hawke remained without pretension. He was still 'Bob' to many friends or 'PM' to those who felt that some deference to the office was required. Hawke became a grandfather, saw more of his wife, knuckled down to a grinding workload and became even thinner and trimmer; but within months the strain on him was betrayed as his thick mane greyed and the lines in his face deepened into crevices.

Yet his relative youth and his fighting instinct made him an aggressive Prime Minister, merciless with the Opposition and censorious of his colleagues' mistakes. Hawke was determined to stay on top. He rejoiced in the realisation of his destiny, yet possessed the maturity to curb the excesses of power. A clever PM, he mastered his brief and relied on common sense. The public service came to him as the agenda of business unfolded. Hawke signed letters and dispatched papers promptly; there was none of the agony of indecision that gripped Fraser. Only rarely, perhaps too rarely, did Hawke throw back the advice. But he was measuring and assessing always. This was a cautious Prime Minister determined to entrench himself for years.

Lacking the interest in policy detail possessed by Whitlam and Fraser, Hawke delegated to his ministers and focused on the central direction. Having delegated, he was receptive to ministerial initiative. On non-vote-switching issues Hawke had a fairly open mind which meant more scope than expected for ministerial autonomy and reform under his Government. He would listen, counsel and advise. Hawke was a superb chairman of Cabinet, controlling the meeting, giving direction to the discussion. But he insisted upon ministerial solidarity and discipline—a major advance on the Whitlam years. Indeed in the first fortnight of office Hawke had secured two seminal changes. Firstly the Caucus agreed to a 13-strong Cabinet selected by the Prime Minister. This meant a significant centralisation of power and enhanced authority for the Prime Minister. Secondly Cabinet agreed at its first meeting on the solidarity principle, which meant that ministers would support Cabinet decisions in Caucus and not attempt to overthrow them. This was a far-reaching advance for Cabinet authority in the teeth of Caucus sovereignty.

The Cabinet, the engine room of Government, to begin with comprised Hawke, Bowen as Trade Minister, Button in Industry and Commerce, Grimes as Social Security Minister, Willis in Employment and Industrial Relations, Keating as Treasurer, Young as Special Minister of State, Stewart West in Immigration, Peter Walsh as Resources Minister, Bill Hayden in Foreign Affairs, Susan Ryan as Education Minister, Evans as Attorney-General and

Gordon Scholes as Defence Minister. John Dawkins as Finance Minister joined Cabinet later.

The tone of this original Cabinet was moderate and pragmatic. It was completely dominated by the right wing and the centre group. The only fully fledged left-wing minister was West. Outside the Cabinet the left was consigned to junior ministries—Uren in Territories, Brian Howe in Defence Support and Arthur Gietzelt in Veterans' Affairs. So the left was far weaker than in the Whitlam Ministry. Significantly the old Hayden centre group was very strong, notably in the Cabinet. Button's objective had been achieved. The centre had made a successful transition from Hayden to Hawke. The proof of this was their Cabinet positions—those of Button, Walsh, Dawkins and Hayden himself—and their junior ministers, John Kerin in Primary Industry, Barry Jones in Science and Technology, Neal Blewett in Health and Michael Duffy in Communications. Yet Button's defection had left a legacy of suspicion towards him; the Button–Hayden rift split and weakened the centre.

The dominant group, however, was the right and it had an obvious NSW leaning. The process was not apparent until mid-year but the key power-relationship in the Cabinet would become the Prime Minister–Treasurer, Hawke–Keating axis, expressed in the direction of economic policy. Other right-wing or centre-unity ministers included Evans in Cabinet and then Kim Beazley in Aviation, Chris Hurford in Housing, Clyde Holding in Aboriginal Affairs, John Brown in Sport and Tourism and Barry Cohen in Environment. The Cabinet itself was not over-endowed with right-wingers, but Hawke and Keating were a powerful alliance. Initially Mick Young operated as an intimate political adviser to Hawke.

Lionel Bowen as deputy was in a unique position, alienated from the old Hayden group yet never a confidant of the Hawke camp. But Bowen's presence, like that of Lynch in the Fraser Government, was essential for stability. Two days after the election Hayden met his centre group to canvass the Walsh–Dawkins strategy devised when he had resigned the leadership—the contesting of the deputy's post. Hayden appeared keen to run; Button was opposed. Hayden could rely upon left-centre votes but he felt constrained to seek Hawke's acquiescence in any move. Hayden saw Hawke five days after the poll. It was a subtle battle in psychology, since Hayden was inevitably relying upon Labor's collective guilt over the leadership issue. And surely such guilt must have lain heavy on the new Prime Minister! But Hawke stayed firm; Hayden never ran and Bowen remained deputy. In fact a Hawke–Hayden team would have defied human emotions and made for conflict.

Within the Caucus a similar breakdown of forces prevailed between right, centre and left. The left, which met as a faction, was the most organised and hence clearly identified. It had about 35 votes out of 105. That is, with right-centre support, Hawke had a majority. But the Hawke Caucus was notable for the entry into Parliament of two outstanding faction organisers, Graham Richardson from the right, the biggest faction, and Gerry Hand from the left. These men quickly became the tactical bosses and numbers men.

Richardson brought to the Caucus all his Irish-Catholic humour, cunning and ruthlessness from his days as NSW Secretary. He wielded an influence far beyond that attached to his backbench position and became more valuable to Hawke than were some ministers. Richardson played a significant part in making Hawke ALP leader and never hesitated to adopt this as a benchmark for their relations. The combination of Keating as Treasurer, Richardson as organiser and Peter Barron as Hawke's adviser gave the NSW right a high and dominant profile.

Hand as the left's organiser faced a trinity of difficulties. The left lacked sufficient numerical support, did not possess leadership personalities to carry either the party or the public and had played no role in the Hawke ascension. In the opening months of the Government it battled to stay a viable force.

Hawke did not hesitate to discipline his ministers—Evans and Scholes for the RAAF flights over Tasmania that had photographed the Gordon-below-Franklin dam site, Brown for criticising the tourist pull of koalas, West for calling for higher wages and, of course, Mick Young. But the acid test of Hawke's disciplinary code came during the emotional debate in November 1983 over uranium. Stewart West, caught between his loyalty to Cabinet on one hand and to the anti-uranium mass movement on the other, sought a dispensation from Cabinet solidarity. Hawke refused. The left took a collective decision and West resigned from Cabinet in order to take an anti-uranium stance in the Caucus. So the left sacrificed its only Cabinet place for its ideological purity.

Hawke had a more measured and less frenetic approach to Government than Fraser. In terms of executive management he reverted to tradition, almost in the Menzies mould. Ministers had their own responsibilities. Treasurer Keating and the Treasury resumed primary control over economic policy, a break from the hijacking of policy pioneered by the Prime Minister's Department under Fraser. Indeed under Hawke the resources of his own department were neither fully utilised nor sufficiently tested. The result was that the quality of the Prime Minister's Department began to deteriorate. Hawke, unlike Fraser, did not demand an alternative view on every issue and lacked Fraser's policy curiosity or administrative drive.

Hawke's great political achievement was to capture that balance between reform and reassurance, innovation and tradition. Herein lay Hawke's genius. He encamped squarely in the middle of Australian politics and constructed a coalition spanning business on the right and the unions on the left. Hawke represented an historic shift of policy and change of ideology for the ALP. As Prime Minister he put into practice the idea of 'consensus' which became a strategy of middle-ground politics. The old Labor Party aligned itself with labour against capital; indeed this was the very rationale for its existence. But Hawke stood this conflict on its head and argued instead for the mutual interests of labour and capital.

During 1983 Hawke succeeded in putting the strategy into place. The key to this duality lay in economic policy. The Government succeeded at home and abroad in cultivating the business and financial community and winning its confidence. Simultaneously it used its ties with the trade union movement to fashion an effective wages policy, a fundamental requirement for sound economic management. On the one hand, the 1983–84 budget deficit of $8,400 million was accepted in financial markets amid a regime of falling interest rates; on the other, the Arbitration Commission and most of the union movement accepted the return to wage indexation and the loss of real wages implicit in the wage pause.

Hawke was very lucky that a favourable environment maximised his audacious ability to construct this remarkable coalition. Fraser had inadvertently picked the trough of the downturn for his election. So Hawke enjoyed the seeds and then the fruits of gradual economic recovery. Employment began to pick up; exports rose, partly due to the gathering momentum of international recovery but also to the breaking of the drought. The countryside was rich and record harvests were produced. The pent-up benefit of Fraser's wage pause was revealed in a falling inflation rate and signs that Australia was beginning to bridge the gap formed by its international uncompetitiveness. Most significantly the lack of private enterprise activity ensured that, as the demand for money fell, so did interest rates. The confidence of Hawke's first year can only be understood in the light of cheaper money, which was the equivalent of a big tax cut for most home owners. Hawke harnessed such optimism to the chariot wheels of his Government.

It was precisely because Hawke's style and substance contrasted with the earlier prime ministerial models of Whitlam and Fraser that confusion abounded in interpretations of his Government. More than either of his predecessors Hawke appealed to, and identified with, mainstream Australia. This is authentic and uncontrived, and sometimes unattractive, because Hawke's own nature and inclinations are so absolutely mainstream. In the political spectrum Bob Hawke is positioned dead centre.

Hawke's political skills were revealed when the platform on which he was elected was cancelled the very day, 6 March, after the election. Treasury Chief John Stone told Hawke and Keating on that day of the $9,600-million deficit estimate for 1983–84 and of the extent of capital outflow. It was a fateful day. These early meetings sowed the seeds for an immediate 10 per cent devaluation, the survival of Stone himself and the abandonment of the campaign programme, notably the tax cuts. Hawke used the $9,600-million deficit figure to establish the political conditions under which he could throw his entire campaign package into the melting pot and start again. His ploy was successful; it was accepted by the community, rather than perceived as an act of slick cynicism. The financial community was impressed and recognised Hawke as a realist. Perhaps the lesson to be learnt is that the voters had been motivated not by Labor's promises but by confidence in Hawke himself.

Hawke's skill as a contemporary politician was revealed during the National Economic Summit. Its enduring value was that Hawke used the meeting to create the psychological climate for his middle-ground politics. He did this as effectively as a competent magician who holds his audience spellbound. Only months later did Hawke's real achievement at the summit become obvious. The financial community had been purged of its inflationary expectations. The combination of economic trends and Hawke psychology had convinced the market that inflation was being beaten. This perception was both domestic and international. A survey of portfolio managers conducted by the Syntec economic group in spring 1983, when inflation was 11.5 per cent, showed the majority expected inflation to average no more than 8.5 per cent over the next five years. This Labor Government had turned normal expectations upside down.

The other historic role for the Summit was to introduce into policy the innovatory ALP–ACTU prices–incomes accord. The accord was designed to stop a wage explosion during an economic upturn. It would work by unions staying within the centralised wages system and, during the early phase of recovery, taking less money than was available through bargaining in the marketplace. The trade-off for this restraint was that during recessions the unions would obtain from the centralised system higher wages than they could win from the market.

It was at the Summit that the real dimensions of Australia's unemployment crisis were illustrated for the entire community. The average levels of jobless during the three years before Labor won office were 5.8 per cent, 6.2 per cent and 8.9 per cent, the latter being the 1982–83 figure. The projections at the Summit for the first three years of Labor Government—under the wages outcome which the accord would produce—were 10.0 per cent,

10.1 per cent and 9.7 per cent. That is, after the first full term under Hawke the predicted result from the preferred policy was that unemployment increases might only be checked. This outcome also envisaged the creation of about 450,000 new jobs, which would be needed to absorb new entrants into the workforce and prevent any further percentage increase in the jobless. It was a sobering picture.

The Summit was presented with inflation and unemployment projections under three wage outcomes—a high-wage scenario, medium-wage scenario (the accord option) and low-wage scenario. The depressing but bracing conclusion for the trade unions was that the three-year outcome which most effectively produced low inflation and low unemployment was the low-wage option. This caused the late chief of the Hooker Corporation, Sir Keith Campbell, to dramatise the situation by calling for a complete clamp on wages and salaries 'if we genuinely care about the jobless and we genuinely wish to incur discipline and sacrifice'.

However it was obvious that Hawke would not accept the low-wage scenario even though it was best for inflation and unemployment. Why was this? Hawke's old friend and employers' representative George Polites knew. He told the meeting with an air of lament that the low-wage option was 'beyond the limits of consensus available at this conference'. In short the wages sacrifice it would demand of the trade unions, representing the 90 per cent employed, in order to create more jobs to help the 10 per cent unemployed was just too great. The Government was remarkably honest in presenting to the Summit and the public these options. They exposed the heart of the prices–incomes accord and the true challenge facing Hawke as the architect of consensus.

The accord is based upon mutual trust which in turn means mutual vulnerability. Its endorsement by the Arbitration Commission in October 1983 gave workers a 4.3 per cent rise based on consumer price index movements. More than 99 per cent of unions gave a written promise to the Commission to forgo any extra demands. Despite sceptics within business the accord held together throughout the period of the first Hawke Government. This was despite some very low, even negative cpi results, due to the effect of the new Medicare health insurance scheme. During 1984 the March and June quarter cpi outcomes were 0.4 per cent and 0.2 per cent respectively. There was no national wage rise for this six months. This meant not only rapidly falling inflation but a controlled emergence from the Fraser Government's wage pause without any pent-up wages breakout.

Both Hawke and Keating told the unions that without the accord the Government would have to revert to orthodox fiscal and monetary tools—

the Fraser approach. That is, Labor would end its efforts to work simultaneously against both inflation and unemployment. Fundamental to the accord was a new approach to Government decision-making in which the unions through the ACTU were taken into the inner councils. The key ACTU officials were Secretary Kelty and Vice-President Crean and these men were akin to ministers without portfolio. They had dual roles as leaders of the trade union movement and generals working with Hawke to maintain the progress of the accord. The more the union movement complied with the orchestrated decisions of the Arbitration Commission the more the authority of the ACTU grew within that movement. The new Government decision-making procedure inaugurated at the Summit was given expression through the setting up of the Economic Planning Advisory Council. Initially business was flattered by its participation on EPAC; but it soon realised that the influence bestowed upon the trade unions was greater.

As 1983 turned into 1984 Hawke's success in entrenching the accord became apparent. The trade union connection which was important in his rise to power became even more important in his use of that power. The paradox of the accord is that it was accepted by unions as a legitimate means of obtaining long-term gains and by business as offering the best avenue to limiting excessive wage costs. The reconciliation of this apparent contradiction was made much easier because Hawke was operating in an environment of economic recovery after a wages pause.

The accord embodied the notion of Bob Hawke as the political fixer. In order to win trade union compliance for moderate wage rises, concessions were made elsewhere to the unions. Costs boomed in the non-wage area—long service leave, workers' compensation, occupational safety and superannuation. In the 1984–45 budget personal income tax cuts worth $1,300 million were explained by the Government as a substitute wage rise for the loss of any late 1984 national wage case. At the same time Kelty foreshadowed that the next major demand by the unions for accord compliance would be Government and employer moves towards a national superannuation scheme. As a result of Hawke's success the real analytical question about the accord became not how long it would survive but, rather, what price the Government would pay to ensure that survival. The Government was able to afford that price in 1983 and 1984 but this was primarily because of the economic pickup.

The accord put the trade union movement in an historic dilemma. While Hawke and Keating recognised that a market system for determining wages was more efficient in theory, they believed the best result in practice was to work through arbitration which is the deeply entrenched Australian system. The question is: if Hawke cannot get this system to work then who can? Any failure of the accord will vindicate the free-market decentralised wages policy advocated by John Howard. The choice for the unions is to scuttle the accord for short-term gain and vindicate the arguments of the Liberal Party right wing or, alternatively, adhere to the system. Certainly the unions chose adherence in 1983 and 1984, thereby allowing Hawke to enter his re-election campaign as the apostle of consensus. Contrary to the views of many critics, Hawke had given consensus genuine meaning through the accord. In political terms it highlighted the contrast between Labor's style of cooperative Government and the confrontationist stamp which still tainted the Liberals. Finally consensus gave the Hawke Government an aura of authority which stemmed from its apparent control over events. The ultimate test is whether Hawke's consensus becomes a powerful political tool to facilitate national progress or merely another antidote to lull Australia into accepting economic mediocrity.

The most critical economic debate in Hawke's first term came at the very start. It occurred in the Cabinet pre-Summit and in the party post-Summit. The issue was the degree of expansion in the first Keating budget. After all, the rationale for the accord was to allow for an expansionary economic policy to create jobs. The expansionist forces were led by Ralph Willis who had the backing of the left and the Victorian Government push, including Premier Cain and Treasurer Rob Jolly, along with the Melbourne Institute of Applied Economic and Social Research and sections of the Melbourne *Age*. There was a sharp exchange in Cabinet between Keating and Willis before the Summit. But the Treasurer prevailed with help from Hawke and, significantly, Hayden, who had returned to hard-headed economics now he was no longer leader and dependent upon left votes.

The critical factor for macroeconomic policy in 1983 and for the character of the Hawke Government was the transformation of Paul Keating from a tentative, unsteady Treasurer into the most dominant of Hawke's ministers. In the early days after the election Keating had confessed to Hawke his doubts whether he could handle the portfolio. He retained the ideological John Stone as Treasury Secretary and endured months of criticism for being Stone's puppet. The bureaucrat so long marked for extinction by the ALP became its principal adviser. But by mid-1983 the maturing of Keating in the post was discernible.

During the winter recess Hawke went overseas and insisted that Keating join him; so did Stone. The time Hawke and Keating spent together at the White House, on the VIP plane, and in top-level financial talks bred a personal friendship and chemistry between these two pragmatists. Moreover it restored Keating's confidence in himself, which had taken such a battering since March as he struggled, without administrative experience and without a theoretical economic position, to handle the Treasury. The Hawke–Keating alliance was sealed on this trip and became the power instrument in the Government which defined economic policy. Significantly it was Keating who put the steel into Hawke and persuaded him that the expansionist push had to be turned back whenever it arose.

The trip also brought to a brief high the Keating–Stone relationship. It is true that Treasury exercised a great influence over its minister; it always does. But the media had missed the story. The Government had not succumbed to Treasury policies; the story was that Treasury, for once, was working for the Labor Party and not against it. It is true that Treasury remained sceptical about Labor and felt its ministers would probably lose their economic nerve in 1984, but political psychology nonetheless meant that Treasury looked towards its new masters with more enthusiasm than past practice would suggest. There were three reasons for this. Treasury was utterly relieved to be rid of Howard, with whom its relations had collapsed; Stone relished his deliverance from execution; and Keating's direct and forceful personality was the right ingredient to combine with Stone and his senior officers and establish a significant rapport.

The August budget was largely a holding operation within parameters already determined. The reshaping of spending priorities was modest; the implementation of Labor reform restrained; the political damage minimal. The Government had pruned the sectional tax rorts offered by Fraser and thereby generated funds for community works and housing in order to create jobs. But it reached the $8,400-million deficit partly through indirect tax rises—the easy road. Finally Hawke and Keating had defeated a strong Cabinet push to impose an income tax surcharge on incomes of more than $25,000 a year. It was a cautious and well-received budget. The left claimed it was too restrictive; Stone in the budget papers warned it was too expansionist. In fact the budget provided a definite stimulus to a very depressed economy.

However, the seminal economic decision came on 12 December when Keating announced the float of the dollar. This was a fundamental and irrevocable break from the ALP tradition of economic regulation. It marked Keating's coming of age as Treasurer since the float was anathema to both Stone and the Labor Caucus. It paved the way for deregulation of the financial system and the entry of foreign banks. It gave Keating the mantle of independence and made him the darling of the financial community. It stunned the Liberal Party and in particular John Howard, who had wanted to float the dollar but had scarcely put it as a serious proposition to the Fraser Cabinet, which suddenly appeared as far too regulatory. The float was a circuit-breaking decision which changed not just perceptions of the Hawke Government but the environment of politics.

Keating's strategy was to expose Australia to the deflationary impact of overseas forces. Implicit in his action was the belief that the Labor Government had to display fiscal restraint and monetary orthodoxy. The exchange rate no longer existed as a policy tool but reflected the strength of the economy and responsibility of the federal Government. Here was the conclusive proof that the Hawke–Keating priority was economic management competence, not the big-spending reform programmes of former Labor Governments.

The Treasurer had educated first Hawke and then other senior ministers to the float. The decision sailed smoothly through the Cabinet. Like other currency issues it was never referred to Caucus beforehand. Stone's hostility to free-floating exchange rates was well known. But his views were shared neither in the Reserve Bank, the Prime Minister's Department nor other senior Treasury ranks. The float signalled the beginning of the end for Stone. It revealed that Keating had outmanoeuvred Stone by establishing strong contact with the line of first assistant secretaries beneath him. The contrast in ministerial style between Keating and Howard was highlighted. Howard had kept his distance from the prickly Stone and his department; Keating had gone to meet them out of necessity and then established command.

The float reinforced the unique political coalition being created by Hawke. It connected the Government to the financial community the way the accord tied it more permanently to the unions. The float also suggested that the enduring reforms by the Hawke–Keating-dominated Government might be right-wing, not left-wing in nature. The feature of Hawke's reforms until the end of 1984 is that they were limited strictly to ideas whose time had come. Their application was curbed to avoid the loss of votes. In fact the approach of the Government seemed to be a curious yet clever blend of reform restrained by conservatism.

One of the enduring achievements was the upholding by the High Court of the Commonwealth's constitutional power to halt the Gordon-below-Franklin dam in Tasmania. This was a landmark decision because the court significantly strengthened its powers in several areas and confirmed the wide view of the external affairs power. It was a classic example of Labor's clear-cut commitment to both environmental protection and Commonwealth power being vindicated. By comparison, the state's-rights stand of the conservatives appeared politically irrelevant and constitutionally outdated. Tasmanian Premier Robin Gray by his intransigence was responsible for this far-reaching boost to Commonwealth powers.

Towards the end of 1983 the Government signalled its determination to use the full Commonwealth powers granted in the 1967 referendum to guarantee Aboriginal land rights. In November the Government moved to vest the title to the Uluru National Park, which contains Ayers Rock, one of Australia's biggest tourist attractions, in the local Aboriginal community. The non-Labor parties began mobilising against the Government's land rights policies. The federal Opposition said that it would weaken the federal land rights law passed by the Fraser Government for the Northern Territory. The Executive Director of Western Mining Corporation, Hugh Morgan, launched a far-reaching assault on Aboriginal land rights in early 1984. Morgan labelled the concept anti-Christian, declared that the wider community would revolt against it and argued that Aborigines were being given ownership of the minerals which was denied to ordinary Australians. As the parties and community polarised on the issue Hawke faced a likely clash with the states after his re-election if the Government persisted with its intentions.

However, the racial issue came to prominence most spectacularly on the immigration front and from an unexpected source, the distinguished historian Professor Geoffrey Blainey. Asked to elaborate on some remarks he made at Warrnambool, Blainey wrote a newspaper article on 20 March 1984 whose defiant tone opened a bitter debate: 'I do not accept the view widely held in the federal Cabinet that some kind of Asian takeover of Australia is inevitable. I do not believe that we are powerless. I do believe that we can with goodwill and good sense control our destiny.'[1]

From the start Blainey appeared to misjudge the political implications of his stand. In fact the Government was not committed to the 'Asianisation' of Australia despite a remark to this effect by a spokesman for Immigration Minister West. Government estimates were, given current trends, that by the year 2000 the Asian segment of the total population would be about four per cent. The thrust of Blainey's argument was that the intake of Asians, notably Vietnamese, was too far ahead of public opinion and that the poorer and unemployed in the cities were the real victims of the programme. Blainey came under attack from two quarters: those who wanted to silence him and critics who repudiated his claims. The upshot was a boilover in federal Parliament. Hawke stood behind the policy and the immigration principle of racial non-discrimination. He was well equipped for the task since the campaign against White Australia had been a key issue in the radicalisation of the young Hawke at university in the 1950s. Opposition leader Andrew Peacock initially promised to restore the racial balance by bringing more European immigrants; then he promised to increase the number of skilled immigrants in order to get the same result.

It seems that Blainey was sucked into the debate by the initial remarks by West's spokesman and then some personal comments by Bill Hayden that

Australia should have a population of 50 million in the 21st century. Once under attack he chose to press ahead rather than retreat. By mid-year Blainey said immigration could be a major issue at the election and 'many swinging seats will be lost on this issue'. Obviously, if swinging seats were to be lost on the immigration issue the nation would experience a racial campaign. Government ministers pointed out the effect of Blainey's remarks was to legitimise the racist campaign of the far right. West, who handled the issue ineptly, produced figures in September 1984 showing the number of Asian settlers had remained steady over the past five years but as a proportion of the total intake they had risen seven per cent to 36 per cent in 1983–84. The size of the overall intake had been reduced under the Fraser and Hawke Governments because of high unemployment. In fact, the hump in Asian immigration was passed about the time Blainey made his comments since it stemmed from the refugees taken from Vietnam which peaked in the late 1970s and the subsequent effect of these refugees using the family reunion programme to bring other members of their families to Australia. Ironically it was on immigration policy, where the Government stuck more closely than usual to Fraser's line, that it suffered one of its most dangerous attacks.

Unlike the Whitlam Government, which espoused universality in welfare, the Hawke Government, aware of the pressure on economic resources, took a more rationalist approach. Its first step, under the influence of Walsh and Dawkins but consistent with Hawke's earlier declaration, was to cut by half the lump-sum superannuation entitlement of retiring federal members—a significant decision which occasioned bitter resentment. Then in its May mini-budget Cabinet checked the superannuation rort by proposing a tax on lump-sum entitlements. This was designed to limit the multiplicity of benefits obtained by people who received a major tax deduction from superannuation during their working lives, a virtual tax-free lump sum on retirement, and who could convert the lump sum into assets, thereby drawing the pension. Dawkins and Keating pioneered the superannuation changes but the final scheme came from Treasury.

In one of the most important concessions won from the Government by the ACTU, the tax proposal was significantly weakened in late 1983. The reform had been conceptually precise and politically saleable with a phase-in period of about 40 years. The tax was not primarily designed to raise revenue but to persuade people to accept a retirement system of annuities. When the tax was watered down so was this incentive.

In the August 1983 budget the Government at Keating's urging announced its intention to introduce an assets test on the pension—a bid to prevent the asset-wealthy claiming on the public purse. Five months later in a unilateral declaration at the National Press Club Hawke retreated with an admission that the particular proposal had been a mistake. He simultaneously reaffirmed his belief in needs-based welfare. The Prime Minister feared a protracted battle over the legislation in the Senate and was sensitive to the worries of the NSW right that an assets test would hurt more in NSW because of its higher property values. Both Richardson and Barron argued the need to protect the Wran Government from adverse federal decisions. The result was that Hawke humiliated Social Security Minister Grimes, who was ignorant of the switch, and Cabinet agreed on a panel of inquiry under Professor Fred Gruen to recommend a better assets test.

In June 1984 Hawke released the Gruen Report but rejected its preferred assets test and excluded rather than included the family home. Cabinet decided that pensioner couples resident in their own homes would receive the full pension unless the market value of their other assets exceeded $100,000. The pension would then taper off until the phase-out point, which is where these other assets reached $175,000. The exemption levels were $50,000 higher for all pensioners not living in their own homes, such as renters or those in nursing homes. In practice the assets test would affect only those pensioners with substantial assets and little income. It was announced after Neville Wran's re-election. The story illustrates Hawke's duality—his acceptance of reform combined with his reluctance to lose votes.

These welfare decisions shocked the free-marketeers among the Liberals, who had demanded such action during the Fraser years only to be told it was politically impossible. One of Malcolm Fraser's axioms was that Government could not take benefits from people. But this was precisely what Hawke was doing. It is true that on both the lump-sum tax and assets test the Government subsequently made concessions. Normally such retreats would be seen as ignominious backdowns, evidence of loss of will. Initially in the Hawke Government they tended to be viewed as consensus in action, evidence of Hawke's reasonableness. The spectre of a Labor Government trying to stream-line the welfare state by cutting benefits was a measure of the transformation within the ALP. Senior Cabinet members such as Keating, Walsh, Dawkins and Button were all advocates of this approach. In his speeches Hawke warned that significant increases in welfare benefits depended upon eliminating payments to the better-off. But, as 1984 closed, doubts arose as to whether the Government really would retain the commitment or nerve to pursue this course.

In other areas reforms reflected Labor's traditional preoccupations. The finest example was Medicare. It provided testimony to the weakening resistance to long-standing Labor policy. Medicare was a refurbished Medibank;

and Medibank had provoked some of the most protracted battles of the Whitlam years in Parliament and the community. This time it faced only minor resistance—outside NSW. In NSW the doctors' revolt came too late although it was assisted by an over-reaction from Premier Wran, who threatened to ban striking doctors from the public hospital system for seven years—a position from which he was forced to retreat.

Political pragmatism prevailed over reform in the school funding area. Hawke and Education Minister Ryan wrestled with this issue for nearly 18 months. In 1983 funds were redistributed from the top 40 private schools to the poorer schools—but party feeling was that Ryan could have sold the switch more effectively and limited the backlash which occurred. In 1984 the Government solved its dilemma over public and private schools by simply spending more money. This time funds were maintained to the wealthy private schools and increased for the Government schools. Ryan unconvincingly declared that the state aid debate was dead. But the Government had defused the opposition of the private school lobby, sections of which now saw Hawke as their champion. It was further proof that the Prime Minister would not implement ALP policy if the price was losing votes.

Hawke was determined to bend Labor policy to his own will whenever it conflicted with either his own predilections or the imperatives of vote winning. His first overseas trip became a *tour de force* of personal assertion. The Prime Minister danced like a cavalier through an odd assortment of capitals. In Jakarta he went soft on self-determination for East Timor and aid to Vietnam. He weakened the party's anti-uranium stand, then hardened it up in a press briefing over the English Channel *en route* to Paris. In Washington Hawke supported President Reagan's policies in central America, and told the President that he had no more constructive ally than Australia. Hawke sounded very similar to Fraser, who had visited Washington the year before. The US press, interested in the new Prime Minister, publicised the trip, even realising he had that old familiar script.

During his speech to the Washington National Press Club Hawke, having established his conservative credentials, proceeded to document his chief political motivatiom—winning. He said the difference between the ALP and British Labour Party is that 'we win'. Hawke continued: 'What we are about in Australia is to make sure that the general philosophy, the general principles of the great Australian Labor Party, are attuned to what the people of Australia want.' Hawke's staff winced; the party back home went wild. This was Hawke as his authentic yet indulgent self, reinforcing the doubts about his political judgement inside the party, but deliberately laying down his philosophy to the left.

However, the Hawke Government sometimes appeared devoid of any real roots in Labor tradition and seemed to be operating without any sense of history. This was revealed in the sensational political event of 1983—the Combe-Ivanov affair. Soviet diplomat Valeriy Ivanov was identified by ASIO as a member of the KGB and expelled partly, or perhaps probably, because of his cultivation of former ALP National Secretary and then lobbyist David Combe. This protracted *imbroglio* probably destroyed Combe's career, precipitated the resignation of Mick Young, briefly endangered Hawke's own political future, exposed the Prime Minister as having misled his own Cabinet, documented ASIO's slipshod techniques and ravaged the conscience of the Labor movement, which saw its own sons being ruined by a Government that acted rapidly on ASIO advice.

ASIO Director-General Harvey Barnett told Hawke that Ivanov was KGB and had a relationship with Combe which had become a 'high security risk'. Barnett put three options to Hawke: call in Combe and warn him off, expel Ivanov discreetly, or expel him publicly. Barnett and Hawke both preferred the latter option and this was accepted by the National and International Security Committee of Cabinet which comprised Hawke, Bowen, Evans, Young, Hayden and Scholes. The committee was briefed orally by Barnett and ministers were not shown the raw intelligence material or the bugged telephone transcripts. Hawke told the full Cabinet and then the ministry that Combe should be denied access to the Government to ensure that party insiders were not seen to have special advantages as lobbyists. Ministers accepted this argument. Yet Hawke had misled them by hiding the real reason for the ban—national security.

The flaw in the Government's approach was that Combe would discover that he had been denied access and would inevitably learn the real reason. The Government said it was actually trying to protect Combe's reputation. In fact, it probably destroyed Combe's livelihood and denied him any chance to defend himself. When the issue became public Hawke referred it for investigation to the Royal Commission on Security and Intelligence under Mr Justice Hope. This opened a pandora's box, whose contents went on display throughout the Canberra winter with a succession of politicians, intelligence operatives and lobbyists giving evidence, and with a series of revelations so spectacular and ultimately so tiresome that the public must have given up in confusion.

Mick Young was forced to resign because he had revealed details about the Cabinet committee's deliberations to his best friend, the lobbyist Eric Walsh. The counsel for the Royal Commission subsequently advised that Young appeared to have breached the Crimes Act. Hawke gave evidence and revealed that he had advised two Canberra businessmen, Bill Butler and

Richard Farmer, not to go into business with Combe and indicated that the Government would ban him. The Prime Minister gave this warning three days after the Cabinet committee had made its decision. Significantly Hawke said he had not revealed any security matters to the businessmen or drawn any connection between Ivanov and Combe. Farmer's own evidence supported the Prime Minister. Obviously if Hawke had revealed any security information or the fact that security was at issue, then he would have been in deep political trouble himself.

The manner in which the Royal Commission was conducted and the interventions of Justice Hope himself caused a profound political backlash within the ALP and the Caucus. The party had no power to help Combe; but it felt an injustice was being done. There was a growing feeling that Young should not be sacrificed and that ASIO must be called to account on grounds of inefficiency and political bias. The Combe-Ivanov affair became a mirror which cast distorted images of the Hawke Government. In mid-year the issue loomed so large there were even suggestions that the Prime Minister might fall.

The Hope Report was a thorough vindication of Hawke's actions. It found the Cabinet committee had acted correctly. Hawke's disclosures to Farmer and Butler were 'neither unauthorised nor improper'. ASIO's case was 'adequate, objective and fair'. Ivanov was found to be a KGB officer attempting to use Combe as an agent of influence. Combe was found to be prepared to enter a 'clandestine' relationship with Ivanov and to have given 'deliberately false' evidence to the Commission; he was entitled to no compensation. Young's disclosures to Walsh were 'unauthorised and improper' and a 'real risk' to national security. Hope declined to advise on whether Young had breached the Crimes Act and left any action in this matter to the Government.

Hawke originally wanted to exile Young to the backbench but found the Caucus was resistant. So he buried his doubts and welcomed Mick back to the fold. Young was sworn in again as a minister; meanwhile Combe had no job and split up with his wife. In an extraordinary speech to Parliament Hawke used the Hope Report to vindicate his actions against Combe and then forgot the Hope Report when it came to Young. He said Young was 'a good man' who had always placed great store by 'mateship'; he had learnt his lesson. Ironically in 1984 Young had to stand aside as minister pending an inquiry into allegations that he improperly filled out a customs declaration and failed to pay duty. Evidently he had not learnt his lesson. The feud between Hawke and Combe was finally put to rest at the mid-1984 National Conference. Despite the drama the affair caused inside the Labor Party the opinion polls revealed the voters were unconcerned.

The big question is whether the Combe–Ivanov issue exposed the real nature of the Hawke Government or was merely an aberration. It revealed in dramatic form, with tragic consequences, all the fears within the ALP that Hawke was an instinctual conservative. Some Labor figures suspected that the decision to isolate Combe was symptomatic of the party's collective will to bury the Whitlam image and therefore represented over-anxiety to prove its credentials to those powers normally worried about Labor's reliability—business, international capital, the United States and the intelligence community. It was a decision conceived in the new Labor Party, proud of its toughness and reliability, and yet it provoked a reaction from the old Labor Party, which began to sharpen its axe in order to swing a decisive blow against ASIO.

It was uranium more than any other issue which fanned the emotions and deepened the turbulence in Hawke's first year. The Prime Minister secured Caucus approval for the new huge uranium mine at Roxby Downs. Relying on right-wing and Cabinet backing he defeated 55–46 the anti-uranium forces seeking a shutdown of the industry. Hawke crushed the left, but he had made concessions to the anti-uranium forces before the vote in order to guarantee his win. The issues of new contracts for existing uranium mines and the supplying of uranium to France were deferred until the following years. In order to get the Roxby Downs go-ahead Hawke agreed that no new mines would proceed in the rich Northern Territory uranium province.

The lesson is that uranium is a running political sore within the ALP. It will not disappear. Almost every year another battle will need to be fought; its potential to sap the unity and extend the divisions in the party should not be underestimated.

One of the keys to the Hawke Government's success is that its legitimacy was accepted in a way denied to the Whitlam Government. Hawke himself was fundamental to such a perception. Success breeds upon itself; the more Hawke radiated the winning spirit the more the media, the middle-class and the financial community accepted his longevity as Prime Minister. In this sense Hawke intuitively understood and rectified one of Labor's intractable difficulties in the Whitlam years. Whitlam had proceeded on the naive assumption that control of the House of Representatives was an adequate base from which to reform Australia. Ultimately felled by the Senate and Governor-General, Whitlam was already weakened before these blows by the institutional forces which he had ignored—by the media whose summer honeymoon soon turned into a long winter of hostility, by business, by international capital which went on strike, by powerful interest groups such as the doctors who fought Medibank, by the insurance sector which fought the proposed Australian Government Insurance Office, by the banks who dissented from economic policy, by the farmers convinced they were being discriminated against, and by a hungry and aggressive Opposition which fed on such extra-parliamentary agitation. Finally Whitlam provoked such opponents by exaggerating his commitment to change and reform.

By contrast Hawke understood the longing for security within the Australian electorate and its suspicion about unnecessary or unexplained change. He was never interested in any pursuit of the Socialist millennium and rarely fooled by visions splendid. In speech after speech Hawke stressed the need for predictability and stability in Government decision-making. Except to Labor audiences, Hawke never presented himself as a champion of reformism. His rhetoric was usually pitched to the middle-ground—the message was always 'we are moderate and sensible people'. Hawke would stress the benefits provided for workers and the responsibilities upon them; a similar tune would then be played for business. Hawke was meticulous in depicting himself as a fair and equitable Prime Minister, a man who governed in the national interest.

While Hawke was shaped by Labor's history, he was remarkably free of its heavy ideological baggage. Hawke's career had been the intellectual reverse of most Labor leaders. Their long exposure to Parliament and the Labor movement meant that on taking office they had deep commitments in most areas. Government became an agony of compromising one's beliefs due to electoral necessity. But Hawke lacked such comprehensive views on taking office; his commitments were more generalised and diffused—consensus, economic growth, middle-ground politics. It was more a commitment to a political strategy than a set of policies. Only in office did Hawke confront the latter, and one of the fascinating features of 1983 was Hawke's gradual embrace of specific policy positions.

However, the NSW right's philosophy of winning through factional dominance inside the party and the appeal of pragmatic policies outside was the path Bob Hawke most favoured. The minister on whom he most relied was Keating; the advisers were Richardson and Barron; and the Premier whom he most tried to help was Wran. Hawke was a frontline participator in the 1983 Queensland and then the 1984 NSW state elections. His aim was to establish a Labor hegemony, to make the ALP the natural party of Government. This aspiration was pure NSW right. While he consulted all his ministers the easy camaraderie he enjoyed with the NSW right provoked bitterness everywhere outside that faction. The result was the dramatic emergence in early 1984 of a new faction under the leadership of Bill Hayden.

While the centre had been an identifiable group in the Caucus as far back as Hayden's 1977 challenge to Whitlam it had never been organised at the federal or state level. Four factors lay behind the formation of the centre-left faction, as it became known. They were the acceptance in the party of proportional representation as a voting system, which had the effect of encouraging factional organisation since it delivered delegates according to rank and file voting strength; the perception of the centre ministers—Hayden, Dawkins, Walsh and Blewett—that the more rational reformist elements in the Government should unite to maximise their influence on Hawke; the fear that warfare between right and left factions could wreck the Government unless a safety valve in the form of a new factional alternative was provided; and finally, the conviction of centre ministers, notably Hayden and Dawkins, that they needed their own power base in the ALP rather than being forced to rely upon votes controlled by others. This was a seminal lesson from Hayden's own failure as leader. Mick Young let his continuing disillusionment with Hawke propel him to join forces with the centre-left and his old adversary, Bill Hayden.

The right watched almost agog with disbelief as the centre-left faction organised itself in the glare of media coverage. Its manifesto said the centre-left was less ideological than the left and less pragmatic than the right. The cynics said it wanted the best of everything—power and social democratic principles. The formative meeting was in Adelaide on 19 February 1984 and others soon followed. Button, once a natural member of this group, stayed aloof, still associated with Hawke and distant from Hayden as a result of the leadership issue. The centre-left was weakest in the big states of NSW and Victoria and strongest in the outlying states. Few doubted that it represented a decisive step towards the creation of a Labor Party divided into three nationally organised factions. Henceforth Labor politics would become both more complex and simpler; complex because majority decisions would always require the support of two of the three factions and simpler because all votes would be marshalled under a factional banner. Senator Peter Cook became the organiser for the centre-left in Caucus, thereby becoming its counterpart to Richardson and Hand.

Hawke declared himself 'totally relaxed' about the new faction. But his NSW right associates were in a repressed fury. Hayden kept insisting the centre-left backed Hawke's leadership in order to weaken resistance to its formation and also deny Hawke's backers the excuse to launch a pre-emptive strike. In fact, the policy orientation of the centre-left ministers was strongly to the Hawke–Keating line, notably in economic policy. There was no immediate issue likely to spark any clash. But both sides privately admitted that power and policy disputes were certain to arise further down the line. The message for the right which had hitherto been able to count on their support was that the members of the centre-left were now organising their own game.

Meanwhile Hawke prepared for his inevitable re-election against the Opposition troika of Andrew Peacock, John Howard and Ian Sinclair. Hawke had a justified excuse for an early election. This was the logic flowing from Fraser's 1983 double dissolution which threw the House of Representatives and the Senate out of kilter. A half-Senate election was due before mid-1985 and this gave Hawke grounds for a late 1984 poll after less than two years in office.

Paradoxically the Government started down another path. Originally it planned to hold referendums in February 1984 that would enable the life of the Senate to be extended until late 1985, thereby permitting Hawke to serve a full three years. The Prime Minister was inclined initially to wait the full term and seek re-election with concrete achievements and having created nearly 500,000 new jobs, which was his biggest promise in the 1983 campaign. But in late 1983 the Government changed course, donned its typical pragmatic guise and set its sights on a late 1984 poll. The Prime Minister signalled his strategy at a Kirribilli House press conference in January 1984 and spent the rest of the year conditioning the voters to the early poll. Unlike Fraser, who promoted election speculation and then denied it, Hawke moved consistently and openly towards his early election.

Hawke was significantly assisted by a package of electoral reforms, the most sweeping since the 1920s and based upon the Wran model in NSW. The Government succeeded in constructing alliances with the Australian Democrats and the National Party on different parts of the package to guarantee its passage. The reforms included public funding of political parties, disclosure of campaign donations, an expanded federal Parliament, simplified voting procedures for the election of both Houses (to reduce the informal vote which must help Labor) and the establishment of an independent Australian Electoral Commission. The combined impact of these electoral reforms was to Labor's advantage; each change had a validity in its own right. The electoral rules which had helped nurture the former Liberal Party hegemony were dissolved.

The combined effect of the electoral redistribution and the expanded Parliament meant Hawke held an even stronger position before he went into the election. This was because the slight bias against Labor was being corrected. When the 1983 election result was superimposed on the proposed new boundaries Labor's existing majority became 28 in a 148-seat Parliament. Labor's winning margin rose from 2.3 per cent to 3.2 per cent. That is, the Opposition required a 3.2 per cent uniform swing to win office. Yet the average swing in the fortnightly Morgan polls during 1984 had been about two per cent away from the Opposition and towards the Government.

Hawke's aim was to increase further his dominance over the coalition and make the margin of victory so great after his 1984 election that the Opposition would not be able to overtake him in one hit. A late 1984 poll meant a subsequent election in early 1988—the bicentennial year. Hawke's timetable was worked out in early 1984. Then he turned his attention to the two primary matters on the political agenda: the ALP National Conference and the 1984–85 budget.

The 99 delegates to the ALP Conference endorsed the Hawke–Keating policies of economic growth and watched the Hayden centre group come of age as a faction. Hawke kept at bay the implicit conflict between the institutions of party and imperatives of Government. If he had been defeated on a major issue such as foreign banks or uranium then the Prime Minister would have stuck by the Cabinet decisions of his Government and flouted the dictates of the party.

The historic decisions by the Conference came on the economic platform with acceptance of foreign banks and deregulation. The most dramatic was endorsement of the liberalised uranium policy, a debate launched when Resources and Energy Minister Walsh declared: 'Delegates, just 10 years ago Jim Cairns went to Iran to sell uranium to the Shah.' On foreign policy Hayden beat off the left's demands to effectively cancel the US alliance and confront Indonesia over the East Timor incorporation. The dominant figures on the floor were Hawke, Hayden and Keating, and the prevailing power axis a coalition of the right and centre-left which combined to defeat the left.

The left was vanquished but far from unhappy. It had 41 or 42 firm votes out of 99, not far from a majority in its own right. Although the left had the weakest representation in the Hawke Ministry it was the strongest faction at rank and file level in the party. Moreover its influence was on the rise.

This highlighted a fundamental problem for the Hawke Government: would the rank and file of the party allow Hawke and Keating to get away with it? The trouble for Hawke–Keating policies as that like everything else in the Labor Party they depended upon numbers. The right-wing position was under attack and its numerical strength in the ALP was eroding. The party was being swollen by recruits from the new left, the middle-class left, interested primarily in issues such as uranium or foreign bases. In 1984 few people were joining the ALP to put their shoulders behind the pragmatic realism of Hawke–Keating policies. Unlike Gough Whitlam, they did not inspire new adherents to the party. The NSW State Conference was the only one controlled by the right wing.

One danger for Hawke was a polarisation in the party between the moderates in Cabinet and the radicals in the branches. For every right-wing victory on uranium, Timor or foreign banks, hostility deepened within the left-dominated branches towards the Prime Minister. Some senior ministers feared that as Cabinet marched to the right the party beneath it moved, in retaliation, to the left. This confronted Hawke with a profound challenge. There were two constituencies vitally important to him and he must hold them both—the voting public and the party faithful. The questions remained whether any ALP leader could reconcile these constituencies, and whether the left would pursue its policy demands if the price was an internal party eruption. The real factional threat to the Hawke Government came not from the Hayden centre but the left wing itself.

The force of the second Keating budget lay in its consistency as a document reflecting the Government's well-established priorities. The deficit was cut moderately from the $7.9 billion outcome the previous year to an estimated $6.7 billion in 1984–85. The unions got a $1.3 billion tax cut. And most ministers were happy with spending increasing an estimated six per cent in real terms. The key to the budget was the big rise in receipts (10.5 per cent in real terms) stemming from the economic recovery. Its catch was that by reverting to a new five-step tax structure the Government would use fiscal drag in subsequent years to guarantee its revenue position. Income earned over $19,500 a year still attracted a marginal tax rate of 46 cents in the dollar.

The unbeatable combination of good luck—taking office at the trough of the economic downturn—and competent management dominated the first period of Hawke Government. In mid-1984 unemployment fell to 8.8 per cent, a far better result than predicted at the National Economic Summit. Inflation was under five per cent and the number of new jobs created had reached 240,000. There was a major transfer of income from wages to profits, thereby creating the potential for new investment. It was true that the overseas recovery, the breaking of the drought and the Fraser wage pause contributed to this outcome. But the Government had displayed a firm touch and both a new style and set of priorities for a Labor administration.

Keating had identified the economic agenda for the next 18 months: the shift to a broadly based indirect tax, a restructuring of federal-state taxation responsibilities and a drive against spending to further cut the deficit. The political ascendancy of the Treasurer over economic policy was merely confirmed when Secretary Stone resigned his post. Stone's credentials as an economic purist were no longer needed. The great strategic challenge facing Keating was to shift policy on to a deflationary course while maintaining the accord.

The Government's greatest asset remained the extraordinary phenomenon at its helm. Despite Hawke's faults his immense political popularity serves as a gigantic buffer to cushion his own and his Government's mistakes. Looking at the 'bottom line', there are five reasons for concluding that the decade of the 1980s will belong to Hawke. Firstly his personal popularity will hold up for longer than that of his Government and, in the process, because he is leader, the Labor vote will remain higher. In the television-age of concentration on leadership, the ALP has the perfect leader. Secondly the Liberals face an acute leadership dilemma with neither Andrew Peacock nor John Howard nor anybody else equipped to match Hawke as a leader. Thirdly Hawke is dominant inside his own party, relying upon the coalition consisting of the right wing and centre-left. Hawke is determined to maintain his ascendancy over the left wing, a course which leads to internal conflict but is the path to power through strength. This strategy is viable, subject to the party being able to contain the growing power of the left wing within the branches. Fourthly the margin of Hawke's dominance could take many years to erode. If he improves at the 1984 election upon his 3.2 per cent safety margin then the Opposition could face an uphill task of bridging the even greater gap at the subsequent poll. Finally the individual and collective quality of the Hawke Ministry, while not outstanding, must be rated as better than average by Australian standards with Hawke having great confidence in his Treasurer.

Overall this means the Government is likely to be more politically durable than its economic performance might justify. Even indifferent economic results will not easily result in Hawke's fall. His capacity to adapt, even to the collapse of the accord, should not be underestimated. Real economic progress might see Hawke break the Menzian structure of politics and make Labor the natural majority party at the federal level. But that will not be easy in an age when world economic fluctuations are more frequent and have a proven ability to demolish Governments.

In many senses the true parallel with Hawke is Menzies. Hawke and Keating are trying to create a new political establishment. They sought from the start to run the country more efficiently and generate more economic growth than the Liberals. They challenged the conservatives on their own terrain. They grasped that the record of the Liberal Party itself in these areas had bordered on the mediocre. Hawke, like Menzies, understands the yearnings for security within the electorate. In foreign policy he became the champion of the US alliance; in domestic politics the advocate of economic progress. Unlike Fraser, who was both aloof from the voters and prone to sharp changes in policy, Hawke tried to establish rapport with the electors and reassure them through consistency of approach. Hawke and Keating worked to sever and then usurp the traditional links which once connected the Liberals to the media corporations, business elite and financial community. Often the Liberals betrayed little understanding of the magnitude of the challenge Hawke posed.

The story of the eight years from 1975 onwards is that our political parties experience cyclical fluctuations while our Prime Ministers tend to be too timid and forgo their full opportunities. It took Labor eight years to recover; it may take the Liberals even longer. Fraser became aware only gradually of his failure to use his power. Hawke faces the historic choice of building upon his successful first term and bringing genuine change to Australia, or retreating down the path of caution, unwilling to use his political mandate or unable to meet the more exacting challenge of 1985 and beyond.

As 1984 closed, Hawke had emerged as a figure of substance. The man considered by many of his own backers in mid-1982 as a 'plunge into the unknown' had developed into an astute and competent Prime Minister. The doubts about his stability and fears about his unpredictability had been put down. The private Hawke was a far more controlled and less exciting figure than the media image which he had enjoyed for so long. The internal wars which had produced emotional instability, physical risk and mental damage had long since been settled. Hawke's emotional nature was revealed again only in September 1984 when he cried twice in two days on the media about claims that he was soft on the drug trade. Yet Hawke was completely purged of the devil of alcohol and no longer had any inclination to drink. He was no more the personality magnet made irresistible by the gleam of self-destruction. The personal sacrifices he had made left only one outlet for his energies—being a successful Prime Minister.

Hawke had easily fulfilled the predictions of his supporters and become Labor's electoral saviour. But in office he was a more complex Prime Minister than the party had expected. It was true that he had displayed both caution and conservatism, yet he was slowly evolving a new set of policy commitments as he settled into Government. The pace may have been measured, but Hawke was adamant that change only came through political strength. He had moved to rationalise the welfare sector, deregulate the financial system, encourage private sector growth by controlling inflation and was talking about tax reform and industry restructuring as steps along the road towards a more dynamic economy. Hawke, in fact, was marching up his own learning curve and was finally reinvesting in his intellectual capital, which he had ignored for so long. He was not a creative thinker but was skilful at mastering his brief. Perhaps the great danger was that his second Government might fall victim to the great luck enjoyed in his first term. Had Hawke and his ministers been trapped into a false sense of confidence? Had economic recovery come too easily? Governments are never tested until put under pressure from economic conditions. That test still lay ahead for the Prime Minister. After his re-election Hawke would no longer have the advantage of a huge economic recovery; he would have the disadvantage of a stronger left wing resisting him in the party.

Hawke's critics still saw him as a demon who would terminate Labor's role as a party of reform. The truth is that Hawke, with Keating's assistance and drawing upon his unique popular standing, had set about fashioning a new Labor Party. The Prime Minister never defined the task in these terms but this is certainly his mission. The Hawke Labor Party is a blend of reformism and conservatism, innovation and tradition. Labor would keep and strengthen its trade union ties but develop a new association and commitment to the financial sector. Two big questions were posed by this process. Would the old Labor Party allow Hawke to get away with it? And was the political strategy that Hawke was following viable for Labor in the long term?

Hawke has displayed immense skill in pioneering his middle-ground politics and winning such public confidence in his leadership. Consensus and nationalism have been his indispensable tools. Much will now depend upon how re-election further changes the man. It can accentuate his natural strengths or further tempt his weaknesses. Hawke is a unique product of Australian democracy. Perhaps, because the public identifies so closely with him, Hawke's progress will reveal our own future as a nation.

Endnotes

Chapter 1 The seeds of conflict

1 Blanche d'Alpuget, *Robert J. Hawke*, Schwartz, Melbourne, 1982, p. 291.
2 Personal interview with Lionel Bowen, 14 July 1983.
3 The accounts of the formative years of both Hayden and Hawke in this chapter are based upon two biographies, *Hayden* by Denis Murphy, Angus & Robertson Publishers, Sydney, 1980, and *Robert J. Hawke* by Blanche d'Alpuget, op. cit. They are also based on *The National Times*, 4 July 1982.
4 Murphy, op. cit., p. 1.
5 Interview with John Edwards, *The Australian Financial Review*, 29 June 1972.
6 ibid.
7 ibid.
8 ibid.
9 ibid.
10 House of Representatives Hansard, 22 October 1975, p. 2360.
11 Personal interview with David Combe, May 1983.
12 Personal interview with Dr Peter McCawley, May 1983.
13 *The Sydney Morning Herald*, 14 January 1976.
14 *The Courier Mail*, 13 February 1976.
15 d'Alpuget, op. cit., p. 303.
16 Personal interview with Bill Hayden, September 1976.
17 *The Sydney Morning Herald*, 21 December 1979.
18 d'Alpuget, op. cit., p. 304.

Chapter 2 Hayden as saviour

1 This chapter draws upon the author's account of the Hayden challenge, 'Who's Who in the Getting of Gough', *The National Times*, 21 March 1977.

2 *The Sydney Morning Herald*, 4 March 1977.
3 Interview with Paul Kelly for *The National Times*, 2 September 1976.
4 Interview with Richard Butler, 12 July 1978.
5 Late in 1976, its hand forced by significant capital outflow, the Fraser Government devalued the dollar 17.5 per cent.
6 Personal interview with David Combe, May 1983. See also Paul Kelly, *The National Times*, 6 June 1977.
7 Personal interview with Clyde Cameron, March 1977.
8 *The Melbourne Sun*, 15 March 1977.
9 Interview with John Ducker, June 1983.
10 *The National Times*, 6 June 1979.
11 *The Sydney Morning Herald*, 4 and 7 October 1977.
12 Discussion with Hawke, 10 December 1977.
13 *The National Times*, 28 November 1977.
14 Chifley is the exception because he led the party for the first time in 1946, the first election after the Curtin Government received its large 1943 wartime majority.

Chapter 3 Born to rule

1 *The National Times*, 15 September 1979.
2 *The Sydney Morning Herald*, 25 November 1979.
3 Interview with Niree Creed, ABC, 2 March 1983.
4 Personal conversation with Reg Withers, August 1978.
5 *The National Times*, 19 August 1978.
6 Don Chipp and John Larkin, *Don Chipp, The Third Man*, Rigby, Adelaide, 1978, pp. 175–6.
7 *The National Times*, 4 November 1978.
8 Michelle Grattan and Patrick Weller, *Can Ministers Cope?* Hutchinson, Melbourne, 1981.
9 Quoted from Michael Sexton, *The Bulletin*, 8 February 1983.
10 *Labor to Power—Australia's 1972 election*, edited by Henry Maher, Angus and Robertson Publishers, Sydney, 1973, pp. 48–59.

Chapter 4 Hayden as leader

1 Max Walsh, *Poor Little Rich Country*, Penguin, 1979, Melbourne, pp. 141–51.
2 *The Sydney Morning Herald*, 22 May 1982.
3 *The National Times*, 24 March 1979.

4   House of Representatives Hansard, 26 September 1979.
5   *The Bulletin*, 13 March 1979.
6   John Laws's interview with Bill Hayden, February 1980.
7   Personal conversation with Bill Hayden, mid-1980.
8   Personal conversation with a senior Labor source to whom Ducker related the exchange.
9   *The National Times*, 28 July 1979.
10 ibid.
11 ALP campaign planning document, October 1979, tabled in Parliament on 22 November 1979.
12 Report from the National Secretary on the 1980 campaign, p. 12.
13 ALP campaign planning document, October 1979, op. cit.

Chapter 5   Boom and bust

1   This report was dated 2 June 1980, and the departments represented were the Prime Minister's, Treasury, Finance, the Reserve Bank, Trade and Resources, Industry and Commerce, National Development and Energy.
2   Fraser's policy speech, September 1980.
3   Total federal taxation as a proportion of GDP rose from 25.8 per cent in 1975–76 to 27.8 per cent in 1980–81.
4   IDC report, 2 June 1980, op. cit.
5   Statement No. 2, 1981–82 budget, p. 48.
6   The estimated deficit for the 1981–82 budget was $146 million with a $1,542 million domestic surplus.
7   This exchange draws upon an article by John O'Hara, *The Sydney Morning Herald*, 1 August 1981.
8   ibid.
9   *The Australian*, 17 December 1981.
10 Statement No. 2, 1982–83 budget, p. 51.
11 ibid., pp. 52–3.

Chapter 6   The irresistible force

1   *The Sydney Morning Herald*, 2 July 1977.
2   ibid.
3   d'Alpuget, op. cit., p. 357.
4   ibid., p. 389.
5   Personal interview with John Ducker, May 1983.
6   House of Representatives Hansard, 22 November 1979, p. 3361.

7   *The Sydney Morning Herald*, 12 November 1979.
8   ibid.

Chapter 7   The Peacock crisis

1   *The Sydney Morning Herald*, 19 December 1981.
2   ibid.
3   John Edwards, *Life Wasn't Meant To Be Easy*, Mayhem, Sydney, 1977, p. 79.
4   *The Sydney Morning Herald*, op. cit.
5   Andrew Peacock, House of Representatives Hansard, 28 April 1981.
6   ibid.
7   Statement by Lee Kuan Yew, 10 September 1980.
8   Andrew Peacock, House of Representatives Hansard, op. cit.
9   Peter Nixon, House of Representatives Hansard, 28 April 1981.
10 ibid.
11 ibid.
12 ibid.
13 Jim Bonner's note to the Prime Minister, 19 April 1981, and David Barnett's note, 26 April 1981.
14 ibid.
15 Andrew Peacock to Malcolm Fraser, resignation letter, 15 April 1981.
16 Peter Nixon, House of Representatives Hansard, op. cit.
17 Malcolm Fraser, press statement and press conference, 15 April 1981.

Chapter 8   Hayden surges

1   *The National Times*, 6 September 1981.
2   *The Age*, 4 September 1981.
3   *The Age*, 2 May 1981.
4   *The Sydney Morning Herald*, 30 November 1981.

Chapter 9   Fraser defeats Peacock

1   *The Sydney Morning Herald*, 29 August 1981.
2   *The Sydney Morning Herald*, 16 September 1981.
3   *The Sydney Morning Herald*, 4 and 5 March 1982.
4   *The Sydney Morning Herald*, 7 April 1982.

Chapter 10   Hayden stumbles

1   Account based on a briefing of ANOP research.
2   From the full correspondence and statements in Malcolm Fraser's press release of 7 June 1982.

3   Malcolm Fraser's press release, 8 June 1982.
4   *The Sydney Morning Herald* and *The Age*, 10 June 1982.
5   *The Sydney Morning Herald,* 23 June 1981, and Bill Hayden's speech to the Australian Institute of International Affairs, 22 June 1981.
6   Bill Hayden, National Press Club speech, 14 March 1981, *The Sydney Morning Herald*, 20 March 1981.
7   *The Age,* 1 May 1982.
8   House of Representatives Hansard, 11 March 1981, pp. 664–6, and 24 March, p. 817.
9   House of Representatives Hansard, 11 March 1981, pp. 666–71.
10 House of Representatives Hansard, 12 March 1981, p. 711.
11 *The Sydney Morning Herald*, 15 June 1982.
12 *The Australian Financial Review*, 25 June 1982.
13 *The Sydney Morning Herald*, 23 June 1982.
14 *The Sydney Morning Herald*, 29 May 1982.
15 Michelle Grattan's interview with Bill Hayden, *The Age*, 30 June 1982.
16 ibid.

Chapter 11   Hawke strikes

1   See Chapters 5 and 9. This refers to cooperation between Hayden and Richardson on issues such as the Lowe by-election, uranium and previous federal conferences.
2   Personal interview with Bob Hogg, May 1983.
3   Keating and Uren have conflicting versions of this conversation and this account represents an effort by the author to paint the most probable picture.

Chapter 12   Hawke on the brink

1   Personal interview with Bob Hawke, 12 July 1982.
2   ibid.
3   *The Age*, 26 June 1982. (However Phillip Adams' classification of Fraser as a 'maddie' seems misplaced.)
4   Brian Toohey, *The Australian Financial Review*, 2 July 1980.
5   Personal interview with Bob Hawke, June 1983.

Chapter 13   The challenge

1   *The Sydney Morning Herald*, 10 and 16 July 1982.
2   *The Age,* Michael Gawenda's report on Bill Hayden's challenge week, 17 July 1982.

3 ibid.
4 ibid.
5 *The Canberra Times*, 16 July 1982.
6 *The Age*, 16 July 1982.
7 The Electoral Strategy Committee was established in autumn 1982 to coordinate Labor's political tactics. It initially comprised seven shadow ministers—the four leaders and Mick Young, Paul Keating and Ralph Willis. Hawke's omission was another display of the 'parliamentary club' suspicion of him. It was politically foolish and Hayden compounded the problem by publicly referring to Hawke's lack of suitable qualifications.
8 Bill Hayden's speech to the South Australian ALP Conference, June 1983.

Chapter 14   Fraser's election strategy

I 'Sunday' programme, National Nine Network, 11 April 1982.
2 Howard's speech to the Premiers' Conference, 24 June 1982.
3 *The Business Review Weekly*, 18 July 1981.
4 *The Sydney Morning Herald*, 19 July 1982.
5 Personal interview with David Barnett, July 1983.
6 *The Sydney Morning Herald*, 11 November 1982.
7 ibid.

Chapter 15   Costigan thwarts Fraser

1 Royal Commission on the Activities of the Federated Ship Painters' and Dockers' Union, Interim Report, No, 4, Vol. 1, p. 39.
2 ibid., p. 48.
3 ibid., p. 56.
4 ibid., p. 62.
5 ibid., pp. 70–1.
6 Peter Bowers, *The Sydney Morning Herald*, September 1982.
7 *The Sydney Morning Herald*, 28 September 1982.
8 *The Sydney Morning Herald*, 17 August 1982.
9 *The Age,* 19 August 1982.

Chapter 16   Election strategy foiled

1 Malcolm Fraser, press release, 30 August 1982.
2 *The Sydney Morning Herald*, 1 October 1982.
3 Briefing given by Malcolm Fraser to journalists on 2 March 1979.

4 *The Australian*, 14 September 1982.
5 ANOP Report, August 1982.
6 ANOP report on Western Australian survey work, dated 1 December 1982.
7 Letter to *The Bulletin*, January 1983.

Chapter 17   The curse of Flinders

1 Interview with Sir Charles Court, 22 April 1983.
2 *The Sydney Morning Herald*, 30 October 1982.
3 House of Representatives Hansard, 11 November 1982.
4 Personal interview with Bill Kelty, June 1983.
5 ANOP report on Western Australian survey work, dated 1 December 1982.

Chapter 18   Recovery, reconstruction and reconciliation

1 ANOP, ALP voter research, August 1982, p. 5.
2 ANOP report on Western Australian survey work, dated 1 December 1982.
3 Letter, Professor L. F. Crisp to Bill Hayden, 21 December 1982.

Chapter 20   Race for power

1 Bill Hayden, 'AM' programme, 12 January 1983.
2 *The Sydney Morning Herald*, 13 January 1983.
3 Personal interview with Simon Crean, June 1983.
4 Personal interview with Bill Kelty, June 1983.
5 ABC, 'Nationwide' interview with Hawke, February 1983.
6 Personal interview with Bill Kelty, June 1983.

Chapter 21   The climax

1 Personal interview with David Barnett, July 1983.
2 Personal interview with Peter Nixon, June 1983.
3 Personal interview with Bob Hawke, May 1983.

Chapter 24   The victor

1 *The Age*, 20 March 1984.

Index